The Black Teacher and the Dramatic Arts

*Participants in the Summer Institute
in Repertory Theatre, 1968*

The Black Teacher and the Dramatic Arts

A DIALOGUE, BIBLIOGRAPHY, AND ANTHOLOGY

William R. Reardon and
Thomas D. Pawley, Editors

NEGRO UNIVERSITIES PRESS
51 RIVERSIDE AVENUE
WESTPORT, CONNECTICUT   06880

Library of Congress Catalog Card Number: 73-90789
SBN: 8371–1850–6
Negro Universities Press, 51 Riverside Avenue, Westport, Conn.
06880
Printed in the United States of America

To Ethel and Peg

contents

dialogue

part 1 The College Situation

part 2 The School and Community Situation

bibliography

anthology

illustrations

preface

IN January, 1967, Dr. Reardon received a grant from the United States Office of Education, Arts and Humanities Institute, to run a summer repertory theatre program at the University of California, Santa Barbara. The purpose was to upgrade the training of secondary school teachers of theatre and drama. Stipends for company members were well beyond those paid to an actor in the average summer stock or off-Broadway company for a repertory of classic plays in excellent new theatres. Between six and seven hundred applications were received from teachers around the nation. Only three applications came from graduates of the more than one hundred traditionally Negro colleges, and only one of these was qualified by terms of the grant.

Where were the black teachers of theatre and drama? Obviously, there should be a great number. As Professor Hobgood noted in a paper delivered at the National Convention of the American Educational Theatre Association in New York in 1967, the rate of growth in this field during the fifties and sixties has been phenomenal, far exceeding the growth rate of higher education in general. Indeed, as of June, 1966, more than half the 1,581 accredited colleges offered degrees in this area. Thousands of teachers in this field are listed in the *AETA Directory*, which was utilized as a part of the mailing list for this project.

Dr. Reardon checked by telephone and letter with Dr. Pawley of Lincoln University and Dr. Dodson of Howard University. It became quite clear immediately that all too few graduates from Lincoln and Howard were going into this area of the teaching field and, even more curiously, that among those who did, even fewer tended to remain. Faced with the fact of an educational profession growing with incredible speed, we could only ask ourselves what was deterring black students from pursuing it as well?

Once assured by Drs. Pawley and Dodson that they would be happy to participate in searching out the answer, Dr. Reardon then drew up and submitted a proposal to the United States Office of Education, Disadvantaged Youth Branch, for an Institute in Black Repertory Theatre to be held on the campus of the University of California, Santa Barbara, in the summer of 1968. The proposal was approved in December, 1967.

In order to contact as many applicants as possible who might be interested in a teaching career in this field, the range for applicants was broadened beyond the normal conditions of government grants. Applications were accepted from senior students in traditionally Negro colleges or black students in white colleges; professional people interested in teaching were also eligible, as were current teachers of theatre and drama and administrators with an interest in the area.

Approximately two hundred inquiries were received, the greatest number of which were from applicants with no dramatic training, experience, or college work in the field. In many cases the applicants were in other areas of the arts and wished to become acquainted with theatre. Of about eighty who met the qualifications to some degree—and that with a considerable latitude in our interpretation of the qualifications—the list finally narrowed to the forty-one who were ultimately selected for the repertory company.

Like any theatre company, we wished to be artistically successful and were determined that we would be. But unlike most theatre companies, we had an educational reason for our existence—a concern for the black teacher. Thus all our decisions had to be acceptable from both an artistic and an educational angle, with neither to be slighted.

In our play selection, we decided to do full-length plays. Obviously a playwright is better able to present the full dimension of his talent when he has the whole evening to do so. In addition, each member of our company was required to act in one play and to serve in a technical capacity in another. In our judgment, performance in either capacity in a full-length play had greater scope and magnitude than in a one-act. For reasons that will be noted later in the dialogue, we were particularly concerned with a fullness of technical involvement for the participants.

Since we were primarily a black company with only a few whites, it seemed only proper that we should focus on black writers. Inasmuch as the government was supplying the bulk of the money, we felt these playwrights should be Americans. Naturally Hansberry, Hughes, Baldwin, and Jones came up for immediate consideration. But it seemed to us that these fine authors have already made the heights. In our particular circumstance, subsidized as we were and removed for just once in our lives from the inexorable pressure of the box office, we believed that we could accomplish more if we presented fine examples of dramatic writing by black authors who were not so well known at the moment as their talents indicated they should be.

No thematic note was imposed. We were looking for good plays and for variety in the repertory. Loften Mitchell's *A Land Beyond the River* was the first play selected. Certainly the story it recounts is a major moment in the black heritage in America. Ted Shine's *Morning, Noon, and Night* was the second to be selected, and it is a fantastic blend of comedy and horror in a rural Texas family dominated by an awesome peg-legged matriarch who is a religious fanatic. For our third choice, we selected the musical play *Fly Blackbird* by C. B. Jackson and James Hatch. With considerable musical talent and dance ability in our company, this mild satire proved an excellent instrument. Furthermore, in case we would have sufficient time, we selected two dramatic readings for potential production: Loften Mitchell's *Tell Pharaoh*, a loving and impassioned story of Harlem, and Ossie Davis' moving account of the black tragedian, *Curtain Call, Mr. Aldridge, Sir*. We did have sufficient time, and the two readings were done.

Of these five plays, only one had been published; the rest were in typescript only. These are now published in the anthology segment of this work. One of the major complaints of participants, as well as spectators at our productions, was the difficulty in nding published full-length plays by black authors. In a country the size of ours, word-of-mouth knowledge of existing typescripts is almost valueless—publication of plays is vital. We believe that the publication of these plays will lead to many further productions of these fine works and to an increased awareness of the talent available among black playwrights.

Another decision made in advance of the arrival of the participants derived from our concern with teachers of drama in the black community. To find what their situations were like, we determined to run a continuing dialogue throughout the summer. In the course of this dialogue, each person presented his experiences as a teacher or a student of the drama in black schools and communities. The reports were given with an openness and a speed that were somewhat revealing. We believe that the dialogue represents a good random sampling of reactions to the teaching of drama in the traditionally Negro schools by both students and teachers intensely concerned with such teaching. As such, it is worthy of attention and consideration if the future is to improve at all.

Although a decision had been made to compile a small bibliography on black drama and theatre for the participants, it became immediately evident that the participants both desired and needed a larger bibliography. In fact the director of the institute was overwhelmed by the stream of letters he received from around the country requesting bibliographical materials. The working bibliography here attempts to provide a listing of approximately a thousand items on the subject. There was neither time nor space for a complete bibliography of such works, but it is hoped that this one will be a helpful tool for teachers and students.

The director of the institute would like to add a personal note. For many years he has been involved with theatre companies, in summer stock as well as in universities. Yet never has he been associated with a company as harmonious and hard-working as was this group. Within forty-eight hours of their arrival, they were an incredibly compatible unit. The absence of prima donnas was a sheer delight—and the presence of talent in both breadth and depth was a revelation.

The participants worked a minimum of eight hours a day in rehearsal and technical activities. Only one formal class was run on a daily basis for four weeks, during which each play in the repertory was thoroughly analyzed and discussed by the company, the directors, the designers, and all involved in the production process. The participants asked for and received a variety of special lectures ranging from the use of new materials in scenic construction to the pertinency of graduate programs in this area throughout the land. The dialogues were held at various hours, sometimes in evening sessions, throughout the summer. The participants came in order to work, and they did work—in a way that was a delight to every member of the staff.

The company was present at Santa Barbara from June 17, 1968, to August 2, 1968. The three plays and two dramatic readings were presented for a total of eighteen public performances, including a touring presentation at the Inner City Cultural Center in Los Angeles. There the playwrights whose works our company had presented were honored at a banquet for their contributions to black drama and theatre. Throughout the summer, the company played to packed houses. The members proved to those of us on the staff of the institute that they were united not only by an artistic interest in the drama, but also by their intense concern with teaching it in the college, the elementary and secondary school, and in the ghetto community itself. A remarkable percentage of them, aided by additional grants from the University of California and from the United States Office of Education, are now involved in qualifying themselves to become teachers by obtaining advanced degrees in this area. Perhaps from this group will come the future leaders of the educational theatre and in the development of drama in the traditionally Negro colleges and schools.

THE EDITORS

acknowledgments

WE ARE indebted to many people for encouragement and help. In the United States Office of Education we thank the following: Drs. Irving Brown, James Spillane, Junius Eddy, Bruce Gaarder, Stu Tinsman, Ralph Ranald, and their staffs. At the University of California, Santa Barbara, our deep appreciation goes to Chancellor Vernon I. Cheadle and his staff, Dean Andrew Bruckner of the Graduate School and his staff, as well as to Arts and Lectures, the Extension Division, and the Division of Public Information. We are also appreciative of the aid given us by President Charles Hitch of the University of California and by Dr. Burton Wolfman of the Berkeley campus.

We acknowledge gratefully the contributions of all the participants in the institute as well as the contributions of Professors Hatlen, Dodson, Glenn, Miller, Baschky, Brown, and Brauner to the entire production schedule. Special thanks go also to Loften Mitchell for his work as critic in residence and to Frank Silvera for his contributions.

For assistance in the bibliographical efforts, we thank Ann Pritchard of the library, University of California, Santa Barbara, and Mrs. Dolores W. Turner, curator of the Negro Collection at Fisk University.

For permission to publish the works in the anthology, we thank The Ira Aldridge Society, Shubert Fendrich of Pioneer Drama Service, and Felix Greissle of the Edward B. Marks Company. For generously contributing a wide selection of photographs to choose from, our thanks go to Harold Bergsohn. We also thank our editors for their patience and understanding: Mrs. Edith Tarcov, Marcia Kovarsky, and Janet Goldberg.

Finally, a very special note of appreciation goes to Mrs. Colleen Ellis, secretary for the institute, for her invaluable contributions.

dialogue

introduction

BECAUSE the dialogue contains some scathing observations on administrators in traditionally Negro schools, we wish to state from the start that everyone involved in these dialogues is *pro* the Negro college. We understand their financial problems and their individual philosophical points of view. Within the context of reality, we would live with them as they resolve the financial problems, but we wish to reject out of hand their philosophical assumptions on the position of drama in their universities.

Probably no administrator would be caught dead admitting he had adequate funds. Yet in all honesty, the administrator in a white university occasionally has access to a wallet whereas his colleague in the black college normally functions from a change purse. Financial restrictions force choices upon all administrators. Unfortunately, these choices in the traditionally Negro colleges have worked overwhelmingly against the training of students in theatre and drama. Furthermore the choices have been accompanied by a series of incorrect philosophical, educational, and sociological assumptions. Adjustment in administrative thinking in the area of finance will be gained only by an arduous and continuous set of compromises with financial reality; adustments in the latter area of incorrect premises are vital and should be made with immediacy.

Commitment to a somewhat standard vocational approach to education for the black student admittedly has conservative appeal to the black mother and father who want to be sure that John and Jane will have jobs when the educational process has finished. It is a thoroughly practical middle-class value. It makes sense—but only if it occurs in its proper perspective in the process of education.

Students have been screaming lately about education, about involvement, about identity. The screams range along a tonal scale from the high pitch of paranoic nonsense to the low resonance of genuine misery. But one common note unites them: *Who am I?* This is 1969 and intuitively they recognize that something of vital importance has happened which is not reflected in their educational process as it should be. In a world where the potential number of vocations has expanded incredibly beyond that available to other generations, and where vocational preparation in any college is yet rigidly limited, the students recognize a flaw. Before they can make a choice, they must know the fullness of their own spiritual and aesthetic dimensions, the range of their talents, and the sphere of their powers. Who you are comes before what you will be.

The Negro college, because of a philosophical commitment to a vocational concept of education, has virtually ignored the drama's potential contribution to the spiritual foundation of the student. Exceptions exist, of course, and they are noted in the course of the dialogues. And there have been individuals who have given a lifetime to espousing the cause of drama: Randolph Edmonds, Owen Dodson, Thomas Poag, Anne Cook, and others. Whatever does exist in the drama in the Negro colleges springs almost totally from their efforts. But it is sad to relate that many who entered this battle were forced to leave the area over the years, resigned to the fact that too little was being gained for the efforts expended.

Nor may the colleges be absolved from guilt for the

Staff members during a dialogue.
Left to right: Thomas Pawley, Owen Dodson,
Frank Silvera, Ted Shine, Theodore Hatlen.

inevitable results of this lack of concern as it has affected the black community. From a sociological standpoint, there is no audience for the drama in the black community. Such a statement passes over the existence of certain small ingroups of theatre devotees; it refers instead to the bulk of the black community which accepts the film but not the stage since the latter was not a part of its educational conditioning. Even now a nineteenth-century attitude toward the drama prevails.

There is a peculiar double irony. Not only has the drama been ignored in the education of the average student in the traditionally Negro university because the university has denigrated or ignored the tremendous contributions of black artists, but by ignoring the drama the university has also ignored the very point it has professed to follow: vocational preparation. For at a time when there is increasing emphasis on expanding vocational opportunities for black Americans in business, education, and the professions, it is painfully apparent that the educational theatre does not attract and train enough black teachers to meet the needs of the black community.

No particular consolation comes from realizing that the failure of the educational theatre to meet this need corresponds with the failure of education in virtually all fields. Indeed such a need is stressed by the findings of the United States Commission on Civil Rights which reveal that racial segregation in education is greater now than in 1954, by the demands of students at the traditionally Negro colleges and universities for more courses in the history, art, and culture of black men, by the urgings of the Southern Regional Education Board that Negro institutions in the South be upgraded to a level with the white, and by the assertions of civil-rights activists both in the community and on the campus that the black man control his own destiny and furnish the leadership in finding solutions for his problems.

Ironically, there is a dearth of persons pursuing careers in educational theatre at a time when the professional theatre, movies, and television are lowering traditional barriers. Concomitantly, the sister arts of music and painting continue to attract many black students. Why not the theatre?

Certainly, today, there are few who would doubt the importance of training in the composite art of drama and theatre. Its place in our cultural heritage is secure. Its meaningfulness as a source of insight into the human condition is recognized on every hand, as is the fundamental reflection it accords of the feelings of past and present times. Cultured men have long applauded this art form which teaches, excoriates, involves, and delights. But as a potential force for depicting the greatness of the black heritage, the triumphs and defeats of black society, and the goals for united aspiration, the art remains almost untapped. As a result, there is not only a deprivation in the realm of ideals, but also, on a cold economic level, black students are not being prepared for hundreds of positions open to them in the educational theatre.

Numerous causes immediately suggest themselves so that the temptation is great to propound answers ex cathedra. But even these answers may not get at ultimate causes. For example, why have not Negro colleges and secondary schools embraced drama as they have athletics and music? Why does theatre continue largely as an extracurricular activity? Why does theatre remain primarily the responsibility of English departments and English teachers? Are the unsophisticated reactions of Negro audiences, bred largely on a diet of movies and television, discouraging the development of the dramatic arts?

To get specific answers to these and other questions, a dialogue on the status of education in the drama in the traditionally Negro college and school was an integral part of a Summer Institute in Repertory Theatre at the University of California, Santa Barbara, between June 17 and August 2, 1968. As genuine practitioners of theatre, the participants brought a solid sense of reality to their comments in the dialogue.

The forty-one participants were joined in the dialogue by four visiting faculty members from black universities. Twenty-two of the participants were students completing bachelor degrees; fifteen members were already engaged as teachers in predominantly Negro junior high schools, high schools, colleges, and universities; the remainder were associated with predominantly white schools. The participants came from twenty different states, most of which were in the East and the South.

Accordingly, either as current student or teacher or as former student or teacher, the members of the group had an intimate knowledge of the dramatic training available in forty traditionally Negro institutions. Furthermore, they were acquainted with the high school, junior high, and community activities in the black community in over sixty cities and towns. Since the participants ranged in age from twenty to sixty-two, they were united not only by a concern for the future of dramatic education in the traditionally Negro college, but were also aware of the past history of this education as well as its present situation.

Two questions were basic to the dialogue: *What are the reasons for the apparent failure of black students to enter educational theatre and drama? What policies should be adopted to remedy this condition?*

Each participant was asked to speak from his training and experience on these basic questions. It was suggested that he organize his thoughts—at all times "telling it like it is"—around five fundamental concerns: (a) the location and definition of the problem, (b) the analysis of the causes of the problem, (c) the analysis of existing criteria and those which should exist, (d) solutions to the situation, and (e) means of implementing changes in the current condition. Having presented an oral report, the participant was then interrogated at length by all members of the dialogue panel.

The reports and discussions covered two areas: (1) college and university programs, and (2) the role of the black teacher in the junior high school, high school, and black community and inner-city activities in drama.

In order to assure ourselves that we were not reporting incorrectly or disproportionately the emphases given in these dialogues, the authors read the full report to the company for any changes which members might feel should be made. The pages that follow are the final approved version of the dialogue.

abstract

THE results of the dialogue are contained in the following pages and are presented under two headings: (1) The College Situation and (2) The Junior High School, High School, and Community Situation. The conclusions on The College Situation follow:

A. The situation is abysmal and an insult to the Negro college student.

B. Administrative echelons appear guilty of some mental commitments hanging over from a day long gone.

C. Colleges are brutally understaffed administratively and are painfully personalized operations.

D. The colleges are incredibly divorced from the reality of the ghetto community which often surrounds them.

To the four conclusions these solutions are suggested:

A. The administrators must make an enormous act of faith in the desires and talents of their black students and recognize that the creative history of the black man in America must be recorded by some of their students. Anything less is sheer stupidity.

B. Administrators must make a commitment to a balanced education in the arts and shake off vestigial practices in favor of an awareness of vocational opportunities now offered by the arts. These opportunities are now almost closed to black students by virtue of their training.

C. The least to which the black student is entitled is a minimal education in the drama. Since 90 percent of the colleges do not offer even this, the American Educational Theatre Association's minimal criteria for training in the drama in a four-year college should be adopted and autonomy given in control of budgets and counseling to the theatre and dramatic specialist.

D. Students wishing to involve themselves in the community and ghetto activities in the drama currently find it almost impossible to do so. The college must become involved in the community through children's theatre, creative dramatics, consulting services to junior and senior high schools, assignment of students to schools for field experience, and liaison with the needs of teachers and community leaders functioning in the field.

The Junior High School, High School, and Community Situation disclosed seven problems reducible here to dual conclusions that interlock with all problems:

A. Whether intentionally or unintentionally, the absence of theatre experience for young black students is a result of the attitudinal deficiencies of higher administrative echelons (boards of education, superintendents, principals) toward the black student.

B. The almost automatic failure of the great majority of the black community to become involved in the dramatic experience is a result of the above.

To these conclusions, the following solutions are proposed:

A. Support of dramatic experiences should be enlarged by alteration of the attitudes of the educational heirarchy so that the potentials of the black student are honored with the same attention as those of the white student. Programs should be upgraded by supporting courses and extracurricular activities, by the use of teachers qualified in the field, by the use of meritorious plays of contemporary pertinence to the students and parents, by an educational usage of state drama festivals, and by early exposure of the child to the world of drama through creative dramatics and children's theatre experiences.

B. The support of the black masses will be increased through attacking the basic problems of housing, food, and education. Theatre should be taken to the people by street theatre groups, by touring groups from colleges, and by the combined efforts of the college, high school, junior high school, and community. Community involvement could also be obtained by the encouragement of black playwrights and production of their plays. This absence of drama experiences is now so pervasive that almost any set of positive experiences will help to eliminate the unsophisticated attitudes toward drama now prevailing in most black communities. A potential model, worthy of close examination by all major cities, for activity in the community is the Los Angeles Inner City Cultural Center.

The final musical number of the last play produced this summer (*Fly Blackbird*) was singularly fitting also for the results of this dialogue. The number was entitled "Wake Up." The status of drama education in the black schools and communities is such that there could be no better theme song. An all-out effort in this cultural field is required from the top echelons of government to the last artist involved. Competent teachers must be trained to develop in this new generation an idea of its heritage, its potential for cultural greatness in the drama, and an understanding of dramatic experience in the life of the whole man.

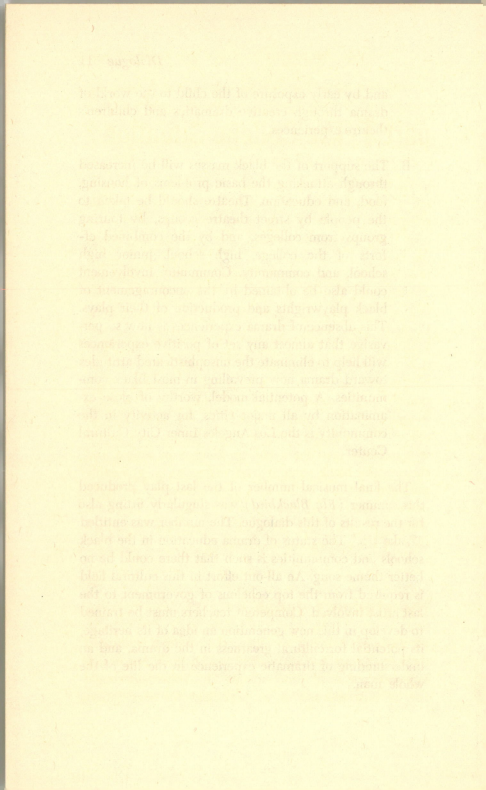

part 1 The College Situation

IN considering why so few black students become teachers of drama and theatre in colleges and universities, one comparison should be kept in mind from the start. Well over thirty major universities offer doctoral degrees in the field of drama under various departmental designations such as Dramatic Art, Speech and Drama, Theatre, Theatre Arts, Drama, or Speech. To name but a few, the degree is awarded by such distinguished universities as Cornell, Yale, Iowa, Northwestern, Indiana, Kansas, Louisiana State, Texas, Stanford, and California. More than quadruple that number of universities offer a master's degree in the area. Among over a hundred traditionally Negro colleges and universities, only Tennessee A and I offers a master's degree in this field, and no school offers a doctoral degree. Since the master's degree is a minimal goal for a college teacher in drama and theatre, the black student who wishes to be genuinely prepared to teach in this area must ultimately, with the one exception noted, attend a white school. To enter the white graduate school, the student must have been qualified by his undergraduate training.

the students speak

BY an overwhelming majority, the students indicated their preference for attending a traditionally Negro college rather than a white college. This statement should not be misconstrued as an argument for segregation, since the phrase "traditionally Negro college" means a college that was once all-Negro but now has varying proportions of white students enrolled. The sense of black identity and personal identity gained within the framework of such a college was considered an invaluable asset. Missing in this environment, or at least mitigated, was the prevalent white image presented by the various media. Nor did the students believe that attendance at a white college held any hope for either black or personal identity. The sentiment of this group was clear: they were where they wanted to be.

In addition to the environment of the Negro college itself, there were inducements of at least equal importance for the black student interested in drama. Weighing heavily in the value scale were the opportunities to be involved in the production of works by black playwrights, to be cast in plays where one's talent, and talent alone, was the sole criterion, and to associate with other artists of similar interests.

But once having stated the positive values of the traditionally Negro college, the students' further comments quickly revealed the unfortunate paradox: they were where they wanted to be but unfortunately the opportunities, for the most part, had not yet arrived.

To be sure, the opportunity to act was present, although not very often in the works of black playwrights. Even this opportunity, however, was limited by a minimal number of play productions each year, or by the whims of directors not overly concerned with students, or by the insistence of administrators that the activity be extracurricular, or by the miserly dispensation of both time and facilities within which to act. Funds in support of production activities were often so meager as to be more appropriately described as nonexistent. Formal classes in acting or group workshops wherein students could develop as actors from their freshman through senior years were present in only a few colleges. As one student expressed it, when he was assigned to teach drama as a high school teacher, he was being "asked to teach what he had never been taught."

By curricular standards of an average department of drama in a white college, the opportunities for actor training in a traditionally Negro college must be described as limited in the best of schools and generally haphazard or pitiful in the others.

It is a matter of supreme irony, then, that this training is unquestionably the major training available to the black student. It is even more ironic that this inadequate training focuses his eye, if it focuses the eye at all, on a professional career in the theatre as an actor. Certainly it aids in perpetuating a continual flow of unprepared persons into the rigorous and precarious career of professional acting. Certainly, too, it is almost worthless in the preparation of producers, directors, designers, technicians, costumers, and other personnel needed by the educational theatre. Walter Mitty emerges victorious; reality is foresworn.

Significantly, and undoubtedly as a result of his training, not one student mentioned a goal orientation toward any of the specialties in theatre mentioned above. Such learning experiences as were available to him in these areas were usually extracurricular. The potential artistic designer for the educational theatre, whether his potential was for settings, costuming, or lighting, was deprived of any opportunity to develop through sophisticated criticism of his talent and its practicality. No courses were open to him for practice; no continued supervision was open for his development. Indeed how could a man conceive of becoming a lighting designer, for example, if, as one student glumly put it, "our stage was lighted by pressing one button." Similarly, the lack of interest in technical positions by students skilled with their hands was also readily comprehensible: the laboratories for such students must be the shop and the stage, and they must have machines and tools. The absence of these necessities wipes out any future technical career interests from the start.

The students consistently reiterated the need for facilities. They felt that they had no "home" on campus for their dramatic activities and that whatever facilities were offered to them were given begrudgingly or on a hit-or-miss basis. Most of them were forced to major in English or in speech (one was even a physical education major by virtual dictate), and by departmental fiat, drama was available only in the extracurricular pattern, and even then, not always approved. Since few of them had attended high schools with well-rounded programs in dramatic arts, the students could see no way in which they might achieve appropriate training with the existent facilities. They resented the realization that they could only be inadequate in their preparation for teaching or for graduate work as a result of their training.

In stating the reasons for a lack of facilities or of curricula in drama in their colleges, the students presented an interesting spectrum. They suggested that administrators of Negro colleges must share a great deal of blame for the status of theatre. The attitudes of administrators were assessed as ranging from utter indifference to enthusiastic support, the latter being a microscopic minority. From the student view, black administrators have little or no respect for dramatic arts as an academic discipline and, out of all proportion, prefer to emphasize athletics and music. The students believe the administrators to be outmoded in their thinking: viewing the drama with a nineteenth-century puritanical eye they find it suspect and hence, are totally unable to comprehend its literary and aesthetic values. Many avowed that the administrators have no conception of the potential of the drama in the contemporary black community, and that those few who do are afraid of the drama because it might disturb the status quo. Finally, they despaired of shaking administrators from a major misconception about the drama and theatre—that the field is only avocational and not vocational.

Human frailties constituted a significant part of the spectrum also. Assigned guilt for obstructing the students' desires for drama were an array of individuals in the following positions of power: a speech department professor who wished only speech to be taught; an English professor whose personal unhappy experiences with the theatre had soured him on it for all others; an advisor–counselor for English and speech who personally crusaded against drama because she disliked the drama teacher; a "tired" professor of speech who could not be bothered to push for what the students wanted; a man who retained things as they were because his "little empire" was as he desired it to be; a chain of command founded on an insurmountable nepotism that defied students and instructor alike; a vague feeling that certain strong departments such as English, music, and athletics were opposed to drama.

Although students suspected during their undergraduate years that they were being inadequately trained, the realiation struck most clearly when they went out to teach or to enter graduate school. It should be stated that the black student who is unfortunate in his geographical or financial position and cannot attend one of less than a dozen traditionally Negro colleges that offer appropriate training in drama must inevitably find himself in deep trouble. (At least 90 percent of the traditionally Negro colleges do not appear to meet the *minimum* quantitative criteria for accreditation by the national professional society in drama and theatre, the American Educational Theatre Association.)

Basically the drama student from the traditionally Negro college finds himself with two alternatives: quit the pursuit of his goal and elect another goal, or proceed to make up the deficiencies of his training.

If he elects the second alternative, as several did, the first painful irony appears. The poor become poorer. In most instances the young black student is in a bad financial position. To pursue his career in graduate school, he has to spend more time and more money to make up deficiencies in order to start at the same level of preparation as his fellow white student.

In most fields of graduate study, the factor of color would not impede the training of the student. While it might be true that the possibility of abrasive personal relationships could remove some of the joy from a graduate career, yet the training would remain the same for white or black. Unfortunately the field of drama poses a partial exception to this general rule. Negroes enrolled in white institutions usually constitute a most visible minority. As the students indicated, they found themselves accepting minor roles or roles written for blacks or none at all. For a person with a major interest in acting, such a situation was inevitably intolerable. Whereas some specific directors used interracial casting in plays in which race was not a factor, the majority still adhered rather strictly to a policy of racial typecasting. Since roles written for blacks in plays about whites are few and relatively insignificant, the black actor found his opportunities for growth and development quite limited. To compound his miseries, plays by black authors require more Negroes than are present in a white department and, accordingly, are not often produced. One young actress put her experience succinctly. After trying out unsuccessfully for plays over a two-year period, she finally read for a children's play that would be acted with masks: she couldn't even get cast as a dog. (In our repertory group, where the talent was far beyond the average college and university level, and where her competition included many older teachers and some professional actresses, the young lady was cast in two major roles.) Other students, whose experiences were a little more fortunate, stressed the necessity to get on the stage in a major role in order to interest other black students in trying out for productions.

This particular feature of training in the white college and university is a deficiency. It is remediable, and efforts are being made to eliminate this weakness. But since the function of the average graduate school is not primarily to train actors but to give acting experiences as a part of the total training of the teacher, this weakness should cause less concern than the fact that the positive areas for development are not effectively exploited by the black student. In graduate school, a student learns dramatic literature and its relationship to all phases of theatrical art such as directing, designing, costuming, lighting, writing, producing, and research. In these areas, color has no existence whatsoever. But due to the lack of facilities involved in his earlier training and the dominance of a stress on acting to the exclusion of the other theatre arts, the black student does not understand the full range of his talents, the possibility of vital careers in any of these areas in educational theatre, or even the full dimensions of the scope of careers now open to him. His earlier training has not geared him toward the vital choices for the teacher in drama and theatre: research orientation, directing orientation, or technical orientation.

It is understandable that the students were confused as to the goals of educational theatre and drama and the criteria which should be pursued. But their genuine interests were evident. They had a strong conviction about the need to present drama and to do drama with children in the elementary grades both to foster self-development and a desire for this cultural endeavor in this newest generation of black children. Not only did they believe that high school drama must achieve a far greater dominant focus in the curriculum than it currently has, but they also vehemently insisted that the college had a duty to involve itself in the community life, as well as in bringing excellence in drama to the community in the college productions and in the sponsoring of professional groups. Presentations of the black heritage and contemporary issues were considered contingent functions of the college drama department. Reiterated constantly throughout the students' remarks was the word "excellence." In fact, many of the negative comments on their training stemmed from the belief that growth and development toward excellence were lacking. Almost like Camus, they seemed ready to issue the death sentence for mediocrity.

the teachers speak

FROM the opening day of the dialogue, it was apparent that the teacher of drama and theatre in the traditionally Negro college is in much the same position as that of his white counterpart during the 1920s when departments of drama and theatre were virtually unknown.

The historic problems that faced the outstanding men in the field at that time (the Drummonds, Kochs, Mabies, and Macgowans) and that were confronted and eliminated by them and their successors in the thirties, now face the black teacher. His problems are the establishment of a new artistic and intellectual discipline and the achievement of academic respectability.

One very articulate young teacher suggested that the problem in the Negro colleges was "a struggle for survival." The implications here are clearly stated in Darwinian terms. In the evolution of the Negro college to a condition of equality, the more traditional attitudes resist the development of a new species to such an extent that the tentative beginnings may be wiped out in the ensuing struggle.

The problems and causes fall roughly into seven areas which naturally vary in significance according to local conditions for the teachers. The areas are the following: (1) administration and fellow educators, (2) budget, (3) lack of scholarship support, (4) family and community attitudes, (5) facilities, (6) instructional overload, and (7) lack of professional ethics.

Put bluntly, the teachers saw the greatest problem—a peculiarly devastating one since it emanates from the conceit of ignorance—stemming from the administration and fellow educators. Surrounded all too often by colleagues and an administration whose own training left them with an enormous cultural gap in the comprehension of dramatic literature and theatre, and who, not knowing that there is a gap, sense no loss, the black instructor's problem is less the student's education than that of his colleagues. A further impediment to the instructor is an equally monstrous obstacle: the educator with no training in drama but who is certain he knows all about it. The latter is particularly detrimental, especially when untrained English teachers are assigned the responsibility for dramatic productions.

The teachers, as had the students, consistently indicted top-level administrators as being either anti-theatre or grossly ignorant of theatre. Such an attitude invariably leads to either no support or minimal support at best. Theatre remains strictly extracurricular, tolerated as window dressing, good for pictures in the yearbook and announcements suggesting the well-rounded program of activities which prospective students may enjoy. It is not, however, to be taken seriously in the academic world. Also, in the administrators' efforts to upgrade their institutions and to overcome years of deprivation, theatre is given a low priority. As one Negro college president said, "In my plan for developing the college, drama is in the third act and we are only in the first." At this particular college, however, it is apparent that the production is a five-act play and theatre is in the epilogue.

The education of the administration and faculty to the point of comprehending and supporting a new field of endeavor in the curriculum can be an arduous and time-consuming process. At one moment this education may require extreme forthrightness and a strong application of faculty political power; at the next, it may need a delicate application of personal interrelationships; at a third, the impact of creative accomplishments and scholarly publications may prove the persuasive force.

This problem has not, for the most part, been met well by the teachers. The reasons are clear. The teacher tends to be a relatively young man in the profession, and he lacks the status that comes with a doctoral degree, years of teaching, and heavy committee involvement. In addition, the young teacher carries a work load of killing dimensions, has no voice (or little voice) in guidance or

budget, and is overwhelmed with minutiae. He has neither the time nor the preparation to fight the major battles that face him. In a sense, even though he transfers
from school to school, the instructor in the drama in the
Negro institutions must face a lifetime of fighting the
first round over and over again. He never gets to come
out for the second round.

The power structure in many of the colleges prevents
the continuance of the battle. Again and again the old
struggle of separating drama from English and then
from speech as an academic discipline is being repeated
in the Negro colleges. Their struggle for identity began
between the two World Wars and has resulted in the establishment of only two departments of theatre. Perhaps
a dozen or so departments of speech and drama have developed. But in the vast majority of colleges, drama is
regarded simply as an extension or subdivision of English. Little wonder, then, that a great deal of the opposition to the expansion of drama comes from within
departments of English. Without their sanction, drama
continues as an extracurricular activity. Thus the drama
instructor's requests for curriculum, budget, or facilities
are dead on arrival.

The problem of administrative censorship was also reiterated by the teachers. Although the teacher is rarely
subjected to outright censorship by administrators in his
selection of plays for production, he is made aware that
certain plays "might disturb society" or that other plays
"may get people emotionally upset." As playwrights
throughout the ages have written with such objectives
in mind, the young drama instructor may be forgiven a
sudden feeling that he is functioning in a slightly schizo-
phrenic world.

On the whole, the instructors were united in believing
that the administration, on virtually all levels, does not

understand the drama and theatre as a literary force and tradition or as a vocational or avocational part of education. Not knowing the field, the administrators fear it.

Budgets constitute the next most pressing problem for the instructor. Almost as a basic policy in the traditionally Negro colleges, students are not charged admission to the plays. Thus a potential source of income for development is eliminated. Ironically, in those few cases where money was made from the plays, it ended up again and again in athletic budgets. When support comes from the incidental fees paid by students, the drama instructor finds himself in some cases with a budget of two or three hundred dollars. One teacher was relatively well off; his allocation was .005 percent of the student fees, the other .995 going primarily to athletics and music.

Under such budgetary situations, acquisitions of equipment for lighting, costuming, and other theatrical needs are either extremely limited or impossible. Even the purchasing of scripts becomes a major outlay. The instructors see little hope of improvement. Until the status of drama changes, the budgets will remain totally inadequate.

Money is again a major consideration for the teachers in the third area of their concern. The average student in the traditionally Negro college is in poor financial condition, and a scholarship is of vital importance. When a field of study is not formally installed in the curriculum, scholarships are not awarded. This lack of support forces many talented drama students into a field of only secondary interest. In some cases, the teachers reported that students on work-study programs, supported in great part by federal funds, could not work in drama because of administrative disapproval. Such an attitude can only eliminate good students from the field.

The teachers were bitter about the lack of scholarships for potential drama students. They indicated that the problems facing them with their students are not comparable to those of their white colleagues in the field. Black students enter college as theatrical virgins from high schools with either no programs in drama or poor programs at best. Indeed, even in 1968, such drama as existed in one community in Georgia was not open to attendance by Negroes. In high schools where there were elective courses, students were not encouraged to take them. Thus live drama was an unknown field, and theatre automatically meant movies and television. Accordingly, the black teacher faces a dual problem: he must not only train drama students, he must also train drama audiences. He starts from scratch with both. In the formative years of the young people who are now his students, professional and community theatre had no part. These were only the playthings of the white middle class.

In his attempt to establish a meaningful theatre program, the teacher sometimes runs headlong into family and community attitudes that deter young people from the selection of theatre as a career and hinder the development of audience support. Parents were often insistent that their offspring enroll in "something practical" that will lead to a good job after graduation. When students suggest that they would like to make a career of theatre, the parents (and some counselors) usually respond with "What are you going to do with it?" This question suggests not only that economic considerations are paramount in the minds of the parents rather than the fulfillment of their childrens innate desires, but also reveals that the positions in educational theatre and in government need to be made known to the counselors as well.

Another attitude of the parents (as well as of some

fellow college students) likewise aggravates the problem for the black teacher; the attitude is the result of centuries of a theatrical heritage where actors were considered rogues and vagabonds. The modern version, fostered in great part by the nineteenth century's concepts, and held by many black parents, is that people in theatre are at worst sexual perverts and at best eccentric. Such assumptions discourage "normal" young men and women from lending their support to theatrical activity.

With such a background in the drama for the average student in a traditionally Negro school, there is little wonder that the frequent complaint was voiced: "The students don't come to see the plays." This was particularly true of colleges in large metropolitan centers or those with a large percentage of students from urban ghettoes. Even here, however, there were exceptions. In the smaller college communities or isolated rural communities which frequently are the loci of the Negro colleges, drama appears to have good audience support. The reason may well be that students come out of curiosity—or perhaps there is nothing better to do.

One director from a northern community college suggested that the lack of audience support in the urban community came from the failure of the theatre to deal with the reality of the black man in contemporary life. Theatre, he said, was dishonest. Admittedly there is little or no drama with which the black man can directly identify. In part this is traceable to the failure of the Negro colleges to develop effective drama departments or to encourage the development and production of plays by black playwrights. There are, of course, plays that do reflect reality, but these are seldom performed. The teachers were in agreement that many of the colleges were guilty of isolating themselves from the ghetto

Preparing sets for Fly Blackbird

and from the issues of the day. The further charge by one teacher that black audiences cannot empathize with Ibsen, Shakespeare, Shaw, and Molière brought sharp rebuttals. To suggest that there is nothing in these playwrights for black audiences is to suggest that they can only appreciate plays about themselves and would inevitably delimit what could be taught to black students. The teachers would concede, however, that the cultural and educational lag may lead to these plays finding little response in the contemporary scene, but that this is only a temporary condition. One point brought definite agreement. The black teacher of drama in the Negro college has a big job facing him in overcoming adverse attitudes.

Insofar as available facilities for drama and theatre are concerned, there is a wide discrepancy in the Negro colleges: from nonexistent to excellent but unequipped. The instructor at one school may be forced to hunt for any vacant room that can be converted for use as a theatre; at another, the teacher will find that he must wait his turn for any stray hours that may be open in the scheduling of the all-purpose auditorium; at a third, the professor may find himself in the position of having a beautiful theatre that unfortunately was never equipped after it was built. Few instructors, however, have theatres.

Without facilities, the black student is unable to obtain proper training which could equip him for a vocational career in educational theatre. The need for equipment, as well as space, for the entire technical area of drama was constantly mentioned by the teachers. As was noted earlier, students complete their training without the opportunity to develop any particular talent in the field other than that of acting. Shops require tools, lumber, muslin, paint—the whole array of materials that go with any major construction effort. Lighting instruments are designed to accomplish specific tasks; their means of electrical control are variable; their positioning and color combinations are relatively intricate. Putting a tin can reflector over a small lamp may answer an immediate pressing need for a production; it scarcely qualifies as appropriate technical education in an electronic age. In terms of facilities, and thereby in terms of training, the teacher in the educational field needs a comprehension of all phases of technical work: construction, lighting, costuming, and design. He needs an awareness of the shop areas, the stage, and the front of the house with its publicity, tickets, printing, and public-relations aspects. The black teacher persists in exercising his ingenuity to cover what he does not have, but the result can hardly be called good educational theatre. Increasingly the attitude of the young black teacher is to chuck it all and get out of the theatre completely. And students, seeing the conditions under which their mentors must work, and recognizing the inferior quality of the education they are receiving, are loath to make a career of educational theatre.

But if the black teacher is lacking in almost every practical requirement for theatre, there is at least one area in which he has a surfeit: his instructional course load. If the teacher spends sixteen hours a week instructing classes in speech or English—rarely indeed in actual courses in drama or theatre—his already full load dictates that any drama activities must be over and beyond the average instructional load in his college. This overload should be translated to fit reality. Presuming that he follows the standard rehearsal time, on any occasion that an instructor directs and produces a full-length play he will spend approximately one hundred hours as a director in rehearsal, and approximately the same amount of time in the reading, research, and preparation of the play prior to rehearsal. To this expenditure must be realistically added the supervision time on the construction of the settings, costumes, and props, the handling of lighting, and the preparation of publicity and other details which vary singularly with the intricacies of the play and locale. It would be unusual for the teacher to achieve this total involvement in less than three hundred hours. It may safely be prophesied that if the young director, man or woman, attempts to present two, three, or four shows a year, as is being done, there will be very few old directors in the traditionally Negro college. In most established departments of drama in the white colleges and universities, teaching credit equivalent to a course is given for each play directed. In addition, the director usually has the services of other faculty in design and construction as well as in publicity areas.

It follows that the instructors share a basic lament. They are spread too thin to accomplish effectively the instructional tasks which they see on every hand. They believe that frustration must be inevitable until such time as they have load schedules that permit the appropriate training of the student. The prevalence of the one-man department, or more correctly the one man assigned to drama, irrevocably inhibits the dramatic training of the black student.

The final area of irritation, that of a lack of professional ethics, is always a gingery one. In the academic world, conflicts of personalities are by no means limited to the traditionally Negro colleges. Nor are they restricted to people in the drama department. But if, on the fancy of a president, a faculty member can be told to be "off my campus in twenty-four hours," if the wife of an administrator dictates the drama and music to be seen and heard, if the lines for curriculum development are controlled at key positions by nepotism, if no change is desired and one is informed that he may leave if he wishes change, if the faculty member with the most advanced degrees in the area has no voice in the curriculum and guidance of the area, if the chairman of the department counsels students against the drama or directs bright students away from it, if success in the drama is greeted by jealous suppression as its reward, there may be some slight impediment to the free exchange of ideas and perhaps even some mild diminution of enthusiasm. Totally apart from the emotional situations that spring from such conflicts, the traditionally Negro school is often overly personalized in its operation, perhaps in direct correlation to the fact that it appears generally to be understaffed administratively. Probably this latter aspect leads to the failure to utilize appropriately those faculty members whose advanced degrees have made them most qualified in the drama. Almost needless to say, the professional waste is appalling. Not only does the college lose by not using the talent it has, but the young teacher with no curricula for teaching in his specialty at his disposal loses vital years when he should be growing professionally.

One of the major tasks, then, which the black teacher sees confronting him is the necessity to educate, in matters concerning the drama, not only the community and the black student, but also his colleagues. He must also reveal the excellent vocational potentials in drama and theatre in the educational world for technicians, directors, producers, critics, scholars, and teachers at all levels. And finally, he must be cognizant of the need to pursue his own personal training through to the most advanced degrees in order to have the professional know-how to establish and evolve curricula that can advance his field.

the administrators speak

THE problems of the theatre administrator merge with and overlap those of the teacher. That they are not separate and distinct is due in large measure to the virtual absence of departments of drama (Howard and Spelman are notable exceptions) and the limited number of departments of speech and/or drama among the more than one hundred traditionally Negro colleges and universities. Consequently the so-called administrator is more likely to be administrator-teacher or a "one-man department." This condition is further attested to by the use of the title "director of drama," rather than chairman or head, by the National Association of Dramatic and Speech Arts. This organization of traditionally Negro colleges prefers this designation for the individual responsible for the theatre program among its member colleges.

Even a casual examination of the evidence leads to the inescapable conclusion that most administrative problems that the theatre administrator faces spring from the fact that theatre is an extracurricular activity in the majority of Negro colleges. Although this is not necessarily a deterrent to its development—athletics and music have done well—the attitudes of many college presidents and deans seem to relegate theatre to the same niche with ping-pong and chess. This attitude helps to explain the paucity of courses in drama, the failure to give academic credit for dramatic productions, the presence of large number of elementary education, mathematics, biology, agriculture, and English majors in the casts of productions, and the continuation of the belief that theatre is an extension of English. It also helps to explain the small budgets available for productions.

The administrators noted that change in attitudes is brought about very slowly. Indeed one college, long regarded as the birthplace of educational theatre among Negro colleges, has neither a speech nor a theatre major. Yet its well-heeled Department of English (in which the drama teacher is an instructor) has a staff of forty persons. This lack of academic status influences both student and faculty attitudes, particularly the latter. Typical of faculty attitudes is the experience of one administrator. When he petitioned the faculty for the addition of a minor in speech and drama, one staid professor of sociology opposed the innovation as merely "increasing the sideshow." Such an objection is ironic when it comes from a man in a field which, measured by academic time, is still in its swaddling clothes. Nonetheless such opinions are in part responsible for the fact that course offerings in drama generally are limited to one or two courses in play production. Speech, however, has fared much better.

Money looms large on the administrative horizon of the Negro college theatre administrator as it does on that of his white counterpart. One administrator recalled the beginning of his career at a college in the Southwest where he was given a budget of one hundred dollars to produce four plays during the school year. When he complained that this would not even pay royalties, he was told, "Oh, we don't pay royalties because we change the names of the plays." College policies frequently preclude the charging of admission which might be used to replenish flagging finances. While money is available nowadays for such things as scripts and royalties—business managers are now aware that they are subject to suits—funds for set construction, lighting equipment, and costumes are at the bare minimum or nonexistent.

Many administrators have used the "annual tour" as a

means of raising funds through off-campus productions at high schools, community organizations, and other colleges. While some of these ventures prove successful, most barely break even and some end up in the red. A further consequence of the inability to charge admission is the attitude among members of the potential audience that drama is "for free" and therefore cannot be worth much. While such an attitude is patently false, it is an additional hurdle for the black administrator since it reinforces traditional attitudes toward the theatre as a worthless institution, valuable perhaps for children and ladies' clubs but meaningless as an educational instrument.

Getting an audience thus becomes a matter of "talking it up" among the student body, requiring attendance through the cooperation of the personnel deans, or motivating students to attend by having them write reviews and reports for English classes. There is something to be said for these devices as means of introducing the culturally deprived student to the theatre; but they are certainly not to be condoned as a means of maintaining an audience.

Still another major problem of the theatre administrator is a lack of staff for technical assistance. The director in the traditional Negro college must be a well-rounded individual. He not only functions in the traditional role of director but also as set designer, light designer, property master, and costume designer for the entire season. In addition to serving on faculty committees, he also carries a full teaching schedule, usually a minimum of twelve hours. Included in his schedule of courses will probably be Fundamentals of Speech and English Composition.

In some instances a knowledgeable and personable director may secure the assistance of the Industrial Arts,

Home Economics, and the Art Departments. For the most part, however, he must rely on one or two dedicated students. The experience of one of the authors is a case in point. A few years ago he was offered a position as director of drama at a prominent Deep South institution, renowned for its sponsorship of the arts. After having been wined and dined by the president, he asked, "Who does your technical work?" The well-intentioned president replied, "Oh, I'm sure you can find a student to help you." This utter lack of appreciation, disregard, and even disdain for theatre crafts may explain, in part, the attitudes of students discussed elsewhere in this report.

In the opinions of the administrators, some of the Negro institutions have adequate production facilities. A few (Howard, Florida A and M, Southern, Grambling, Spelman, Hampton, Philander Smith) have theatres. Still others have theatres under construction or in the planning stage. But by and large the typical theatre is an all-purpose auditorium or auditorium-gymnasium which must be shared with the ever-present band or choir, convocations, movies, and other activities ad nauseam. Some of these facilities have adequate stages for dramatic productions; unfortunately they are ill-equipped and lack shop space for the construction and painting of scenery, for making costumes, and for storage space. Perhaps the principal inadequacy is that they lack rehearsal space and are unavailable to the theatre group until the week prior to the production or available only in the late evening hours when other activities have ended. The director is thus forced to rehearse in the most outlandish places so that when he does reach the stage he must practically reblock his show. This absence of facilities cannot be attributed to the unenlightened college administrator alone. Blame must be shared by the board of trustees that regards drama as a frill or of low priority in the scheme of the developing Negro institutions.

Growing out of the basically conservative, traditional, and even reactionary attitudes on many campuses is the specter of censorship. Some colleges have drama committees whose duty it is to supervise the selection and production of plays. In others the censorship takes a more subtle form. It is simply understood that certain plays are not done or are done only with the approval of some higher authority. These plays include those which might incur the wrath of the white or Negro community or the board of trustees. The administrator thus increasingly finds himself caught between student demands for plays by LeRoi Jones and James Baldwin and the avant-garde plays of Genet with their frank treatment of sex, race, religion, and politics, on the one hand, and the conservative academic community, which at times seems only too eager to regard the theatre as immoral and dirty, on the other. Sometimes the administrator finds the situation somewhat ludicrous as with the young director of drama at a North Carolina College. She was told that she could not do *Goodbye My Fancy* for fear of insulting the president of the college. Apparently the drama committee saw something in the play that paralleled closely the behavior of its esteemed leader.

The problems of the administrator-teacher will not disappear overnight. They will be solved as the traditionally Negro colleges assume equal status with their sister institutions in the South and border states. This will mean a complete reorientation of boards of trustees, college administrations, and faculty toward the arts in general and drama and theatre in particular. The status quo will change with even greater rapidity when parents recognize the value of theatre in the development of the whole man, and insist that the Negro colleges divest themselves of their apathy, distrust, ignorance, or disdain for the theatre as an institution.

conclusions and solutions

THE first conclusion on the situation in drama in the traditionally Negro college is patently evident: the situation is abysmal. It is an insult so to deprecate the cultural life of the black college student as to offer him neither the opportunity to participate fittingly and fully in the dramatic experience or to enjoy its best dimensions as a spectator. This blind administrative policy represents nothing more or less than a sentence to fifth-rate citizenship in the full cultural and aesthetic dimensions of society. The black artist had better be a born genius because his own college is not going to give him much help.

The second conclusion is that the administrative echelons may be guilty of some out-moded ideas. With no attempt to attack the sister art of music, the question, nonetheless, constantly arises. Why the totally disproportionate emphasis on music in relation to the arts of drama, sculpture, or painting? Admittedly there was a day when the choir singing spirituals induced benevolence in the hearts of philanthropists and loosened pursestrings. Admittedly, too, there was a day, perhaps still existent, where the nubile young lady waving a baton jiggled her way along in front of a massive and gaudily outfitted marching band and the attending legislators and dignitaries felt that their support of the institution was thereby justified. If, in this political world, politics must still be practiced, then one sighs and reluctantly accepts a degree of pragmatism—but not at the expense of the education of the whole man. There is strong suspicion that the emphasis on athletics in the American scene has been too easily utilized by administrators to attract support to their colleges. If the black student is five feet eight inches tall, weighs 145 pounds, and is not particularly coordinated, he will be massacred in the sports world of Wilt Chamberlain, Jim Brown, and Willie Mays. Probably the majority of American boys dream of a career in sports—the black youth perhaps even more than most because of the spectacle of attainment presented by such great athletes. It is not, however, the province of a college to foster delusion because it is more pleasant than reality, and it smacks of chicanery when an overemphasis is given to athletics out of a budget all too meager to attend to the needs of a full education.

The third conclusion of this dialogue is that the traditionally Negro college is too woefully understaffed on its administrative levels for effective and imaginative leadership. As a result, the operation of the college becomes overly personalized, progress is impeded by dogmatism, jealousy, and departmental strictures, and control of the "empire"—usually by English professors—in relation to drama becomes more important than the training and education of the student. To maintain a proper pride and dignity in the awareness of one's self-development and growth is virtually impossible for the student or teacher of drama in the Negro college. It is painful to be a second-class citizen among one's peers; yet that is what the administrative policy has dictated for those who follow this area of our cultural heritage.

A fourth conclusion is that the Negro college is incredibly divorced from a concern with the community or ghetto which often physically surrounds it. It is walled in by academic inaction, and from the dialogue it seems that Milton's lines are brutally applicable:

Others apart sat on a hill retir'd,
In thoughts more elevate, and reason'd high
Of providence, foreknowledge, will, and fate,
Fix'd fate, free will, foreknowledge absolute,
And found no end, in wand'ring mazes lost.

As the black community sees it, drama comes from television and movies—and in these media there is very little that reflects reality to the black community. The black writer, actor, director, and technician who should be combining their talents to educate the black community to an appreciation of drama by works relating to their present lives and past heritage, as well as to an appreciation of the great classics, who should be training children, high school students, and adults, are themselves not being trained by the colleges. Even worse than not training students to a level of competency is the realization that the Negro college is afraid of the drama's potential. "Don't rock the boat" is a dismal philosophy for 1969. Must every black artist become a social worker?

Other conclusions could be stated, but having stated the above, they become less relevant. More important is the question: what are the solutions?

To the first conclusion—the abysmal situation in drama training—one enormous act of faith must be made by the administrations in the traditionally Negro colleges: the black student's desire and talent for the art of drama is every bit as powerful and deep as that of any white student. He does not need to be coddled with some kind of "safe" materialistic goal; he does not need to be taught a "standard trade." The dramatist and the poet record the moment; the actors and all the crafts of theatre rivet that moment again and again in time; the teachers and researchers recall it again and again. Any nation or any group that leaves the recording of its creative history to anyone other than itself is guilty of an act of enormous stupidity. And it is singularly true of the drama that there has never been a great dramatist who was not great in his own day—he had to have actors to perform his work, men to produce all phases of it, and audiences to react to it in order for him to grow in his creative talent. More than enough black dramatic talent has gone down the drain in the last fifty years through lack of opportunity and total apathy. The administrators must face a duty: the dramatic artist must be developed. What other alternative can possibly exist but the continued lopsided presentation of the white image? And he has an added duty—to overcome his fear, and to foster the polemic of LeRoi Jones, the humanity of Lorraine Hansberry, the poetic flare of Owen Dodson, the intense rural portraits of Ted Shine, the heritage concerns of Loften Mitchell, that is, the whole spectrum of insights and varieties of expression that flow from an increasing number of excellent writers. To produce these writers' works and those of other young men and women who will be coming up through the colleges, there must be persons of talent and training to serve as producers and audiences ready to view them. One does not come without the other.

As to the second conclusion—the disproportionate emphasis on music and athletics—the most important need is for a balanced commitment to education in the arts, and for shaking off vestigial practices that are no longer essential to the continuance of the college. It might be helpful also if the Negro administrator would realize that training in the drama is not basically avocational unless a person so desires it. For throughout the nation today there are innumerable opportunities for a trained teacher in the drama on all levels from creative dramatics through college and university researchers. Indeed in the colleges the need is very high for trained technicians and designers. In addition there are openings for graduates in drama and theatre in government service, setting up centers for theatre in overseas communities, and openings in community theatre throughout the country. The drama student is no longer limited to the professional theatre itself. The employment possibilities are good today—perhaps more realistically so than for either athletics or music.

The third conclusion stated that the traditionally Negro college was woefully understaffed administratively and overly personalized in its structure. These factors have perpetuated the status of drama as an extracurricular activity. It has been starved budgetarily, peremptorily refused admission to the curriculum, and contemptuously relegated to whatever spare facility happened to be handy. If the person in charge of decisions affecting the fate of drama was one whose main concern was music, speech, or English, his own area was understandably advanced while drama was held stagnant.

For the administrator who would like to be sure that the students receive appropriate training in drama, the following description constitutes the Minimum Criteria (Quantitative) established by the Board of Directors of the American Educational Theatre Association pursuant to Bylaw 27, Section "b" for a Senior College (United States Office of Education Class II).

1. *Curriculum:* Not fewer than thirty semester hours, or equivalent, of theatre or drama content courses.

   a. These to be exclusive of dramatic literature, broadcasting and film, public speaking or forensic courses.

   b. Courses to be offered regularly and taught by qualified instructors who are regular members of a theatre or theatre-speech department faculty.

c. Content and Distribution of courses in curriculum, at least three semester hours in each subject.

(1) Introduction to Theatre. (This should consist of a survey of drama and the art and craft of theatre. It should not include practice in applied theatre, nor should it be designed to give students "thorough knowledge of play production.")

(2) Introduction to Technical Production. (This should involve theory and practice of building, painting, rigging, and shifting scenery; construction and use of properties; familiarity with lighting instruments and their control.)

(3) Theatre Speech. (This should include study of and practice in using the actor's voice, breath control, articulation-enunciation-pronunciation, phonetics, and projection. It should not involve speech correction, preparation of speeches for public speaking, or forensic courses.)

(4) Theatre and Drama History

(5) Directing

(6) Beginning Acting

(7) Technical Production

(8) Elective. Advanced Theatre or Drama Courses: e.g., Playwriting, Dance, Costume, History, Dramatic Literature, etc.

2. *Library:* Adequate reference facilities. (See AETA Bibliographies, Lists of Plays, etc.)

3. *Staff:*

a. Training: Drama instructors to have M.A.

degree, or equivalent, with no fewer than forty-five semester hours of drama content courses, at least twenty-one of which will be graduate level courses from an accredited college. (Professional training or experience as approved by individual institutions may be substituted for degree requirements.)

b. Teaching Load: Teaching load not to exceed twelve semester hours of classroom instruction. Drama instructors responsible for production as director or technician to be granted a three-semester-hour credit on the teaching load.

c. Number: A minimum of three full-time faculty members or equivalent in charge of the program, and a student scholarship or work-aid program sufficient to carry on the production schedule recommended below.

4. *Physical Plant:* Adequate physical plant and production facilities to present open stage, arena, or proscenium productions.

5. *Production:* Annually four long plays (directed by regular faculty members) and three short plays or one interdepartmental production.

Surely these minimal criteria are not overwhelming. They are within the province of any administrator to achieve for his college. Once achieved, he could assume with some degree of assurance that the graduates of his college would not present themselves to a graduate school for admission without appropriate preparation. Is not a black student entitled to at least minimal preparation for his career?

One additional note is vital to the success of the program outlined above. An average annual budget for production which permits at least one relatively lavish show, two more standard productions, and one of minimal requirements seems necessary. The program will founder and sink if budgetary control and guidance of students are not within the function of the theatre members comprising the staff. A major degree of autonomy is of absolute import if the esprit de corps of both faculty and students is to be maintained. Nothing could have been clearer from the dialogue reports.

Naturally in these difficult times for securing qualified teachers, any administrator might pause at implementing a new program for fear that he could not adequately staff it. The authors of this report wish to note the following fact. Of the thirty-one members of this repertory company (the other ten are not considered because they were either too old to start graduate study or were involved in positions of importance outside the educational framework), fifteen men and women have requested permission to pursue graduate work to the master's and/or doctoral degree in dramatic art at the University of California. This group is a remarkably bright and talented collection of teachers and prospective teachers in the field. Operating both individually and as a collective group with identical interests, they could perform wonders in the traditionally Negro colleges in the field of drama. During each of the next three years, some of them will complete their training. They would prefer to make their impact felt in the traditionally Negro school, but if they make the sacrifices entailed to achieve the higher degrees and find that the colleges have not moved to develop the area, there is no question in the minds of the authors where these young people will go to teach: to white colleges that will be delighted to have them. This generation will no longer wait. And the administrator who thinks they will, unfortunately will find himself running Mediocrity University.

As to the fourth conclusion, the isolation of the college

from this community and its concerns, one might easily dismiss this as the traditional, and somewhat eternal, separation of town and gown if it involved white colleges and the white community. But with the significant social problems of the ghetto today, the failure of colleges to involve themselves intimately and to establish a rapport between the black community and the college community was a source of constant recrimination by the students in the dialogue. Again administrative pressures, voiced or unvoiced, were major factors in this enforced isolation. Students would like to have gone into the community, to the elementary, junior high, and high school grades—even to the community centers—to work with children and adults in dramatic activities. But there was little effort on the part of the universities to encourage or to aid such ventures, and it is a bit saddening to report that those members of the dialogue who were most intimately involved in bringing drama to the disadvantaged child were older women who accomplished it at a personal sacrifice in time and money. Nor did the colleges attempt to establish a liaison with the teachers in junior highs or high schools or with community activities; those who most needed guidance and help looked in vain for it from the colleges who should have been providing the leadership.

As the reports in the dialogue clearly revealed, last year was not a good year in the traditionally Negro school. Unrest and turbulence among the student bodies were more the rule than the exception. One of the better lines of personal communication can be through the presentation of dramatic events that have a verity for the audience. It shows that the university does care, that it does understand, that it does empathize with those outside its halls. There is much that can be done, much that needs to be done, and the university which relates to the community through its drama will have established one vital line of rapport in a day when rapport must be established.

part 2 The School and Community Situation

SINCE one of the primary objectives of educational theatre is the preparation of secondary school teachers, an evaluation of the status of theatre on this level must necessarily follow. It is presented in three phases, none of which is mutually exclusive: (1) The Nature of the Problem, (2) The Causes, and (3) The Solutions.

nature of the problem

SEVEN basic problems affect the secondary school theatre. Among these, the absence or denial of the theatre experience is the fundamental issue. Again and again teachers from as far north as Pennsylvania to deep southern Louisiana voiced this complaint. As a result, persons with degrees or training in theatre are prevented from developing the drama program and are instead forced to teach courses in English and speech. In many schools dramatic experience is limited to a once-a-year preparation of a one-act play for the state festival. And even this production was often assigned to the person who happened to supervise extracurricular activities, even if he happened to be the head of the department of social sciences. In some instances the production of a play occurs primarily as one of several devices for raising funds to be used for other projects. There is a singular lack of courses, and in the very few schools that do offer courses in drama, the offerings are electives and generally carry no credit toward the high school diploma.

Administrators, including both superintendents and principals, constitute a second major problem that prevents the fostering of theatre in secondary schools. In the Deep South there is still a residue of the attitude that Negroes should receive only vocational training in agriculture and industrial arts, that they should develop skilled hands since few of them can absorb a liberal education. When this view prevails, it is likely to be held by the white superstructure. Principals themselves are largely oriented toward athletics, and tolerate drama only as it is required for maintenance of membership in the high school activities association of which athletics is a part. This toleration of drama is limited to participation in the state festival, which the director, incidentally, is under pressure to win since this will enhance the school's prestige. Administrators evince an abysmal ignorance of the goals of educational theatre, frequently equating it with acting in movies, television, and on the professional stage. These same administrators have been known to prescribe the kind of plays which should be produced.

A frequent complaint of teachers, black and white, is that black students do not participate in drama, whether by choice or by exclusion. They are sometimes encouraged to take courses in theatre (in the rare instances where they are offered) in lieu of more rigorous courses that they have failed to pass. The expectation that incompetent students could hope to understand the literature, memorize the roles, and achieve any dimension of characterization, indicates the depth of administrative ignorance about the drama. Where theatre is strictly extracurricular, students are likely to equate it with acting and are unaware of the variety of arts involved in play production. In some desegregated schools in which they are an ethnic minority, black students are ignored and even subtly discouraged from participating. In other desegregated schools where they would be welcomed, the very nature of the situation makes them hesitant to become involved. An outstanding exception to this general complaint is a parochial school in Atlanta, Georgia, where two-thirds of the all-black student body rallied to the support of the white drama teacher. It should be noted, however, that in this school there was no athletic program, and the students were from a comfortable financial background.

Four other problems are inherent in the development or lack of development of theatre on the junior-senior high school level and may be telescoped as follows. One barrier is a lack of quality plays, especially short plays. This is further aggravated by a lack of time in which to produce, a lack of money for productions, and the constant demand of the state festival. Further compounding the problem are inadequate facilities for productions. Teachers lament also the failure of parents to support the theatre and the woefully inadequate background of both the junior and senior high school students for participation in theatre.

the causes

AN analysis of these seven problems and the assessment of their causes suggest these tentative conclusions. Unlike the dialogue on the college, there were no high school students participating; thus there could be a tendency to oversimplify what is admittedly a very complicated problem with serious economic, sociological, and psychological implications.

The first two problems are closely connected. Why do junior and senior high schools omit drama from their curricula and limit it (where it exists) to the sphere of extracurricular activities? And why do the administrators of predominantly Negro schools thwart and restrict the development of meaningful programs in the dramatic arts?

In the secondary schools, too, it is the administrators (boards of education, superintendents, and principals) who are basically responsible for the low state of drama. They, even more than the college president, set the policies under which our public schools operate. It should be remembered that it is the public school systems in which the bulk of Negro students are enrolled. White superintendents and white boards of education are prone to regard theatre as unnecessary or an extravagance for Negroes. In one major northern city there was considerable dramatic activity in white schools but not in those schools within the ghetto. Administrators often stress the philosophy that the Negro should develop manual skills. (Several participants pointed out that this outmoded philosophy has led to the neglect of a contemporary technical education and created many unemployed in this century of the computer.) Whether or not there are courses or plays is largely the prerogative of the principal, and he is not likely to challenge the ruling junta unless pressured. Should he happen to be partial to the same philosophy, he is unlikely to yield to the pressure. More than likely he is oriented to athletics and its perennial auxiliary, the marching band. Talented young black athletes are avidly sought by universities from Minnesota to California and more recently in the Deep South which now has begun to preserve its own rich natural resources; an athletic grant-in-aid means prestige for the high school as well as a chance for a college education and a career in professional athletics for the student. Since athletics and drama are both under the supervision of the state high school activities association, and since schools are required to participate in all of these activities, the principal will give only the nominal support to drama needed to ensure continued participation in football and basketball. Again, as pointed out by one teacher, appropriations are made on the basis of the number of activities sponsored by the school and the principal is given wide latitude in the distribution of funds once they are received.

Here too, since drama is often regarded as an aspect of English and speech, the principal feels he has satisfied its need by having courses and activities in these other areas. Again since dramatic productions are expensive and since the school board may not have given him sufficient funds with which to operate, he curtails whatever he considers nonessential. Consequently, even in those instances in which the principal is sympathetic to the development of theatre programs, he may not be able to give it adequate support. In other instances he may not have faculty trained in theatre, and knowing that he must assign the drama contest play to an unwilling English teacher, he simply confines his support to the annual play festival.

Administrative attitudes and actions are both a cause and a result. In all fairness to the administrators, their actions may stem from ignorance of the values of the dramatic arts in the development of well-rounded students. As a nation we have given only lip service to the arts until recent years. Administrators, then, may simply reflect our national apathy.

High school theatre teachers must also share the onus for the absence of drama in the curriculum and its preeminent status as an extracurricular activity. As several members of the dialogue pointed out, some of their colleagues accept all too willingly an inferior status and fail to press for a meaningful theatre program either out of fear of losing their jobs or because they suffer from battle fatigue. Thwarted and weary over the continual denial of their efforts, they accept complacently their assignment as an English or speech teacher. Since neither students nor their parents are overly concerned about the omission of drama programs or the attitudes and actions of administrators or teachers, theatre continues to be the ugly duckling of the arts in secondary schools.

The failure of young Negroes to participate in theatre in both predominantly Negro and in integrated secondary schools arises from a variety of causes. That there is little or no theatregoing tradition, and therefore little knowledge of or interest in theatre in the black community, is certainly a contributing factor. It may be observed, on the other hand, that talent shows emphasizing musical virtuosity attract more than their share of Negroes in schools in and out of the ghetto. The image of the many successful singers, musicians, and performers and the influence of millions of records have contributed to this. Not so in opera or symphony, however, for here the image is blurred by the passing marching bands and choirs.

One teacher in a northern California high school, in which Negroes are one of many racial minorities, suggested that the young black male regards theatre as a threat to his masculinity and is therefore partial to athletics, which reinforces it. Then too, high school stages show a dominance of the feminine since girls do support theatre to a greater degree than boys. A teacher from southwestern Georgia stated that young Negroes there are obsessed with sports to the exclusion of theatre. Here again the young person may be reflecting the national hysteria which has led to the current explosion of professional athletics. Parental attitudes, teacher attitudes, which are themselves the products of prior conditioning, may also influence the young black student to regard drama as trivial, insignificant, and unworthy of his time in the educational scheme.

Reasons for inadequate facilities and meager financial support have already been suggested. Drama requires money. When boards of education are faced with the prospect of cutting the "frills" out of the budget, drama is likely to be the first excised. The new auditorium (rarely a theatre) becomes an auditorium-gymnasium on the grounds of economy. Later both disillusioned boards and superintendents know better. When there is a little theatre, it will seat one hundred persons in comfortable cushioned chairs; here they may view a bright polished hardwood stage, a nightmare for a theatre man. Here, too, they will find rows of borderlights that some manufacturer has convinced the school board they need —and that will impede productions for years to come. In the absence of trained personnel to advise him, the superintendent or principal simply earmarks what he regards as adequate funds for constructing the theatre wing or for conducting the drama program. Money earmarked for dramatic arts is sometimes diverted to the band, choir, or football team since the dividends in terms of public appreciation are likely to be greater. Ignorance of the costs of providing high-quality theatre is certainly a contributing factor.

One of the most urgent needs of the high school teacher is quality plays, particularly one-act plays written for Negroes. Teachers in predominantly Negro schools feel that the lack of plays with characters and themes with which ghetto students can empathize is a major factor in the lack of interest in the theatre. They say it is impossible, considering the backgrounds of the majority of Negro students, that an interest in theatre could be developed through plays written for and by whites. The dialogue members unanimously reject this conclusion in view of the experience of the Los Angeles Inner City Cultural Center in successfully presenting Shakespeare and the classics to ghetto youngsters. It is certainly true, however, that there is a dearth of good plays for secondary schools and also of plays about Negroes. If plays about Negroes will motivate an interest in the theatre then by all means let us have more of them. But this should not be an end in itself, since the larger aim of the theatre is the illumination of understanding of the man universal.

The failure of parents to support the theatre either by their attendance at plays or by encouraging their children to participate is not difficult to comprehend. As one dynamic young teacher long active in the civil-rights movement in Louisiana suggested, the problems of Negroes are by and large the problems of poor people, and the poor are concerned with obtaining the basic necessities of life—food, clothing, and housing—rather than indulging in cultural activities. Again many black people regard theatre as a leisure-time activity designed for the classes rather than the masses. To be more exact, it is an activity by and for white people. The whole concept militates against its support by Negroes—the beautiful theatre setting, the social atmosphere, the manner of dress and speech of the audience—all of these are calculated to engender feelings of inferiority or embarrassment. Since poor people also have pride and dignity they avoid those things which might destroy them.

That this assessment is true is attested to by a teacher from Albany, Georgia, who reported that Negroes "are not permitted" to attend the little theatre through such devices as the sale of season tickets, a "grandfather clause" "for whites only" in the sale of tickets, charters establishing the theatre as a private club—all familiar machinations in maintaining racial segregation. Actions such as these help to explain the attitudes and actions of the administrative superstructure. Theatre, like the country club, is reserved for the upper classes, so that while there may not be a "white only" clause in the constitution, Negroes just simply do not apply.

A vice-principal advanced the monetary consideration as a reason for the failure of Negro parents to attend plays in a southern California community. She felt that the admission fee was prohibitive even in the rare instances in which black students appeared in plays in the local high school. While this may be a partial explanation, it is not a primary cause in view of the substantial support given by Negro audiences to professional sports and professional singers and musicians. By and large black audiences are absent from professional theatre. Accordingly, it is not surprising that they do not attend the average school production. Indeed, the advertising industry has discovered that as a class Negroes buy high-quality merchandise whether it be Johnny Walker or an Eldorado. Lack of a theatregoing tradition and educational background are likely to be more significant as explanations for the lack of attendance at plays, whereas lack of education is not a barrier to the appreciation of Ray Charles or Willie Mays.

It was also suggested that the black parent is simply not interested in what his children are doing. A former teacher in an all-Negro school whose clientele was drawn from middle-income black families was puzzled by the failure of parents to attend their productions. Her experience with these youngsters, who avidly supported her program in spite of parental disinterest, is itself highly instructive. In the same city another teacher reported that about 40 percent of parents supported her productions. A possible explanation of why a so-called middle-class Negro group failed to support their children as a comparable white group does may be explained, at least partially, by the fact that income rather than income plus education is the determining factor in the Negro middle class. A parent with an eighth-grade education might well have the resources to maintain a fine automobile and an expensive home but lack the understanding or background to enjoy a play by Sartre. Again, to maintain his status the Negro frequently holds two jobs so that he does not have the time to see his son or daughter perform. Respect for the teacher has long been a characteristic of the Negro parent, however, so that if Miss Tatum says that Johnny ought to participate in dramatics and that she will expect to see the parents there, they will be present.

With rare exceptions the Negro college is not affecting community attitudes toward the drama. This is especially true of the "black Ivy League" colleges, some of which have bona fide departments of drama. However, in view of the problems inherent in maintaining theatre programs on the college level, this is not surprising. Nevertheless, this need is a duty that confronts them. Perhaps projecting themselves into the community might be the salvation of college drama departments since it would lead ultimately to greater student and community interest.

A problem that challenges the high school director in those schools which do have programs in theatre is the elementary school background of students. Creative dramatics, which is excellent for introducing children to theatre, is not included in the educational program of the typical all-Negro school—neither is children's theatre nor theatre for children, both of which are fundamental ways by which a child is exposed to drama. Exceptions to this general rule apparently exist in Nashville, Tennessee, and Tallahassee, Florida. School operettas do seem to be a part of the tradition but the emphasis here is on the music. The first real theatre experience is likely to come in the secondary schools, and since this, too, is impoverished, the result is predictable. For many students it is entrance into college that provides the first meaningful contact with good theatre so that the college is forced to do what the elementary and secondary school should have done. This same problem is not unknown to college English, speech, and mathematic teachers. But these at least have the support of all concerned in the educational process.

The narrow educational experience, the culturally deprived home background, difficulties in reading, writing, speaking, and listening are part of the ghetto experience of a very large number of black junior and senior high school students. And these are inadequate preparation for high school theatre—for participants and audiences.

solutions

WHAT, then, needs to be done to provide meaningful theatrical experiences for young Negroes in junior and senior high schools?

Since there is only minimal support for educational theatre among the black masses, the first effort must be directed toward enlarging that support. This is a herculean task that involves overcoming the cultural lag resulting from years of segregation, discrimination, and neglect. Obviously, then, theatre will be enhanced to the degree that the problems of the ghetto existence are eliminated through better housing, better education, and better jobs.

It will also be aided by taking the theatre to the people in the manner of Mohammed and the mountain. Street theatre such as that projected for the current summer in Atlanta and St. Louis and touring groups such as the Young Peoples Theatre of Philadelphia and the Free Southern Theatre group might be helpful in this regard. But above all the traditionally Negro college has a duty and an opportunity to enlarge its base of operations and become deeply involved in speaking the gospel of good theatre among the black community. This would be mutually helpful since not only will it enlarge the audience, but it will also serve to motivate students to study theatre in Negro colleges and to become teachers.

The support of the black masses will also be gained by writing and producing plays about the common man and his problems, by plays that present an honest picture of the black man and avoid the ancient stereotypes still abounding in our theatre. Some means must be found of giving encouragement to the writing of plays about black people by talented playwrights. Young writers need recognition and professional credits. Such needs may be met by contests for plays which award not only monetary prizes but also production of the plays at the colleges involved.

Support will also be gained through the institution of programs in dramatic arts in the elementary schools of the ghetto, through such teaching devices as creative dramatics, by attendance and participation in children's theatre productions, and by field trips to community and professional theatres.

A second major point of attack must be directed toward the educational hierarchy of our public schools:

Running lights during a performance

boards of education, superintendents and principals, and in some instances state or city officials who influence public policy, particularly in the southern and border states. The attitudes of those who administer our schools must be altered to the end that black youngsters are provided the same opportunities for cultural development as white youngsters. This implies establishing theatre on both a curricular and extracurricular basis. It means the regular production of plays. It means employing competent, well-trained teachers of theatre with adequate budgets, financial support, and production facilities. In other words, it means spending money and a lot of it or in many cases simply achieving a balance of expenditure so that the cultural needs are met.

Furthermore, the dominant attitude of administrators that theatre means acting must be upset by publicizing the vocational opportunities available in educational theatre, government service, drama therapy, and recreation. It also must be made clear to students, teachers, and parents that theatre, which is inevitably a collective art, means a total involvement in an eclectic discipline embracing dancing, painting, sculpture, music, and poetry. It thus can utilize the talents and skills of a wide range of varying abilities.

As a third point of departure, schools already having programs in theatre must be upgraded. They must raise their production standards and expand their curricular offerings.

As a temporary expedient while money is short, teachers might use the services, talents, and facilities present in their departments of home economics, industrial arts, and art. Principals could be very helpful here in encouraging such departments to support actively the production schedule in drama.

Teachers must combat the attitude of principals typified in the experience of an Atlanta teacher who was told that she was working her students too hard and trying to make professionals out of them. That same principal would no doubt cut out his tongue before he said the same thing to the football coach. Our educational philosophy should be that anything worth doing should be done to the best of our ability. Nothing less than excellence within the means at our disposal must be the motto of the teacher in the black secondary schools. Affiliation with strong professional organizations currently providing national leadership, such as the Secondary School Theatre Conference of the American Educational Theatre Association and the National Thespian Society, will give the teacher and the school good professional contacts and help to keep them abreast of innovations and changes. Perhaps seeking to have secondary school programs accredited by state speech and drama associations will touch the conscience of those in authority. Strict adherence to standards, where they exist, for the certification of drama teachers and vigorous actions to upgrade them, where they are inadequate, are also indicated. If the school participates in the state drama contest or festival, it should adopt the philosophy that this is a learning experience for the benefit of the students and not a chance for the director to exhibit his prowess or to enhance himself in the eyes of a principal imbued with the you've-got-to-win-them-all philosophy.

Both directly and indirectly throughout this report, allusions have been made to parents and to other members of the black community with reference to attitudes about drama.

It would be ridiculous to belabor the obvious. As a result of the minimal exposure to drama and theatre which the black community has had, attitudes toward it are basically unformulated, participation and utilization of it as a community activity are at best haphazard, and the so-called "unsophisticated" black audience could be nothing other than it is. Participant after participant commented upon this lack of sophistication in his audiences, particularly as it related to audiences talking back to characters onstage throughout performances and generally failing to observe conventional theatre "manners." These manifestations were not traceable primarily to crudeness or exhibitionism tendencies. They were instead related to the audiences' lack of acquaintance with the convention of the "fourth wall" and to the desire to participate directly in the activity on the stage before them. (Some good playwrights should be able to utilize this desire with enormous effectiveness.)

Educational experience definitely changes this attitude. Whereas the participants reported that freshmen tended to follow this pattern (and the report indicates that students had experienced virtually no live theatre before arriving at college), by their junior year this habit pattern had been eliminated through their new awareness of the drama and theatre. Since this reaction pattern is also exhibited among freshmen and sophomores in many white schools, it is probable that the lag resulting from the lack of dramatic experience at an earlier period for the black student leads to this phenomenon in college years. During the course of the stage productions of this institute at Santa Barbara, groups of young black students under various Head Start and Youth Opportunity programs had the opportunity to see their first live stage show and some of them did occasionally address the actors during performance. On the regular production nights, since both the black and white community members present were older, there was less audible reaction. But occasionally it did occur, and it was wryly amusing to watch the distress of the white audience members when it did. It is a pattern familiar to any producer who has toured shows in overseas military installations where the young men, white and black, are meeting a new experience and follow a response pattern that is natural but intrusive because a convention other than the natural one exists for this medium.

An excellent focus for scholarly work would definitely be a study of the behavioral patterns of black audiences since they are probably the result of a complex of educational and sociological causes. Indeed, on this point of studies, an overwhelming need of both the audience and the teachers was recognized at this institute. The director of the institute found himself barraged with requests for *written* information about black writers, black theatre history, black drama, and black heritage. Every effort must be made to write that record, to make writings and plays available for use. The development and support of black scholars and their research efforts, and the continued development of bibliographical works are vital to the immediate future if the black community is to know its own artists and accomplishments.

Along this line, in closing, attention should be called to one of the most distinctive and encouraging projects now under way in Los Angeles—the Inner City Cultural Center. Now less than three years old, the project is attempting to answer many of the needs indicated by this report, and if its initial success continues, it may well serve as a model for other major cities throughout the land. The Inner City Cultural Center is located in the heart of an almost perfectly balanced racial neighborhood representing not only black but also Mexican, Oriental, and Indian cultures. It has its physical entity—an old rebuilt theatre—right in the neighborhood, a source of neighborhood pride. Furthermore, not only does it concentrate on excellence in its theatre programs and in its support of all artistic aspects of society, but it interlocks professional, educational, and cultural purposes at all levels. During the year, over 35,000 high school students are exposed to the best of drama, and adults have ample opportunity also. It maintains training programs with vocational ends for high school graduates, and constantly fosters lectures, special demonstrations, and photographic and artistic exhibits. Finally, it is deeply involved in the establishment of a library—the Langston Hughes Memorial Library—to make accessible to all the significant documents that have emanated from the minority community. The entire project is guided and controlled by people who know the conditions in Los Angeles, and is wisely supported by such diverse sources as the Ford Foundation, the United States Office of Education, and the National Endowment for the Arts and Humanities. In the opinion of the participants and of the authors of this report, it is the most promising activity currently being undertaken on the national scene for the purposes of cultural education in the drama and the arts for minority groups.

More Inner City Cultural Centers are needed. But as this report shows, the job must also be done by the junior high schools, high schools, and colleges throughout the black community. The talent for dramatic art—indeed, for all the arts—lies abundantly within this community. We cannot afford to let it die. And the fifteen participants in this institute who wish to continue toward advanced degrees are united in believing that they can and will constitute a strong core of united professional concern for this field. They are young; they are vital. Their ultimate impact on the teaching of drama in the traditionally Negro college could be significant.

appendix
NDEA Institute in
Repertory Theatre

STAFF

DR. WILLIAM R. REARDON, Director of the Institute
Professor of Dramatic Art, University of California, Santa Barbara, California

DR. THOMAS PAWLEY, Director of the Dialogue
Chairman, Division of Fine Arts and Humanities, Lincoln University, Jefferson City, Missouri

MR. LOFTEN MITCHELL, Critic-in-Residence
Professional playwright

DR. THEODORE W. HATLEN, Producer
Professor of Dramatic Art, University of California, Santa Barbara, California

DR. OWEN DODSON, Director
Professor of Dramatic Art, Howard University, Washington, D.C.

DR. STANLEY L. GLENN, Director
Chairman, Department of Dramatic Art, University of California, Santa Barbara, California

MR. EUGENE MILLER, Director
Lecturer in Dramatic Art, University of California, Santa Barbara, California

MR. RICHARD BASCHKY, Designer
Lecturer in Dramatic Art, University of California, Santa Barbara, California

MR. LEON I. BRAUNER, Costume Designer
Assistant Professor of Dramatic Art, University of California, Santa Barbara, California

MR. WILLIAM BROWN, Designer
Associate Professor of Dramatic Art, Howard University, Washington, D.C.

PARTICIPANTS

GEORGIA ALLEN, Instructor of English and Drama, C. L. Harper High School, Atlanta, Georgia

JEANETTE BARNES, student, Lincoln University, Jefferson City, Missouri

ANN BOUKIDIS, Dean of Girls, Raymond Cree Junior High School, Palm Springs, California

ADRIENNE BRITT, Instructor, Morgan State College, Baltimore, Maryland

ALFREDINE BROWN, Drama Specialist in Recreational Therapy, St. Elizabeth's Hospital, Washington, D.C.

ROBERT BROWN, student, Xavier University, New Orleans, Louisiana

URLENE BROWN, student, The College of Wooster, Wooster, Ohio

CHARLES BRYANT, Instructor of English and Drama, Paul Lawrence Dunbar High School, Washington, Louisiana.

WINSTON BUTLER, student, California State College at Los Angeles, Los Angeles, California

BETTY COLEMAN, student, Spelman College, Atlanta, Georgia

GLORIA DANIEL, Motivation Coordinator, William Penn High School, Philadelphia, Pennsylvania

SANDRA DILLARD, Instructor, Newlon Elementary School, Denver, Colorado

DONNIEL DOSTER, Chairman of Department of Social Sciences, River Road Junior High School, Albany, Georgia.

EDWARD FISHER, Professor of Speech, Jackson State College, Jackson, Mississippi

H. D. FLOWERS, Instructor, South Carolina State College, Orangeburg, South Carolina

RUTH ANN GAINES, student, Clarke College, Dubuque, Iowa

TOMMIE HARRIS, student, Jackson State College, Jackson, Mississippi

WILLIAM HARRIS, student, University of California, Santa Barbara, California

JOHN HOLMES, Instructor, Bartlett Junior High School, Philadelphia, Pennsylvania

WILLIAM HUNTER, Instructor, Williamsburg Training School, Greeleyville, South Carolina

RAYMOND JACKSON, student, University of Toledo, Toledo, Ohio

ANNE JENKINS, Instructor of English, Severna Park Senior High School, Severna Park, Maryland

HARRY JOHNSON, student, University of Maryland, College Park, Maryland

JILL KAMP, student, New York University, New York, New York

JAMES KILGORE, Assistant Professor of English, Cuyahoga Community College, Cleveland, Ohio

WALTER MARLIN, student, Texas Technological College, Lubbock, Texas

SISTER M. AVILA MCMAHON, Chairman, Department of Speech and Drama, Marygrove College, Detroit, Michigan

HELEN T. MORGAN, Supervisor, Department of Public Assistance, Philadelphia, Pennsylvania

ETHEL PITTS, Instructor of Speech, Southern University, Baton Rouge, Louisiana

EVA PITTS, student, Morgan State College, Baltimore, Maryland

GEORGE PUMPHREY, professional actor, Center Stage, Baltimore, Maryland

SISTER M. CHARLOTTE RODGERS, Instructor, Bishop McCort High School, Johnstown, Pennsylvania

TED SHINE, Assistant Professor, Prairie View College, Prairie View, Texas

ROBERT STEPHENS, student, Howard University, Washington, D.C.

ANTHONY SWEETING, Instructor of Drama, Palm Springs Junior High School, Hialeah, Florida

JACQUELYN TAYLOR, student, Winston-Salem State College, Winston-Salem, North Carolina

WYETTA TURNER, student, Indiana University, Bloomington, Indiana

JAN VAN HEE, Chairman, English and Speech Arts Department, Grant High School, Sacramento, California

DELORES WASHINGTON, Instructor, Bartlett Junior High School, Philadelphia, Pennsylvania

JEROME WILLIAMS, Principal, Cole Elementary School, St. Louis, Missouri

JOHN WILLIAMS, Instructor of Speech, L. B. Landry Junior-Senior High School, New Orleans, Louisiana

bibliography

introduction

THE authors hope that this working bibliography of materials on black theatre and drama will prove a useful tool for teachers and students. Primary emphasis was placed upon books, plays, and articles written by black authors. The emphasis is not exclusive, however, and many entries by white authors will be found.

Although no attempt was made to prepare a comprehensive bibliography, the authors did hope to show the diversity of sources which treat the topic, and this variety is indicated in part by the more than 40 journals and periodicals that are represented among the more than 950 entries.

The decision to present the bibliography in a chronological fashion came in the process of compilation. Such a pattern will provide interesting potentials for comparative research by students. It also helps to reveal attitudes toward the black artist and changes in those attitudes in later years. The growth in treatment of the black artist in both depth and breadth is also indicated by this style. It should aid in depicting the varied dimensions of the black spirit in dramatic art and theatre with greater clarity. Certainly the quantitative growth of concern for black theatre and drama is immediately discernible through the chronological approach.

Scholarly theses are listed because they are often sources of significant research findings. Plays are listed according to the date of their publication, not of their composition. In the listing of articles, the order is strictly alphabetical by author, when he is known, and by title when he is not. Although no annotation has been attempted, a descriptive name or subject may be found alongside entries where it was felt that such a description might save time for the reader.

pre-1930

BOOKS

DU BOIS, W. E. B. *The Souls of Black Folk: Essays and Sketches.* Chicago: A. C. McClurg, 1908.

ISAACS, EDITH J. R. *Theatre: Essays on the Arts of Theatre.* Boston: Little, Brown, 1927.

LOCKE, ALAIN. *The New Negro: An Interpretation.* New York: Albert and Charles Boni, 1925.

————. and Gregory, Montgomery, eds. *Plays of Negro Life.* New York: Harper, 1927.

NELSON, JOHN HERBERT. *The Negro Character in American Literature.* Lawrence Kans.: University of Kansas, Department of Journalism, 1926.

ROWLAND, M. *Bert Williams—Son of Laughter.* London: English Crafter, 1923.

SCHOLARLY THESES
None.

PLAYS

BONNER, MARITA. *Exit, an Illusion. Crisis* 36 (October, 1929):335-336, 352

————. *The Pot-Maker. Opportunity* 5 (February, 1927): 43-46.

————. *The Purple Flower. Crisis* 35 (January, 1928):9-11.

BRUCE, RICHARD. *Sahdji—An African Ballet.* In *Plays of Negro Life,* edited by Alain Locke and Montgomery Gregory.

COTTER, JOSEPH S. *Caleb, the Degenerate.* Louisville: Bradley, West, 1903.

————. *On the Fields of France. Crisis* 20 (June, 1920):77.

CULBERTSON, E. H. *Rackey.* In *Plays of Negro Life,* edited by Alain Locke and Montgomery Gregory.

DUNCAN, THELMA. *The Death Dance.* In *Plays of Negro Life,* edited by Alain Locke and Montgomery Gregory.

EASTON, WILLIAM E. *Christophe*. Los Angeles: Grafton, 1911.

GAINES-SHELTON, RUTH. *The Church Fight*. *Crisis* 32 (May, 1926):17-21.

GRAHAM, OTTIE. *Holiday*. *Crisis* 26 (May, 1923):12-17.

GREEN, PAUL. *In Abraham's Bosom*. In *Plays of Negro Life*, edited by Alain Locke and Montgomery Gregory.

————. *The No 'Count Boy*. In *Plays of Negro Life*, edited by Alain Locke and Montgomery Gregory.

————. *White Dresses*. In *Plays of Negro Life*, edited by Alain Locke and Montgomery Gregory.

HILL, LESLIE P. *Toussaint L'Ouverture*. Boston: Christopher, 1928.

JOHNSON, GEORGIA D. *Blue Blood*. In *Fifty More Contemporary One-Act Plays*, edited by Frank Shay. New York: Appleton, 1928.

————. *Plumes*. *Opportunity* 5 (July, 1927):200-201, 217-218. Also in *Plays of Negro Life*, edited by Alain Locke.

LIPSCOMB, C. D. *Frances*. *Opportunity* 3 (May, 1925): 148-153.

LIVINGSTON, MYRTLE A. *For Unborn Children*. *Crisis* 32 (July, 1926):122-125.

MATHEUS, JOHN. *Black Damp*. *Carolina Magazine*, vol. 49 (April, 1929).

————. *'Cruiter*. In *Plays of Negro Life*, edited by Alain Locke and Montgomery Gregory.

MILLER, MAY. *Scratches*. *Carolina Magazine*, vol. 49 (April, 1929).

NELSON, ALICE DUNBAR. *Mine Eyes Have Seen*. *Crisis* 15 (April, 1918):271-275.

O'NEILL, EUGENE. *The Dreamy Kid*. In *Plays of Negro Life*, edited by Alain Locke and Montgomery Gregory.

————. *The Emperor Jones*. In *Plays of Negro Life*, edited by Alain Locke and Montgomery Gregory.

RICHARDSON, WILLIS. *Compromise*. In *The New Negro*, edited by Alain Locke.

————. *The Broken Banjo*. In *Plays of Negro Life*, edited by Alain Locke and Montgomery Gregory.

————. *The Deacon's Awakening*. *Crisis* 21 (November, 1920):10-15.

————. *The Flight of the Natives*. In *Plays of Negro Life*, edited by Alain Locke and Montgomery Gregory.

_____. *The Idle Head. Carolina Magazine,* vol. 49 (April, 1929).

ROGERS, J. W. *Judge Lynch.* In *Plays of Negro Life,* edited by Alain Locke and Montgomery Gregory.

SPENCE, EULALIE. *The Fool's Errand.* New York: French, 1927.

_____. *The Starter.* In *Plays of Negro Life,* edited by Alain Locke and Montgomery Gregory.

_____. *Undertow. Carolina Magazine,* vol. 49 (April, 1929).

TOOMER, JEAN. *Balo.* In *Plays of Negro Life,* edited by Alain Locke and Montgomery Gregory.

TORRENCE, RIDGLEY. *Granny Maumee.* In *Plays of Negro Life,* edited by Alain Locke and Montgomery Gregory.

_____. *The Danse Calinda.* In *Plays of Negro Life,* edited by Alain Locke and Montgomery Gregory.

_____. *The Rider of Dreams.* In *Plays of Negro Life,* edited by Alain Locke and Montgomery Gregory.

WHITE, LUCY. *The Bird Child.* In *Plays of Negro Life,* edited by Alain Locke and Montgomery Gregory.

WILSON, FRANK. *Sugar Cane. Opportunity* 4 (June, 1926):201-203. Also in *Plays of Negro Life,* edited by Alain Locke and Montgomery Gregory.

ARTICLES

ANDERSON, GARLAND. "How I Became a Playwright." In *Anthology of the American Negro in the Theatre* (1968), edited by Lindsay Patterson, pp. 85-86. Reprinted from *Everyman.* London: May, 1928.

COVINGTON, FLOYD C. "The Negro Invades Hollywood." *Opportunity* 7 (April, 1929):111-113.

DAY, CAROLINE BOND. "What Shall We Play?" *Crisis* 30 (September, 1925):220-222.

DENIG, LYNDE. "A Unique American Playhouse [Lincoln]." *The Theatre* 23 (June, 1916):362.

"*Dramatis Personae: Florence Mills.*" *Crisis* 34 (September, 1927):229, 248.

"*Dramatis Personae: In Abraham's Bosom.*" *Crisis* 34 (March, 1927):11-12.

"*Dramatis Personae: Josephine Baker et al.*" *Crisis* 34 (May, 1927):85-86.

"*Dramatis Personae: Rose McClendon.*" *Crisis* 34 (April, 1927): 55, 66-67.

"Dramatis Personae: The Rivals." *Crisis* 34 (June, 1927):128.

DU BOIS, W. E. B. "Drama Among the Black Folks." *Crisis* 12 (August, 1916):169-173.

"First Steps Toward a National Negro Theatre." *Current Opinion* 62 (May, 1917):328-329.

GALE, ZONA. "The Colored Players and Their Plays." *Theatre Arts Magazine* 1 (May, 1917):139-140.

GREGORY, MONTGOMERY. "For a Negro Theatre." *New Republic* 28 (November 16, 1921):350.

HARRISON, HUBERT. "The Significance of *Lulu Belle*." *Opportunity* 4 (July, 1926):228-229.

HARTE, ROLLIN LYNDE. "The Negro in Drama." *Crisis* 24 (June, 1922):61-64.

HUTTON, LAWRENCE. "Negro on the Stage." *Harper's Monthly* 79 (June, 1889):131-145.

JELLIFFE, ROWENA. "The Gilpin Players." *Opportunity* 6 (November, 1928):344-345.

JOHNSON, CHARLES S. "Ira Aldridge." *Opportunity* 3 (March, 1925):88-90.

JOHNSON, EDWIN D. "The Jewel in Ethiope's Ear [dramatic criticism of Negro theatre]." *Opportunity* 6 (June, 1928):166-168.

"Krigwa Players Little Negro Theatre." *Crisis* 32 (July, 1926):134-136.

LEVINSON, ANDRÉ. "The Negro Dance." In *Theatre: Essays of the Arts of the Theatre*, edited by Edith J. R. Isaacs, pp. 235-245.

LOCKE, ALAIN. "Steps Toward the Negro Theatre." *Crisis* 25 (December, 1922):66-68.

_____. "The Drama of Negro Life." *Theatre Arts Monthly* 10 (October, 1926):701-706.

_____. "The Negro and the American Theatre." In *Theatre: Essays*, edited by Edith J. R. Isaacs, pp. 290-303.

MATTHEWS, BRANDER. "The Rise and Fall of Negro Minstrelsy." *Scribners* 57 (June, 1915):754-759.

O'NEIL, RAYMOND. "The Negro in Dramatic Art." *Crisis* 27 (February, 1924):155-157.

"Othello, the African." *Crisis* 32 (June, 1926):67-68.

"Poetry and Drama." *Crisis* 34 (July, 1927):158.

Pool, Charles. "A Negro Art Theatre [The Shadows Art]." *Drama* 16 (November, 1925):54-55.

"Ridgley Torrence's Negro Plays." *New Republic* 10 (April 14, 1917):325.

SCOTT, ESTHER FULKS. "Negroes as Actors in Serious Plays." *Opportunity* 1 (April, 1923):20-23.

SEYBOLT, MARK. "Playwriting." *Crisis* 29 (February, 1925):164-165.

"The Theatre: *Lulu Belle.*" *Crisis* 32 (May, 1926):34.

TORRENCE, RIDGLEY. "The New Negro Theatre." *Crisis* 14 (June, 1917):80-81.

VAN VECHTEN, CARL. "Beginning of Negro Drama." *Literary Digest* 48 (May 9, 1914):1114.

"Why Not a Negro Drama for Negroes by Negroes?" *Current Opinion* 72 (May, 1922):639-640.

YOUNG, STARK. "Negro Material in the Theatre." *New Republic* 50 (May 11, 1927):331-32.

1930-1939

BOOKS

BRAWLEY, BENJAMIN. *The Negro Genius: A New Appraisal of the Achievement of the American Negro in Literature and the Fine Arts.* New York: Dodd, Mead, 1934.

BROWN, STERLING. *Negro Poetry and Drama.* Washington, D.C.: Associates in Negro Folk Education, 1937.

CUNARD, NANCY. *Negro Anthology 1931-1933.* London: Wishart, 1934.

EDMONDS, RANDOLPH. *Shades and Shadows.* Boston: Meador, 1930.

————. *Six Plays for a Negro Theatre.* Boston: Baker, 1934.

JOHNSON, JAMES W. *Along This Way.* New York: Viking Press, 1933.

————. *Black Manhattan.* New York: Knopf, 1930.

LEE, GEORGE WASHINGTON. *Beale Street—Where the Blues Began.* Introduction by W. C. Handy. New York: R. O. Ballou, 1934.

LOCKE, ALAIN. *Negro Art: Past and Present.* Washington, D.C.: Associates in Negro Folk Education, 1936.

————. *The Negro and His Music.* Washington, D.C.: Associates in Negro Folk Education, 1936.

LOGGINS, VERNON. *The Negro Author: His Development in America.* New York: Columbia University Press, 1931.

RICHARDSON, WILLIS. *Plays and Pageants from the Life of the Negro.* Washington, D.C.: Associated Publishers, 1930.

————. and Miller, May, eds. *Negro History in Thirteen Plays.* Washington, D.C.: Associated Publishers, 1935.

ROBESON, ESLANDA GOODE. *Paul Robeson, Negro.* London: Gollancz, 1930, New York: Harper, 1930.

WITTKE, CARL FREDERICK. *Tambo and Bones.* Durham, N.C.: Duke University Press, 1930.

SCHOLARLY THESES

BOND, FREDERICK W. "The Direct and Indirect Contribution Which the American Negro Has Made to the Drama and the Legitimate Stage, With the Underlying Conditions Responsible." Ph. D. dissertation, New York University, 1938.

LAWSON, HILDA J. "The Negro in American Drama." Ph.D. dissertation, University of Illinois, 1939.

WESTMORELAND, BEATRICE FULTZ. "The Negro in American Drama." Master's thesis, University of Kansas, 1937.

PLAYS

BOND, FREDERICK W. *Family Affair.* Institute, West Virginia: West Virginia State College, 1939.

BURKE, INEZ. *Two Races* [pageant]. In Richardson, Willis, *Plays and Pageants from the Life of the Negro.*

CUNEY-HARE, MAUD. *Antar of Araby.* In Richardson, Willis, *Plays and Pageants from the Life of the Negro.*

DUNCAN, THELMA. *Black Magic.* In *Yearbook of Short Plays.* New York: Row, Peterson, 1931.

————. *Sacrifice.* In *Plays and Pageants from the Life of the Negro,* edited by Willis Richardson.

EDMONDS, RANDOLPH. *Bad Man.* In *Six Plays for a Negro Theatre,* edited by Randolph Edmonds.

————. *Bleeding Hearts.* In *Six Plays for a Negro Theatre,* edited by Randolph Edmonds.

————. *Breeders.* In *Six Plays for a Negro Theatre,* edited by Randolph Edmonds.

————. *The Devil's Price.* In Edmonds, Randolph, *Shades and Shadows.*

————. *Everyman's Land.* In Edmonds, Randolph, *Shades and Shadows.*

————. *Hewers of Wood.* In Edmonds, Randolph, *Shades and Shadows.*

————. *Nat Turner.* In Edmonds, Randolph, *Six Plays for a Negro Theatre.*

————. *The New Window.* In Edmonds, Randolph, *Six Plays for a Negro Theatre.*

————. *Old Man Pete.* In Edmonds, Randolph, *Six Plays for a Negro Theatre.*

————. *The Phantom Treasure.* In Edmonds, Randolph, *Shades and Shadows.*

————. *Shades and Shadows.* In Edmonds, Randolph, *Shades and Shadows.*

————. *The Tribal Chief.* In Edmonds, Randolph, *Shades and Shadows.*

EDWARDS, H. F. V. *Job Hunters. Crisis* 38 (December, 1931): 417-420.

GILBERT, MERCEDES. *Environment.* In *Selected Gems of Poetry, Comedy, and Drama* by Mercedes Gilbert. Boston: Christopher, 1931.

GUNNER, FRANCES. *The Light of the Women* [pageant]. In *Plays and Pageants from the Life of the Negro,* edited by Willis Richardson.

HARLOW, S. RALPH. *It Might Have Happened in Alabama. Crisis* 40 (October 1933):227-229.

HARRIS, HELEN WEB. *Genefrede.* In *Negro History in Thirteen Plays,* edited by Willis Richardson and May Miller.

HUGHES, LANGSTON. *Don't You Want to Be Free? One-Act Play Magazine,* 2, October 1938.

————. *Scottsboro Limited: Four Poems and a Play in Verse.* New York: Golden Stair, 1932.

JOHNSON, GEORGIA D. *Frederick Douglass.* In *Negro History in Thirteen Plays,* edited by Willis Richardson and May Miller.

————. *William and Ellen Craft.* In Richardson, *Negro History in Thirteen Plays,* edited by Willis Richardson and May Miller.

MATHEUS, JOHN. *Ti Yette.* In *Plays and Pageants from the Life of the Negro,* edited by Willis Richardson.

MCCOO, EDWARD. *Ethiopia at the Bar of Justice* [pageant]. In *Plays and Pageants from the Life of the Negro,* edited by Willis Richardson.

MILLER, MAY. *Christophe's Daughters*. In *Negro History in Thirteen Plays*, edited by Willis Richardson and May Miller.

_____. *Graven Images*. In *Plays and Pageants from the Life of the Negro*, edited by Willis Richardson.

_____. *Harriet Tubman*. In *Negro History in Thirteen Plays*, edited by Willis Richardson and May Miller.

_____. *Riding the Goat*. In *Plays and Pageants from the Life of the Negro*, edited by Willis Richardson.

_____. *Samory*. In *Negro History in Thirteen Plays*, edited by Willis Richardson and May Miller.

_____. *Sojourner Truth*. In *Negro History in Thirteen Plays*, edited by Willis Richardson and May Miller.

PRICE, DORIS. *The Bright Medallion*. In *University of Michigan Plays*, edited by Kenneth T. Rowe. Ann Arbor: University of Michigan Press, 1932.

_____. *The Eyes of the Old*. In *University of Michigan Plays*, edited by Kenneth T. Rowe. Ann Arbor: University of Michigan Press, 1932.

_____. *Two Gods: A Minaret*. *Opportunity* 10 (December, 1932):380-383, 389.

QUINN, DOROTHY. *Out of the Dark* [pageant]. In *Plays and Pageants from the Life of the Negro*, edited by Willis Richardson.

RICHARDSON, WILLIS. *Antonio Maceo*. In *Negro History in Thirteen Plays*, edited by Willis Richardson and May Miller.

_____. *Attucks the Martyr*. In *Negro History in Thirteen Plays*, edited by Willis Richardson and May Miller.

_____. *The Black Horseman*. In *Plays and Pageants from the Life of the Negro*, edited by Willis Richardson.

_____. *The Elder Dumas*. In *Negro History in Thirteen Plays*, edited by Willis Richardson and May Miller.

_____. *The House of Sham*. In *Plays and Pageants from the Life of the Negro*, edited by Willis Richardson.

_____. *The King's Dilemma*. In *Plays and Pageants from the Life of the Negro*, edited by Willis Richardson.

_____. *In Menelik's Court*. In *Negro History in Thirteen Plays*, edited by Willis Richardson and May Miller.

_____. *Mortgaged*. In *Readings from Negro Authors*, edited by Otelie Cromwell, Eve Dykes, and Lorenzo Fuller. New York: Harcourt, Brace, 1931.

_____. *Near Calvary*. In *Negro History in Thirteen Plays*, edited by Willis Richardson and May Miller.

STEPHENS, NAN BAGBY. *The Green Vine*. New York: Row, Peterson, 1939.

STREATOR, GEORGE. *Two Plays:* "New Courage"; "A Sign." *Crisis* 41 (January, 1934):9

ARTICLES

ANDREWS, CYRIL BRUYN. "Ira Aldridge." *Crisis* 42 (October, 1935):308, 318.

BELCHER, FANNIN S. "Negro Drama, Stage Center." *Opportunity* 17 (October, 1939):292-295.

BENNETT, GWENDOLYN. "The Emperors Jones [Wayland Rudd]." *Opportunity* 8 (September, 1930):270-271.

BRAWLEY, BENJAMIN. "The Promise of Negro Literature." *Journal of Negro History* 19 (January, 1934):53-59.

BROWN, STERLING A. "Six Plays for a Negro Theatre [Randolph Edmonds]." *Opportunity* 12 (September, 1934):280-281.

————. "The Atlanta University Summer Theatre." *Opportunity* 12 (October, 1934):308-309.

BUCK, PEARL. "Wanted: True Drama of the Negro Race." *Opportunity* 17 (April, 1939):100-101.

CLARK, ELEANOR GRACE. "Racial Antagonism in Shakespeare." *Opportunity* 14 (May, 1936):138-140, 157.

CLINE, JULIA. "Rise of the American Stage Negro." *Drama* 21 (January, 1931):9-10.

COOK, MERCER. "*Imitation of Life* in Paris." *Crisis* 42 (June, 1935):182, 188.

COOKE, ANNE. "Third Moscow Theatre Festival." *Opportunity* 14 (February, 1936): 58-59, 63.

COX, LEONORE. "Scanning the Dance Highway [Kykunkor]." *Opportunity* 12 (August, 1934):246-247.

CUNARD, NANCY. "*Stevedore* in London [Paul Robeson]." *Crisis* 42 (August, 1935):238.

CUNEY-HARE, MAUD. "Musical Comedy." *Negro Musicians and Their Music*. Washington, D.C.: Associated Publishers, 1936. Also in *Anthology of the American Negro in the Theatre* (1968), edited by Lindsay Patterson, pp. 36-49.

DALE, EDGAR. "The Movies and Race Relations." *Crisis* 44 (October, 1937):294-296, 315-316.

DALY, VICTOR. "Green Pastures and Black Washington." *Crisis* 40 (May, 1933):106.

DEUTSCH, HELEN, and HANAU, STELLA. "The Provincetown Theatre and The Negro." *Crisis* 38 (October-November, 1931): 373-374, 396.

EDMONDS, RANDOLPH. "Education in Self-Contempt." *Crisis* 45 (August, 1938):262-263, 266-278.

_____. "Out-of-Date Colleges." *Crisis* 45 (November, 1938): 351-353, 362.

_____. "Some Reflections on the Negro in American Drama." *Opportunity* 8 (October, 1930):303-305.

_____. "Some Whys and Wherefores of College Dramatics." *Crisis* 37 (March, 1930):92-94.

_____. "What Good Are College Dramatics." *Crisis* 41 (August, 1934):232-234.

"For a Negro Theatre." *Theatre Arts Monthly* 17 (July, 1933): 486, 491.

"The Gilpin Players of Cleveland." *Crisis* 37 (June, 1930):191-192, 214.

GOOD, CHARLES HAMLIN. "The First American Literary Movement." *Opportunity* 10 (March, 1932):76-79.

GRANT, GEORGE C. "The Negro in Dramatic Art." *Journal of Negro History* 17 (January, 1932):19-29.

HADDON, ARCHIBALD. "Centenary of Negro Drama [Ira Aldridge]." *Crisis* 41 (February, 1934):35-36.

HALLIBURTON, C. D. "Imitation Ruins the Negro Star." *Opportunity* 17 (October, 1939):308, 316-317.

HUBERT, LEVI C. "Harlem WPA Group Sings Opera." *Crisis* 43 (July, 1936):203, 214.

JETER, OLYVE L. "De Lawd on Broadway." *Crisis* 38 (April, 1931):118-120.

KARA-MOURSA, SERGIUS. "Ira Aldridge in Russia." *Crisis* 40 (September, 1933):201-202.

KNIGHT, RAPHAEL. "Stage Spotlights Harlem Housing [*One-Third of a Nation*]." *Crisis* 45 (May, 1938):143-144.

LAWSON, EDWARD. "A Show Every Negro Should See [*Sing for Your Supper*]." *Opportunity* 17 (May, 1939):149.

_____. "He Crashed the Color Line [Perry Watkins, designer]." *Opportunity* 17 (February, 1939):52-53.

_____. "The Negro Actor on Broadway." *Opportunity* 16 (November, 1938):331-333.

_____. "Theatre in a Suitcase [Harlem Suitcase Theatre]." *Opportunity* 16 (December, 1938):360-361.

LYMAN, JOHN. "A Negro Theatre [Repertory Playhouse]." *Opportunity* 12 (January, 1934):15-17.

MCDOUGALD, J. F. "The Federal Government and the Negro Theatre." *Opportunity* 14 (May, 1936):135-137.

MILLER, LOREN. "Hollywood's New Negro Films." *Crisis* 45 (January, 1938):8-9.

————. "Uncle Tom in Hollywood." *Crisis* 41 (November, 1934):329, 336.

OVINGTON, MARY WHITE. "Dudley and His Mule." *Crisis* 39 (June, 1932):189, 203-204.

POWELL, ANNE. "The Negro in the Federal Theatre." *Crisis* 43 (November, 1936):340-341.

RANSDELL, HOLLACE. "The Soap Box Theatre." *Crisis* 42 (April, 1935):122, 124-125.

RAUCH, LAWRENCE LEE. "Triple-Threat Artist [Clarence Muse]." *Opportunity* 17 (September, 1939):275-276.

RIVERS, W. NAPOLEON, JR. "Gautier on Aldridge." *Crisis* 39 (January, 1932):459-460.

————. "Toussaint L'Ouverture in French Drama." *Opportunity* 10 (April, 1932):112-114.

ROSENBERG, CHESTER. "Duke Ellington." *Crisis* 43 (February, 1936):40-41, 60.

RUDD, WAYLAND. "Russian and American Theatre." *Crisis* 41 (September, 1934):270-278.

SCHLICH, ROBERT. "Theatre and the Arts." *Crisis* 39 (March, 1932):90.

SCHUYLER, GEORGE S. "*Not* Gone With the Wind." *Crisis* 44 (July, 1937):205-206.

SILVERA, JOHN D. "Still in Blackface." *Crisis* 46 (March, 1939): 71-72, 89.

SPRATLIN, VALAUREZ B. "The Negro in Spanish Literature." *Journal of Negro History* 19 (January, 1934):60-71.

THOMPSON, LOUISE. "The Soviet Film [*Black and White*]." *Crisis* 40 (February, 1933):37, 46.

WILLIAMSON, HARVEY M. "The Gilpin Players." *Crisis* 42 (July, 1935):205-206.

1940-1949

BOOKS

BOND, FREDERICK W. *The Negro and the Drama*. Washington, D.C.: Associated Publishers, 1940.

BROWN, STERLING A.; DAVIS, ARTHUR P.; and LEE, ULYSSES. *The Negro Caravan*. New York: The Dryden Press, 1941.

HANDY, W. C. *Father of the Blues*. New York: Macmillan, 1941.

ISAACS, EDITH J. R. *The Negro in the American Theatre*. New York: Theatre Arts, 1947.

MCKAY, CLAUDE. *Harlem: Negro Metropolis*. New York: Dutton, 1940.

MYRDAL, GUNNAR, with RICHARD STERNER and ARNOLD ROSE. *An American Dilemma*. New York: Harper, 1944.

NOBLE, PETER. *The Cinema and the Negro*. London: 1948. (A special supplement to *Sight and Sound*. Index series, No. 14.)

_____. *The Negro in Films*. London: Skelton Robinson, 1948.

ULANOV, BARRY. *Duke Ellington*. New York: Creative Age Press, 1945.

WATKINS, SYLVESTER C., ed. *Anthology of American Negro Literature*. New York: Modern Library, 1944.

SCHOLARLY THESES

BELCHER, FANNIN S., JR. "The Place of the Negro in the Evolution of the American Theatre, 1767-1940." Ph.D. dissertation, Yale University, 1945.

COLLINS, LESLIE M. "A Song, a Dance, and a Play—An Interpretative Study of Three American Artists [Negro performers]." Ph.D. dissertation, Western Reserve University, 1945.

GARTON, CHRISTIANA. "The Portrayal of Negro Character in the American Drama and Novel." Master's thesis, University of Colorado, 1942.

PAWLEY, THOMAS D., JR. "Experimental Productions of a Group of Original Plays." Ph.D. dissertation, University of Iowa, 1949.

PEMBROOK, CARRIE D. "Negro Drama Through the Ages." Ph.D. dissertation, New York University, 1946.

PETTIT, PAUL B. "The Important American Dramatic Types to 1900. A Study of the Yankee, Negro, Indian and Frontiersman." Ph.D. dissertation, Cornell University, 1949.

POAG, THOMAS E. "The Negro in Drama and Theatre." Ph.D. dissertation, Cornell University, 1943.

TROESCH, HELEN D. "The Negro in English Dramatic Literature on the Stage and a Bibliography of Plays with Negro Characters." Ph.D. dissertation, Western Reserve University, 1940.

PLAYS

BUTCHER, JAMES. *The Seer.* In *The Negro Caravan,* edited by Sterling A. Brown, Arthur P. Davis, and Ulysses Lee.

DODSON, OWEN. *Divine Comedy.* In *The Negro Caravan,* edited by Sterling A. Brown, Arthur P. Davis, and Ulysses Lee.

EDMONDS, RANDOLPH. *Bad Man.* In *The Negro Caravan,* edited by Sterling A. Brown, Arthur P. Davis, and Ulysses Lee.

LAMB, ARTHUR C. *Portrait of a Pioneer* [radio play on Aldridge]. *Negro History Bulletin* 12 (April, 1949):162-164.

PAWLEY, THOMAS D., JR. *Jedgement Day.* In *The Negro Caravan,* edited by Sterling A. Brown, Arthur P. Davis, and Ulysses Lee.

RICHARDS, STANLEY. *District of Columbia. Opportunity* 23 (April-June, 1945): 74-77.

STEPHENS, NAN BAGBY. *Lily.* New York: Row, Peterson, 1940.

WARD, THEODORE. *Big White Fog.* In *The Negro Caravan,* edited by Sterling A. Brown, Arthur P. Davis, and Ulysses Lee.

WRIGHT, RICHARD and GREEN, PAUL. *Native Son: A Play in Ten Scenes.* New York: Harper, 1941.

ARTICLES

"Actors Show How." *Negro Digest* 2 (April, 1944): 63-64.

ARVEY, VERNA. "Hall Johnson and His Choir." *Opportunity* 19 (May, 1941):151, 158-159.

"The Bard at Karamu." *Ebony* 3 (October, 1948): 36-40.

BERCH, BARBARA. "Lena Hits the Jackpot." *Negro Digest* 1 (January, 1943):13-15.

"Birth of a Musical [producer Clarence Muse]." *Ebony* 1 (April, 1946):47-50.

BOAS, FRANZISKA. "The Negro and the Dance as an Art." *Phylon* 10 (First Quarter, 1949):38-42.

BONTEMPS, ARNA. "Langston Hughes." *Ebony* 1 (October, 1946): 19-23.

————— and CONROY, JACK. "Karamu." *Any Place But Here.* New

York: Hill and Wang, 1945. Also in *Anthology of the American Negro in the Theatre* (1968), edited by Lindsay Patterson, pp. 111-115.

"The Boy with Green Hair [film on racial prejudice]." *Ebony* 4 (December, 1948):60-62.

BRAGGIOTTI, MARY. "No Midnight for Cinderella." *Negro Digest* 2 (February, 1944):13-15.

————. "Siren in Sepia [Hilda Simms]." *Negro Digest* 3 (December, 1944):45-47.

BROWN, STERLING A. "The Federal Theatre." From official reports of the Myrdal-Carnegie Study, Carnegie Foundation, 1940. Also in *Anthology of the American Negro in the Theatre* (1968), edited by Lindsay Patterson, pp. 101-107.

————. "The Negro Actor Attempts Legitimate." From official reports of the Myrdal-Carnegie Study, Carnegie Foundation, 1940. Also in *Anthology of the American Negro in the Theatre* (1968), edited by Lindsay Patterson, pp. 123-125.

BUCKMASTER, HENRIETTA. "A Forgotten Othello: Ira Aldridge." *Crisis* 51 (March, 1944):84-85.

The Burning Cross [film exposing KKK]. *Ebony* 2 (September, 1947):36-41.

"Canada Lee Back in the Ring." *Ebony* 2 (August, 1947):16-17.

"Canada Lee in Whiteface." *Ebony* 2 (January, 1947):38-39.

"Canadian Home of the Original Uncle Tom." *Crisis* 54 (March, 1947):81.

CARTER, PHIL. "It's Only Make-Believe." *Crisis* 53 (February, 1946):44-45, 61.

"Casbah [Katherine Dunham in film]." *Ebony* 3 (March, 1948): 36-38.

"Cass Timberlane [Maid in Hollywood films]." *Ebony* 3 (November, 1947):23-24.

COOK, MERCER. "De Lawd and Jazz." *Crisis* 47 (April, 1940): 112-114.

————. "Will Marion Cook: He Helped Them All." *Crisis* 51 (October, 1944):322, 328.

COOKE, ANNE. "The Atlanta University Summer Theatre." *Opportunity* 19 (November, 1941):331-333.

"Crusader for the Classics [Dean Dixon, music]." *Ebony* 1 (February, 1946):47-50.

Curtis, Constance, and Glasgow, Adele. "A Legitimate Theatre for Harlem." *Crisis* 51 (October, 1944): 321.

"Dancing School [Henry Le Tang]." *Ebony* 3 (March, 1948):45-48.

"A Date with Anna [Hilda Simms]." *Ebony* 1 (December, 1945):17-23.

"A Day at Home with a Chorus Girl [Carmen Alexander]." *Ebony* 1 (February, 1946):18-23.

DELAHANTY, THORNTON. "Reform in Movieland." *Negro Digest* 1 (January, 1943):63-65.

DENIS, PAUL. "The Negro in Show Business." *Negro Digest* 1 (February, 1943):34-39.

"Duffy's Tavern [Eddie Green]." *Ebony* 4 (March, 1949):23-26.

"The Duke and Duchess of the Music World [Ellington and Horne]." *Ebony* 4 (October, 1949):20-24.

"Dunham Dances at Pompeii." *Ebony* 4 (October, 1949):49-50.

EDMONDS, RANDOLPH. "The Negro Little Theatre Movement." *Negro History Bulletin* 12 (January, 1949):82-86, 92-94.

ELLIS, ROBERT. "Broadway's Battle Against Prejudice." *Negro Digest* 6 (December, 1947):63-66.

————. "How Radio Discriminates Against Negroes." *Negro Digest* 7 (June, 1949):64-66.

FERRER, JOSE. "Race in the Theatre." *Negro Digest* 4 (March, 1946):27-28.

FIELD, SIDNEY. "A Toughie Gets Tougher [Canada Lee]." *Negro Digest* 1 (February, 1943):15-16.

"Gentleman's Agreement [film on racism]." *Ebony* 3 (January, 1948):17-18.

GREEN, EDDIE. "My Biggest Break." *Negro Digest* 7 (September, 1949):31.

GREENE, MARJORIE. "Young Man of the Theatre and His Left Hand [Owen Dodson]." *Opportunity* 24 (Fall, 1946):200-201.

"Harlem Meteor [*Anna Lucasta*]." *Negro Digest* 3 (March, 1945):9-10.

HARMON, JOHN H. "Black Cowboys Are Real." *Crisis* 47 (September, 1940):280-281, 301-302.

HARRIS, AVENELLE. "I Tried to Crash the Movies." *Ebony* 1 (August, 1946):5-10.

"He Didn't Stoop to Conquer [Paul Robeson]." *Negro Digest* 2 (December, 1943):11-12.

HENLE, FRITZ. "Photo Salon: Four Studies of Canada Lee." *Negro Digest* 5 (February, 1947):95-98.

HILL, J. NEWTON. "The Achievement of the Negro in Drama." *Negro History Bulletin* 12 (February, 1949):100-102, 119.

HOLLIDAY, BILLIE. "I'm Cured for Good." *Ebony* 4 (July, 1949):26-32.

"Home of the Brave [film]." *Ebony* 4 (June, 1949):59-62.

HUGHES, LANGSTON. "Backstage." *Ebony* 4 (March, 1949):36-38.

————— et al. "Is Hollywood Fair to Negroes?" *Negro Digest* 1 (April, 1943):16-21.

—————. "The Need for Heroes." *Crisis* 48 (June, 1941):184-185, 206.

—————. "Simple and Me." *Phylon* 6 (Fourth Quarter, 1945): 349-353.

"Janet Collins [dancer]." *Ebony* 4 (September, 1949):53-54.

JEFFERSON, MILES M. "The Negro on Broadway, 1944." *Phylon* 6 (First Quarter, 1945):45-52.

—————. "The Negro on Broadway, 1945-46." *Phylon* 7 (Second Quarter, 1946):185-196.

—————. "The Negro on Broadway, 1946-47." *Phylon* 8 (Second Quarter, 1947):146-159.

—————. "The Negro on Broadway, 1947-48." *Phylon* 9 (Second Quarter, 1948):99-107.

—————. "The Negro on Broadway, 1948-49." *Phylon* 10 (Second Quarter, 1949):103-111.

KAMP, STELLA. "Langston Hughes Speaks to Young Writers." *Opportunity* 24 (Spring, 1946):73.

KAREV, G. "Russia Remembers Ira Aldridge." *Negro Digest* 5 (September, 1947):80-82.

LANDRY, ROBERT J. "Racial Stereotypes in Dramatic Writing." *Opportunity* 23 (April-June, 1945):72-73.

LANE, WILLIAM C. "Leading Man at Seventeen [Earle Hyman]." *Crisis* 55 (July, 1948):204, 220.

LASH, JOHN S. "The Negro and Radio." *Opportunity* 21 (October, 1943):158-161, 182-183.

"Lazy Lips [Pearl Bailey]." *Negro Digest* 4 (September, 1946):47-48.

LEE, CHAUNCEY. "USO Camp Shows and the Soldier." *Crisis* 51 (February, 1944):50, 61.

"Lena Horne Begins a New Movie." *Ebony* 1 (March, 1946):14-20.

LEONARD, CLAIRE. "Dark Drama." *Negro Digest* 2 (August, 1944):81-82.

LEWIS, LLOYD. "Life with Uncle Eggs [Bert Williams]." *Negro Digest* 4 (July, 1946):19-22.

LOCKE, ALAIN. "A Contribution to American Culture." *Opportunity* 23 (Fall, 1945):192-193.

LOVELL, JOHN, JR. "Democracy in a Hit Revue [*Call Me Mister*]." *Crisis* 54 (March, 1947):76-77.

————. "Negro Drama: Double Take [on Edith Isaacs' book, *The Negro in the American Theatre*]." *Crisis* 54 (November, 1947):334-336.

————. "New Curtains Going Up." *Crisis* 54 (October, 1947): 305-307, 315-316.

————. "The Operatic Stage." *Crisis* 55 (February, 1948):42-44, 59-62.

————. "Roundup: The Negro in the American Theatre [1940-1947]." *Crisis* 54 (July, 1947):212-217.

————. "Singing in the Streets [musical]." *Crisis* 54 (June, 1947):172-174, 188.

————. "Sources of Broadway." *Crisis* 54 (September, 1947): 268-270, 283-284.

MATTHIAS, BLANCHE C. "Katherine Dunham." *Opportunity* 19 (April, 1941):112-113.

MCCLAIN, WILLIAM A. "Cincinnati's Theatre Doors Are Opened." *Crisis* 48 (December, 1941):382-383, 389.

MCCONNELL, FANNY. "Broadway Taboo Is Lifted." *Opportunity* 22 (Fall, 1944):175.

"Meet the Real Lena Horne." *Ebony* 3 (November, 1947):9-14.

"Moonrise [Rex Ingram film]." *Ebony* 3 (July, 1948):51.

"Movie Maids [on menials in films]." *Ebony* 3 (August, 1948):56-59.

NATHAN, GEORGE JEAN. "Color Takes the Stage." *Negro Digest* 4 (December, 1945):37-40.

"Negro Movies Hit Pay Dirt." *Ebony* 1 (September, 1946):42-44.

"*The Negro Sailor* [documentary film of World War II]." *Ebony* 1 (July, 1946):11-14.

NOBLE, PETER. "The Negro on the Stage." In *The Negro in Films*, pp. 13-27.

"Nothing Too Big for Bigger [Canada Lee]." *Negro Digest* 3 (February, 1945):77-80.

ORTIZ, FERNANDO, and MARQUINA RAFAEL. "The Negro in the Spanish Theatre." *Phylon* 4 (Second Quarter, 1943):144-152.

OTTLEY, ROI. "Greta Garbo of the Arab World [Takia Koriem]." *Negro Digest* 7 (November, 1948):36.

PAWLEY, THOMAS D., JR. "I Am a Fugitive from a Play." *National Theatre Conference* 10 (July, 1948):9-12.

————. "Stage Craft in Negro Colleges." *Negro College Quarterly* 4 (December, 1946):193-199, 217.

"The Peanut Man [about G. W. Carver]." *Ebony* 2 (July, 1947):48-50.

"Perry Watkins [stage designer]." *Ebony* 2 (June, 1947):20.

"Pinky [film on "passing"]." *Ebony* 4 (September, 1949):23-25.

"Poets." *Ebony* 4 (February, 1949):41-45.

"Radio and Race." *Ebony* 1 (January, 1946):41-43.

"Rainbow over Broadway [*Finian's Rainbow*]." *Ebony* 2 (May, 1947):38-40.

"Romeo and Juliet in Television [Hilda Simms]." *Negro Digest* 5 (December, 1946):19-22.

ROSE, BILLY. "Box Office Color Line." *Negro Digest* 6 (December, 1947):19-20.

"Ruby Hill." *Ebony* 1 (May, 1946):14-19.

"The Schoolmarm Who Glorified Leg Art [Katherine Dunham]." *Ebony* 2 (January, 1947):14-18.

SCHUYLER, GEORGE. "America Caught Up with Him [Lucky Roberts]." *Crisis* 49 (June, 1942):194-195.

"Shakespeare in Whiteface [Ira Aldridge]." *Negro Digest* 2 (April, 1944):39-40.

"Showcase of Harlem [Apollo Theatre]." *Ebony* 4 (July, 1949):13-18.

SMITH, WILLIAM THOMAS. "Hollywood Report." *Phylon* 6 (First Quarter, 1945):13-16.

STILL, WILLIAM GRANT. "How Do We Stand in Hollywood?" *Opportunity* 23 (April-June, 1945):74-77.

STRICK, ANNE. "*Kingsblood* from Novel to Play." *Negro Digest* 6 (February, 1948):40-43.

————. "Tolerance in the Theatre." *Negro Digest* 6 (January, 1948):80-82.

"Trial by Fire [play by Fr. Dunne]." *Ebony* 2 (June, 1947):31-35.

TRUMBO, DALTON. "Blackface, Hollywood Style." *Crisis* 50 (December, 1943):365-367, 378.

"Two Decades with the Duke." *Ebony* 1 (January, 1946):11-19.

WILDBERG, JOHN. "Broadway's Iron Curtain." *Negro Digest* 5

(December, 1946):41-43.

_____. "Talent and Tolerance in the Theatre." *Negro Digest* 4 (April, 1946):43-44.

WILSON, EARL. "Dressing Room Shrine [Ethel Waters]." *Negro Digest* 3 (February, 1945):89-90.

WINSLOW, THYRA SAMTER. "Color Takes the Stage." *Negro Digest* 4 (May 1946):43-45.

1950-1959

BOOKS

ANDERSON, MARIAN. *My Lord, What a Morning.* New York: Viking, 1956.

BARDOLPH, RICHARD. *The Negro Vanguard.* New York: Rinehart, 1959.

BUTCHER, MARGARET JUST. *The Negro in American Culture.* New York: Knopf, 1956.

FLETCHER, TOM. *100 Years of the Negro in Show Business.* New York: Burdge, 1954.

GAMMOND, PETER. *Duke Ellington, His Life and Music.* New York: Roy Publishers, 1958.

JEROME, VICTOR JEREMY. *The Negro in Hollywood Films.* New York: Masses and Mainstream, 1950.

MARSHALL, HERBERT, and STOCK, MILDRED. *Ira Aldridge, the Negro Tragedian.* New York: Macmillan, 1958.

SETON, MARIE. *Paul Robeson.* New York: Dobson, 1958.

WATERS, ETHEL. *His Eye Is on the Sparrow.* New York: Doubleday, 1951.

SCHOLARLY THESES

ARCHER, LEONARD C. "The National Association for the Advancement of Colored People and the American Theatre. A Study of Relationships and Influences." Ph.D. dissertation, Ohio State University, 1959.

DAVIDSON, FRANK C. "The Rise, Development, Decline and Influence of the American Minstrel Show." Ph.D. dissertation, New York University, 1952.

GARY, J. VAUGHN, JR. "The Integration of the Negro on the New

York Stage Since 1940." Master's thesis, Columbia University, 1958.

KUHLKE, WILLIAM. "They Too Sing America: The New Negro as Portrayed by Negro Playwrights, 1918-1930." Master's thesis, University of Kansas, 1959.

LINNEHAN, E. G. "We Wear the Mask: The Use of Negro Life and Character in American Drama." Ph. D. dissertation, University of Pennsylvania, 1953.

LUCK, JAMES WILLIAM. "The Contribution of the Negro to the Legitimate Theatre in America." Master's thesis, Emerson College, 1953.

SANDLE, FLOYD L. "A History of the Development of the Educational Theatre in the Negro Colleges and Universities, 1911-1959." Ph. D. dissertation, Louisiana State University, 1959.

WILLIAMS, EDDIE RAY. "The Rise of the Negro Actor in the American Theatre from 1900-1950." Master's thesis, Tennessee A & I, 1951.

PLAYS

HANSBERRY, LORRAINE. *A Raisin in the Sun.* New York: Random House, 1959.

HUGHES, LANGSTON, and MARTIN, DAVID. *Simply Heavenly.* New York: Dramatists Play Service, 1957.

JOHN, ERROL. *Moon on a Rainbow Shawl.* London: Faber & Faber, 1958.

KOMAI, FELICIA (in collaboration with Douglas, Josephine). *Cry, the Beloved Country* (A verse adaptation from Paton's novel.) London: Edinburgh House Press, 1954.

MCBROWN, G. P. *Birthday Surprise [Paul Dunbar]. Negro History Bulletin* 16 (February, 1953):102-104.

PETERSON, LOUIS S. *Take a Giant Step.* New York: French, 1954.

ARTICLES

"Actress in the Making." *Our World* 5 (August, 1950):24-26.

"African Ballet Upsets New York." *Ebony* 14 (May, 1959):37-42.

"Aftermath: Here Is Marva." *Our World* 8 (July, 1953):12-13.

ALAN, ROBERT. "Paul Robeson: The Lost Shepherd." *Crisis* 58 (November, 1951):569-573.

ALLEN, STEVE. "Talent Is Color-Blind." *Ebony* 10 (September, 1955):41-49.

"Amos 'n' Andy on Television." *Ebony* 6 (May, 1951):21-24.

"André Drew School of the Dance." *Ebony* 11 (June, 1956):27-30.

"Anna Belle Hill." *Ebony* 5 (March, 1950):49-51.

"*Anna Lucasta* [film—Eartha Kitt and Sammy Davis]." *Ebony* 14 (December, 1958): 72-76.

"Anna Lucasta, the Tenth [Mauri Lynn]." *Our World* 8 (July, 1953):28.

"Ballerina De Lavallade." *Our World* 8 (July, 1953):49-50.

"Ballet Star [Arthur Mitchell]." *Ebony* 15 (November, 1959): 122-126.

"Belafonte Becomes Big Business." *Ebony* 13 (June, 1958):17-24.

BELCHER, FANNIN S., JR. "The Negro Theatre: A Glance Backward." *Phylon* 11 (Second Quarter, 1950):121-126.

BENNETT, LERONE, JR. "Hollywood's First Negro Movie Star [Sidney Poitier]." *Ebony* 14 (May, 1959):100-108.

————. "Wonderful 'Mr. Wonderful'." *Ebony* 12 (December, 1956): 40-49.

"Billie Holliday's Tragic Life." *Ebony* 11 (September, 1956):47-51.

"Billy Daniels." *Ebony* 5 (September, 1950):40-44.

"Birthday for Sarah [Vaughan]." *Ebony* 7 (July, 1952):108-110.

"*Blackboard Jungle* [Poitier film]." *Ebony* 10 (May, 1955):87-93.

"Booking Agent [Ben Waller]." *Ebony* 8 (December, 1952):120-126.

"Broadway 'Oriental' [Juanita Hall]." *Ebony* 14 (March, 1959):128-130.

"Broadway's Newest Golden Boy [Belafonte]." *Our World* 9 (May, 1954):43-47.

BROWN, G. F. "Decline of Negro Show Business." *Sepia* 7 (January, 1959):36-39.

BROWNLEE, L. "*A Raisin in the Sun*." *Sepia* 7 (May, 1959):68-71.

"Buddy Bradley [teaching dance in Britain]." *Ebony* 5 (July, 1950):61-62.

"Butterbeans and Susie [oldest Negro Comedy Team]." *Ebony* 7 (April, 1952):59-63.

"Cakewalk King [Charles E. Johnson]." *Ebony* 8 (February, 1953):99-106.

"Can Sammy Davis, Jr., Crash Network TV?" *Ebony* 9 (October, 1954):33-40.

CANTOR, EDDIE. "The Best Teacher I Ever Had [Bert Williams]." *Ebony* 13 (June, 1958):103-106.

CARTWRIGHT, MARGUERITE. "No Type-Casting—Frederick O'Neal Scores Again." *Negro History Bulletin* 18 (October, 1954):3-4.

"Cat-Like Miss Kitt." *Ebony* 12 (July, 1957):24-26.

"Chance of a Lifetime [Diahann Carroll]." *Our World* 9 (May, 1954):12-17.

"Child Star Grows Up [Leslie Uggams]." *Ebony* 15 (December, 1959):115-120.

"Comeback for Lena Horne." *Ebony* 6 (August, 1951):29-32.

COUCH, WILLIAM, JR. "The Problem of Negro Character and Dramatic Incident." *Phylon* 11 (Second Quarter, 1950):127-133.

COWAN, M. F. "Some Unknown Plays About the Negro." *Negro History Bulletin* 14 (June, 1951):200-204ff.

CROSBY, BING. "What Show Business Owes the Negro." *Negro Digest* 9 (August, 1951):3-6.

"*Cry, the Beloved Country* [film]." *Ebony* 6 (July, 1951):57-62.

"Dance Version of *Porgy.*" *Ebony* 8 (September, 1953):99-101.

"Dance Virtuoso [Eunice Cain]." *Ebony* 12 (February, 1957):32-37.

"The Dancing Holders." *Ebony* 13 (February, 1958):117-122.

"Dandridge Gets Red Carpet Treatment." *Ebony* 11 (August, 1956):24-29.

"Danish Play by Negro College." *Negro History Bulletin* 15 (June, 1952):187.

DARMSTADER, KARL D. "An Englishmen Reviews *Uncle Tom's Cabin* in 1853 and Prophesies about 1953." *Negro History Bulletin* 17 (January, 1954):83.

DAVIS, ARTHUR P. "The Tragic Mulatto Theme in Six Works of Langston Hughes." *Phylon* 16 (Second Quarter, 1955):195-204.

"Dazzling New Star of Dance Drama [Matt Turney]." *Ebony* 13 (July, 1958):28-32.

"*The Decks Ran Red* [Dorothy Dandridge movie]." *Ebony* 14 (November, 1958):60-64.

"*The Defiant Ones* [Poitier movie]." *Ebony* 13 (October, 1958):80-84.

DELPECK, JEANINE. "An Interview with Native Son [Richard Wright]." *Crisis* 57 (November, 1950):625-626, 678.

"*Demetrius and the Gladiators* [William Marshall film]." *Ebony* 9 (November, 1953):91-96.

"Do Negroes Have a Future in Hollywood?" *Ebony* 11 (December, 1955):24-30.

"Do You Remember . . . Stepin Fetchit?" *Negro Digest* 9 (November, 1950):42-43.

DODSON, OWEN. "College Troopers Abroad [Howard Players]." *Negro Digest* 8 (April, 1950):47-49.

"Donald McKayle—Dancer." *Crisis* 60 (April, 1953):212.

"Dorothy Dandridge." *Ebony* 9 (December, 1953):100-103.

"Dorothy Dandridge's Greatest Triumph [Academy Award nomination]." *Ebony* 10 (July, 1955):37-41.

DOVER, CEDRIC. "The Importance of Georgia Douglass Johnson." *Crisis* 59 (December, 1952):633-636, 674.

DU BOIS, W. E. B., and WHITE, WALTER. "Paul Robeson: Right or Wrong." *Negro Digest* 8 (March, 1950):8-18.

"Dunham Dance Graduates." *Ebony* 8 (June, 1953):48-53.

"Eartha Kitt."*Ebony* 7 (June, 1952):60-64.

"Eartha Kitt Takes Off." *Ebony* 11 (March, 1956):24-29.

EDDY, JUNIUS. "A Theatre for All People [Karamu]." *Wisconsin Stage* 8 (Fall, 1954):26-34.

"Edna McGriff." *Ebony* 8 (December, 1952):35-38.

"*The Egyptian* [de Lavallade film]." *Ebony* 9 (August, 1954): 83-86.

"Eleanor Martinez—Talented Dancer." *Our World* 7 (November, 1952):6-7.

ELLIS, ROBERT. "A Hollywood Director Speaks Out [*Home of the Brave*]." *Negro Digest* 9 (January, 1951):42-44.

"Europe's Dancing Doll [Frances Taylor]." *Ebony* 7 (September, 1952):60-66.

"Faculty Frolics [Virginia Union Teachers]." *Ebony* 12 (March, 1957):112-114.

"$50,000 a Day [Nat Cole]." *Ebony* 8 (October, 1953):85-92.

FORD, NICK AARON. "How Genuine Is *The Green Pastures?*" *Phylon* 20 (First Quarter, 1959):67-70.

"Frank Silvera." *Ebony* 7 (March, 1952):51-55.

"From Actor to College Prof [Juano Hernandez]." *Ebony* 8 (November, 1952):122-128.

"From Vera to Viejah." *Our World* 10 (April, 1955):14-15.

GARDNER, A. "Sammy Sends Me." *Our World* 10 (December, 1954-January, 1955):48-52.

GAREY, DORIS B. *"The Green Pastures* Again." *Phylon* 20 (Second Quarter, 1959):193-194.

GIBSON, RICHARD. "Is the Negro Writer Free?" *Negro Digest* 9 (September, 1951):43-45.

"Girl with the Big Bass Voice [Ann Weldon]." *Ebony* 10 (July, 1955):107-109.

"Golden Year on Broadway." *Our World* 5 (September, 1950):30-34.

GOODMAN, P. "They are Bought." *Liberation* 4 (December 1959): 5-6.

"Grace Through Exercise [Dorothy Dandridge]." *Ebony* 14 (March, 1959):33-36.

"The Great Sammy Davis Comeback." *Ebony* 10 (April, 1955):26-31.

"Greater Philadelphia's Newest TV Star." *Color* 11 (December, 1955-January, 1956):5.

"Hadda Brooks." *Ebony* 6 (April, 1951):101-105.

HARRIS, MARK. "Shaw Speaks of the Negro." *Negro Digest* 8 (February, 1950):52-55.

————. "What Shakespeare Wrote About Negroes." *Negro Digest* 8 (January, 1950):34-38.

"Harry Belafonte's Best Year." *Ebony* 11 (March, 1956):56-60.

HEPBURN, D. "How Evil Is Eartha?" *Our World* 9 (September, 1954):9-15.

"The High Mountain [radio show]." *Crisis* 61 (April, 1954):226-229, 250.

"Hollywood's 'Hottest' Negro Actor [Juano Hernandez]." *Ebony* 5(August, 1950):22-26.

"Hollywood's New Glamour Queen [Dorothy Dandridge]." *Ebony* 6 (April, 1951):48-50.

"How Linda Darnell Fights Jim Crow." *Color* 11 (March, 1956):19-21.

INGRAM, REX. "I Came Back from the Dead." *Ebony* 10 (March, 1955):48-55.

"Integration Showcase [Frederick O'Neal]." *Ebony* 14 (August, 1959):71-74.

"Island in the Sun [Dandridge/Belafonte film]." *Ebony* 12 (July, 1957):33-37.

IVY, JAMES W. "First Congress Negro Writers and Artists." *Crisis* 63 (December, 1956):593-600.

"Janet Collins' Dance School." *Ebony* 11 (January, 1956):28-30.

JEFFERSON, MILES M. "The Negro on Broadway, 1949-50." *Phylon* 11 (Second Quarter, 1950):105-113.

————. "Empty Season on Broadway, 1950-51." *Phylon* 12 (Second Quarter, 1951):128-136.

————. "The Negro on Broadway, 1951-52: Another Transparent Season." *Phylon* 13 (Third Quarter, 1952):199-208.

————. "The Negro on Broadway, 1953-54: A Baffling Season." *Phylon* 15 (Third Quarter, 1954):253-260.

————. "The Negro on Broadway, 1954-55—More Spice Than Substance." *Phylon* 16 (Third Quarter, 1955):303-312.

————. "The Negro on Broadway, 1955-56—Pits and Peaks in an Active Season." *Phylon* 17 (Third Quarter, 1956):227-237.

————. "The Negro on Broadway, 1956-57." *Phylon* 18 (Third Quarter, 1957):286-295.

"Josephine Baker Comes Home Again." *Ebony* 6 (May, 1951):74-78.

"Juanita Hall [Bloody Mary]." *Ebony* 5 (July, 1950):29-32.

"June Richmond [comedienne in Sweden]." *Ebony* 8 (November, 1952):141-144.

KAPLAN, SIDNEY. "Herman Melville and the American National Sin: The Meaning of *Benito Cereno*." *The Journal of Negro History*. Part I, 41 (October, 1956):311-338; Part II, 42 (January, 1957):11-37.

"Katherine Dunham Spices Up Dance Review." *Ebony* 10 (August, 1955):25-27.

"Kid Entertainers." *Ebony* 5 (September, 1950):67-70.

"King Cole's Wife Goes Back to Work." *Ebony* 11 (December, 1955):132-138.

"Lavinia Williams [dancer's work in Haiti]." *Ebony* 9 (February, 1954):94-98.

"Lena Horne Enjoys Longest Vacation." *Ebony* 10 (December, 1954):64-70.

"Lena Horne Returns to Broadway." *Ebony* 13 (January, 1958):74-78.

"Lena Horne's New Singing Style." *Ebony* 5 (October, 1950):35-36.

"*Lights Out* [film on racial bias]." *Ebony* 6 (December, 1950):87-90.

"*Lost in the Stars* [Broadway musical]." *Ebony* 5 (February, 1950):26-28.

"Louis Takes a Giant Step." *Our World* 9 (January, 1954):45-48ff.

"*Mambo* [Katherine Dunham movie]." *Ebony* 10 (December, 1954):83-86.

"Man Who Created Emperor Jones." *Sepia* 6 (May, 1958):41.

"Marpessa Dawn [stars in Europe]." *Ebony* 15 (November, 1959):85-90.

"Matt Turney—Dancer." *Crisis* 65 (April, 1958):212-215.

"*The Member of the Wedding* [Ethel Waters film]." *Ebony* 8 (December, 1952):47-51.

"Memory Lingers On." *Our World* 9 (September, 1954):46-49.

"Men in My Life [Ethel Waters]." *Ebony* 7 (January, 1952):24-32.

MIERS, EARL SCHENCK. "Paul Robeson: Made by America." *Negro Digest* 8 (October, 1950):21-24.

"Million Dollar Beauty, Lena Horne." *Sepia* 6 (January, 1958):7-13.

"Miss Dunham Trains Dancers for New Film." *Ebony* 13 (October, 1958):121-124.

"Miss Waters Regrets." *Ebony* 12 (February, 1957):56-60.

"Mr. Duncan Returns to B'Way." *Our World* 5 (March, 1950):32-34.

"Moondongo—A New Dance Group's Version of an Old African Theme." *Our World* 9 (June, 1954):8 ff.

MORRISON, ALLAN. "Ethel Waters Come Back to Broadway." *Negro Digest* 8 (April, 1950):6-10.

_____. "W. C. Handy." *Ebony* 9 (November, 1953):59-70.

_____. "Who Will Be the First to Crack Met Opera?" *Negro Digest* 8 (September, 1950):52-56.

MORTIMER, OWEN. "Ira Aldridge: Shakespearean Actor." *Crisis* 62 (April, 1955):203-214.

"Movie-Maker Belafonte." *Ebony* 14 (July, 1959):94-100.

"Muriel Rahn's Dance of the Seven Veils." *Ebony* 10 (January, 1955):66-73.

"Mystery of Dorothy Dandridge." *Color* 11 (March, 1956):7-9.

"Nat King Cole Turns Actor." *Ebony* 12 (June, 1957):74-76.

"Negro Actors Star in Off-Broadway Play." *Crisis* 66 (January, 1959):36-37.

"Negro and TV." *Our World* 9 (February, 1954):17-23.

"The Negro in Literature: The Current Scene." *Phylon* 11 (Fourth Quarter, 1950). This special issue is devoted to an overall examination of writers.

"Negro Playwrights." *Ebony* 14 (April, 1959):95-99.

"Negro Progress in 1953." *Ebony* 9 (January, 1954):17-24. (An annual feature in January issues.)

"New Faces [Eartha Kitt]." *Ebony* 9 (May, 1954):30-34.

"New Faces in Show Business." *Ebony* 9 (June, 1954):45-48.

"Newest Ballet Star [Jamie Bower]." *Ebony* 10 (November, 1954):36-40.

NICHOLS, CHARLES. "The Origins of *Uncle Tom's Cabin.*" *Phylon* 19 (Third Quarter, 1958):328-334.

"*No Way Out* [film]." *Ebony* 5 (March, 1950):31-34.

"*Of Men and Music* [Marian Anderson film]." *Ebony* 6 (May, 1951):49-52.

"Off-Stage with Eartha Kitt." *Our World* 8 (January, 1953):44-45.

"The Old-Timers." *Ebony* 12 (December, 1956):63-66.

"Opera Singers [leading Negro artists]." *Ebony* 15 (November, 1959):27-34.

"Otto Sterman, the Man of a Hundred Faces." *Our World* 10 (February, 1955):17-23.

OWENS, W. H., JR. "Philosophy of Dramatic Education in Our Schools." *Negro Education Review* 3 (October, 1952):171-174.

"Passing of Beulah." *Our World* 8 (February, 1953):12-15.

"*Passion Play* [Chicago's all-Negro play]." *Ebony* 5 (May, 1950):25-28.

PAWLEY, THOMAS D., JR. "Theatre Arts and the Educated Man." *Central States Speech Journal* 8 (Spring, 1957):5-11.

"Pearl Bailey." *Ebony* 5 (May, 1950):21-24.

"Pearl Bailey Returns to Broadway [*House of Flowers*]." *Ebony* 10 (April, 1955):60-64.

"Pearl Primus." *Ebony* 6 (January, 1951):54-58.

"Pearl's Prodigy [Percival Borde]." *Ebony* 14 (March, 1959):46-50.

"*Porgy* Amid Pyramids [touring show]." *Ebony* 10 (June, 1955):40-46.

"*Porgy and Bess* [controversy]." *Ebony* 8 (November, 1952):98-102.

"Psychology Predicts Stage Careers." *Ebony* 14 (January, 1959):24-28.

"Radio Producer [Robert Hodges]." *Ebony* 7 (March, 1952):81-84.

"Requiem for the Kingfish [Tim Moore]." *Ebony* 14 (July, 1959):57-64.

RICHARDS, AGNES. "The Black Swan [Elizabeth Taylor Greenfield]." *Negro Digest* 9 (November, 1950):73-75.

ROBINSON, FANNIE. "I Remember Bojangles." *Ebony* 8 (February, 1953):49-60.

ROWAN, CARL. "Has Paul Robeson Betrayed the Negro?" *Ebony* 12 (October, 1957):31-42.

"*St. Louis Blues* [Nat Cole movie]." *Ebony* 13 (May, 1958):27-32.

"Salome [danced by Carmen de Lavallade]." *Our World* 5 (December, 1950):24-26.

"Sammy and Friends." *Ebony* 13 (November, 1957):25-30.

"Sammy Davis, Jr." *Ebony* 6 (December, 1950):45-49.

"Satchmo Goes 'Back Home' [African tour]." *Ebony* 11 (September, 1956):31-34.

"School for Child Entertainers." *Ebony* 8 (August, 1953):62-66.

SCHUYLER, GEORGE S. "What's Wrong with Negro Authors." *Negro Digest* 8 (May, 1950):3-7.

"Screen Test [Dorothy Dandridge]." *Ebony* 9 (September, 1954):37-42.

"*See How They Run* [Dorothy Dandridge film]." *Ebony* 8 (April, 1953):43-48.

"Shakespeare Play Barred in Southern Colleges [Negroes in cast]." *Crisis* 57 (April, 1950):228-229, 270.

"*Show Boat* [film debut of William Warfield]." *Ebony* 6 (June, 1951):69-71.

"Silas Green of New Orleans [southern tent show]." *Ebony* 9 (September, 1954):68-73.

SISSLE, NOBLE. "How Jo Baker Got Started." *Negro Digest* 9 (August, 1951):15-19.

"Sissle and Blake [40 years in vaudeville]." *Ebony* 10 (March, 1955):112-118.

SMITH, WILLIAM GARDINER. "Phylon Profile XXI: Ethel Waters." *Phylon* 11 (Second Quarter, 1950):114-120.

SPINGARN, A. B. "Books by Negro Authors, 1950." *Crisis* 58 (February, 1951):80-84. (This excellent compilation has been a regular feature for years.)

SPINKS, WILLIAM C. "Bert Williams: Brokenhearted Comedian." *Phylon* 11 (First Quarter, 1950):59-65.

"Stage Manager for *Fanny* [Charlie Blackwell]." *Ebony* 12 (August, 1957):37-38.

"Stepin Fetchit Comes Back." *Ebony* 7 (February, 1952):64-67.
"Sugar Hill on Broadway." *Our World* 7 (January, 1952):36-43.
"*Take a Giant Step* [movie]." *Ebony* 14 (September, 1959):48-51.
"Television [job opportunities]." *Ebony* 5 (June, 1950):22-25.
"That Certain Feeling [Pearl Bailey]." *Ebony* 11 (January, 1956):75-79.
"This Is Show Business." *Our World* 8 (September, 1953):32-36ff.
THOMPSON, ERA BELL. "Why Negroes Don't Like *Porgy and Bess.*" *Ebony* 14 (October, 1959):50-54.
"Trailer Theatre [American Negro Repertory]." *Ebony* 5 (October, 1950):52-54.
"Trenier Twins [comedy team]." *Ebony* 9 (July, 1954):31-34.
"Trial [Juano Hernandez as a judge]." *Ebony* 11 (November, 1955):29-32.
"Trials of a TV Actress [Abbie Shuford]." *Ebony* 10 (March, 1955):104-110.
TUCKER, MARTIN. "*Mister Johnson* vs. Mr. Hyman." *Crisis* 65 (January, 1958):13-16, 61.
TUCKER, SOPHIE. "How Negroes Influenced My Career." *Ebony* 9 (December, 1953):80-92.
"TV Floor Manager [Fred Lights]." *Ebony* 9 (April, 1954):104-106.
"TV Technicians." *Ebony* 9 (August, 1954):25-30.
"Twelve Years to Broadway [Barbara McNair]." *Ebony* 13 (May, 1958):69-74.
WEALES, GERALD. "Pro Negro Films in Atlanta, Georgia." *Phylon* 13 (Fourth Quarter, 1952):298-304.
"*West Side Story* [Negro dancers]." *Ebony* 13 February, 1958):49-53.
"What Makes a Star? [panel discussion]." *Ebony* 13 (November, 1957):143-146.
"When Mahalia Sings." *Ebony* 9 (January, 1954):34-38.
WHITE, A. "From Tom-Toms to Television." *Our World* 6 (February, 1951):30-38.
"Why Negroes Don't Like Eartha Kitt." *Ebony* 10 (December, 1954):29-38.
"William Marshall, De Lawd's Gift to Hollywood." *Our World* 6 (December, 1951):12-14.
YOUNG, A. S. "Dorothy Dandridge Marries." *Sepia* 7 (September, 1959):39-43.

_____. "Harry Belafonte's Debut as a Hollywood Producer."
Sepia 7 (July, 1959):34-39.

YOUNG, L. M. "Apollo Story [theatre]." *Our World* 9 (June,
1954):74-81.

_____. "Negroes Who Work on Broadway." *Our World* 7 (July,
1952):34-38.

ZAHN C. "What's My Crime?" *Liberation* 1 (February, 1957):
15-17.

1960

BOOKS

SHAW, ARNOLD. *Belafonte: An Unauthorized Biography.* New
York: Chilton, 1960.

SCHOLARLY THESES

None

PLAYS

None

ARTICLES

"*All the Young Men* [Poitier movie]." *Ebony* 15 (August,
1960):83-88.

BRADLEY, B. "Making of a Broadway Star." *Sepia* 8 (July,
1960):58-60.

"Broadway U.S.A. [Hilda Simms USO Tour]." *Jet* (November
10, 1960):59.

COTTON, LETTIE JO. "The Negro in the American Theatre." *Negro
History Bulletin* 23 (May, 1960):172-178.

"D.C.'s Dean of Show Biz [Shep Allen]." *Ebony* 16 (November,
1960):89-93.

ELKIN, FREDERICK. "Censorship and Pressure Groups." *Phylon* 21
(First Quarter, 1960):71-80.

HEPBURN, D. "They Call Him a Genius [Harold Scott]." *Sepia* 8
(November, 1960):32-34.

"The Last Angry Man [Billy Dee Williams]." *Ebony* 15 (January,
1960):42-44.

"Lena's Daughter Makes Stage Debut." *Ebony* 16 (November, 1960):129-134.

LUCAS, B. "Mr. and Mrs. Broadway [Ruby Dee and Ossie Davis]." *Sepia* 8 (9) (April, 1960):51-53.

MORRISON, ALLAN. "Mother Role Brings Broadway Fame [Claudia McNeil]." *Ebony* 15 (May, 1960):97-102.

"The Pretender [James Earl Jones]." *Jet* (June 9, 1960):60.

"*Raisin in the Sun* Sets Record [number of performances]." *Jet* (June 16, 1960):58.

"See How They Run [Tennessee A & I Players]." *Jet* (March 10, 1960):41; (April 28, 1960):60.

"The Star-Maker [Phil Moore]." *Ebony* 16 (November, 1960):120-128.

"Tambourines to Glory [Hazel Scott in lead]." *Jet* (July 21, 1960):62.

"*Toys in the Attic.*" *Ebony* 15 (July, 1960):125-128.

TURNER, DARWIN T. "The Negro Dramatist's Image of the Universe, 1920-1960." *CLA Journal* (September, 1960). Also in *Anthology of the American Negro in the Theatre* (1968), edited by Lindsay Patterson, pp. 65-74.

"TV Schoolmarm to 24,000 Children [Norma Anderson]." *Ebony* 15 (April, 1960):60-64.

WEBB, A. "How TV Is Missing the Boat on Tan Stars." *Sepia* 8 (9) (May, 1960):19-22.

"A Wreath for Udomo [at Karamu]." *Jet* (March 31, 1960):60.

YOUNG, A. S. "Hollywood School for Actors." *Sepia* 8 (9) (March 1960):72-76.

YOUNG, M. "The Cool World." *Sepia* 8 (9) (May, 1960):36-40.

1961

BOOKS

None

SCHOLARLY THESES

ABRAHAMS, ROGER DAVID. "Negro Folklore from South Philadelphia, a Collection and Analysis." Ph.D. dissertation, University of Pennsylvania, 1961.

SILVER, REUBEN. "A History of the Karamu Theatre of Karamu House, 1915-1960." Ph.D. dissertation, Ohio State University, 1961.

PLAYS

DAVIS, OSSIE. *Purlie Victorious.* New York: French, 1961.

ARTICLES

BALDWIN, JAMES. "James Baldwin on the Negro Actor." *Urbanite* (April, 1961). Also in *Anthology of the American Negro in the Theatre* (1968), edited by Lindsay Patterson, pp. 127-130.

"Ballet Ballads [Carmen de Lavallade]." *Ebony* 16 (May, 1961): 34-35.

BARKSDALE, RICHARD K. "White Tragedy—Black Comedy." *Phylon* 22 (Third Quarter, 1961): 226-233.

BENNETT, LERONE, JR. "The Soul of Soul." *Ebony* 17 (December, 1961):111-120.

"*Black Maturity* [Langston Hughes song-play] Opens Off-Broadway." *Jet* (December 28, 1961):56.

CLAYTON, EDWARD T. "The Tragedy of Amos 'n' Andy." *Ebony* 16 (October, 1961):66-73.

"Dance History from Cakewalk to Watusi." *Ebony* 16 (August, 1961):32-38.

"Dick Gregory." *Ebony* 16 (May, 1961):67-72.

"Dyerettes Train Successors [dancers]." *Ebony* 16 (April, 1961): 35-36.

EPSTEIN, B. R. "Stereotypes [TV]." *Community* 21 (September, 1961):9-10.

GANT, HERMAN. "Why I Turned Down Stardom in Paris." *Negro Digest* 11 (December, 1961):45-48.

HANSBERRY, LORRAINE. "American Theatre Needs Desegregating, Too." *Negro Digest* 10 (June, 1961):28-33.

"*Hawaii* [Juanita Hall film]." *Jet* (January 19, 1961):60.

HEPBURN, D. "Vinnette Carroll, Woman on the Run." *Sepia* 10 (October, 1961):57-60.

HUGHES, LANGSTON. "The Need for an Afro-American Theatre." In *Anthology of the American Negro in the Theatre* (1968), edited by Lindsay Patterson, pp. 163-164. Reprinted from *Chicago Defender* (June 12, 1961).

"King Kong." *Ebony* 17 (December, 1961):80-86.

LEAKS, SYLVESTER. "Purlie Emerges Victorious." *Freedomways* 1 (Fall, 1961):347.

"Mr. and Mrs. Broadway [Ruby Dee and Ossie Davis]." *Ebony* 16 (February, 1961):110-114.

PHILLIPS, WALDO P. "The Emperor Jones Recrowned [W. H. Ellis]." *Negro History Bulletin* 24 (May, 1961):183-184.

POITIER, SIDNEY. "Why I Became an Actor." *Negro Digest* 11 (December, 1961):80-97.

"Prima Donna from Mississippi [Leontyne Price]." *Ebony* 16 (April, 1961):96-100.

"A Raisin in the Sun [movie]." *Ebony* 16 (April, 1961): 53-56.

ROBINSON, LOUIE. "First Lady of Jazz [Ella Fitzgerald]." *Ebony* 17 (November, 1961):131-139.

SCOTT, JOHN A. "On the Authenticity of Fanny Kemble's Journal of a Residence on a Georgian Plantation in 1838-1839." *Journal of Negro History* 46 (October, 1961):233-242.

"A Taste of Honey [play]." *Ebony* 16 (April, 1961):53-56.

"Unusual Appeals Bring Broadway Cash [Producer Oscar Brown, Jr.]." *Ebony* 16 (June, 1961):73-80.

"West Indies Limbo Queen [Roz Croney]." *Ebony* 16 (March, 1961):119-121.

"A Wreath for Udomo [Broadway preparation]." *Jet* (March 2, 1961):59.

1962

BOOKS

REISNER, ROBERT G. *Bird: The Legend of Charlie Parker.* New York: Citadel Press, 1962.

Schomburg Collection, Dictionary Catalog. Boston: Hall, 1962.

SCHOLARLY THESES

DAVIS, BR. JOSEPH MORGAN. "A Compilation and Analysis of Views Concerning the Contributions of the Negro to the American Theatre in 1950-1960." Master's thesis, Catholic University, 1962.

PLAYS

HULT, RUBY. *The Saga of George W. Bush. Negro Digest* 11 (September, 1962):88-96.

ARTICLES

"African-American Cultural Exchange." *Ebony* 17 (March, 1962):76-79.

"Behind the Laughter of Jackie (Moms) Mabley." *Ebony* 17 (August, 1962):88-91.

"*The Blacks* [off-Broadway stage]." *Ebony* 17 (September, 1962):47-53.

"Broadway's Newest Star [Diahann Carroll]." *Ebony* 17 (July, 1962):40-45.

"Committee for the Employment of the Negro Performer (CENP)." *Freedomways* 2 (Summer, 1962):310.

DAVIS, OSSIE. "Purlie Told Me!" *Freedomways* 2 (Spring, 1962): 155-159.

"For the Queen and Commoners [Sammy Davis, Jr.]." *Ebony* 17 (January, 1962):30-34.

"Gallery of Dancers." *Negro Digest* 11 (May, 1962):73-75.

"Great Lady of Opera." *Negro Digest* 11 (August, 1962):3-9.

"High School for Aspiring Artists." *Ebony* 17 (January, 1962): 54-62.

"*The Intruder* [film on school integration]." *Ebony* 17 (May, 1962):76-79.

"Juano Hernandez in *Young Man*." *Sepia* 11 (March, 1962):16-18.

"Katherine Dunham's New Show." *Sepia* 11 (November, 1962): 70-74.

KINNEMAN, JOHN. "The Negro Renaissance." *Negro History Bulletin* 25 (May, 1962):197-200.

LACY, E. "I Almost Starred with Errol Flynn." *Negro Digest* 11 (August, 1962):10-14.

MAPP, EDWARD. "The Image Makers [Negro stereotype]." *Negro History Bulletin* 26 (December, 1962):127-128.

MILLSTEIN, GILBERT. "Dick Gregory: The Race-nik Comedian." *Negro Digest* 11 (March, 1962):25-30.

"New Musical Star in Old Vienna [Olive Moorefield]." *Ebony* 18 (November, 1962):61-66.

"Purlie Victorious." *Ebony* 17 (March, 1962):55-60.

ROBINSON, LOUIE. "The Private World of Dorothy Dandridge." *Ebony* 17 (June, 1962):116-121.

ROGERS, RAY. "The Negro Actor." *Freedomways* 2 (Summer, 1962):310-313.

"Roland Hayes—A Lifetime on the Concert Stage." *Ebony* 17 (September, 1962):42-46.

SAUNDERS, DORIS. "Command Performance of Williams and Walker." *Negro Digest* 11 (March, 1962):16-21.

"Selection and Use of Children's Literature in Teaching Intergroup Relations." *Journal of Intergroup Relations* 3 (Summer, 1962):244-252.

"She Sings Along with Mitch [Leslie Uggams]." *Ebony* 17 (March, 1962):40-46.

"Symposium: The Negro in the American Theatre." *Negro Digest* 11 (July, 1962):52-58.

TODD, ARTHUR. "One of Our National Treasures." *Ballet Annual, 1962*. Also in *Anthology of the American Negro in the Theatre* (1968) edited by Lindsay Patterson, pp. 215-226.

1963

BOOKS

HUGHES, LANGSTON. *Big Sea*. New York: Hill and Wang, 1963.

SCHOLARLY THESES

BRADLEY, GERALD S., JR. "The Negro in American Theatre." Master's thesis, Carnegie Institute of Technology, 1963.

PLAYS

FIEBLEMAN, PETER S. *Tiger, Tiger Burning Bright*. Cleveland: World Publishing, 1963.

HUGHES, LANGSTON. *Five Plays*. Edited and introduced by Webster Smalley. Bloomington, Ind.: Indiana University Press, 1963. Includes *Mulatto, Soul Gone Home, Tambourines to Glory, Little Ham*, and *Simply Heavenly*.

MITCHELL, LOFTEN. *A Land Beyond the River*. Cody, Wyo.: Pioneer Drama Service, 1963.

REED, EDWENA. *A Man Always Keeps His Word. Negro History Bulletin* 26 (January, 1963):138-140.

ARTICLES

BARROW, WILLIAM. "Gallery of Leading Men." *Negro Digest* 12 (October, 1963):45-48.

————. "Introducing the Concept: New Theatre in Detroit." *Negro Digest* 12 (May, 1963):77-79.

————. "Man of Many Faces: Frank Silvera." *Negro Digest* 12 (September, 1963):40-43.

"*Broc Peters* [film success]." *Ebony* 18 (June, 1963):106-112.

"*The Cardinal* [Ossie Davis movie]." *Ebony* 19 (December, 1963):126-132.

DALTON, FLETCHER E. "Why TV Is a Wasteland for Negroes." *Negro Digest* 12 (June, 1963):27-29.

DELLINGER, D. "Death and Taxes Lead to Rebirth of Living Theatre." *Liberation* 8 (November, 1963):9-10.

"Edric Connor, Theatrical Genius." *Sepia* 12 (December, 1963): 52-55.

FEINSTEIN, HERBERT. "Lena Horne Speaks Freely." *Ebony* 18 (May, 1963):61-67.

"Hollywood Hires a Negro Director." *Sepia* 12 (April, 1963): 35-38.

"How Liberal Is Show Business?" *Sepia* 12 (March, 1963):40-43.

HUDSON, BENJAMIN F. "Another View of 'Uncle Tom'." *Phylon* 24 (First Quarter, 1963):79-87.

HUTSON, JEAN BLACKWELL. "The Schomburg Collection." *Freedomways* 3 (Summer, 1963):431-435.

KAISER, ERNEST. "The Literature of Harlem." *Freedomways* 3 (Summer, 1963):276-291.

————. "The Literature of Negro Revolt." *Freedomways* 3 (Winter, 1963):36-47. (Mr. Kaiser and Mr. Clarke publish regular articles on *Recent Books* in *Freedomways*—a very fine listing.)

"Leading Negro Artists." *Ebony* 18 (September, 1963):131-140.

"*Lilies of the Field* [Poitier film]." *Ebony* 18 (October, 1963): 55-58.

"The Living Premise [off-Broadway spoof]." *Ebony* 19 (November, 1963):59-62.

"Miriam Makeba." *Ebony* 18 (April, 1963):74-80.

MITCHELL, LOFTEN. "The Negro Theatre and the Harlem Community." *Freedomways* 3 (Summer, 1963):384-394.

MONFRIED, WALTER. "The Great Ira Aldridge." *Negro Digest* 12 (March, 1963): 67-70.

MORRISON, ALLAN. "One Hundred Years of Negro Entertainment." *Ebony* 18 (September, 1963):122-128.

MOSS, CARLTON. "The Negro in American Films." *Freedomways* 3 (Spring, 1963):134-142.

"Myrna White Scores Dance Success." *Ebony* 18 (April, 1963):59-64.

WILLIAMS, JIM. "The Need for a Harlem Theatre." *Freedomways* 3 (Summer, 1963):395-404.

WILLIAMS, JOHN A. "The Negro in Literature Today." *Ebony* 18 (September, 1963):73-76.

YOUNG, A. S. "Sammy Davis Speaks Out." *Negro Digest* 12 (June, 1963): 19-25.

"Young Troupers Make Hit Debut [Chicago Players]." *Ebony* 18 (May, 1963):156-161.

1964

BOOKS

CLARKE, JOHN HENRIK, ed. *Harlem U.S.A.* New York: Seven Seas Books, 1964.

GREGORY, DICK. *Nigger.* New York: Dutton, 1964.

HUGHES, LANGSTON. *I Wonder as I Wander.* New York: Hill and Wang, 1964.

SANDLE, FLOYD L. *The Negro in the American Educational Theatre: An Organizational Development: 1911-1964.* Ann Arbor: Edwards Bros., 1964.

SCHOLARLY THESES

SHERMAN, ALFONSO. "The Diversity of Treatment of the Negro Character in American Drama Prior to 1860." Ph.D. dissertation, Indiana University, 1964.

PLAYS

BALDWIN, JAMES. *Blues for Mr. Charlie.* New York: Dial, 1964.

DUBERMAN, MARTIN. *In White America.* Boston: Houghton Mifflin, 1964.

JONES, LEROI. *Dutchman* and *The Slave.* New York: Morrow, 1964.

ARTICLES

"Actors' New Boss [Fred O'Neal]." *Ebony* 19 (June, 1964):58-63.

108   *The Black Teacher and the Dramatic Arts*

"Barbara McNair: The Acting Debut of a Singer." *Sepia* 13 (April, 1964):74-78.

"Black Actor in Norway [Earle Hyman]." *Negro Digest* 13 (February, 1964):32-36.

"*Black Like Me* [film]." *Ebony* 19 (May, 1964):37-44.

"*Blues for Mr Charlie*." *Ebony* 19 (June, 1964):188-193.

"*Blues for Mr. Charlie* [criticism]." *Negro Digest* 13 (September, 1964):34-40.

BRADLEY, GERALD. "Goodbye, Mr. Bones: The Emergence of Negro Themes and Characters in American Drama." *Drama Critique* (Spring, 1964). Also in *Anthology of the American Negro in the Theatre* (1968), edited by Lindsay Patterson, pp. 12-20.

CLARKE, J. B. "Alienation of James Baldwin." *Journal of Human Relations* 12 (First Quarter, 1964):30-33.

CORBETT, DEMETRIUS M. "Taras Shevchenko and Ira Aldridge." *Journal of Negro Education* 33 (Spring, 1964):143-150.

DERBY, DORIS; MOSES, GILBERT; and O'NEAL, JOHN. "The Need for a Southern Freedom Theatre." *Freedomways* 4 (Winter, 1964):109-112.

DUBERMAN, MARTIN. "History and Theatre." *Columbia University Forum* (Fall, 1964). Also in *Anthology of the American Negro in the Theatre* (1968), edited by Lindsay Patterson, pp. 199-204.

FARNUM, GEORGE T. "Shakespeare and the Blacks." *Freedomways* 4 (Fall, 1964):479-486.

FULLER, HOYT W. "The Negro Writer in the United States." *Ebony* 20 (November, 1964):126-134.

"Hollywood What Now?" *Negro Digest* 14 (December, 1964):72-78.

"Home Life of Mai Britt and 'Golden Boy'." *Ebony* 20 (December, 1964):136-146.

"James Baldwin: A Literary Assessment." *Negro Digest* 13 (January, 1964):61-68.

"James Earl Jones' Goal Is to Become a Great Actor." *Sepia* 13 (February, 1964):72-76.

KENT, G. E. "Baldwin and the Problem of Being." *CLAJ* 7 (March, 1964):202-214.

LEAKS, SYLVESTER. "In White America." *Freedomways* 4 (Spring, 1964):280-281.

LINDSAY, POWELL. "We Still Need Negro Theatre in America." *Negro History Bulletin* 27 (February, 1964):112.

MOSS, CARLTON. "The Negro in American Films." *Harlem, U.S.A. 1964.* Also in *Anthology of the American Negro in the Theatre* (1968), edited by Lindsay Patterson, pp. 229-247.

"NAACP vs. Hollywood." *Sepia* 13 (March, 1964):66-71.

"Negroes on Broadway." *Ebony* 19 (April, 1964):186-194.

"*No Strings* for Barbara." *Ebony* 19 (January, 1964):42-50.

"*None but the Brave* [film with Rafer Johnson]." *Ebony* 19 (October, 1964):110-115.

O'BRIEN, J. "Let Us Have a New American Theatre." *Negro Digest* 13 (March, 1964):44-47.

OLIVA, L. JAY. "Ira Aldridge and Théophile Gautier." *Journal of Negro History* 48 (Spring, 1964):229-231.

" 'Raceless' Bill Cosby." *Ebony* 19 (May, 1964):131-140.

REDDEN, CAROLYN L. "The American Negro: An Annotated List of Educational Films and Filmstrips." *Journal of Negro Education* 33 (Winter, 1964):79-82.

"*Robin and the Seven Hoods* [Sammy Davis movie]." *Ebony* 19 (June, 1964):90-100.

ROBINSON, LOUIE. "38 Years of Serious Music [William Grant Still]." *Ebony* 19 (February, 1964):102-106.

SANDERS, CHARLES L. "Requiem for 'Queen Dinah'." *Ebony* 19 (March, 1964):146-154.

SONKOR, SHELBY. "Hollywood Race Revolt." *Flamingo* 3 (1964):44-45.

STRALEY, GEORGE H. "Mr. Kean's Black Boy [Ira Aldridge]." *Show* 4 (February, 1964):24-25.

TALBOT, WILLIAM. "Every Negro in His Place: The Scene on and off Broadway." *Drama Critique* (Spring, 1964). Also in *Anthology of the American Negro in the Theatre* (1968), edited by Lindsay Patterson, pp. 207-211.

"Top Actor of the Year [Poitier]." *Ebony* 19 (March, 1964):123-129.

WHITMIRE, GEORGIA E. "Bibliography." *Journal of Negro Education* 33 (Fall, 1964):421-435. (Excellent bibliographies by this writer appear as a regular feature in the *Journal.*)

1965

BOOKS

BONTEMPS, ARNA, and CONROY, JACK. *Any Place But Here.* New York: Hill and Wang, 1965.

DAVIS, SAMMY, JR. *Yes I Can.* New York: Farrar, Straus and Giroux, 1965.

HORNE, LENA. *Lena.* New York: Doubleday, 1965.

The Negro in the United States: A List of Significant Books. 9th rev. ed. New York: The New York Public Library, 1965.

SCHOLARLY THESES

ABRAMSON, DORIS E. "From *Harlem* to *A Raisin in the Sun:* A Study of Plays by Negro Playwrights, 1929-1959." Ph.D. dissertation, Columbia University Teachers College, 1965.

EIKLEBERRY, BURTON. "The Negro Actor's Participation and the Negro Image on the New York Stage, 1954-1964." Master's thesis, University of Kansas, 1965.

PLAYS

ACQUAYE, SAKA. *Obadzeng Goes to Town.* London: Evans Bros., Ltd., 1965.

AMIS, LOLA JONES. *Three Plays: The Other Side of the Wall, The Places of Wrath,* and *Helen.* New York: Exposition, 1965.

EASMON, SARIF R. *Dear Parent and Ogre.* London: Oxford, 1965.

HANLEY, WILLIAM. *Slow Dance on the Killing Ground.* New York: Random House, 1965.

HANSBERRY, LORRAINE. *The Sign in Sidney Brustein's Window.* New York: Random House, 1965.

HILL, ERROL, ed. *Caribbean Plays,* Vol. 2. Extra Mural Department, University of West Indies, 1965. (Contains six one-act plays by Hill, Hillary, Labastade, Redhead, Sealy, and Wolcott.)

LAPIDO, DORE. *Three Yoruba Plays.* Adapted to English by Ulli Beier. Ibadan: Mbari Publications, 1965.

OLAYOKE, OLU D. *The Iwako-Man and the Wood-Carver.* London: Evans Bros., Ltd., 1965.

SOYINKA, WOLE. *Five Plays.* London: Oxford, 1965.

————. *The Road.* London: Oxford, 1965.

ARTICLES

"Bubbles Bounces Back." *Ebony* 20 (January, 1965):49-54.

"The Cool World [film]." *Ebony* 20 (July, 1965):43-46.

DAVIS, OSSIE. "The Significance of Lorraine Hansberry." *Freedomways* 5 (Summer, 1965):397-402.

"Emperor Jones in Norway." *Sepia* 14 (March, 1965):47-51.

"Farewell, Marian Anderson." *Ebony* 20 (June 1965):39-46.

FEAGANS, J. "Atlanta Theatre Segregation: A Case of Prolonged Avoidance." *Journal of Human Relations* 13 (Second Quarter, 1965):208-218.

FRANCE, ARTHUR. "A Raisin Revisited." *Freedomways* 5 (Summer, 1965):403-410.

FULLER, HOYT W. "*The Toilet* and *The Slave*." *Negro Digest* 14 (July, 1965):49-50.

_____. "Up in Harlem: New Hope." *Negro Digest* 14 (October, 1965):49-50 ff.

_____. "World Festival of Negro Arts." *Negro Digest* 14 (March, 1965): 49-50.

GIBSON, WILLIAM. "Certain Fictions . . . And Uncertain Hopes." *Liberation* 10 (October, 1965):12-13.

"Girl on the Go in Paris [Marpessa Dawn]." *Ebony* 20 (May, 1965):100-105.

HILL, HERBERT. "*Uncle Tom*—An Enduring American Myth." *Crisis* 72 (May, 1965):289-295, 325.

"How Movies Break Up Marriages [Poitier and Carroll]." *Ebony* 20 (September, 1965):98-108.

HUGHES, LANGSTON. "That Boy LeRoi." *Chicago Defender* (January 11, 1965). Also in *Anthology of the American Negro in the Theatre* (1968), edited by Lindsay Patterson, pp. 205-206.

"I Spy [first Negro costar in TV]." *Ebony* 20 (September, 1965): 65-71.

"James Earl Jones—Actor Still Climbing." *Ebony* 20 (April, 1965):98-106.

LEWIS, JOHN. "Paul Robeson—Inspirer of Youth." *Freedomways* 5 (Summer, 1965):369-372.

MERIWETHER, L. M. "The Amen Corner." *Negro Digest* 14 (January, 1965):40-47.

MITCHELL, LOFTEN. "Alligators in the Swamp." *Crisis* 72 (February, 1965):84-87.

"NAACP vs. *The Birth of a Nation*," *Crisis* 72 (February, 1965):96-97, 102.

"*Nothing but a Man* [Dixon and Lincoln film]." *Ebony* 20 (April, 1965):198-201.

"The Owl and the Pussycat [Diana Sands]." *Ebony* 20 (February, 1965):98-103.

"Preservation Hall," *Ebony* 20 (May, 1965):64-72.

RECORD, WILSON C. "The Negro Creative Artist." *Crisis* 72 (March, 1965):153-158, 193.

"Reri Grist—Toast of Two Continents [opera singer]." *Ebony* 20 (March, 1965):84-90.

ROBESON, PAUL. "It's Good to Be Back." *Freedomways* 5 (Summer, 1965):373-377.

ROBINSON, LOUIE. "The Life and Death of Nat King Cole." *Ebony* 20 (April, 1965):123-134.

STEVENS, HOPE R. "Paul Robeson—Democracy's Most Powerful Voice." *Freedomways* 5 (Summer, 1965):365-368.

"The Task of the Negro Writer as Artist (includes Ossie Davis)." *Negro Digest* 14 (April, 1965):54-83.

1966

BOOKS

DAVIS, JOHN P., ed. *The American Negro Reference Book.* Englewood Cliffs, N.J.: Prentice-Hall, 1966.

MILLER, ELIZABETH W. *The Negro in America: A Bibliography.* Cambridge, Mass.: Harvard University Press, 1966.

The Negro Handbook. Compiled by editors of *Ebony.* Chicago: Johnson, 1966. (Cf. Section 14 on Creative Arts, pp. 355-373.)

SELBY, JOHN. *Beyond Civil Rights.* Cleveland: World Publishing Co., 1966 (on Karamu House).

WELSCH, EREVIN K. *The Negro in the U.S.: A Research Guide.* Bloomington: Indiana University Press, 1966.

SCHOLARLY THESES

BLITZGEN, SR. MARY JOHN CAROL. "Voices of Protest: An Analysis of the Negro Protest Plays of the 1963-64 Broadway and Off-Broadway Season." Master's thesis, University of Kansas, 1966.

PLAYS

WARD, DOUGLAS TURNER. *Two Plays: Happy Ending* and *Day of Absence.* New York: Dramatists Play Service, 1966.

ARTICLES

"Advent of the Negro Actor on the Legitimate Stage in America. *Journal of Negro Education* 35 (Summer, 1966):237-245.

"Apollo Story." *Sepia* 15 (January, 1966):14-20.

BALDWIN, JAMES. "Theatre: The Negro In and Out." *Negro Digest* 15 (October, 1966):37-44.

BONTEMPS, ARNA. "Harlem in the Twenties." *Crisis* 73 (October, 1966):431-434, 451-456.

————. "The Negro Contribution to American Letters." In *The American Negro Reference Book,* edited by John P. Davis, pp. 850-878.

BROWN, MARION E. "The Negro in the Fine Arts." In *The American Negro Reference Book,* edited by John P. Davis, pp. 766-774.

BULLINS, ED. "Theatre of Reality." *Negro Digest* 15 (April, 1966):60-66.

BURG, ROBERT. "Young Actor on the Way Up [James Earl Jones]." *Negro Digest* 15 (April, 1966):26-31.

"Carol Cole." *Ebony* 21 (July, 1966):114-120.

CHILDRESS, ALICE; LINCOLN, ABBEY; MARSHALL, PAULE; and WRIGHT, SARAH E. "The Negro Women in American Literature." *Freedomways* 6 (Winter, 1966):14-19.

COLE, MRS. NAT KING. "Why I Am Returning to Show Business." *Ebony* 21 (January, 1966):45-52.

CONSTANTINE, J. ROBERT. "The Ignoble Savage, An Eighteenth-Century Literary Stereotype." *Phylon* 27 (Second Quarter, 1966):171-179.

DAVIS, OSSIE. "Flight from Broadway." *Negro Digest* 15 (April, 1966):14-19.

DEE, RUBY. "The Tattered Queens." *Negro Digest* 15 (April, 1966):32-36.

"Diana Sands: Collecting Acting Prizes Is Her Hobby." *Sepia* 15 (May, 1966):60-63.

"A Diva's Date With Destiny [Leontyne Price at Met]." *Ebony* 22 (December, 1966):184-192.

"Enroute to the Future [Negro actors in white roles]." *The New York Times* (July 31, 1966). Later reprinted in *Negro History Bulletin* 30 (April, 1967).

FULLER, HOYT W. "World Festival of Negro Arts." *Ebony* 21 (July, 1966):96-106.

GEORGE, ZELMA. "Negro Music in American Life." In *The American Negro Reference Book,* edited by John P. Davis, pp.

731-758. Also to be noted is the same author's *Bibliographical Index to Negro Music*, a card catalog of 9,952 titles of published Negro thematic material, and history and criticism of Negro music. The master catalog is located in the Moreland Collection of the Howard University Library, Washington, D.C.

GREAVES, WILLIAM. "First World Festival of Negro Arts." *Crisis* 73 (June-July, 1966):309-314, 332.

"Harlem Fine Arts School." *Ebony* 21 (May, 1966):80-86.

HILL, HERBERT. "Stuff of Great Literature." *Crisis* 73 (February, 1966):99, 110-114.

HORNE, LENA. "The Three Horned 'Dilemma' Facing Negro Women." *Ebony* 21 (August, 1966):118-124.

HUGHES, LANGSTON. "The Negro and American Entertainment." In *The American Negro Reference Book*, edited by John P. Davis, pp. 826-849.

HUNTER, R. G. "Hollywood and the Negro." *Negro Digest* 15 (May, 1966):37-41.

JONES, LEROI. "Blues, Jazz and the Negro." In *The American Negro Reference Book*, edited by John P. Davis, pp. 759-765.

————. "In Search of the Revolutionary Theatre [Black Arts Repertory]." *Negro Digest* 15 (April, 1966):20-24.

KING, WOODIE, JR. "Problems Facing Negro Actors." *Negro Digest* 15 (April, 1966):53-59.

"Leading Man at the Met." *Ebony* 21 (January, 1966):84-90.

MOORE, WALTER. "Needed: A Negro Film Movement." *Negro Digest* 15 (January, 1966):45-48.

MORRISON, ALLAN. "Negro Women in the Arts." *Ebony* 21 (August, 1966):90-94.

"New Girl on Broadway [Thelma Oliver in *Sweet Charity*]." *Ebony* 21 (October, 1966):52-57.

"A New Playwright [Ronald Milner]." *Negro Digest* 15 (October, 1966):49-50.

O'NEAL, FREDERICK. "Problems and Prospects: The Negro in Today's Theatre." *Negro Digest* 15 (April, 1966):4-12.

ROBINSON, LOUIE. "Dorothy Dandridge, Hollywood's Tragic Enigma." *Ebony* 21 (March, 1966):70-82.

"Sammy Davis, Jr.: Busiest Man in Show Business." *Ebony* 21 (April, 1966):165-178.

WARD, DOUGLAS TURNER. "American Theatre: For Whites Only?" *The New York Times* (August 14, 1966). Also in *Anthology of the American Negro in the Theatre* (1968), edited by Lindsay Patterson, pp. 81-84.

1967

BOOKS

BEIER, ULLI, ed. *Introduction to African Literature*. London: Longmans, 1967.

HUGHES, LANGSTON and MELTZER, MILTON. *Black Magic: A Pictorial History of the Negro in American Entertainment*. Englewood Cliffs, N.J.: Prentice-Hall, 1967.

MITCHELL, LOFTEN. *Black Drama: The Story of the American Negro in the Theatre*. New York: Hawthorne, 1967.

MPHABELE, EZEKUL, ed. *African Writings Today* (some plays included). London: Penguin, 1967.

ROLLINS, CHARLEMAE HILL. *Famous Negro Entertainers of Stage, Screen, and TV*. New York: Dodd, Mead, 1967.

WATSON, DEREN, with STEPHENSON, LEON. *The Story of the Ink Spots*. New York: Vantage, 1967.

SCHOLARLY THESES

COLLE, ROYAL. "Negro Image and the Mass Media." Ph.D. dissertation, Cornell University, 1967.

ZIETLON, EDWARD ROBERT. "Wright to Hansberry: The Evolution of Outlook in Four Negro Writers." Ph.D. dissertation, University of Washington, 1967.

PLAYS

BALDWIN, JAMES. *Amen Corner*. New York: Dial, 1967.

CLARK, JOHN PEPPER. *Ozide*. London: Oxford, 1967.

JOHN, ERROL. *Three Screen Plays: "Farea Majende," "The Dispossessed," "Hasta Luego."* London: Faber & Faber, 1967.

JONES, LEROI. *The Baptism* and *The Toilet*. New York: Grove, 1967.

————. *Slave Ship: An Historical Pageant*. In *Negro Digest* 16 (April, 1967):62-74.

MACKEY, WILLIAM W. *Behold! Cometh the Vanderkillins*. New York: Azaziel Books, 1967.

SOYINKA, WOLE. *Kongi's Harvest*. London: Oxford, 1967.

ARTICLES

ADELMAN, LYNN. "A Study of James Weldon Johnson." *Journal of Negro History* 52 (April, 1967):128-145.

CRIPPS, THOMAS R. "The Death of Rastus: Negroes in American Films Since 1945." *Phylon* 28 (Fall, 1967):267-275.

DENT, THOMAS C. "The Free Southern Theatre." *Negro Digest* 16 (April, 1967):40-44 ff.

"Diana Sands: First Tan Cleopatra." *Sepia* 16 (August, 1967):18-20.

GAFFNEY, FLOYD. "The Black Actor in Central Park." *Negro Digest* 16 (April, 1967):28-34.

"Gallic-American Spectacular [Diahann Carroll]." *Ebony* 22 (April, 1967):36-42.

GREENWOOD, FRANK. "Burn, Baby, Burn!" *Freedomways* 7 (Summer, 1967):244-247.

HANAU, D. "Ghetto Theatre: Vital Drama or Social Therapy?" *Community* 26 (April, 1967):7-10.

JEANPIERRE, WENDELL A. *"Who's Got His Own* [Ronald Milner play]." *Crisis* 74 (October, 1967):423.

JONES, LEROI. "What the Arts Need Now." *Negro Digest* 16 (April, 1967):5-6.

KGOSITSILE, K. W. "Towards Our Theatre: A Definitive Act." *Negro Digest* 16 (April, 1967):14-16.

KING, WOODIE, JR. "Black Theatre: Weapon for Change." *Negro Digest* 16 (April, 1967):35-39.

LA BRANT, LOU. "Untapped Resources of Negro Students." *Negro American Literature Forum* 1 (Winter, 1967):15-17.

"Lola Falana: The World Is Her Oyster." *Ebony* 22 (July, 1967):114-118.

MEYER, HOWARD N. "A Play for All Regions [*In White America*]." *Crisis* 74 (March, 1967):89-93.

MILNER, RONALD. "Black Magic: Black Art." *Negro Digest* 16 (April, 1967):8-12 ff.

―――――. *"Who's Got His Own."* *Crisis* 74 (January-February, 1967):31-34.

"*Mission Impossible's* Greg Morris." *Ebony* 23 (December, 1967): 99-100.

MITCHELL, LOFTEN. "Black Drama." *Negro Digest* 16 (April, 1967):75-87.

―――――. "The Season Is Now [*Who's Got His Own* and *My Sweet Charlie*]." *Crisis* 74 (January-February, 1967):31-34.

MORRISON, ALLAN. "A New Surge in the Arts." *Ebony* 22 (August, 1967):134-138.

"New 'Bad Guy' of the Movies [Raymond Saint-Jacques]." *Ebony* 22 (June, 1967):171-178.

"New Star in the TV Heavens [Nichelle Nichols]." *Ebony* 22 (January, 1967):71-76.

"Opportunity Please Knock [Oscar Brown, Jr.]." *Ebony* 22 (August, 1967):104-108.

PETERS, ART. "Comeback of an Ex-Star [Frankie Lyman]." *Ebony* 22 (January, 1967):42-50.

RAMBEAU, DAVID. "Concept East and the Struggle Against Racism." *Negro Digest* 16 (April, 1967):22-27 ff.

ROBINSON, LOUIE. "Redd Foxx: Crown Prince of Clowns." *Ebony* 22 (April, 1967):91-98.

"Schomburg's Ailing Collection [on the famous library]." *Ebony* 22 (October, 1967):55-60.

"*Sweet Charity's* Exciting Paula Kelly." *Sepia* 16 (May, 1967):24-27.

"*To Sir, with Love* [Poitier film]." *Ebony* 22 (April, 1967):68-74.

TURNER, DARWIN T. "The Failure of a Playwright." *CLAJ* 10 (June, 1967):308-318.

WARD, DOUGLAS T. "Needed: A Theatre for Black Themes." *Negro Digest* 17 (December, 1967):34-39.

"You're so Lovely . . . [Florence Mills]." *Crisis* 74 (October, 1967):411.

1968

BOOKS

COUCH, WILLIAM, JR., ed. *New Black Playwrights*. Baton Rouge: Louisiana University Press, 1968.

PATTERSON, LINDSAY, comp. and ed. *Anthology of the American Negro in the Theatre*. International Library of Negro Life and History. Under the auspices of The Association for the Study of Negro Life and History. New York: Publishers Company, Inc., 1967-1968.

PLAYS

AHMAD, DOROTHY. *Papa's Daughter. The Drama Review* 12 (Summer, 1968):139-145.

BULLINS, ED. *A Son Come Home*. *Negro Digest* 17 (April, 1968):54-73.

———. *Clara's Ole Man*. *The Drama Review* 12 (Summer, 1968):159-171.

———. *Goin' a Buffalo*. In *New Black Playwrights*, edited by William Couch, Jr.

———. *How Do You Do: A Nonsense Drama*. Mill Valley, Cal.: Illuminations Press, 1968.

CALDWELL, BEN. *Four Plays: Riot Sale, The Job, Top Secret, Mission Accomplished*. *The Drama Review* 12 (Summer, 1968):40-52.

ELDER, LONNE. *Ceremonies in Dark Old Men*. In *New Black Playwrights*, edited by William Couch, Jr.

GARRETT, JIMMY. *And We Own the Night*. *The Drama Review* 12 (Summer, 1968):62-69.

GUNN, BILL. *Johnnas*. *The Drama Review* 12 (Summer, 1968): 126-138.

JONES, LEROI. *Home on the Range*. *The Drama Review* 12 (Summer, 1968):106-111.

———. *Police*. *The Drama Review* 12 (Summer, 1968):112-115.

KENNEDY, ADRIENNE. *A Rat's Mass*. In *New Black Playwrights*, edited by William Couch, Jr.

———. *Funnyhouse of a Negro*. In *Anthology of the American Negro in the Theatre*, edited by Lindsay Patterson.

MACKEY, WILLIAM W. *Family Meeting*. In *New Black Playwrights*, edited by William Couch, Jr.

MILNER, RONALD. *The Monster*. *The Drama Review* 12 (Summer, 1968):94-105.

SANCHEZ, SONIA. *The Bronx Is Next*. *The Drama Review* 12 (Summer, 1968):78-83.

STOKES, HERBERT. *The Uncle Toms*. *The Drama Review* 12 (Summer, 1968):58-60.

WARD, DOUGLAS T. *Happy Ending* and *Days of Absence*. In *New Black Playwrights*, edited by William Couch, Jr.

WHITE, EDGAR. *The Cathedral of Chartres*. *Liberator* 8 (July, 1968):16-19.

WHITE, JOSEPH. *Old Judge Mose Is Dead*. *The Drama Review* 12 (Summer, 1968):151-156.

X, MARVIN. *Take Care of Business*. *The Drama Review* 12 (Summer, 1968): 85-92.

ARTICLES

BAILEY, PETER. *"Daddy Goodness* [review]." *Black Theatre* 1 (October, 1968):31.

———. "Is the Negro Ensemble Company *Really* Black Theatre?" *Negro Digest* 17 (April, 1968):16-19.

———. "The Electronic Nigger." *Ebony* 23 (September, 1968): 97-101.

"Black Playwrights Get a Break." *Sepia* 17 (November, 1968):20-23.

BULLINS, ED. "A Short Statement on Street Theatre." *The Drama Review* 12 (Summer, 1968):93.

———. "Black Theatre Groups: A Directory." *The Drama Review* 12 (Summer, 1968):172-175.

———. "Black Theatre Notes." *Black Theatre* 1 (October, 1968):4.

CAMPBELL, DICK. "Is There a Conspiracy Aganist Black Playwrights?" *Negro Digest* 17 (April, 1968) :11-15.

CRIPPS, THOMAS R. "Negroes in Movies: Some Reconsiderations." *Negro American Literature Forum* 2 (Spring, 1968):6-7.

DODSON, OWEN. "Playwrights in Dark Glasses." *Negro Digest* 17 (April, 1968):31-36.

FERGUSON, JOHN. "Nigerian Drama in English." *Modern Drama* 11 (May, 1968):10-26.

"For Love of Ivy [Poitier and Lincoln]." *Ebony* 23 (October, 1968):52-59.

FULLER, HOYT W. "Black Theatre in America: An Informal Survey." *Negro Digest* 17 (April, 1968):83-93.

HARRIS, HENRIETTA. "Building a Black Theatre." *The Drama Review* 12 (Summer, 1968):157-158.

HATLEN, THEODORE, and REARDON, WILLIAM. "Beautiful Black." UCSB *Alumnus* (Fall, 1968):22-29.

HOLLY, ELLEN. "How Black Do You Have to Be?" *Contact* 1 (October, 1968): 7-12. Reprinted from *The New York Times*.

HUGHES, CATHARINE. "Poet in Motion [Arthur Mitchell]." *Ebony* 23 (October, 1968):210-217.

JONES, LEROI. "Cummunications Project." *The Drama Review* 12 (Summer, 1968):53-57.

KAISER, ERNEST. "Selected Bibliography of the Published Writings of Langston Hughes." *Freedomways* 8 (Spring, 1968):185-191.

KING, WOODIE, JR. "Black Theatre: Present Condition." *The Drama Review* 12 (Summer, 1968):117-124.

LABRIE, PETER. "Legacy of Otis Redding." *Negro Digest* 17 (April, 1968):37-40.

LANTZ, RAGNI. "Hello, Dolly!" *Ebony* 23 (January, 1968):83-89.

LEWIS, C. L. "Black Knight of the Theatre: Ira Aldridge." *Negro Digest* 17 (April, 1968):45-47.

MASON, CLIFFORD, with MACBETH, ROBERT, and BULLINS, ED. "The Electronic Nigger Meets the Gold Dust Twins." *Black Theatre* 1 (October, 1968):24 ff.

MILLER, ADAM DAVID. "It's a Long Way to St. Louis." *The Drama Review* 12 (Summer, 1968):147-150.

MILNER, RONALD. "Black Theatre, Go Home!" *Negro Digest* 17 (April, 1968):5-10.

MITCHELL, LOFTEN. "An Informal Memoir for Langston Hughes and Stella Holt." *Negro Digest* 17 (April, 1968):41-43, 74-77.

NEAL, LARRY. "Cultural Nationalism and Black Theatre." *Black Theatre* 1 (October, 1968):8-10.

————. "The Black Arts Movement." *The Drama Review* 12 (Summer, 1968):29-39.

O'NEAL, JOHN. "Motion in the Ocean: Some Political Dimensions of the Free Southern Theatre." *The Drama Review* 12 (Summer, 1968):70-77.

PATTERSON, LINDSAY. "Not By Protest Alone." *Negro History Bulletin* 31 (April, 1968):12-14.

————. "The Waste Lands." In *Anthology of the American Negro in the Theatre*, edited by Lindsay Patterson, pp.269-270.

PIERCE, PANCHITTA. "Lena Horne at 51." *Ebony* 23 (July, 1968):125-135.

REARDON, WILLIAM, and HATLEN, THEODORE. "The Black Teacher and the Drama [pamphlet]." University of California, Santa Barbara, Calif. (October, 1968):28 pp.

RILEY, CLAYTON. "Arts: Television's Negroes." *Liberator* 8 (November, 1968):21.

————. "*Daddy Goodness* [review]." *Liberator* 8 (July, 1968):21.

————. "*Ladies in Waiting* [review]." *Liberator* 8 (August, 1968):21.

_____. "Three Short Plays by Ed Bullins [review]." *Liberator* 8 (May, 1968):20.

SANDERS, CHARLES L. "Sidney Poitier: Man Behind the Superstar." *Ebony* 23 (April, 1968):172-182.

SPINGARN, ARTHUR B. "Books by Negro Authors in 1967." *Crisis* 75 (March, 1968):81-87, 99-101. (This resume may be found yearly in *Crisis*. An excellent reference tool.)

TEER, BARBARA ANN. "The Great White Way Is Not *Our* Way—Not Yet." *Negro Digest* 17 (April, 1968):21-29.

"The Visitation: Controversial Opera Probes Dilemma of the Black Man." *Ebony* 23 (June, 1968):76-82.

X, MARVIN. "An Interview with LeRoi Jones." *Black Theatre* 1 (October, 1968):16 ff.

_____. *"Moon on a Rainbow Shawl* [review]." *Black Theatre* 1 (October, 1968):30.

anthology

introduction

THE plays contained in this anthology are beautifully suited to production by traditionally Negro colleges or high schools with large enrollments of black students. Indeed, traditionally white colleges, with any kind of growing enrollment of black students, should find these plays singularly compatible for their production purposes, as should many high schools and community groups.

These are good plays: forceful, entertaining, and dramatic. They are also educational in that the authors have disclosed varied aspects of the black spirit and heritage in this country. The educational qualities spring from the plays and characters themselves rather than by imposition of theme upon the material.

Insofar as the individual plays are concerned, they differ remarkably. *Fly Blackbird*, the musical play first produced in 1963, fits admirably the need of almost any production program for a vivacious and meaningful night of entertainment. Most schools desire one musical on their annual program, primarily because American audiences love them and the students need this kind of training. *Fly Blackbird* can be done with piano accompaniment alone, or as it was at Santa Barbara, with a small combo. The show fits a small theatre or is readily capable of expansion to a larger auditorium. This flexibility in staging is an outstanding asset. So, too, with its settings—they may be extremely simple and selective or may be amplified to the point where the scenic element is a resplendent aspect of the production. Choreography is vital, however, and needs full attention to the youthful exuberance that characterizes the dance required in this show. Finally, the potential for brilliant costuming and lighting is inherent in the show.

The story is simple. It starts with the mystical cabalism of a lodge ceremony in which Sweet William Piper, the old Negro movie star, is inducted as Exalted Grand Bull of the Caribou Lodge. He is also slated to become an honorary member of the Royal Order of Taurus, "the first one of our people" to be so honored. As befits such an honor, Piper proudly sings the virtues of waiting in the song "All in Good Time."

Arriving late for his induction ceremony, Piper's daughter Josie, a Sarah Lawrence girl, encounters Carl Eldridge, a student who is serving as a part-time janitor at the lodge. Though they jar each other on this first meeting, they are obviously destined for future meetings. The scene breaks away to a park where a group of youngsters, black, white, and Japanese-American, are forming an organization, the keynote to which is the song "Now." Officer Jonsen, a benevolent Negro, tries to quiet them down and goes off with their promise. Into the scene comes Big Betty—an almost automatic show-stopper with her expansive song and dance—"Big Betty, Loud and Wrong." Incorporating her into their organization, the group now starts its drive for integration. Into this meeting comes the white man, Sidney Crocker, who is "Sick of the Whole Damned Problem." He is joined in his song by Sweet William. Now the young and old are set for combat, and the story follows through as the young people meet, are jailed, rise from their despondency, and go forth exultant to the conflict. In beautiful counterpoint throughout are the songs of Sweet William, "There's a Right Way and a Wrong," "Who's the Fool— Them or Me?" played against the surging strength of the young people with their "Rivers to the South," "Fly Blackbird," and "Wake Up."

There is a love theme of course—what would a musical be without it? Carl and Josie sing "Couldn't We?" and "The Lilac Song" as their initial conflict grows into love. And there is comedy with the brilliantly incisive satires of Piper's films on the late show, or the shock of the white police matron and Officer Jonsen when they find they are related in "Natchitoches, Louisiana" and "All Alone in the Twilight Zone." There is conflict and triumph in the dream sequence, as the spell of Dr. Crocker's Love Elixir is finally broken when Carl sings of "Old White Tom" who just didn't realize his time had come, and leads the symbolic burial behind their Cadillac headstones of both Crocker and Sweet William. At the finale, Josie joins with Carl in the wave of the future, and the entire company and audience join in the play's triumphant call to "Wake Up." Naturally any musical needs good voices, but *Fly Blackbird* seems well within the range of any college group, its major problem focusing on Sweet William Piper, a musical role of some demanding dimensions. It will be a long time before audiences forget Big Betty, Sweet William, Josie and Carl, Officer Jonsen and Matron Jonsen, Crocker and the Blackbirds.

The first of the dramatic readings, *Curtain Call, Mr. Aldridge, Sir* proves eminently successful. One might readily anticipate that the dialogue would flow smoothly, for the author is none other than the renowned Ossie Davis, internationally known actor and author of *Purlie Victorious*. Working from the simplified format of five lecterns for five performers, who will carry all parts, Davis has presented a very moving portrait of this renowned and overlooked tragedian.

The reading requires one actor for Aldridge, one voice for the women's roles, two voices for other male roles, and one voice, preferably that of a white actor, for lines assigned to various white people. It is a short reading, encompassing a little more than thirty minutes, but an effective one. Taking us from the total anonymity of Aldridge, insofar as standard American references are concerned, to the birth of Aldridge into a ministerial family, Davis swiftly moves through incisive moments in the life of Aldridge as his aspirations for the stage grow, but are rebuffed by the society that surrounds him in America.

Although his father is hurt and upset by his son's desire to pursue a career other than the ministry—and particularly acting—nonetheless he magnanimously consents. At eighteen, Aldridge is off for London and within a year is performing at the Old Vic. But there was opposition in England also, and in Ireland, to the idea of a black man becoming distinguished in theatrical art. Confident of his ability, Aldridge asks that he be judged by none other than the great Edmund Kean. When Kean is overwhelmed by Aldridge's talent, Ira gains his London appearance. Eight years after leaving America, his apprenticeship served and his talent now acknowledged, he appears at Covent Garden with Ellen Tree in *Othello*.

Even here, of course, there was bigotry to overcome, and in spite of an overwhelming performance, the victory was not yet complete. Nonetheless it was a triumph. Davis follows Aldridge through his distinguished career in England until he leaves for Europe in 1852. For years he played Europe with astonishing results, and then, in 1858, came his greatest acclaim with his trip to Russia.

Having brought Aldridge to the pinnacle of his success, Davis now asks him what was his greatest triumph. While acknowledging all the honors and merits bestowed upon him by royalty and other actors, the moment that remained strongest in Aldridge's memory was one of "that kinship of the spirit which maketh all men one," the moment when the Jewish people, led by their chief rabbi in the Ukraine, thanked him for his understanding of Shylock.

At his death and honored burial in Poland, we can feel only the great loss that was America's, for Aldridge never returned here and never displayed his art in our land. Although it is indeed a very late date for clarification, Mr. Davis has helped set the record straight. This man Aldridge was a part of our black heritage that should have been—and wasn't. Certainly this memorial to a great artist deserves to be produced again and again. From a production standpoint, there is no problem whatsoever with *Curtain Call, Mr. Aldridge, Sir*. It is designed for minimal staging, lighting, and sound, and not only theatre groups but also groups more basically interested in oral interpretation will find this an excellent and challenging work. The work could readily be produced on a bill of one-acts, or as a curtain raiser to an evening's program that was not overly extensive. It might well be that it fits best as it was done at Santa Barbara—in conjunction with another dramatic reading of longer duration, Loften Mitchell's *Tell Pharaoh*.

Tell Pharaoh may be performed in intimate surroundings but is also capable of being expanded for production in huge auditoriums. The key to this expansion lies in the producer's decision as to how the music should be handled. Large choral groups are definitely a potential for this show (the St. Albans Children's Choir was used in the original production), and music may be rendered by guitar accompaniment or *a cappella*. It is so tightly written that if the producer desires, and if the young

woman and the young man are also singers, the entire
show can be done with four people. However, even a
quick reading will indicate the possibility for added
magnitude present in the musical aspects of the show,
and probably either choral groups or sound tapes of choral groups will be utilized most often. The staging itself
is reasonably minimal, relying mainly upon the lecterns
with an open area for the occasional scene that is played
thereon. Some further potentials for effectiveness exist in
the use of lighting designs for the areas.

Mitchell loves Harlem. No one who reads any of his
works on Harlem can doubt that. But *Tell Pharaoh* is
more than a loving depiction of Harlem—it is an impassioned cry for liberation, for justice. It shows a Harlem
that is the hub of the black America to which stream the
exploited looking for a life with some hope for themselves and their children. It shows, too, how from its
very start, Harlem has been sold out and its people
" 'buked and scorned" by those who sought only avari-
cious gain from the locale and the inhabitants. History
is called forth to attest to those who sold out the Negroes—the British, particularly, who, having seized New
Amsterdam, brought into existence very severe slave
codes. Even after glorious participation in the Revolution, harassments continued with the attacks of hoodlums on the African Grove Theatre and the African Free
School. Even later, the contributions of the Negro to the
battles in the Civil War were conveniently ignored.

To many people, the idea of Harlem as a suburban
carriage and mansion area in the late nineteenth century
will seem quite unusual. The exploitation of Harlem by
real estate interests who knew how desperately the
Negro needed an area for homes is not only stated but
movingly depicted in scenes of a mother desirous of her
daughter not being beat up on her way home from

school, or of a father who, returning home angry, is told by his wife to "Go fight where you got mad!" and answers only, "If I did, you'd be a widow before you could bat an eye!" The Negro needed Harlem—and he paid for it at triple the normal price.

Still there was happiness—when the battling was over. And there were moments of great nostalgia as the beautiful people strolled on their Sunday walks, or indulged in their private language. But the harmony was disrupted beneath the blast of economic enslavement that came from foreclosures and refusals to grant loans on mortgages. As Mitchell puts it, "the rape of the black American was complete." But still the black community survived, and still, as World War II ends the first act, its young men go forth to fight for a democracy which is not theirs at home.

In his second act, Mitchell concerns himself with a problem of a more national scale—the decisions stemming from DeLaine's battle in South Carolina. The seeds of rebellion burst forth throughout the land, and although met by increased indignities and attempts at suppression, they will not be prevented from flowering. In the midst of his passion, Mitchell interjects the leavening humor of Black Sam the Cowboy and rises from that moment to a paean commanding Pharaoh to let my people go—all my peoples, everywhere, throughout the earth. *Tell Pharaoh* can be an intensely moving experience and affords an excellent opportunity for drama and musical groups to collaborate on production.

There is only one play in this anthology which dates prior to 1963: Loften Mitchell's *A Land Beyond the River*. Originally this play opened at the Greenwich Mews Theatre in New York in 1957 where it was a definite success. In the dozen years which have passed since its opening, tremendous strides have been made in civil rights. It is now clear that Mitchell has written a heritage play—a portrait of an historical moment of great significance. Today, history is being made so rapidly in this area that it is a bit difficult to gain perspective—particularly when only a dozen years have intervened. Yet Mitchell has riveted for our enjoyment the historic battle of the Reverend Dr. Joseph A. DeLaine in his struggle for schooling for his parishioners. From this battle came the decisive Civil Rights decisions of 1954.

Knowing that the story would be familiar to his audiences, Mitchell elected to explore the character dimensions of the people involved in this battle, using a simple but fascinating device—the repairing of a rotten schoolroom floor. In trying to repair that which cannot be repaired, these patient and disparate characters find a common bond for their anger and frustration. When he sees that the men need leadership beyond that which he has been giving them, Layne decides to escalate his campaign from buses to a demand for equal schools.

One of the ways by which we get to know Mitchell's characters is through his use of love. Love weaves its way throughout *A Land Beyond the River*. There is love for the Lord evident in prayer and song; there is love for youth as for the two rambunctious youngsters, and for age, as is seen in the great respect shown by all for Grandma Simms. There is youthful love in the developing courtship between Ben and Laura; marital love in many phases, as in the mature devotion of Layne and Martha, the strong familial bond between Mary and Bill, and the tumultuous, oftentimes humorous, love of Duff and Ruby. There is even love and compassion for Philip Turnham, though he has persecuted Layne and harmed his own people, and there is love reciprocated between the doctor and the people. Even at the moment of greatest anguish, Layne calls on his parishioners for a forgiving love toward the bigots who have harassed them endlessly.

Battering against these decent people are the bitter and painful dramatic incidents. Threats, assaults, house-burnings, child-beating, and murderous gunfire are but a part of the actual persecution. To the psychological and political pressures exerted by Cloud and Turnham are added economic reprisals to dim the enthusiasm of the group for justice. Bolstered by Layne's faith, they endure and they conquer. The strength and courage of Layne shine forth in this drama and assure Mitchell of a lasting place in the role of dramatists who have recorded the black heritage in this land.

In terms of its setting, *A Land Beyond the River* requires a careful composite design, with much attention paid to ease of shifting. There are ample opportunities for effectiveness in lighting to enhance the theatrical elements in the play. The costuming, for the best authenticity, will normally be in period.

The final work in this anthology, Ted Shine's *Morning, Noon, and Night,* is an extraordinary combination of fantasy, comedy, and horror. When first produced at Howard University, the play was done proscenium. In its next production at Santa Barbara, the setting was in three-quarter staging. Under both conditions the play proved remarkably effective.

Shine writes very tightly and this play is particularly compact. There are only four characters: Gussie, the boy Ben, the aunt Ida, and the traveling evangelist Sister Sue. The plot itself is relatively simple and revolves around Gussie's attempt to acquire both the home and the boy for her own and the extent to which she will go to secure them. Only Ben's ultimate independence stands between her and triumph.

Simple though the plot is, the characters prove memorable indeed. Gussie gives an actress an opportunity for a tour de force seldom encountered. Peg-legged, powerful, capable of coaxing at one moment and threatening horrendously at another, fanatical in her religiosity, singing and dancing with a vitality that is overwhelming, Gussie is always a challenge. And yet her impact on an audience is nothing less than awesome, for Shine has drawn this character with singular originality. Gussie rings true, as do Shine's other characters, all taken from the rich, rural areas of Texas he knows so well.

Sister Sue is a bizarre creation. Coming back yearly to await the coming of Ben's manhood, she prods and feels him as though testing a prize horse, exclaiming on his teeth and his increasing growth, and warning him always to drop everything and head for her when he feels the approach of manhood. She, too, just as Gussie, has destined the boy for preaching and looks forward not only to marrying him but to a partnership with him.

In Ida Ray, the most "normal" of the characters in this play, Shine achieves a strong rapport with the audience. Ida is a woman who labors to keep this home together, who is searching for some tiny bit of love and happiness for herself, and finds that the pressures around her mount beyond her control. Ida Ray is a good woman, but she is no match for the diabolism of Gussie, and is bound to be swallowed up by such a dominant woman.

But it is Ben who provides the major conflict with Gussie. Ben is a peculiar character in whom Shine has conceptualized brilliantly what a "mature boy of eleven" should be. Both at Howard and at Santa Barbara, audiences unhesitatingly accepted this conceptualization even though the role, in both instances played by the same actor, was handled by a man in his mid-twenties. Rather than the reality of the eleven-year-old boy, what is required is the conceptualization of an eleven-year-old, and this necessitates a remarkable job of acting. Though seemingly a realist in his tight play structure, Shine imbues his work with elements of fantasy and nonrealism that should be recognized, as in the case of this conceptualization, if his greatest effectiveness is to come forth. In the truest sense of dramatic writing, Shine is a poet; his world is one beyond sheer realism.

Fly
Blackbird

a musical play
in two acts by
C. B. Jackson and
James Hatch

ADDITIONAL MATERIAL BY JEROME ESKOW

synopsis of scenes

The place is a northern city in the United States, the time is today.

characters

(All members of the cast are Negroes unless otherwise identified)

SWEET WILLIAM PIPER, a man in his late fifties
OFFICER JONSEN, a dignified, middle-aged man
CARL ELDRIDGE, a virile young college man
JOSIE PIPER, an attractive young college girl
TAG, a small, vivacious sixteen-year-old girl
GAIL, a young white girl
CAMILLE, an attractive girl of about nineteen or twenty
PALMER, a tall, good-looking young man
PAUL, a vibrant youth
GEORGE, a young Japanese-American
ROGER, a bright youth
GLADYS, a young white girl
BETTY, a tall, extremely energetic girl—Tag's older sister
LOU, a young white student
SIDNEY CROCKER, a white man in his mid-fifties
POLICE MATRON, a middle-aged, attractive, white, southern
WHITE COP
Also extra chorus members as desired. Roles doubled as needed
for Lodge Members, Students, Crocker Boys and Crocker Girls.

music

ACT ONE

ACT TWO

Act One

scene 1. *The Caribou Lodge. As the curtain opens a mysterious ritual is gradually revealed in silhouette and phosphorescence. We see what might be an ancient rite. Men move rhythmically. A strange animal horn is heard. Suddenly a pinspot captures one figure.*

Brother Sweet William Piper, a Negro man in his late fifties, is being installed as "Exalted Grand Master of the Caribou." He, like the others, is dressed in a long flowing robe. In one hand he holds the sacred sword, in the other, the triple scepter of the Lodge. His neck is ringed with the official surplice and near his hand rests the miter of the Master Caribou. The total impression given is one of a man overburdened, but for Mr. Piper it is a moment of glory. He is beaming with self-satisfaction. When the lights come up, Mr. Jonsen, a dignified-looking middle-aged Negro, is holding the miter over the head of Piper, who stands before the grand throne. The other Lodge members surround him.

JONSEN

With all the authority vested in me by the Royal Order of Caribou, I crown thee Exalted Grand Bull!

FIRST LODGE MEMBER

C . . .

SECOND LODGE MEMBER

A . . .

THIRD LODGE MEMBER

R . . .

FOURTH LODGE MEMBER

I . . .

FIFTH LODGE MEMBER

B . . .

SIXTH LODGE MEMBER

O . . .

SEVENTH LODGE MEMBER

U . . .

ALL

Caribou!

FIRST LODGE MEMBER

C . . .

JONSEN

Is for the courage that we cherish.

SECOND LODGE MEMBER

A . . .

JONSEN

Is for ambition we hold high.

THIRD LODGE MEMBER

R . . .

JONSEN

Is for the right; let it not perish.

FOURTH LODGE MEMBER

I . . .

JONSEN

Is for ideals that never die.

FIFTH LODGE MEMBER

B . . .

JONSEN

Is for brotherhood's endeavor.

SIXTH LODGE MEMBER

O . . .

JONSEN

Is obligations to be true.

SEVENTH LODGE MEMBER

U . . .

JONSEN

Is to be useful now, forever
And all together they spell . . .

ALL LODGE MEMBERS

Caribou!

PIPER

I've always known there'd come a time
when Life would open all its doors to me.
And now I know what Life can bring.
Now I know that anything

you wish with all your heart for can come true . . .
Some wishes do come true.

Everything comes to those who wait.
ALL IN GOOD TIME!
Carefully choose the path you take
and you will find
the moon will be yours, the stars will be mine.
Won't that be fine!

The Heavens will light the darkness of night,
the sun will shine.

Everything comes to those who wait.
ALL IN GOOD TIME!
ALL IN GOOD TIME!

There may be times things go wrong
and every sky looks cloudy and gray.
But patience lives to see the day
when all the clouds have gone away.
And I am sure that come what may or might
the stars will shine tonight.

Everything comes to those who wait.
ALL IN GOOD TIME!
Carefully choose the path you take
and you will find
the moon will be yours, the stars will be mine.
Won't that be fine!

The Heavens will light the darkness of night,
the sun will shine.

Everything comes to those who wait.
ALL IN GOOD TIME!
ALL IN GOOD TIME!

Now I have found and you'll find too
that patience is a blessing in disguise.
Just you wait and you will see
how beautiful this world can be.

How wonderful
How marvelous
How grand!
The world is in our hands.

ALL

Everything comes to those who wait.
ALL IN GOOD TIME!
Carefully choose the path you take
and you will find
the moon will be yours, the stars will be mine.

PIPER

Won't that be fine!

ALL

The Heavens will light the darkness of night.

PIPER

The sun will shine.

ALL

Everything comes to those who wait.
ALL IN GOOD TIME!
ALL IN GOOD TIME!

PIPER

ALL IN GOOD TIME!
(*The Lodge Members applaud.*)

PIPER

Thank you. Thank you. I . . . what can I say? This honor,
this position you've awarded me. . . . I only wish my
dear wife were alive to share this moment. My daughter—
who's away at Sarah Lawrence—where she's head of her
class—couldn't be here. So I share my enthusiasm with
you.

LODGE MEMBERS

(*Touched*) Hear! Hear!

PIPER

Brother Caribou, this is a twice glorious week for me. Not
only have you crowned me Master Caribou, but tomorrow
—tomorrow I shall set foot upon a different ladder. Tomorrow the Royal Order of Taurus is extending to me—as
the first one of our people—an honorary membership in
their lodge.

LODGE MEMBERS

(*Enthusiastically*) Hear! Hear!

PIPER

My friends, this is the year nineteen hundred and sixty-nine, and we have finally arrived!

ALL

Everything comes to those who wait.
All in good time.
The moon is yours
The stars are mine
The sun will shine
All in good time.
ALL IN GOOD TIME!

(*As Piper, Jonsen, and the Lodge Members exit singing, Carl, a young Negro in his early twenties, enters. He wears a white waiter's jacket. He sings softly as he begins to empty the ashtrays, etc.*)

CARL

C-A-R-I-B-O-U.
Everything comes to those who wait . . .
All in good time. . .

(*Carl picks up a cigar case which Piper has left behind. Assuming a mock-dignified pose he addresses the audience.*)

CARL

My friends, this is the year nineteen hundred and sixty-nine, and we have finally arrived. May I add to all of you brothers in the South—and in the North—who haven't arrived—be patient. Don't push—

(*Carl's speech is interrupted by the entrance of Josie Piper, young, attractive, refined, the daughter of Sweet William Piper.*)

JOSIE

I beg your pardon . . .

CARL

Oh, hi.

JOSIE

Hi. (*Seeing no one else in the room*) To whom were you speaking?

CARL

To whom? Why to youm, Miss—er—what's your name?

JOSIE

What's *your* name?

CARL

There must be an echo in here.

JOSIE

I'm looking for the new Grand Master.

CARL

Can you keep a secret?

JOSIE

Yes.

CARL

The new Grand Master of the Caribou . . . is *me*.

JOSIE

Unless I'm mistaken, that's my father's cigar case.

CARL

Oh. You're Josie. Miss Piper. Daughter, you missed my coronation.

JOSIE

This is absurd. Where's my father?

CARL

Don't you know your own father, child? My motto emblazoned on my cigars: "Don't rock the boat!"

> (*Josie tries to cross the room, angered now by Carl's flippancy, but he blocks her path.*)

JOSIE

Would you mind getting out of my way! (*Tries to push him aside.*)

CARL

That's a good right arm. What did you major in, Phys Ed?

JOSIE

Oh, you're impossible!

> (*Piper, returning for his cigar case, enters. He is now dressed in street clothes.*)

PIPER

Josie! Josie, is that you?

JOSIE

Poppa!

PIPER

(*As they embrace warmly*) What a surprise!

JOSIE

I'm sorry I couldn't be here for the coronation.

PIPER

But you're here now and that's the important thing. How nice you look.

JOSIE
(*Noting Grand Master's surplice*) You got it!

PIPER
(*Modestly*) Everything comes to those who wait.

JOSIE
All in good time.

JOSIE AND PIPER
Carefully choose the path you take and you will find

PIPER
The moon will be yours

JOSIE
The stars will be mine

JOSIE AND PIPER
Won't that be fine!

CARL
(*Clearing throat*) Amen!

PIPER
(*Really noticing Carl for the first time*) Oh, Carl! Forgive
me. Have you met my daughter?

JOSIE
Yes, Poppa, we've already met.

PIPER
Josie is a Sarah Lawrence girl. Carl here is putting himself
through college by helping out around here.

JOSIE
(*Sarcastically*) How nice.

PIPER
What are you studying at college, Carl?

CARL
Political science.

PIPER
Ah, they call it a science now, eh? To my way of thinking,
politics is an art.

CARL
The art of the possible.

PIPER
Yes, that's true. It's all in knowing what you can do and
when. Twenty years ago I would never have been accepted as an honorary member of the Taurus Lodge. . . .
But today . . . we've come a long way. In another fifty
years . . . all of us may be members.

JOSIE

Poppa, it's getting late.

PIPER

All right, dear.

CARL

(*Handing Piper his cigar case*) This is yours, I believe, Sir.

PIPER

Thank you, Carl. You keep up the good work . . . and remember . . . everything comes to those who wait.

JOSIE

(*Acidly*) Nice meeting you, Mr.—?

CARL

Eldridge. Nice to have met you.

PIPER

Goodnight. (*Piper and Josie exit.*)

CARL

"Sarah Lawrence girl" huh. Maybe in fifty years we'll all be Sarah Lawrence girls. Mr. Piper, Sir . . . in fifty years I'll be dead. If there's a job, I want a chance to earn a decent living.

> (*A section of the Caribou Lodge set is broken away, and Tag, a small Negro girl about sixteen years of age, comes running in.*)

TAG

Now!

CARL

(*Removing waiter's jacket*) If there's a school, I want the best education I can get.

> (*Another section of the Lodge is broken away. Gail, a young white girl, enters.*)

GAIL

Now!

CARL

(*Building in intensity*) If there's a house for rent, don't tell me "sorry but we don't rent to colored."

> (*Another section of the Lodge set is broken away. Camille, a Negro girl of nineteen or twenty, enters.*)

CAMILLE

Now!

CARL

It makes me mad!

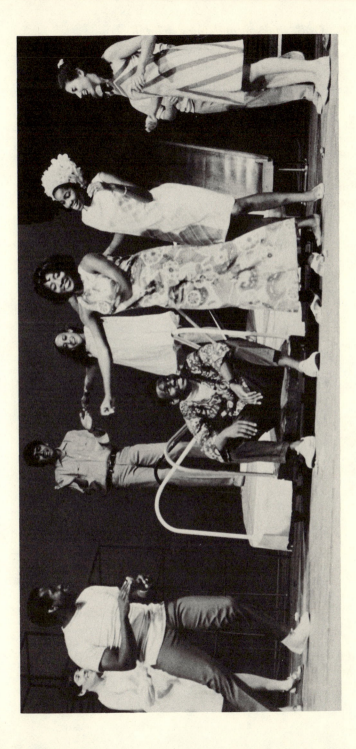

Students singing in the park

SCENE 2. *The entire body of Students come rushing forward as the last section of the Caribou Lodge set is broken away. We find that the scene has been transformed to a public park somewhere near the campus of a northern college. The Students are dressed in normal spring attire: sweaters, sport jackets, etc. There are benches, trees, a fountain, etc. A row of fine apartment buildings can be seen in the distance. The group gathers around Carl.*

GROUP

Now!

TAG

Not another hour.

GROUP

Now!

CAMILLE

Not another day.

GROUP

Now!

CARL

Not a minute longer but now!

GROUP

Right now! Right now! (*Continue under.*)

CARL

(*Leaping onto bench*)

We've waited two hundred years or more
But the time is drawing near
When we will stand up and say—
Today is the day!

GROUP

The time is here!
Now! Not another hour
Now! Not another day
Now! Not a minute longer but now!

TAG

We've got to do something to let people know how we feel.

PALMER

(*A tall, good-looking Negro youth*) Right! As long as we keep our mouths shut, things'll stay just as they are:

GROUP

See no evil! Hear no evil! Think no evil! Know no evil!

CAMILLE

(*Haughtily*) I think it's a shame the way they treat (*to Paul*) *your* people down south.

PAUL

(*A young Negro*) I don't know about that . . . but the way they treat *your* people up north is wicked.

GEORGE

(*A young Japanese-American*) This is supposed to be the melting pot of the world. All right, let's melt!

GROUP

We've waited two hundred years or more,
but the time is drawing near
when we will stand up and say
Today is the day!
The time is here!
Now! Not another hour
Now! Not another day
Now! Not a minute longer but now . . .
Right away!

(*At the conclusion of the song the Students break into noisy chattering. A Negro policeman, Mr. Jonsen of Scene I, enters.*)

OFFICER JONSEN

Hey, you kids. Come over here. I wanta talk to you. (*The Students gather around him.*) Look, you're gonna have to keep the noise down. This is a public park and there are other people here besides yourselves.

CARL

You're right, Officer. We'll quiet down. Right . . .

GROUP

(*Whispered*) Now!

OFFICER JONSEN

Just what are you up to anyway?

CAMILLE

We're gonna form an organization.

TAG

An organization to establish a greater degree of communication between people from various cultural and socioeconomic backgrounds.

OFFICER JONSEN

That's very interesting. You sound like a bright kid.

CARL

Sure she is. Her IQ must be over 172 . . .

PAUL

. . . and that was on a bad day.

TAG

And Officer, that's white man's IQ, measured by his language, his culture, and his words . . .

OFFICER JONSEN

Then your Negro IQ must be over 200.

ROGER

(*A young Negro boy*) Officer, do you realize that the Negro unemployment rate is two and a half times that of—

OFFICER JONSEN

I know.

GLADYS

(*A young white girl*) But Officer, do you realize that a Negro worker forty-five years of age or over who loses his job will probably never again be gainfully employed?

OFFICER JONSEN

Thank you for the information. Now just so I don't become one of those statistics . . . (*Gathers Group in close around him, then whispers*) . . . Keep it down. (*Exits*)

ROGER

(*Enthusiastic and loud*) Hey, he was a nice cop, wasn't he? (*The volume of the Group's chatter rises again.*)

CARL

(*Quieting Group*) Well, let's keep him that way. Look, if we're gonna form an organization, let's get started.

GAIL

I'm for that.

TAG

We'll get started today.

PALMER

That lets me out. I have to study today.

TAG

Study tonight like everybody else.

PALMER

Can't. Betty and I are going to a party at the Licorice Lounge.

CAMILLE

By the way, where is that sister of yours, Tag?

TAG

(*Shrugs*) I don't know. She said she'd be here at two o'clock.

CARL

Do you have to go tonight, Palmer?

PALMER

(*Takes balloon from his pocket and blows it up.*) I already have a (*Holds up balloon*) ticket.

CARL

That?

PALMER

Yeah! Every Thursday the Licorice Lounge knocks a dollar off the admission price if you bring one of these balloons. (*Carl grabs balloon and breaks it.*) . . . Hey! What are you doin'?

CARL

The Licorice Lounge has got to go!
(*Betty, a tall and extremely energetic young Negro girl, Tag's older sister, enters. She carries an armful of blown-up balloons.*)

BETTY

The Licorice Lounge *does* go, man! Who needs discount tickets?

TAG

Betty, you're late. It's after three o'clock. You said you'd be here at two.

BETTY

Be cool, Baby. It's only two o'clock C.P. Time.

GEORGE

(*Puzzled*) C.P. Time?

BETTY

Colored People's Time, plumpit.

CARL

Yeah. Just a little bit behind everybody else. (*He grabs balloons from Betty.*)

BETTY

Hey! Gimme those!

CARL

Betty, we've decided to do something worthwhile for a change.

CAMILLE
We're forming an action group.

CARL
Right! So forget the Licorice Lounge and let's get to work.

BETTY
(*Astounded*) Work? Carl Eldridge, go wash your mouth out with soap. That nasty word. Aren't you ashamed of your—

CARL
Betty, will you shut up a minute and listen!

BETTY
Shut up? Are *you* tellin' *me* to shut up? Do you realize who you're talkin' to? This is Big Betty.

CARL
Can't you ever be serious about anything?

CAMILLE
Carl was trying to say something important.

BETTY
Loud and wrong. (*She has begun to dance.*)

GAIL
Oh, why fight it.
(*The Students are gradually being drawn into Betty's dance.*)

BETTY
This is Big Betty.

PALMER
(*Shifting blame to Betty, but joining in eagerly*) Once she gets going, you can't stop her.

CARL
You guys make me sick.

BETTY
Loud and wrong.

TAG
Oh, oh! Here she goes!

GROUP AND BETTY
(*Except Carl*)
So stand back. Look out. Get outta the way!

BETTY
'Cause this is Big Betty's song.
I don't do the waltz

GROUP
Nor the gavotte.

BETTY

I can't stand the shag.

GEORGE

Don't play no ragtime music!

BETTY

Never cared for the minuet
and you can bet
I'm not about to do no foxtrot . . .

But I can rock 'n' roll
from pole to pole
'cause I've got cinnamon
in my soul,
so when I start to move
if you don't approve
just stand back!

'Cause this is Big Betty
This is Big Betty
This is Big Betty
Loud and Wrong!

> (*She dances. Unable to resist, the other members of the Group join her. The dance builds to a wild, noisy pitch.*)

ALL

Stand back!

BETTY

This is BIG BETTY!
This is BIG BETTY!
Loud and wrong!

BETTY

Now that's what I call an action group.

> (*Officer Jonsen crosses behind the group, eyeing the Students suspiciously. They greet him sheepishly, holding their breaths until he exits.*)

CARL

Betty, instead of wasting all that energy, why don't you use it for something constructive?

BETTY

(*Sexily*) What'd you have in mind?

CAMILLE

Doing something about discrimination in this country.

TAG

(*Coming forward with picket sign she has improvised. It reads: "BRING LOUISIANA BACK INTO THE U.S.A."*) Right! We're marching south!

PALMER

(*Reading*) "Bring Louisiana back into the U.S.A."?

GAIL

We're going to Washington to see the President.

(*The Students have formed a line of march.*)

ROGER

The President of the United States of America.

(*Lou, a young white student has leaped onto a bench. He assumes a presidential air.*)

TAG

Let me talk to him.

LOU

Yes, my dear, what can I do for you?

TAG

Don't you think the Southern Negro should be allowed to vote?

GROUP

Yes!

LOU

(*Pondering deeply*) Uh . . . for which party?

TAG

Ah, you get down. Let me be President. (*She climbs onto bench.*) My friends, my fellow Americans—all you dedicated young people—Yes, I mean you with the brown eyes. Tell me, will you do everything in your power to bring about a state wherein every American, regardless of race, sex, creed, or previous economic condition, has equal and unobstructed access to the vast material and intellectual resources of this great nation?

GROUP

Yes!

TAG

Even at the risk of your own immediate comfort and well-being?

GROUP

Yes!

TAG

Then I pronounce you full and equal citizens . . . as of . . .

GROUP

Now!

TAG

Not another hour.

GROUP

Now!

CARL

Not another day.

GROUP

NOW! Not a minute longer but now.
Right now!
Right now!
Right—

> (*The reprise of the song is interrupted at this point by the appearance, from the Audience, of Sidney Crocker, a white man in his mid-fifties. The Group freezes into whatever positions they happen to be in at the time of his interruption. Crocker is expensively dressed, indicating a position of affluence. He wears a black Homburg and an impeccable gray suit of the finest material. He carries a light topcoat on his arm.*)

CROCKER

(*Coming from Audience*) Hold it! Hold it! Let's stop this before it goes any further. (*He climbs onto the stage and addresses Audience directly.*) What are they complaining about? (*Indicating frozen figures of Students*) We're living in the richest country in the world. We've never had it so good. You know, that's the whole damned trouble with people. They're never satisfied. No matter how much they have, they always want more.

Let's look at the facts. I'm a businessman and I like to see things down in black and white. (*Leafing through a small notebook which he takes from his pocket*) Now the average income in the United States is about five thousand dollars a year. The average for the Negro is two to three thousand. I realize that's below what you and I make, but remember . . . it's considerably above the average for the hemisphere.

Did you know that the per-capita income for Mexico and Brazil is less than three hundred dollars . . . and in Bolivia they live on one hundred dollars a year! What if you and I had to exist on that? Five hundred dollars is a year's wage in Puerto Rico and . . . that other island . . . you know the one I mean—a good example of where this kind of thing can lead.

I'm sick of the whole damn problem.

(*The Students unfreeze and begin to tango mechanically in the now dimly lit background. As Crocker's song progresses, some of them gradually exit.*)

The whole damn thing has gotten out of hand.
I can't bear another syllable on the subject.
I've had about as much . . . as I can stand.

It's driving me insane
Driving me mad
I simply can't believe the situation is that bad!

What the heck
Do they expect?
They're still a whole lot better off than many on this earth.

They have cars.
Radios and television sets.
'Course a lot of those things aren't paid for yet,
But that's what the Credit Card is for . . .
So everybody can have a few goodies.

They're not the only ones with problems
What are they making so much noise about?
Why should I listen to them weep and moan?
I've got problems of my own.
But who would care if I began to shout:

Oh, I'm oppressed!
I'm mistreated!
I'm a victim of an unjust circumstance!

No!
I take my medicine like a man
and take misfortune by the hand,
politely say:
"Miss Fortune, shall we dance?"

(*Crocker dances a tango, backed up by the remaining Students.*)
Now, don't get me wrong.
I don't have a prejudiced bone in my body.
That's a fact in which I've always taken pride.
I don't care if you're short, tall, fat, or lean,
black, brown, red, or green. . .
Just as long as you're . . . white *inside!*

It's (*Throwing topcoat to ground in rage*)
driving me insane, driving me mad (*Tramples coat*)
I simply can't believe the situation is that bad!

I'm sick of the whole damn problem.
The whole thing's gotten out of . . .
(*Is about to throw Homburg to ground, but thinks better of it and plops down on bench instead.*)
(*Piper enters. He is as nattily dressed as Crocker. He wears a white Homburg. He recognizes the figure seated exhausted on the bench, rushes over to him.*)

PIPER

Sid?

CROCKER

Bill! Am I glad to see you. How the devil are you?

PIPER

Fine! I haven't seen you since I did that benefit for your lodge.

CROCKER

The boys still talk about it, Bill. You were great.

PIPER

Still feel the pains.

CROCKER

The kids of today could learn a lot from you old-timers. What's the matter with them? All this nonsense about "freedom." (*Becoming agitated again*) Freedom to do what?

PIPER

Now take it easy, Sid. You're getting yourself all excited about nothing. I know these kids can be annoying, but take my word for it, it's just a passing phase that everybody'll have forgotten in a few months.

CROCKER

I suppose so. How about your daughter, Josie . . . she's not mixed up with these crazy kids, is she?

PIPER

A Sarah Lawrence girl? (*They both laugh.*)

CROCKER

I forgot. You know, Bill, if there were more people like you, there wouldn't be any Negro problem.

PIPER

I know how you feel, Sid. I've seen these kids—waving banners, singing . . .

CROCKER

They're creating a big disturbance, a completely unnecessary fuss. I think it's a real affront to decent people like us.

PIPER

I know exactly what you mean, Sid . . . exactly what you mean, and I'm

Sick of the whole damn problem!

CROCKER

That's just what I was saying!

PIPER

The whole damn thing has gotten out of hand.
I can't bear another syllable on the subject.
I've had about as much . . .

CROCKER

That's two of us.

PIPER

As I can stand.

CROCKER AND PIPER

It's driving me insane, driving me mad
I simply can't believe the situation is that . . .
(*Piper breaks off, interrupts Crocker.*)

PIPER

Oh, it's not even worth talking about. Sid, I've got to run. Almost forgot . . . I have to pick up Josie.

CROCKER

Could I drop you? I've got my car.

PIPER

Is that your Cadillac parked over there?

CROCKER

(*Modestly*) Yeah, the black one.

PIPER

A beautiful car. 1968, isn't it?

CROCKER

Yes, it is.

PIPER

Well, that's my Cadillac parked beside yours.

CROCKER

The white one?. . . Side by side. Well, we'll both drive. Separate but equal!

PIPER

But mine's a '69. (*Crocker does a take.*)

CROCKER

So what's the problem?

CROCKER AND PIPER

We're sick of the whole damn problem.

PIPER

The whole damn thing is rotten.

CROCKER

It's better off forgotten.

CROCKER AND PIPER

The whole damn thing has gotten out of . . .

(*Piper politely hands Crocker his Homburg. They start to put on their hats, but notice that Piper has mistakenly given Crocker his own white Homburg and he holds Crocker's black one. They exchange Homburgs, correcting the situation.*)

PIPER

(*To Audience*) It goes with the car.

CROCKER AND PIPER

. . . hand!

(*They do a vaudeville-style exit. The Students reenter in the mechanical tango, then freeze. On their reentrance, some carry placards. Piper reappears in a spotlight downstage right.*)

PIPER

(*Indicating frozen Students*) Look at 'em. Who's the fool them or me?

They think they've got the world by the tail,
Think they're gonna change things overnight.
Well, that's all right with me
I've done things differently . . . myself.

I learned a long time ago
that anger doesn't get you anywhere.
There's no use beating your head against a wall
if you intend to get anywhere at all.

They're doing things so differently.
Who's the fool . . . them or me?
>   (*The lights come up. Piper steps into the center-
>   stage area. The Students spring to life.*)
>   TAG

All right, let's have some action.
>   (*The Students get to work painting signs, etc. Gail,
>   crossing, bumps into Piper.*)
>   GAIL

(*Embarrassed*) Oh! Excuse me.
>   PIPER

What a pretty little girl. What does your sign say?
>   GAIL

"End Segregation."
>   PIPER

Oh, I agree with that. (*Indicating Group*) But, there
doesn't seem to be any . . ."segregation" here. (*The other
Students gather around.*) What's this all about?
>   TAG

We're fighting for freedom. (*Group expresses agreement.*)
>   PIPER

(*Good humoredly*) Fighting for freedom indeed. Well,
there's no doubt about the fact that that's what we need . . .
but tell me . . . are you sure this is the best way to go about
getting it?
>   TAG

What do you mean?
>   (*The whole Group responds to Piper's statement,
>   e.g., "If we don't do something, nothing'll ever get
>   done," "It's about the best way I can think of to
>   show people what we mean," "Do you know of any-
>   thing better?" etc.*)
>   PIPER

You know . . . there's a right way and there's a wrong

in everything you do.
You can catch more flies with honey
than by shoutin', yellin', makin', everybody mad.

There's a good way and there's a bad.
Here's my advice to you.
Suit the method to the goal
and watch your dreams unfold before your very eyes.

Ever try to put salt on a robin's tail?
GROUP
That's impossible; it can't be done.
PIPER
I can show you a method that'll never fail.
GROUP
Can't be done! Can't be done!
PIPER
Have you ever tried birdseed?
GROUP
Birdseed?
PIPER
Or breadcrumbs?
GROUP
Breadcrumbs?
PIPER
And if you feel like diggin' up worms . . .
That'll work too.
GROUP
How true!
Why didn't we think of that.
PIPER
You think the lion tamer works with whip and gun?
GROUP
(*Truly entertained by Piper's anecdote, they join in with enthusiasm.*)
That's the version we're accustomed to.
PIPER
Neither whip nor gun makes the lion run.
GROUP
What does the lion tamer do?
PIPER
He tries to fill the lion to the brim
so the lion couldn't possibly swallow him,
GROUP
(*Laughter*)
PIPER
Because a hungry lion can

make a lion tamer look bad.
GROUP
(*Mock sorrow*)
How sad!
PIPER
But a well-fed lion will eat right out of your hand!
GROUP
We understand!
PIPER AND GROUP
There's a right way and there's a wrong
in everything you do.
You can catch more flies with honey . . .
PIPER
Than by shootin' off your mouth
at the wrong times and places,
wavin' those signs in people's faces.

When I was but a little tyke upon my mother's knee
she told me what the world was like
and that was her advice to me.
GROUP
There's a right way and there's a wrong way
You can catch more flies with honey . . .
PIPER
In my day we did the mess around . . .
BETTY
But today we kids know how to really go to town!
(*All dance a few measures.*)
PIPER AND GROUP
You can catch more flies with honey
than with vinegar!
PIPER
Catch 'em!
BETTY
Say . . . who are you, Mister?
PIPER
William Piper's my name.
TAG
Oh, I know! That's Sweet William Piper!
PIPER
Ah . . . you've been reading your *Ebony*.

TAG

I saw you last night on TV . . . in *Safari*.

PALMER

So did I.

ROGER

(*To Group*) I saw it too. It was him. (*To Piper*) I wouldn't have recognized you, Mr. Piper.

PIPER

(*Embarrassed*) That picture was made many years ago. (*Anxious to avoid discussion of the film*) Well . . . it was nice to have met you all. I hope I'll see you again. (*Backing away*) Good-bye! (*He exits.*)

TAG

Gee, he's gotten old.

CARL

Older, but no different.

PALMER

(*To Betty*) You should've seen that movie . . . (*Deep-voiced*) SAFARI!

> (*The lights dim. The Students take up positions behind fountain, under benches, etc., creating imaginary jungle setting. They produce various jungle sounds.*)

BETTY

(*With phony British accent*) Oh, Charles, this infernal heat is driving me mad.

PALMER

The jungle is no place for a white woman, my deah. (*Calling offstage*) . . . Boy!

BETTY

Is Maloka coming?

PALMER

I think so, my deah. (*Paul enters, shuffling.*) Boy, go see what that noise is. (*Referring to a lion roar which Group produces*)

PAUL

Oomgawa, B'wana. (*Shuffles over to fountain.*)

> (*When Paul reaches fountain, the Group produces a blood-curdling roar, leaps wildly at him. Paul shrieks, disappears behind the fountain. Betty agonizes and Palmer comforts her.*)

PAUL

(*Leaping onto the fountain*) Hey, what about that spy picture he played in—PORT SAID! (*Paul exits. Group forms a train.*)

TAG

(*Slinking up to George, who is pacing nervously in front of the Group, looking very shady*) Zee bomb ees on zee trrain.

GEORGE

(*Nods in satisfaction, then glances at an enormous brown purse that Tag carries.*) You fool! You left zee wrrong bag! Zee bomb ees een zees one! (*Grabs purse from Tag, gazes around wildly.*) Porter! Porter!

PAUL

(*Shuffles in, wearing a porter's cap.*) Vouse called mwah, monsoor?

GEORGE

(*Forcing the purse into Paul's hand*) Take zees bag to zee trrain! Queekly! (*George returns his attention to Tag. Paul stands waiting, hand extended, for tip.*)

TAG

I sought eet was een zee white bag.
(*Group produces ticking sound, which increases in speed and intensity.*)

GEORGE

No! No! Zee brown bag.

TAG

I am sure eet was zee white bag,

GEORGE

Brrown bag! (*Tag glances over, sees Paul. George follows her gaze, sees Paul, does a take.*) Go! Queekly! (*Digs around in his pocket for some money, pushes it into Paul's hand. Paul grins, nods, then shuffles over to the "train."*)

TAG

Eet was zee white bag.

GEORGE

Brrown—
(*Once more, Paul disappears behind the fountain. Group produces an explosion noise, hurling the porter's cap into the air.*)
(*George gives Tag a smug look, Tag responds with kittenish shrug. They smile.*)

CARL

Hey! Bet you never saw Piper do his love duet in the picture HIGH COTTON!

All day long I just sweep
Trying to earn my board and keep
Chasin' away the blues
Dancin', dancin' . . . with crumbs in my shoes.

TAG

Oh, how happy I would be
if you would only marry me
What would you have to lose
With me in your arms

CARL

And crumbs in my shoes.
(*Josie enters during the song.*)

JOSIE

Hi.

CARL

(*Embarrassed, trying to quiet the Students*) Oh, hi.

JOSIE

Say, you're quite a dancer.

CARL

Just fooling around with these kids here.

JOSIE

That song sounded awfully familiar.

CARL

Well it should, it's one of your fa— Say, how's the Phys Ed major?

JOSIE

About the other night—I was terribly rude. I'd like to apologize.

CARL

My fault. I'm sorry. (*Carl and Josie argue back and forth about whose fault it was for a moment.*) Look, why don't we pretend that other night never happened. What are you doing around here anyway?

JOSIE

I was supposed to meet my father here. I had no idea I'd run into you again.

CARL

It's destiny.

JOSIE
(*Not understanding*) I beg your pardon.

CARL

Like Romeo and Juliet. Fate hurls us together like two
stars that clash in the night.

JOSIE

I'd better go look for my father.

CARL

It's her! I'd know her anywhere
by her soft blue eyes and her golden hair.

JOSIE

He's the one for me!
My knight in shining armor,
the perfect charmer I've waited for.

GROUP

It's love at first sight,
that's the refrain.
Never before and never again.

JOSIE AND CARL

It's LOVE AT FIRST SIGHT

GROUP

That's the refrain.

JOSIE AND CARL

Never before

ALL

And never again
(*Carl takes Josie by the waist.*)

JOSIE

What are you doing?

CARL

We dance. Never saying a word.

JOSIE

(*Afraid the game is getting out of hand*) It's been lovely.
But I really must go home.

CARL

I'll take you home. (*Dances her around, seats her on
bench.*)

GROUP

It's LOVE AT FIRST SIGHT
That's the refrain
Never before . . . and never again.

CARL
There. Right on your doorstep.

JOSIE
On my *balcony*.

CARL
I love you! I love you!
Always be mine!

At that moment your mean father calls.

JOSIE
He's not mean.

CARL
Oh, yes he is. He takes you inside and locks the door, but later we meet secretly in the park. I propose. Marry me!

JOSIE
My father would never consent.

CARL
We'll run away.

JOSIE
Where?

CARL
To the desert. Or the mountains.

JOSIE
I like the sea.

CARL
Good! I have a cottage there.

JOSIE
We could settle down in a little green cottage
by the sea
Couldn't we?

CARL
Couldn't we?

JOSIE
A little green cottage
with a welcome mat by the door.

CARL
And windows that let the sun come through.

CARL AND JOSIE
Waves pounding on the shore.

CARL
Hear them roll . . .

CARL AND JOSIE
Hear them roar . . .

We'd run down to the beach and welcome the morning
tide.
Wouldn't we? Wouldn't we?
We'd fly down the sand like sea gulls on the wing.

When night falls, we'll see the mirror of the moon glis-
tening on the water.
CARL
And the stars twinkling in the sky . . .
CARL AND JOSIE
We could settle down in a little green cottage by the
sea.
CARL
Couldn't we?
CARL AND JOSIE
COULDN'T WE?
BETTY
(*Inviting Palmer to do a takeoff on Carl and Josie*)
Wouldn't it be wonderful to live by the sea?
PALMER
Splendid, dahling.
CAMILLE
What sea?
PALMER
The Black Sea, stupid!
JOSIE
What's wrong with wanting a decent place to live?
PALMER
Not a thing, honey. (*In falsetto*)

We could settle down
in a little green cottage by the sea . . .
GAIL
I don't know why anyone would want to live where
they're not wanted.
LOU
It's not that I object, but what would my neighbors think?
GAIL AND LOU
You've got to think about property values.
BETTY AND PALMER
(*Palmer in falsetto, Betty in bass voice*)
A little green cottage with a
welcome mat by the door . . .

PALMER
I'd like to settle down
by the old East River.
Serve cocktails and hors d'oeuvres
and sautéed chicken livers.

BOYS
And the only friends you'd see would have
East River—

GIRLS
Olé!

BOYS
Personality!

JOSIE
Why not!

GROUP
You tell me!

BETTY, TAG, AND GAIL
Why can't we have a place
along the beach.
With the sea, surf, and sand
within our reach.

CAMILLE
I've often heard that Oyster Bay . . .

GROUP
Would be the place to live and play!
(*Gail assumes sunbather's pose, starts lathering up with suntan oil.*)

BETTY
(*To Gail*) Hello!

GAIL
Oh, how d'you do.

TAG
Mind if we share your sunshine?

GAIL
Not at all. (*Noting their complexion*) Oh, how marvelous. Sea and Ski?

BETTY AND TAG
Heredity! (*Gail screams.*)
(*The three do a lively dance.*)

CAMILLE
(*Interrupting*) Hey! I read in *The New York Times* that Negroes don't want integration.

BETTY, TAG, AND GAIL
Is that so!

CAMILLE
It seems they've been having difficulty getting Negro families to move into the new middle-income housing.

BETTY, TAG, AND GAIL
That's where the rent comes from. Right out of the ough! *Middle!*

GROUP
Landlord fill the flowing bowl
Flowing bowl, flowing bowl.
Landlord fill the flowing bowl
'til the cup runs over!
(*Repeat*)
(*The singing and dancing reach a frenzied pitch. Officer Jonsen enters, observes the scene in disbelief for a moment, then blows the whistle. The Students freeze. Officer Jonsen points with his club. Drooping, but still dancing, the Students begin to change the scene. They remove fountain, benches, trees, etc. Huge jail bars, which cover the face of the proscenium are moved into place from the sides of the stage. The lights gradually fade to blackout. They come up on:*)

SCENE 3. *Police Station—Office. As the lights come up, we hear the syrupy strains of Stephen Foster's "Old Black Joe." The bars open and we find a police matron seated behind a desk downstage left. She is middle-aged, attractive, white, southern. On the desk are several books, flowers, a radio (presumably the source of the Foster melody). The Matron holds a book in her hand, but is at the moment totally entranced by the music. Officer Jonsen enters.*

JONSEN
(*Politely*) Pardon me. (*The Matron does not respond.*) . . . Pardon me, are you the matron on duty here?

MATRON
(*Indicating radio*) Listen. (*She turns the volume up.*)

JONSEN
I've got a wagonful of screaming kids out there.

MATRON
Pardon?

JONSEN

I just arrested a herd of . . . (*Screaming*) . . . if you'd
turn that damn thing down you could . . . (*Matron turns
volume down, leaving Jonsen screaming into silence.*) . . .
hear me!

MATRON

What?

JONSEN

I can't talk against all that noise.

MATRON

That was Stephen Foster. (*Jonsen grimaces.*) Y'all
oughtn't to be ashamed of yoah heritage.

JONSEN

My what?

MATRON

You should be proud of yoah past.

JONSEN

What's Stephen Foster got to do with my past?

MATRON

It's all here in this book—*The Nigrah and You.*

JONSEN

The Negro and who?

MATRON

(*Sheepishly*) . . . and me. It says Stephen Foster was
one of the best friends the Nigrah ever had. Why, he
wrote hundreds of beautiful songs glorifyin' the people of
yoah race. Oh, I can just see him . . . sittin' in the big
house on the plantation, his loyal and beloved slaves clus-
tered around his feet . . . listenin' to the songs he wrote
for them . . . and for you . . .

JONSEN

Sorry . . . but I don't like Stephen Foster.

MATRON

If you don't like Stephen Foster, you must be a bitter man.

JONSEN

Look, lady . . . I didn't come in here to discuss music. I've
got a wagonload of screaming kids waiting outside, so let's
get down to business.

MATRON

Rush! Rush! Rush! Why is everybody in this city always in
such a hurry? Where are y'all going?

JONSEN
With a little cooperation from you (*Sits down.*) . . . home
to rest my feet.

MATRON
If you didn't rush around so much your feet wouldn't
bother you. Where I come from people take things easier
and live a lot longer.

JONSEN
Maybe you have a point. I was raised in a small town myself.

MATRON
Where are you from?

JONSEN
Natchitoches, Louisiana.

MATRON
Natchitoches? Why, that's my hometown.

JONSEN
I should have known.

MATRON
Gee. I haven't been there in years.

JONSEN
We used to live down on Front Street. Know where that is?

MATRON
Sure I do. Why—do you remember that big house on the
edge of town . . . right by the lake?

JONSEN
The one the hurricane turned around?

MATRON
That's it. I've been trying for days to think of the name of
the man who owned that place . . . the one who used to
walk his fence with a shotgun.

JONSEN
Old Man Miller?

MATRON
Old Man Miller.

MATRON AND JONSEN
Nat-chi-toches, Louisiana
Is the place where my mother gave birth to me . . .

MATRON
Her only child

JONSEN
My mother had eight.

MATRON AND JONSEN
'Twas there I spent my childhood years
With all the hopes and all the fears
Of innocence in a strange new world.
MATRON
I used to walk to Sunday school
Just to listen to the teacher
JONSEN
With his big bass voice.
MATRON
No! She was a lady with silken hair
That gleamed in the sun like silver.
JONSEN
I used to fish in the river, wade in the stream,
Drink from the cooling waters of the brook.
MATRON AND JONSEN
Natchitoches, Louisiana
Is the place where my mother gave birth to me.
(*Going into separate reminiscing*)
MATRON
One-room school house
JONSEN
I was terrible in arithmetic
MATRON
I was awful in arithmetic
JONSEN
But I could outspell anybody in my grade
I still remember the plans I made . . .

I was gonna be spelling champion of the world.
MATRON
I'll bet that Melba Dean Anderson is still mad because I
was elected class president . . . She thought just because
her father was president of the bank, the kids would vote
for her.
JONSEN
I'll never forget the fight I had with that red headed freck-
le-faced kid from South Street. He had no business calling me that name.
MATRON AND JONSEN
I didn't care who (her) (his) father was . . . (*They
laugh.*)

Natchitoches, Louisiana
Is the place where my mother gave birth to me . . .
    MATRON
Her only child.
    JONSEN
Wonder what my brother Charlie is doing.
    MATRON AND JONSEN
'Twas there I spent my childhood years
With all the hopes and all the fears
Of innocence in a strange new world.
Innocence in a strange new world.
    JONSEN
Oh, my gosh! I forgot all about those kids! (*He runs out, then returns with Students. Gail and Tag carry signs.*) All right, none of your lip. Line up and give your names to the matron. Hurry up.
    MATRON
(*To Palmer*) What's yoah name, boy?
    PALMER
Boy?. . . *Mister* Boy!
    JONSEN
Your name!
    PALMER
Palmer. . . Blackbird.
    MATRON
Palmuh . . . Blackbird?
    PALMER
I'm half Indian . . . on my father's side.
    JONSEN
Next.
    ROGER
Roger. Roger Blackbird—
He's my brother.
    MATRON
(*To Gail*) You look like an intelligent girl—what's yoah name?
    GAIL
Gail Blackbird.
    MATRON
What?
    GAIL
We're blood brothers.

MATRON

What is this?

JONSEN

(*To Carl*) All right. I warned you I didn't intend to become a statistic. Now what's *your* name? Your real name?

CARL

Carl Blackbird. We're all one tribe.

(*Students sit, arms and legs folded, "Indian" style and begin chattering in pig Latin.*)

MATRON

We'll see about this. Officer, may I speak to you in private, please.

(*Students remain seated, look at each other conspiratorially.*)

CARL

Four and twenty Blackbirds

GROUP

Yeah!

PALMER

Couldn't get off the ground,

GROUP

Yeah!

PALMER

Couldn't get off the ground.

GROUP

Yeah!

PALMER

Up jumped one, said this ain't no fun,
I'm gettin' sick and tired of bein' held down!

BETTY

Four and twenty Blackbirds
Couldn't get off the ground!
Up jumped Joe and said come on, let's go!
Look out . . . we're skyward bound!

GROUP

Fly Blackbird, Fly Blackbird
Fly Blackbird, rise into the air.
(*Repeat*)

BETTY

Four and twenty Blackbirds
Sittin' in a pie
Some sang low

GROUP
Some sang low
BETTY
Some sang high
GROUP
Some sang high
BETTY
Some sang rebop
GROUP
Some sang rebop
BETTY
Oop Shoop
GROUP
Oop Shoop
BETTY
Razz-a-ma-tazz
GROUP
Razz-a-ma-tazz
BETTY
And all that jazz!
GROUP
And all that jazz!
Fly Blackbird, Fly Blackbird
Fly Blackbird, rise into the air.
CARL
Four and twenty Blackbirds
PALMER
Said, we do believe
CARL
That the Pharaoh's walls
Are cracking up
BETTY
And it ain't gonna grieve me.
CARL
Sally, don'tcha leave me
GROUP
Don't leave!
BETTY
We're gonna . . .
GROUP
Fly Blackbird, Fly Blackbird
Fly Blackbird, rise into the air.

BETTY
Now flap your wings
GROUP
Flap your wings
BETTY
Stand and shout
GROUP
Stand and shout
BETTY
Wiggle your toes
GROUP
Wiggle your toes
BETTY
We're moving out
GROUP
We're moving out
BETTY
Now gimme some skin
GROUP
Gimme some skin
BETTY
Now c'mon in
GROUP
C'mon in
BETTY
When I give the word
GROUP
Give the word
BETTY
We'll sing another chorus of Fly Blackbird.
ROGER
(*Getting overenthusiastic*)
Fly Blackbird, Fly Blackbird, Fly Black—
BETTY
(*Restraining Roger*)
Hold it! (*Pause*) Now!
GROUP
Fly Blackbird, Fly Blackbird
Fly Blackbird, rise into the air.
CARL
Now the bumblebee's stinger is ten feet long
GROUP
The bumblebee's stinger is ten feet long???

CARL

And the Blackbird has a beak

GROUP

The Blackbird has a beak

BETTY

Mister Charlie got pecked by a little blackbird

GROUP

Mister Charlie got pecked by a little blackbird

CARL

And couldn't sit down for a week!

GROUP

Whoo!
Fly Blackbird, Fly Blackbird,
Fly Blackbird, rise into the air.

Fly Blackbird, Fly Blackbird,
Fly Blackbird . . .
See the Blackbird rise into the air . . .
FLY BLACKBIRD?

(*Students are chattering together as Matron and Jonsen return.*)

BETTY

How about that?

MATRON

Look at this mess!

BETTY

What's the matter?

MATRON

Look what you've done to my floor!

TAG

(*Inspecting the floor*) I don't see anything.

MATRON

This floor was freshly waxed. Look at it now!

TAG

Gee, you sound just like my mother.

MATRON

I beg yoah pahdon!

GAIL

All right, so you sound like *my* mother.

BETTY

(*Jokingly, playing "Mama" to Tag*) You just get right down here and clean this up.

JONSEN

You two have just volunteered. The mop is in the closet at the end of the hall.

BETTY

Hey!

JONSEN

The rest of you—into the tank. Let's go!

PALMER

Hey, we get a phone call.

JONSEN

Long as you're from the Blackbird tribe, you can send your messages by drum! Now get in there!

GROUP

We want a phone call! We want a phone call! (*They continue chanting as Jonsen herds them out.*)

MATRON

(*To Betty and Tag*) You'll find the wax with the mop.

BETTY

(*In rich dialect*) Ma'am, we don't mind doin' this if it's just day work—but if you want somebody to sleep in, I don't think we—

JONSEN

(*Reenters, interrupts Betty.*) The closet at the end of the hall. (*Betty and Tag exit.*)

MATRON

What are they charged with?

JONSEN

Disturbing the peace! I warned them.

MATRON

(*Noticing sign Gail has left behind*) Would you look at this sign.

JONSEN

"Bring Louisiana back into the U.S.A."

MATRON

This generation has no conception of the fine traditions which you and I as southerners are trying to uphold.

JONSEN

I left Natchitoches.

MATRON

But you loved it, Officer. . . uh . . . what *is* your name?

JONSEN

Jonsen

MATRON

Jonsen! From Natchitoches?

JONSEN

Did you know my folks?

MATRON

No, but my name's Jonsen too—we spell ours the Danish
way—S-E-N.

JONSEN

So do we.

MATRON

Danish?

JONSEN

Well, there must be hundreds of Danes in Natchitoches.

MATRON

What was your father's name?

JONSEN

Helgar.

MATRON

Helgar!

JONSEN

He was named after my great-grandfather, Helgar Aksel
Jonsen.

MATRON

My heavens!

JONSEN

What's wrong?

MATRON

That was the name of *my* great-grandfather too!

JONSEN

Helgar Aksel Jonsen. . . . You mean that you and I had
the same—

MATRON

It can't be the same man! He wouldn't do a thing like that.

JONSEN

Well how many Helgar Aksel Jonsens can there be in a
town that size?

MATRON

But *my* great-grandfather was a Baptist!

JONSEN

So was mine.

MATRON

Oh Lord! Lord! That would mean that I'm . . . No, it's

not true. Even if it was the same man. You'll see. I'll look
it up.

JONSEN

Look what up?

MATRON

It's all here in this book. (*Holds up* The Negro and You.)
You read it.

JONSEN

"Who Is Legally a Negro"?

MATRON

If you and I are related . . .

JONSEN

It would mean that I'm . . . white?

MATRON

No. That I'm . . . No. It can't be! Hurry, Officer Jonsen!
Hurry!

JONSEN

Let's see . . . in North Dakota and Indiana you're a
Negro if you have twenty-five percent Negro blood . . . in
Mississippi and in Florida—

MATRON

Louisiana?

JONSEN

In Louisiana . . . it's . . . one drop.
(*Matron faints. Tag and Betty enter. They carry
mops and brooms and wear aprons, kerchiefs, and
are ready to clean up as instructed.*)

JONSEN

Help me with the Matron.
(*The Matron, having revived, notes the color of
Betty and Tag, and frantically declines their help.
Jonsen helps the Matron out the door.*)

BETTY

What happened to Scarlett O'Hara?

TAG

Miz Scarlett? She is gone. All gone. (*Tag picks up book
that Jonsen dropped when Matron fainted. Reads title.*)
The Negro and You. Mh mh mh! (*Replaces it on desk.
Notes other books there.*) She's got quite a collection here.
(*Reading*) *Uncle Remus in the Briar Patch, Magnolia
Manor, Little Black Sambo,—*

BETTY

Oh, that's one of my *favorite* stories.

TAG

(*Reading*) "Black Mumbo ate 36 pancakes. Black Sambo's father, Black Jumbo, ate 92 pancakes. But Little Black Sambo was so hungry that he ate 962 pancakes."

BETTY

Who wrote that book?

TAG

Aunt Jemima! (*Replaces it on desk.*)
          (*Voices are heard offstage.*)

COP

Right in that door.

GEORGE

But I wasn't doing anything
          (*Enter George and White Cop.*)

GEORGE

You didn't arrest anybody else.

COP

(*To Tag and Betty*) Where's the officer on duty here? (*They don't answer immediately. The Cop has mistaken them for cleaning women, and prods impatiently.*) You work here, don't you?

BETTY

(*Playing along*) Oh, yassuh, we does. De ossifuh, he step out fo' a bit. Don't he? (*Nudges Tag.*)

TAG

(*Getting Betty's message, but also getting a bit carried away*) Oh yassuh. But befo' he go, he say go clean dat room. He say, you clean dat room good. He say, you gonna make dat room shine like a policeman's boots! Yas SUH! He say, you gonna clean up dat room fo' me 'til it gleam, he say—

BETTY

(*Grabs Tag by the skirt, hauls her away from her tirade.*) Yeah, dat's exactly what he say. (*Glares at Tag.*)

TAG

(*Sheepishly*) Dat's what he say.

COP

(*To George*) All right. You sit down and don't move.

(*Cop exits. Betty moves in behind George.*)

BETTY

Say dere, boy, what yo' in fo'?

GEORGE

Pardon? . . . Betty!

TAG

Hi, George.

GEORGE

Tag! I thought you got away.

TAG

We thought you did.

BETTY

No time for small talk. Come on. You heard that man. He thinks we work here. We're dancin' outta here wif crumbs in our shoes.

TAG

We gotta fix a . . . for . . .

BETTY

Right! (*Taking glasses from Matron's desk*) Here.

TAG

(*Taking hat from hatrack*) This'll help.

BETTY

Good idea.

GEORGE

Why?

TAG

(*Has taken coat from hanger on wall.*) Hold your arms out.

BETTY

Now this! (*Draws moustache on him.*)

GEORGE

Hey, that tickles.

TAG

(*Draws beard*) And this!

BETTY

(*Putting on finishing touches*) Now. Baby, you look great! (*Turns him to face Audience.*)

TAG

Quick George, out this way.

GEORGE

What am I disguised as?

BETTY

You now famous oriental detective.

TAG
Like Charlie Chan!
GEORGE
Oh, no!
BETTY
Oh, yes! (*Holds up bucket.*)
GEORGE
What's that?
BETTY
A gong.
GEORGE
A what?
TAG
A gong, George. Why, all famous oriental detectives must
have a gong!
BETTY AND TAG
Ah so!

> The oriental detective is always
> accompanied by a gong.
> And temple blocks
> and a melody built on a pentatonic scale.
> Nyn nyn nyn nyn nyn (*etc.*)
> Have you ever been to a Hollywood moving picture?
> BETTY
> Then you know what I mean
> TAG
> You know what I mean.
> BETTY, GEORGE, AND TAG
> That's the way it always is
> on the Hollywood movie screen.
> GEORGE
> The oriental detective is always
> accompanied by a gong.
> BETTY
> Look at Charlie Chan
> That famous policeman
> TAG
> From the Orient
> BETTY, GEORGE, AND TAG
> The mysterious east!

BETTY

Then there is Fu Manchu.

TAG

When he blinks those eyes at you . . .

BETTY, GEORGE, AND TAG

The chills begin to trickle down your spine!

GEORGE

Terry and the Pirates and the Dragon Lady . . .

BETTY AND TAG

She's kinda shady

BETTY

Not like Rosie O'Grady, the girl next door.

BETTY, GEORGE, AND TAG

The girl next door!

TAG

To who?

BETTY

Not you!

BETTY, GEORGE, AND TAG

And then we had *The World of Susie Wong*
And once again, we had . . . the gong.

The oriental detective is always
accompanied by a gong.

GEORGE

Why must it always be a gong? Why can't it ever be the samisen or the sho?

BETTY

What's a samisen, man?

GEORGE

Well, it's like a . . . guitar. Or the koto?

TAG

What's a koto, Mister Moto?

GEORGE

Ah . . . the koto is a long, narrow stringed instrument which is plucked. And the most amazing thing about it is that it can be retuned during performance!

BETTY AND TAG

Wow!

GEORGE

Or how about the hichiriki, which is like an oboe, or the kokyu, or the shakuhachi. But . . .

BETTY, GEORGE, AND TAG

Why does it always have to be a gong?

How come an oriental detective is always
accompanied by a gong.
And temple blocks
and a melody built on a pentatonic scale?
Nyn nyn nyn nyn nyn
nyn nyn nyn nyn nyn nyn nyn nyn
nyn . . . nyn
Nyyaaaaahh!

BETTY

Come on. Let's go!

GEORGE

What about the others?

BETTY

Too risky!

(*The Matron enters, somewhat recovered from her
faint.*)

MATRON

Are you girls almost done?

(*Betty and Tag have dropped to their knees and
are scrubbing diligently, humming snatches of Stephen Foster tunes.*)

TAG

Oh, yassum. Jest about, Ma'am.

MATRON

(*To George*) . . . and who are you?

GEORGE

Thousand pardons, Missie. Must introduce self. Am Lou
Man Fang. Special Investigator.

MATRON

Can I help you?

GEORGE

Confucius say, "Lovely woman can always be of help."

MATRON

(*Flattered*) How charmin'. What is it you want, Mr. Fang?

(*George is flustered, but Tag comes to his aid.*)

TAG

Maybe, Mistah Detective, suh . . . you wants de students.

GEORGE
The students? Ah so. Yes. I have orders for the release of the students to me.

MATRON
Oh! Who are the orders from?
(*Unnoticed, Officer Jonsen has entered.*)

GEORGE
Orders, ah . . . orders from . . . ah . . .

TAG
Day's orders from headquarters.

BETTY
Da's right.

TAG
Da's right.

GEORGE
Da's right.

JONSEN
All right! What's going on here? (*Betty, Tag, and George try to sneak away.*) Hold it! (*To George*) I said hold it!

MATRON
You mean even the Chinese are mixed up in this?

TAG
He's a Japanese-American, Ma'am.

MATRON
Don't contradict me!

TAG
I was just trying to help.

MATRON
It doesn't matter. I don't know what anybody is anymore anyway. Would you book him, Officer Jonsen? I'll put these two in the tank with the rest of the Blackbirds.
(*Exits with Betty and Tag.*)

JONSEN
(*To George*) Well, what have you got to say for yourself?
(*Jail bars have started to close.*)

GEORGE
(*Nervously*) I pledge allegiance to the flag of the United States . . .

(*Blackout*)

SCENE 4. *The cells. When the lights come up we find the Students grouped around the bars which cover the face of the proscenium. The lighting is low-keyed. The mood is one of general depression.*

TAG

(*Sadly*) Four and twenty blackbirds
Couldn't get off the ground.

> (*She decides to try to cheer everyone up. Sneaks up behind Gail.*)

Boo!

GAIL

Aw, Tag! (*Turns away.*)

TAG

Hey, George, how does it feel to be a jailbird? (*He ignores her.*) This sure is a cheery bunch. Come on, Betty. Flap your wings!

BETTY

Tag, cut it out!

PALMER

Yeah, act with a little dignity for once.

BETTY

(*Defending her sister*) Who asked you?

PALMER

(*To Betty*) If it hadn't been for your horsing around, we wouldn't be here.

BETTY

My horsing around?

PALMER

That's what I said!

CARL

(*Intervening*) All right. It's doesn't matter. We're here now.

CAMILLE

My folks'll never forgive me for this. (*There are murmurs of agreement from the Students.*)

JOSIE

(*After a pause*) Would somebody mind telling me what that little gathering in the park was all *about*?

ROGER

(*Sadly*) We were going to form an organization.

CARL

We *are* going to form an organization.

JOSIE
To do what?

TAG
To stand up for our rights.

BETTY
The rights of all!

JOSIE
(*Bursts into laughter.*)

BETTY
What's so funny?

JOSIE
I do believe you're serious. (*Laughs*)

BETTY
I got a feelin' me an' Miss Sarah Lawrence ain' gon' get along. (*Grabs Josie by the shoulder.*)

JOSIE
(*Rising to meet the challenge*) Don't handle the threads, honey. I'm liable to blow my cool . . . and I know you don't wanna see that happen.
(*The Group is impressed by her knowledge of slang.*)

BETTY
Talk that talk!

PALMER
Hot damn!

LOU
Don't she sing pretty though!

JOSIE
Look! Just because I don't come on down home doesn't mean I don't know where down home is.

BETTY
(*Walking away—gives Josie a friendly pat on the back.*)
Well, go 'head on, Miss Thing.

JOSIE
Now, seriously. What were you doing out there in the park? The signs, that whole bit? Did you really think anybody would pay attention?

PALMER
They'll pay attention.

GAIL
They'll have to.

JOSIE

Says who?

CARL

Says me!

JOSIE

Oh! (*Beat*) And may I be so bold as to inquire . . . who *me* might be?

ROGER

Only the greatest guy you'll ever have the privilege to run across in these here *Yew*nited States of America . . .

PALMER

Ladies and Gentlemen . . .

GLADYS

Carl Eldridge!

GROUP

Rah!

CARL

Broom-pusher extraordinaire!

GAIL

Honor student!

CARL

Nobody! I'm nobody! We're nobody! (*The Group starts to protest.*) But that's the point. (*Turns to Josie.*) All of us nobodies are beginning to think we're somebody. All of us nobodies all over the world beginning to push out our chests a little bit and sayin', "Hey! Look at me!" For the first time in our lives, startin' to talk above a whisper. (*Yells*) Yahoo! Hey! Look at me!" And every once in a while one of us'll walk up to a Mr. Already Somebody and give him a quick poke right in the eye. (*Quoting Mr. Already Somebody*) "Hey! What'd you do that for?" (*Back to his own voice*) "You know, I can't remember right offhand . . . but I know I had a good reason. It'll come to me after a while. Maybe I just did it to see if anybody'd notice."

PALMER

All over the world.

CARL

Africa

CAMILLE

Asia

ROGER

The Middle East.

JOSIE

What about the South?

PALMER

Oh, there are mighty rivers to the south—
Rivers deep and long.

CARL

I have listened to the rivers of the South
heard them singing:
"New day, new day, new time, new way
coming soon."

GROUP

New day, new day, new time, new way
coming soon.

PALMER

I have followed the rivers of the South
rushing down to the sea.

GROUP

New day, new day.

CARL

I have followed the rivers of the South.
Come follow me!

GROUP

To a new day, new day
A new time and a new way
coming soon.
Stood on the banks of the Mississippi.

PALMER

New day.

CARL

New day.

GROUP

Heard the waters of the bayou,
dark and cold.

PALMER

New day!

CARL

New day!

GROUP

Crossed the wide Missouri.

Listened to the Chippewa, ages old.

CARL

New day!

PALMER

New day!

GROUP

New day!

PALMER

New time!

GROUP

New time!

CARL

New way!

PALMER

New way!

GROUP

New way coming soon!

PALMER

Little drops of rain fall from the branches,
form a pool at the bottom of a tree.

CARL

The pool flows into the babbling brook,
The brook flows into the stream.

GROUP

Then the stream plunges down the side
of the mountain into the river,
filling the river.

PALMER

I have seen the mighty rivers of the South filled to the
brim by a driving rain.

GROUP

New day! New day!

CARL

When the dam breaks,

GROUP

New day!

PALMER

The cup runneth over.

GROUP

New day!

CARL

The river will rise and flood the shore!

GROUP

New day! New day!

PALMER

River foam!

GROUP

New day!

CARL

River roar!

GROUP

New day! New day! New day! New day!

CARL

Ah, . . . Oh, there are mighty rivers to the South, rivers deep and long.

GROUP

Listen to the rivers of the South.

PALMER

Hear them sing. . .

GROUP

Ah . . .

New day, new time, new way . . .

CARL

Coming soon!

(Curtain, end Act I)

Act Two

SCENE 1. *When the set opens, the bars which cover the face of the proscenium are closed. Behind the closed bars the Matron is seated at her desk. Officer Jonsen in a chair beside her. They are listening to the singing of the Students, who are grouped behind a smaller set of bars at the left of the house (stage left) in the auditorium itself.*

GROUP

We could settle down in a little green cottage
by the sea . . . .

(*Josie and Carl enter from opposite sides of the stage in front of the bars. They stop at the center of the stage as though separated by an invisible barrier.*)

JOSIE AND CARL

See the green tree standing on the hill
with its arms outstretched
to the summertime breezes.

Oh, oh, bumblebees sting the gentle lilac
but oh, oh, honey is sweet.

JOSIE

There's a blackbird hidden in the tree
with a sharp pointed beak
and a broken wing.

Oh, oh, bumblebees sting the gentle lilac
but oh, oh, honey is sweet.

JOSIE AND CARL

There's a young man underneath the tree
standing arm to arm with a willowy maiden.

Hear them sing!
oh, oh . . .
oh, oh . . .

196

How they sing!
oh, oh . . .
oh, oh . . .
See the blackbird rise into the air!
          JOSIE
See the green tree standing on the hill.
Oh . . . . (*Exiting*)
          CARL
Oh . . . . (*Exiting*)
          (*As Carl and Josie exit, the lights go down on the*
          Students. The bars open.)

SCENE 2.
          MATRON
(*Sigh*) There's nothing in the world so beautiful as
colored people singing.
          JONSEN
You oughta know.
          (*Voices are heard offstage—Piper and Crocker.*)
          PIPER
(*Offstage*) Do you think I don't know my own daughter?
She would never be involved in such a thing. (*Enters with*
Crocker.) Here we are. Who's the precinct officer here?
(*Recognizes Jonsen.*) Fred. Fred Jonsen!
          JONSEN
(*Rising to shake hands*) Bill Piper?
          PIPER
Fred, am I glad to see *you!*
          JONSEN
What are you doing here?
          PIPER
Josie's been arrested!
          JONSEN
Josie?
          PIPER
My daughter Josie!
          JONSEN
Here? I don't think . . . we picked up some kids in the
park . . .
          PIPER
She didn't have anything to do with that.

JONSEN

. . . who wouldn't give their names.

PIPER

Josie wasn't involved.

JONSEN

Then I doubt that she's here.

PIPER

(*Angrily*) Don't you know who you arrested?

CROCKER

(*Trying to intercede*) Bill, maybe—

PIPER

Josie was arrested by mistake. A friend of mine saw it happen. Why do you say she's not here?

JONSEN

I didn't say that!

PIPER

Fred, either you did or you didn't arrest Josie!

JONSEN

Look, I hardly know the girl! If she's one of those kids—

PIPER

I told you, she wasn't involved.

CROCKER

(*Condescendingly*) Bill, let me talk to him. (*To Jonsen*) Officer, do you think we could arrange to have a look at the prisoners . . . just to relieve Mr. Piper's mind?

JONSEN

Sure! Why not? I never said you couldn't (*Starts to exit.*)

PIPER

(*Following Jonsen*) Josie wouldn't! She's a Sarah Lawrence girl. (*Exit Jonsen and Piper.*)

CROCKER

(*To Matron*) What a character. They're a wonderful people, if you know how to handle them.

MATRON

What do you mean "handle them"?

CROCKER

Well, colored people are very sensitive, you know—

MATRON

(*Sharply*) How would *I* know! (*Catching herself*) I mean . . . no more so than anyone else.

CROCKER

I've known Bill for years. Of course, Bill isn't really like

the others. I've known him for years. You know, most of
the time he doesn't act any more like a Negro than *you* do.

MATRON

(*Startled*) What a ridiculous thing to say!

CROCKER

(*Puzzled by her strange reactions*) From the South,
aren't you?

MATRON

Louisiana. Why?

CROCKER

Louisiana? No wonder? You wouldn't understand the kind
of relationship Bill and I have. Down there you don't know
what it is to get close to The Negro.

MATRON

Oh, I don't know—we get pretty close!

(*Jonsen and Piper are heard offstage.*)

PIPER

(*Offstage*) Josie was not creating any public disturbance!

(*Jonsen and Piper enter.*)

JONSEN

They all were.

PIPER

Fred . . . you and I are members of the same Lodge. You
know I'm a responsible man. Release Josie in my custody.

JONSEN

Bill, to do that I'd need an order from the magistrate.

PIPER

Fred, do a brother Caribou a good turn!

JONSEN

I'd like to help, Bill. But I . . . I just can't release her
without an order.

PIPER

You can but won't!

CROCKER

Bill, we better call my lawyer.

PIPER

(*Disdainfully, to Jonsen*) And you call yourself a Caribou!

CROCKER

There's no point arguing, Bill.

JONSEN

I'd help you if I could.

PIPER
That's mighty white of you. (*Piper and Crocker exit.*)
JONSEN
(*Shaken, to Matron*) How did he know?
MATRON
Maybe that was just a figure of speech.
JONSEN
No. He suspects. I can tell.
MATRON
That friend of his kept looking at me strangely.
JONSEN
How am I going to tell my wife?
MATRON
Tell her what?
JONSEN
That for the past eight years she's been married to a white man.
MATRON
Officer Jonsen . . .

What are we gonna do?
JONSEN
I can't believe it's true.
MATRON
Oh, I could sit right down and cry.
JONSEN
Where do we go from here?
MATRON
How I'd like to disappear from view.
MATRON AND JONSEN
We're all alone in the Twilight Zone.
MATRON
Oh, woe, woe . . . woe is me.
JONSEN
What a catastrophe.
MATRON
What have I done to merit this.
JONSEN
Sad, sad, oh, sad am I.
MATRON
Lady Luck has passed me by. I'm through!

MATRON AND JONSEN
Out here we stand . . .
In no man's land.

MATRON
I used to walk along the street
smile at folks that I'd meet.
Life was just a bowl of cherries.

JONSEN
I'm quite beyond recovery
since I made the discovery
that cherries have a pit.

MATRON
I'm it!

MATRON AND JONSEN
Oh, what a mockery!
Fate, what have you done to me?
Life has dealt a crushing blow.
Sadness and misery,
The heavens high have laid me low.

JONSEN
There's nothing more worth living for
when you find you're neither nor.

MATRON
I can see the surprise
In everybody's eyes
when they discover that I'm Nature's little
compromise!

MATRON AND JONSEN
We're all alone
in the Twilight Zone!
(*Jonsen exits.*)

MATRON
(*Throwing her hands up in despair*) O Lawd, what is
I gonna do?

VOICE
(*Offstage*) I'm glad you asked that question, Lady.

SCENE 3. *The lighting becomes low, mysterious.*

MATRON
Who said that? Officer Jonsen? Officer Jonsen?
(*A figure appears in the darkness behind the closed*

bars. It is Crocker dressed in a white top hat and tails. He carries a cane.)

CROCKER

I'll tell you what you're going to do.

(*The Matron comes over to bars to see better who it is. Crocker taps bars with his cane. They open. The stage is bare.*)

MATRON

(*Puzzled*) Where am I?

CROCKER

(*Produces flowers as if by magic from thin air.*) . . . In the Twilight Zone! (*Calling offstage*)

Sweet William!

(*Piper propels himself onstage aboard what was the Matron's desk, mounted on wheels. Draped around the desk is a banner that reads: "Dr. Crocker's Love Elixir."*)

CROCKER

Don't be frightened, Lady.

PIPER

(*He wears a derby, a striped polo shirt, brightly colored trousers, in the manner of a circus barker.*)

Are you ready, Dr. Crocker?

CROCKER

All yours, Sweet William.

PIPER

Everything comes to those who wait.

All in good time.

(*The Crocker Boys, formerly the Students, dressed in brightly colored band uniforms, strut in.*)

PIPER

Carefully choose the path you take

And you will find . . .

(*The Crocker Boys place gaily colored banners around the stage.*)

PIPER

(*To Audience*) Here we are, all set for the Dr. Crocker Medicine Show—in living color. Just sit close and watch as Dr. Crocker, the world-famous physician and healer, brings you not only song and dance, not only stories and merriment, but the most exciting innovation of the century: Dr. Crocker's Love Elixir!

CROCKER BOYS

Doctor Crocker's Love Elixir
is the most successful trouble-fixer known . . .
to mortal man.

PIPER

Have you got troubles? Do you have headaches? Do you
have pain?

> (*The Crocker Girls, formerly Students, enter, bring-
> ing with them a wagon similar to a parade float.
> Above the float there is a large drawing of Crocker
> and the words: "Dr. Crocker's Medicine Show."
> Some of the girls ride on the float. Some walk pret-
> tily beside it. They wear long, brightly colored
> dresses and bonnets, simulating the costume worn
> in the late nineteenth century when Medicine Shows
> were popular in the United States.*)

CROCKER BOYS

It will take away your troubles,
leave you floating on a bubble of champagne!

PIPER

You'll feel good again!

CROCKER GIRLS

We're lovely, we're charming, delightful to see!

CAMILLE

Doctor Crocker's Love Elixir
has done this for me.

CROCKER GIRLS

We're lovely, we're charming, delightful to see!

CAMILLE

Doctor Crocker's Love Elixir
has done this for me.

I used to be dissatisfied and unhappy. Nothing seemed
right to me, I was mad at the world. Then I discovered
Crocker's Love Elixir! "Why, there's nothing wrong with
the world," I said. "It's me! It's been me all along!" But
now . . . I've found peace and . . . love.

CROCKER GIRLS

Doctor Crocker's Love Elixir
has done this for me.

PIPER

So I ask you, friend and neighbor . . .

PAUL

Why not do yourself a favor?

LOU

You'll love it!

GEORGE

It'll do you good!

ROGER

It'll knock you out!

PIPER

You'll be a new man!

PIPER, CROCKER BOYS AND GIRLS

We ask you not to hesitate.

A minute more may be too late.

It's going fast!

PAUL

It's a blast!

CROCKER BOYS AND GIRLS

Doo-Waaaah!

PIPER

And now the creator of the Elixir of Love, the balm which heals all wounds, may I present my friend and yours, Dr. Sidney J. Crocker!

CROCKER

(*With a gesture, invites Matron to have a seat at side of stage.*) Thank you, Sweet William (*To Audience*) Here . . . (*Picks up an elegant crystal bottle from the desk. Smoke is streaming out of it.*) . . . in this little bottle is the famous power potion, the Dr. Crocker Love Elixir. Ladies and gentlemen, you've seen remedies purported to cure lumbago, arthritis, painful backache, but you've never seen a medicine that can cure the ills of an agonized soul, a tempest-tossed mind, an . . . aching heart. Ladies and gentlemen, here it is . . . (*Pours some into a crystal goblet. It smokes and sputters.*) . . . the Doctor Crocker Love Elixir! (*Holds goblet up triumphantly.*) My friends! Who here is unhappy in his work? Who here is having trouble with his neighbors?

PALMER

(*From a seat in the auditorium*) Mister, I am!

CROCKER

(*Eagerly*) I hear a voice. A young man's voice . . . (*Spots Palmer.*) . . . Ah, my colored friend. Come a little closer please. (*Palmer hesitates.*) Do you have trouble with your white neighbors?

PALMER

Yeah, Mister . . . the trouble is . . . I don't have any!

CROCKER

What's your name, boy?

PALMER

Boy.

CROCKER

All right, Boy, if you'll come up here . . .

PALMER

Hey . . . wait a minute. That's MISTER Boy!

CROCKER

Mister Boy. (*He gestures to Crocker Girls.*) Ladies! (*Several Crocker Girls rush forward, pose enticingly for Palmer's benefit.*) Mister Boy, if you'll come up here, I'll give you a free sample of my Love Elixir so you can testify to the power of this sweet remedy. (*Palmer, who has moved down the aisle in response to Crocker Girls, now hesitates.*) Come, Mister Boy. Come now, there's nothing to be afraid of . . . why, some of my best friends are colored people.

PALMER

All my best friends are colored people.

CROCKER

The Elixir can change that! (*Palmer climbs up on stage, extends hand to Crocker.*) How do you do! (*Shakes Palmer's hand, then wipes off his own hand subtly. Palmer notices and also wipes his hand.*) My friends (*To Audience*) you are about to witness the awesome power of this remedy.

CROCKER BOYS AND GIRLS

Doooo—waaah!

CROCKER

Watch the change that envelops Mister Boy as he drinks the Elixir.

CROCKER BOYS AND GIRLS

Doooo—waaaah!

(*Betty brings Palmer the goblet of Elixir on a tray.*)

PALMER

(*Picking up goblet, examining it suspiciously*) What's in this stuff?

CROCKER

The essence of Love.

PALMER

Will . . . this make you and me brothers?

CROCKER

(*Cheerfully*) Yes, it will!

PALMER

(*Puts goblet back on tray.*) Then I don't want any!
(*Starts to leave the stage.*)

CROCKER

(*Shocked*) Wait a minute! Don't you want to be friends
with all men and . . . women? (*Crocker Girls move forward
seductively.*)

PALMER

(*Returns*) Well . . . since you put it that way . . .

CROCKER

This Elixir will fill your life with Peace and Harmony.
(*Betty hands Palmer the goblet again.*)

CROCKER

Come on , drink it!

PALMER

(*Drinks, and reacts immediately.*) OOOOOO!

CROCKER BOYS AND GIRLS

OOOOOOOOooooooooooooooo!

PALMER

This stuff's pretty good!

CROCKER

Drink some more!

PALMER

(*Drinks.*) OOOOoooooo-weeeeeeeeeeee! (*He collapses
over the desk, falling behind it out of sight of the audience.
The Crocker Boys and Girls surround him. While hidden
from sight, he does a change of costume, shedding the
street clothes he has been wearing.*)

CROCKER BOYS AND GIRLS

OOOOoooooo-weeeeeee! (*When Palmer has completed
his change, they open the circle.*) OOOOOOOOOO-
OOOOOOOH!

(*Palmer leaps over the desk. He now wear bright
yellow overalls with red polka-dot patches.*)

CROCKER BOYS AND GIRLS

Dooo—waah!

PALMER

Ah feels fine! Thankya Doctah Crockah, suh!

CROCKER

Filled with peace?

PALMER

Yas suh! Peace and Harmony!

CROCKER

Good boy! (*Testing him*) Say . . . is that a speck of dust on my shoe?

PALMER

Why it sho' is, suh. Here, lemme dust it off fo' ya.
> (*Palmer falls to his knees and is about to rub the shoe with his hand.*)

CROCKER

No! No! Wait! (*Pulls handkerchief from his pocket, hands it to Palmer.*) Now.

PALMER

(*Taking handkerchief*) Oh, thank you, suh!

CROCKER

Thank *you*, boy! (*Palmer begins polishing Crocker's shoes with enthusiasm.*) . . . And there you are, folks, the white race and the colored race living side by side in love and friendship!

> When I go walking with Mister Boy
> I wear a smile on my face
> because there's nothing better
> in the whole wide world
> than a colored man . . . in his place!
> O' Mister Boy!

PALMER

> (*Following Crocker around the stage*)

Yes, Doctor Crocker?

CROCKER

Oh, Mister Boy!

PALMER

Yes, Doctor Crocker?

CROCKER

> When we walk down the street
> all the people we meet say:
> "How ya doin', Boy?"
> "Good morning, Doctor Crocker!"

We're livin' in the promised land.
CROCKER GIRLS
Oh, Mister Boy!
CROCKER BOYS
Yes, Doctor Crocker?
CROCKER GIRLS
Oh, Mister Boy!
CROCKER BOYS
Yes, Doctor Crocker?
CROCKER
When we walk down the street
all the people we meet say:
GIRLS
How ya doin', Boy?
BOYS
Good mornin', Doctor Crocker
BOYS AND GIRLS
We're livin' in the promised land!
CROCKER
They got a whole lotta trouble in Africa,
they got trouble in Tennessee,
because the colored man is gettin' outta hand,
my friends, you better listen to me.

He's got to be pacified!
He's got to be dominated!
He's got to be willin' to do what I tell him to
'cause this is the order that God created.
BOYS AND GIRLS
He's got to be pacified!
CROCKER
Pacified!
BOYS AND GIRLS
He's got to be dominated!
CROCKER
Dominated!
BOYS AND GIRLS
He's got to be willin' to do what I tell him to
'cause this is the order that God created.
PALMER
Now, just a minute, Doctor Crocker,
there's one thing wrong

and other folks think so too.
From what I can see, you won't listen to me . . .
How come I gotta listen to you?
> CROCKER

Give that boy a shot of the Love Elixir!
> (*Roger pulls out a billy club and slams Palmer over the head with it.*)
> CROCKER BOYS AND GIRLS

WHOP!
He's got to be pacified!
Convinced he's satisfied!
> CROCKER

He's got to be willin' to do what I tell him to
'cause this is the Law that God implied.
> (*Crocker Boys and Girls kneel in a tight group facing the Audience, their hands clasped.*)
> CROCKER
> (*Piously*)

Now I realize that the colored man
hasn't always been treated right.
But I can guarantee Equality . . .
If we separate black from white!
> CROCKER BOYS AND GIRLS
> (*They leap apart. Whites to one side of the stage, Negroes to the other. George, the Japanese-American, is left stranded in the middle, not knowing to which side he should go.*)

We've got to be separated
And kept dis-integrated!
> CROCKER

As long as they're willin' to do
what I tell 'em to
they'll find themselves well situated.
> (*Tag has brought George over to the Negro side but Palmer shoves him out. Roger whacks Palmer with billy club.*)
> BOYS AND GIRLS

WHOP!
> CROCKER

When I go walkin' with Mister Boy
I wear a smile on my face.
> CROCKER AND BOYS AND GIRLS

Because there's nothing better

in the whole wide world . . .
CROCKER
Than a colored man . . . in his place!
GIRLS AND CROCKER
Oh, Mister Boy!
BOYS AND PALMER
Yes, Doctor Crocker?
GIRLS AND CROCKER
Oh, Mister Boy!
BOYS AND PALMER
Yes, Doctor Crocker?
CROCKER
When we walk down the street
all the people we meet say,
GIRLS
How ya doin', Boy?
BOYS
Good mornin', Doctor Crocker!
CROCKER
We're livin' in the promised land!
CROCKER AND BOYS AND GIRLS
We're livin' in the promised land!
CROCKER
Ladies and gentlemen, you have seen what love can do!
MATRON
Love? That's got nothing to do with love!
CARL
(*Comes running down the aisle through the Audience*)
You are so right, lady! (*He leaps onto stage.*)
MATRON
Why, it's Carl Blackbird!
(*Fanfare*)
CROCKER
Sweet William!
PIPER
Yes, Doctor Crocker?
CROCKER
If ever I saw a man in need of the Love Elixir, it's this
one.
CARL
(*To Audience*) This guy is a fraud . . . a fake! Listen to
me! Don't be fooled! What he's selling has nothing to do

with love. (*Piper gestures to Crocker Boys. They rush forward and pick Carl up bodily.*) . . . No! . . . HAAAAAlp! (*Struggles.*)

MATRON

(*Rushing to Carl's assistance*) You put that boy down!

CARL

Put *who* down?

MATRON

(*Politely*) Oh, I beg your pardon. (*Aggressively again*) You put Carl down!

CROCKER

(*To Crocker Boys*) Let him go! (*They obey instantly, dropping Carl with a thud, and return to their places.*) Madam, this young man was trying to disrupt the show.

CARL

You're darn right I was. I don't know what you've done to Palmer, but if you know what's good for you. . . . (*Shakes fist at Crocker.*)

CROCKER

Young man, violence is no solution! (*Snaps his fingers. Crocker Boys rush forward again menacingly.*)

MATRON

(*Planting herself in front of Crocker Boys*) Stop!

CARL

It's all right, Ma'am. Doctor Crocker is right . . . violence is not the answer. (*A bench comes sliding onstage as though of its own volition. Carl takes one end of it.*) Come on, Miss . . .?

MATRON

It's Matron Blackbird!

CARL

Grab the other end, Matron Blackbird. (*They move bench to the center of the stage.*) . . . over here!

MATRON

What are we doing?

CARL

(*Gallantly offering her a seat on bench*) Sitting! (*They sit.*)

CROCKER

(*Rushing over*) Are you just going to sit?

CARL

Just sit.

Crocker Boys lifting Carl

CROCKER

Will you get that cotton-pickin' bench out of the way so we can go on with the show! (*Carl and Matron ignore him.*) Boy, if you just want to sit . . .

CARL

(*Correcting him*) Sit . . . *in!*

CROCKER

Why don't you do as everyone else does and sit *in* the audience.

MATRON

I've spent my whole life sitting out in the audience. Sitting out there is like . . . (*Gropes for the word.*)

CARL

Sitting still. (*Matron nods happily.*) But sitting-*in* is like moving!

CROCKER

What are you driving at?

CARL

We're driving *to* that promised land. (*To Matron*) You with me, Miss Blackbird?

MATRON

All the way!

CARL

Off we go! (*Pantomimes starting a car and driving off. Carl and Matron jounce merrily along, bouncing occasionally as though having hit a bump.*)

CROCKER

Sweet William, do you understand them? (*Piper shrugs.*) (*To Crocker and Boys and Girls*) Do you? Understand them? (*They shrug. Crocker turns to the Audience.*) Do *you* understand them? (*Audience shrugs.*)

MATRON

(*Imitating a horn*) Beep! Beep!

CROCKER

(*Furious*) Give 'em an inch and they take a mile! Ladies and gentlemen, I beg you to be patient. The show will go on. There are many wonderful songs, dances, and heart-warming testimonials—

CARL

(*Rising*) Hey, how about letting me do a song?

CROCKER

I've had just about enough of your nonsense!

CARL

I'm serious. I'd really like to do a song for your show.

CROCKER

(*Suspicious, but also hatching a plot of his own*) What kind of a song did you have in mind?

CARL

(*Winking at Matron*) How about an old plantation song.

CROCKER

(*Winking at Piper*) A little plantation music please (*To Crocker Boys and Girls*) 1—2—3 . . .

(*Crocker Boys and Girls move forward, the girls humming a sweet intro to "Old Black Joe." Crocker escorts Matron to her original seat on the stage-right apron.*

The music picks up tempo.)

CARL

(*To Crocker Boys and Girls*) That's the idea!

CROCKER

Sing it, boy!

CARL

This is the song of Old White Tom
and it's never been sung before.
Some say he was a friend to the colored man
but it's never been proven for sure.

When there was work to be done
in the cotton fields
he was nowhere to be seen.
He was stretched out on a holler log
just a-pickin' his fingernails clean.
(*A spot is focused on Crocker and Piper.*)

CROCKER

Let the slaves do the dirty work. That ain't no job for a white man. After all . . . the dirt don't show up so much on them. (*Crocker and Piper laugh raucously. The spot fades. They exit.*)

CARL

Old White Tom he went along through life . . .
Thinkin' he was better than the black man,
Thinkin' he was better than the red man,
Better than the yellow man.
Hot damn!

This is the song of Old White Tom,
just didn't realize his time had come.

CROCKER BOYS AND GIRLS

Just didn't realize his time had come.

CARL

Now the old folks say that when Tom was born
the devil stood by his side . . .
and the very first words he was heard to say
were: "The Devil's gonna be my guide!"
The Devil touched his heart with a fiery finger
Little Tommy let out a yell
"Devil take my soul, because I'm ready to roll.
I'm gonna give these black folks hell!"

CARL, CROCKER BOYS AND GIRLS

Old White Tom he went along through life

GIRLS

Thinkin' he was better than the black man

BOYS

Better than the red man

GIRLS

Better than the yellow man

BOYS AND GIRLS

Hot damn!

CARL

This is the song of Old White Tom
who didn't realize his time had come,

CROCKER BOYS AND GIRLS

Just didn't realize his time had come.

CARL

Tom jumped outta bed and he grabbed a sheet
and wrapped it around his face.
He said: "Gimme a gun, I'm gonna have some fun.
I'm gonna run all the black folks offa this place."

CAMILLE

"Then who'll do the work?" said his poor old mother.

CARL

"Oh, I never thought a' that!" said he.

GLADYS

"We gotta have slaves, Lord knows we do."

CARL

"Or all the work will fall on me!"

CARL, CROCKER BOYS AND GIRLS

Old White Tom he went along through life
Thinkin' he was better than the black man,
Thinkin' he was better than the red man,
Thinkin' he was better than the yellow man.
Hot damn!

CARL

This is the song of Old White Tom
who didn't realize his time had come.

CROCKER BOYS AND GIRLS

Just didn't realize his time had come.

CARL

(*Tenderly*)

The stars had never shone for Tom.
The sun had never shined.
One day lightning struck
and gosh darn the luck . . .
it turned Tom . . . color blind!

CROCKER BOYS AND GIRLS

(*Sadly*) Nearly drove him outta his . . .
(*Breaking into a broad smile*) . . . mind!

> (*Crocker enters. There is a bright flash, like an explosion on his entrance. At the explosion the Crocker Boys and Girls reassume their regular places and attitudes as part of Crocker's troupe.*)

CROCKER

(*To Carl*) Splendid, my boy! That was magnificent!
(*Carl is confused by Crocker's reaction.*) Sweet William, bring this boy a contract.

> (*The comments of the Crocker Boys and Girls are interwoven with the dialogue between Carl and Crocker.*)

CROCKER

What's your name, boy?

CROCKER BOYS AND GIRLS

(*Whispered breathily*)
Isn't he cute?

CARL

Carl.

TAG

Isn't he sweet? (*The Crocker Boys and Girls swirl around Carl.*)

CROCKER

Carl. Too common. We need something more descriptive.

BETTY

Look at his eyes!

PAUL

Dig the suit!

GIRLS

Satchmo . . .

BOYS

Bojangles . . .

GIRLS

Step-and-fetchit!

CROCKER BOYS AND GIRLS

Isn't he cute?

TAG

Isn't he sweet?

CROCKER

How would you like to make a thousand dollars a week . . . plus carfare?

CARL

Swell!

CROCKER

Tell me, can you act?

CARL

No.

CROCKER

Have you ever danced?

BETTY

Look at his eyes!

PAUL

Dig the suit!

CROCKER BOYS AND GIRLS

Isn't he cute?

TAG

Isn't he sweet?

CARL

Not really.

CROCKER

Never sung professionally?

CARL

Never.

CROCKER

My boy, you'll be a star!

BETTY

Look at his eyes!

PAUL

Dig the suit!

CROCKER BOYS AND GIRLS

He's a . . .

GIRLS

Doll!

CARL

(*Posing with Crocker Girls for picture which Paul takes with flashbulb camera*) But it's Carl Blackbird.

CROCKER
That's it! Carl Blackbird!

CROCKER BOYS AND GIRLS
(*Lifting Carl to their shoulders*) YAAAAY!

CROCKER
The television star . . .

CROCKER BOYS AND GIRLS
YAAAAY!

CROCKER
. . . the movie star!

CROCKER AND BOYS AND GIRLS
YAAAAY!

TAG
(*Holding up imaginary microphone*) Mister Blackbird, would you care to say something to your fans across the nation?

CARL
Yes! (*Tag hands him the imaginary mike.*) Civil rights is one of the most important issues confronting Americans today. (*Reaching into pocket*) I have here a petition—(*He is dropped with a thud.*)

BETTY
Well, I never!

GLADYS
Entertainment and politics just don't mix!

CAMILLE
Who's Carl Blackbird anyway?

PAUL
Nobody!

ROGER, GEORGE, AND LOU
(*Pointing accusingly*) You're nobody!

CROCKER BOYS AND GIRLS
(*Backing away and exiting*) Nobody . . . nobody . . . nobody . . . nobody . . . nobody . . .

CAMILLE
(*Offstage*) Who's Carl Blackbird anyway? (*Lights dim.*)

CROCKER BOYS AND GIRLS
(*Offstage*) Nobody!
> (*Crocker snaps fingers. Josie appears in a spot up-stage. She holds a goblet of the Elixir. She moves, as in a trance, downstage toward Carl.*)

JOSIE
(*Softly*)
We could settle down
in a little green cottage by the sea.
Couldn't we?
CARL
Couldn't we?
JOSIE
A little green cottage
with a welcome mat by the door . . .
CARL
And windows that let the sun come through.
CARL AND JOSIE
Waves pounding on the shore.
CARL
Josie . . . (*Reaches for her. Piper enters.*)
PIPER
Come along, Josie. You can't marry a nobody. (*As Piper and Josie turn to exit, Josie hands Carl the goblet.*)
CARL
(*Alone in the middle of the dimly lit stage*)
We'd run down to the beach
and welcome the morning tide.
We'd fly down the sand
like sea gulls on the wing.
When night falls,
we'll see the mirror of the moon. . . .
(*He drinks the elixir.*)

MATRON
No, Carl! No!
(*Carl, his trance broken, turns toward the Matron, bewildered. Suddenly he doubles over, coughing. The Crocker Boys and Girls enter.*)

CROCKER BOYS AND GIRLS
(*Softly*)
Doctor Crocker's Love Elixir
Is the most successful trouble fixer known . . .
to mortal man.
(*Betty helps Carl, still coughing, offstage. Crocker enters.*)

CROCKER

(*Crocker Boys and Girls hum softly in background.*)

Ladies and gentlemen, a few moments ago you saw upon this stage a young man filled with pain. Bitterness enveloped him like an angry cloud.

In all my years of conversion to harmony, never have I been presented with so difficult a challenge. Never have I encountered anyone as hate-filled, as unwilling to see the light as this young man. But now he will taste success . . . and success will help him to see the world with greater . . . clarity. He has been saved, my friends, he has been SAVED! Ladies and gentlemen, I . . . I . . . look at me . . . I'm crying . . . crying with JOY! Ladies and gentlemen, I give you . . . the best loved Negro entertainer in the world. I give you . . . UNCLE TOM!

CROCKER BOYS AND GIRLS

Doooo-waaah!

(*They part. Carl is standing in a spot. He wears white lip makeup, a huge bow tie, white gloves, derby, etc.*)

CROCKER

Come on down here, Tom.

CARL

Oh, yas suh! (*Hop-steps downstage, slapping his knees rhythmically.*)

CROCKER

Say something for the folks!

CARL

Watermelon!

CROCKER

(*Laughing raucously*) Isn't he a card, folks? Say something else!

CARL

(*Winding up*) Shortnin' bread.

CROCKER

(*To Audience*) Didn't I tell you he'd be great? Say, you got a little song for us, Tom?

CARL

Yas suh!

CROCKER

Well, let's not keep these good people waiting. They came

here to be entertained and we've got to see that they get their money's worth. Take it away!

CARL

(*Somewhat sluggishly*)
Gone are the days
When my heart was young and gay.
Gone are my friends
From the cotton fields away . . . .

CROCKER

(*Cuts him off.*) What's the matter with you, Tom? You've got to put more life into it. Give it more oomph! You've got rhythm, boy, let's see a little of it. Here. Let me show you.

CROCKER

(*Enthusiastically*)
In the evenin' by the moonlight
you could hear those darkies singin'.
In the evenin' by the moonlight
you could hear those banjos ringin'.
(*A la Jolson*)
Mammy!
See what I mean? Now you try it!
(*The Crocker Girls, except for Camille, exit quietly.*)

CARL

Oh, yas suh. You mean like dis.
(*Sadly*)
In the evenin' by the moonlight
you could hear those "darkies" singing . . .
(*A spot focuses on Camille who stands upstage center surrounded by the men who are posed dramatically.*)

CAMILLE

(*With strength*)
No more auction block for me!

MEN

No more! No more!
(*The Girls reenter. They, like Camille, have removed their bonnets.*)

GIRLS

Steal away! Steal away!

CARL

(*Wipes off lip makeup. Removes gloves, hat.*) Or do you mean like this . . . Doctor Crocker . . .

(*Strongly*)

In the evening by the moonlight
You could hear those banjos ringing. . . .

GROUP

O Freedom! O Freedom!
We shall overcome some day!

CARL

But Old White Tom, he went along through life. . .

GROUP

(*Surrounding Crocker*)

Thinkin he was better than the black man,
red man,
yellow man,
Hot damn!

CARL

This is the song of Old White Tom
who didn't realize his time had come!

(*The men lift Crocker, outstretched as though dead, to their shoulders. The Group begins a funeral procession around the stage. There is much crying and weeping.*)

CROCKER

Put me down! (*Struggling*) Have you all gone mad?

(*Camille and Gail exit and return with Crocker's gravestone. It is designed like the front end of a new Cadillac—black. Crocker is gently deposited in front of the gravestone, then tenderly covered with a white sheet.*)

CARL

Brethren . . .

GROUP

(*Moaning*) Oh . . .

CARL

We are gathered here this evening to mourn . . .

GROUP

Oh . . .

CARL

To mourn the loss of one we knew so well . . .

GROUP

Ooooohhhh!

(*Crocker's head pops up.*)

CROCKER

What is this, a joke?
(*Tag tenderly forces his head back down and recovers him with sheet.*)

CARL

Let no man speak against him in this hour.

GROUP

No man!

CARL

He was a good man . . .

GROUP

A good man . . .

CARL

Too bad!

GROUP

Too bad!

CARL

Too bad!

GROUP

Too bad!

CARL

Too bad!

GROUP

Ooooohhhhh! (*Led by Carl, they sing with great emotion.*)
Old White Tom, he went along through life . . .
(*The Men, in pantomime, begin shoveling dirt on Crocker. Suddenly Piper comes running in.*)

PIPER

No! No! Stop that! What are you doing? You can't bury Dr. Crocker!

CARL

Give Mr. Piper his stone!
(*Camille and Gail exit and quickly return with Piper's gravestone. It is designed like the front end of a new Cadillac—white. Piper is gently forced down in front of the gravestone, then tenderly covered with a black sheet.*)

PIPER

Stop! Stop!

CARL

Rest easy, Mr. Piper.

PIPER

(*His head pops up.*) But . . . I ain't ready yet.

CARL

We know that . . . but the faithful servant . . .

GROUP

Oohh!

CARL

Is always buried with his master.

GROUP

Amen.

> (*There is a sudden flash of light. The whole scene begins to dissolve. The Group begins whirling madly about. The light fades. The bars begin to close.*)

CROCKER

(*As lights fade*) No, you can't leave me here. I've loved you. Come back, please. Come back! Come back!

SCENE 4. *As the center stage area blacks out, the lights come up on the Matron, still seated on the downright apron. She is obviously just awakening as from a nightmare.*

MATRON

Don't leave me! Carl come back, please! Officer Jonsen! Officer Jonsen!

> (*Jonsen enters. Overjoyed at seeing him, she clutches him frantically, begins to sing as though her life depended on it.*)

Natchitoches, Louisiana is the place where
My mother gave birth to me, her only child.

JONSEN

It's going to be all right. I talked it over with my wife, and she says since I've been passing as a Negro all these years I might as well just go on doing that . . . and I guess you oughta do the same.

MATRON

Sing, Officer Jonsen! Sing!

> (*Bewildered, he joins her.*)

MATRON AND JONSEN

'Twas there I spent my childhood years

with all the hopes and all the fears
of innocence in a strange new world. . . .
(*Piper, dressed in street clothes, enters.*)

PIPER

I've got it! Good morning, Fred . . . Matron. Here it is—
an order for Josie's release.

JONSEN

She's already been released. She's down in the park with
the rest of those kids.

PIPER

Good. Thank you Fred. See you at the Caribou meeting
next Thursday.

JONSEN

By the way . . . these kids have given me an idea. Could
you put me on the agenda of one of the meetings?

PIPER

(*Laughs*) All in good time, Fred. (*Exits*) All in
good time.

JONSEN

Brother Piper, you've had your good time.
(*Matron picks up the sign left behind by Tag:
"Bring Louisiana back into the U.S.A."*)

JONSEN AND MATRON

(*To Audience, holding the sign between them*)
'Twas there I spent my childhood years
with all the hopes and all the fears
of innocence in a strange new world. . .
innocence in a strange new world.

SCENE 5. *The lights fade on Jonsen and the Matron. The
bars that cover the face of the proscenium open, revealing
the park. Josie is seated on a bench alone, downstage left.
Piper enters.*

PIPER

Josie.

JOSIE

Papa, I'm out!

PIPER

So I see. What a night. I haven't had a wink of sleep. We
saw the lawyers and then the magistrate. When I finally
did get to bed, I tossed and turned. . . . (*Notices that she*

is not listening.) Josie, are you listening to me?

JOSIE

See the sky over there?

PIPER

What sky?

JOSIE

The sun's gonna shine this morning.

PIPER

I'm glad you're in such good spirits, young lady.

JOSIE

I am! I really am. We spent the night singing.

The night will be no more.

PIPER

Josie, now don't get carried away. Those kids are headed for trouble.

JOSIE

Carl says that trouble is inevitable when you're trying to change something.

PIPER

Carl?

JOSIE

Carl Eldridge! You remember, you introduced me to him. . . .

He's wonderful, Papa. I've never known anyone like him.

PIPER

I see.

JOSIE

Why don't you march with us this morning?

PIPER

March?

JOSIE

We're gonna march uptown. Let people know how we feel!

PIPER

Josie, you just got out of jail.

JOSIE

We can't be afraid anymore.

PIPER

Being afraid has nothing to do with it. What I'm talking about is what kind of future you . . . and this Carl . . . will have . . . in jail, outta jail, in jail, outta. . . .

JOSIE

Papa, don't be a fool! (*Realizes what she has said.*) I'm sorry, Papa . . . I'm sorry! (*Backing away*)

PIPER

There've always been . . . two points of view. . . .

JOSIE

Carl's waiting for me, Papa.

PIPER

One old . . . one new.

JOSIE

I have to go. (*She exits.*)

PIPER

They're doing things so differently.
Who's the fool . . . them or me?

They think they've got the world by the tail.
Think they're gonna change things overnight.
Well, that's all right with me.
I've done things differently myself.

I learned a long time ago
that anger doesn't get you anywhere.
There's no use beating your head against a wall
if you intend to get anywhere
at all.

They're doing things so differently.
Who's the fool . . . them or me?

Yes. I've shuffled.
I had to.
Shuffled high, shuffled low.
Shuffled fast, shuffled slow.
But I shuffled my daughter
right through one of the finest schools in the country
so she'll never have to shuffle for anybody . . .
white or black.

Look at 'em!
Proud, handsome,
with that "bow to no man" kinda walk.
Go on! Sing your song of sixpence.

I've sung mine.
Everybody has to pay the Piper . . . some way.

They're doing things so differently.
Who's the fool . . . them or me?
> (*Piper exits. Carl enters. He carries a sign which reads "Now!" He walks to the edge of the stage, sings directly to the Audience.*)
> CARL

I do believe . . .
that the sun can shine
in the middle of the night.
We're gonna walk.

> JOSIE
> (*Has entered, carries a sign saying "Wake up!"*)

We're gonna walk!
> CARL

We're gonna talk!
> JOSIE

We're gonna talk!
> CARL AND JOSIE

There is a new day waiting
at your door.
> JOSIE

The sun's gonna shine this morning.
The night will be no more. . .
I'm gonna open my window wide.
> CARL AND JOSIE

See the new day waiting
at your door.
> CARL

We're gonna walk
> JOSIE

We're gonna walk
> CARL

We're gonna talk
> JOSIE

We're gonna talk
> CARL AND JOSIE

We're gonna sit at the table
with our heads up high!

CARL
We're gonna sing.

JOSIE
Sing!

CARL
Shout!

JOSIE
Shout!

CARL AND JOSIE
All about
the new day waiting at your door.

CARL
We're gonna walk

JOSIE
Walk!

CARL
Talk!

JOSIE
Talk!

CARL
Laugh!

JOSIE
Laugh!

CARL
Cry!

JOSIE
Cry!

CARL AND JOSIE
Sit at the table with our heads up high!

CARL
We're gonna sing!

JOSIE
Sing!

CARL
Shout!

JOSIE
Shout!

CARL AND JOSIE
All about
the new day waiting at your door.

CHORUS
Wake up!
The dawn is coming.

Rise up!
Sleep no more!
Stand up!
Meet the morning.
There's a new day waiting at your door.

CHORUS | CARL AND JOSIE
Wake up! | Wake up! Brothers,
The dawn is coming. | Wake up!
Rise up! | Rise up! Rise up!
Sleep no more. | Sleep no more.
Stand up! | Stand up! Sisters,
Meet the morning. | Stand up!
There's a new day | There's a new day
waiting at your door. | waiting at your door.

(*From this point on, if appropriate, an attempt should be made to get the Audience to join in. This is more easily done if the Students enter through and remain among the audience until the final choruses.*)

CARL
There are those who say the dawn will never come.

CHORUS
There are those who say the dawn will never come.

CARL
I can hear it rollin' like a mighty drum.

CHORUS
I can hear it rollin' like a mighty drum.

CARL
I can hear it callin' like a risin' wind.

CHORUS
I can hear it callin' like a risin' wind.

CARL
"Open your window and let me in!"

CHORUS
"Open your window and let me in!"

CARL
If you believe the very same as I . . .

CHORUS
If you believe the very same as I . . .

CARL
Lift your voices and let 'em fly.

CHORUS
Lift your voices and let 'em fly.

CARL
We're gonna travel the word to every mine and mill.

CHORUS
We're gonna travel the word to every mine and mill.

CARL
Through the valley and over the hill.

CHORUS
Through the valley and over the hill.

CARL
We're gonna travel from Georgia to the coast of Maine.

CHORUS
We're gonna travel from Georgia to the coast of Maine.

CARL
Run through Alabama like a hurricane.

CHORUS
Run through Alabama like a hurricane.

CARL
Got a brand new train. Got a brand new track.

CHORUS
Got a brand new train. Got a brand new track.

CARL
Got twenty million passengers back to back.

CHORUS
Got twenty million passengers back to back.

CARL
Everybody on it is singin' this song.

CHORUS
Everybody on it is singin' this song.

CARL
There's a new day comin' and it won't be long.

CHORUS
There's a new day comin' and it won't be long.

ALL
Wake up!
The dawn is coming.
Rise up!
Sleep no more.

Stand up!
Meet the morning.
There's a new day waiting at your door.
  (*The final chorus is repeated three times with building intensity, to end.*)

  (*Blackout, end Act II*)

Curtain Call, Mr. Aldridge, Sir

a dramatic
reading by
Ossie Davis

BASED ON MATERIAL SUPPLIED BY MILDRED STOCK

STAGE NOTES: *There should be five lecterns for five perform-ers. The actor who is to read Aldridge should either be in dead center, with two lecterns on either side of him, or off to one side with a row of four lecterns somewhat separate from his.*

The narrative will be carried by the performer who reads Aldridge. The other parts will simply be designated as Voice #1, Voice #2, Voice #3, and Voice #4.

Voice #1 should be read by a woman. The remaining voices should be men.

Voice #4 should be a white actor, if possible.

> VOICE #1
Call for Ira Aldridge!
> VOICE #2
Call for Ira Aldridge!
> VOICE #3
Call for Ira Aldridge!
> VOICES #1 AND #2
Call for Ira Aldridge!
> VOICES #1, #2 AND #3
> (*Building to crescendo*)
Call for Ira Aldridge!
> VOICE #4
> (*Putting a stop to the tumult*)
I am sorry! . . . I cannot find your Mr. Ira Aldridge any-where.
> VOICE #1
Did you look in the *Encyclopedia Britannica?*
> VOICE #4
I did.
> VOICE #2
Did you seek him out in the *Dictionary of American Biog-raphy?*
> VOICE #4
I did.
> VOICE #3
Did you search for him in *Who's Who in the Theatre?*

VOICE #4

I looked in all those places, and in more besides: I have found no hide nor hair of Your Mr. Ira Aldridge, and, as for the record of who he was, and what he was, and what he did—it is to me a mystery! Ira Aldridge, Agh! for all I know, or can find in the standard reference works of our times—Ira Aldridge never existed!

IRA ALDRIDGE

But you are wrong, sir: I am Ira Aldridge. I did exist.

VOICE #1

He lived, was born; was black; learned, loved, worked, suffered, and died!

VOICE #2

Ira Aldridge acted in more different countries than any other actor in the world before or since.

VOICE #3

Ira Aldridge received more honors from monarchs and princes and heads of state than any other actor in the world.

VOICE #1

Not only was he the first Negro ever to play Othello, but also to play Lear, and Macbeth—yes, and even Hamlet—

VOICE #2

When he played Shylock in the Ukraine, the entire Jewish community, led by their Rabbi, came out to thank him for the understanding and sympathy he brought to the part . . .

(*There is a moment's pause.*)

IRA

I see, sir, we make no headway with your memory. Let me repeat it, then: I am Ira Aldridge—black tragedian . . .

VOICE #1

Called by some the greatest Shakespearian actor America ever produced.

VOICE #3

Born in America, in New York, Year of our Lord 1807 . . .

VOICE #2

And yet, America, his home—the land which, until his death in Poland, he loved with all his heart . . .

VOICE #1

America has no memory of him!

IRA

Don't you remember, O my country America—don't you recall, O this land of mine, what it was like to be born a Negro in 1807.

VOICE #1

I thank God my son was not born a slave.

VOICE #2

And to that I say Amen. Whatever the heavy burden it is to be black, our son at least is free.

VOICE #1

He's a lot like you, Daniel, especially when he hollers.

VOICE #2

He knows I want somebody to step into my pulpit when I am gone. I will raise him up in the tabernacle of the Most High, and dedicate his life unto the Lord . . . and I hope his congregation will see fit to feed him much more amply than they feed me at Zion Chapel.

IRA

But my brother Joshua and I were never quite the dedicated churchgoers my father wanted us to be. The world was too full of exciting things, and we wanted to taste of them all. For instance, one day we met a Mr. Brown, who had been a steward on a ship out of Liverpool, but had since retired and set up what he called "The African Theatre." One night he let Joshua and me in for nothing. I was beside myself!

IRA

Look, Joshua, look!

VOICE #3

Ira, come on. It's getting late!

IRA

Just a little longer, Joshua just a—oh, will you look at that!

VOICE #3

Ira, come on! Pa will kill us if we're not home before church let's out!

IRA

And had not my brother dragged me away almost bodily, I might have spent the night. My life was never to be the same—I had met the Theatre, and had fallen in love forever. I saved every penny I could and tried to get into some of the other theatres in New York City.

Mister—er—Mister!

VOICE #4

Yes.

IRA

What's the price for a boy like me?

VOICE #4

Sorry, son. Dogs and niggers not allowed.

IRA

Oh, well, it probably wasn't a good show anyway. Some theatres, like the Park Theatre, were not so strict. There was a small section in a top balcony where Negroes were permitted. Here I saw some of the top actors of the day. There was Matthews . . .

VOICE #2

"O! that this too too solid flesh would melt,
Thaw and resolve itself into a dew;
Or that the Everlasting had not—(*Fading out*)

IRA

There was Wallack . . .

VOICE #3

"O judgment! thou art fled to brutish beasts,
And men have lost their reason. Bear with me;
My heart is in the coffin there with Caesar,
And I must pause till it comes back to—(*Fading out*)

IRA

And the greatest of them all, Edmund Kean, of London, England!

VOICE #4

"And say besides, that in Aleppo once,
When a malignant and a turban'd Turk
Beat a Venetian and traduc'd the state
I took by the throat the circumcised dog,
And smote him thus."

IRA

The more I saw, the more I heard, the more my own desire to act raged, like a flame out of control, within me. I joined an amateur all-Negro theatre group and finally got to appear onstage as Rolla in Sheridan's *Pizarro*. I did many other parts large and small; but it was when we came to Shakespeare that I was in my glory. I remember one night I was onstage, doing Romeo, to the prettiest Juliet, white or black, that I have ever played with—

VOICE #1
"Romeo—"

IRA
"My dear?"

VOICE #1
"At what o'clock tomorrow shall I send to thee?"

IRA
"At the hour of nine."

VOICE #1
"I will not fail. 'Tis twenty years till then.
I have forgot why I did call thee back."

IRA
"Let me stand here till thou remember it."

VOICE #1
" 'Tis almost morning. I would have thee gone,
And yet no farther than a wanton's bird;
who let's it hop a little from her hand,
And with a silk thread plucks it back again,
So loving-jealous of his liberty."

IRA
"I would I were thy bird."

VOICE #1
"Sweet, so do I,
Yet I should kill thee with much cherishing.
Good night, good night! Parting is such sweet sorrow,
That I shall say good night till it be morrow."

IRA
"Sleep dwell upon thine eyes, peace in thy breast—
Would I were sleep and peace, so sweet to rest! . . .
Hence will I go to my ghostly father's . . .

VOICE #2
(*Suddenly, loud interruption*)
Hey you up there, Blackie. Get off that stage—

IRA
(*Stumbling a bit*)
". . . Hence will I—Hence will I to" . . .

VOICE #2
I said get off that stage!

VOICE #3
Get off that stage!
(*The voices build to a crescendo, then fade away.*)

IRA

One by one, the little Negro theatres—in which we had played and found pleasure, so painfully built, so dearly bought, so tenderly cared for—were closed up, or torn down by hoodlums, who found in the color of our black faces offenses enough to vent their hatred upon.

VOICE #2

I'm sorry, Son. I saw it coming— But I didn't want to upset you. But, since theatres for Negroes in New York are done with, now maybe we can seriously set out to get you into the ministry.

IRA

. . . No, Dad.

VOICE #2

But you must know what my plans for you have been all along?

IRA

Yes, sir. But even so, I cannot go with you into the ministry!

VOICE #2

Come now, boy, surely you were not thinking of acting as a serious career?

IRA

Why not?

VOICE #2

It's not for a man, my son—acting is child's play!

IRA

Child's play! Oh, no. You are mistaken, sir. Acting is—is more even than art. Acting is life!

VOICE #2

I never thought I'd live to see the day! And even if acting is all the things you say, it has no future for you. The "good white" folks don't want you in their theatres; and the "bad" ones won't even let you in your own! What will you do?

IRA

I'll go to England!

VOICE #2

What!

VOICE #1

Ira, my son, you can't be serious.

IRA

It's got to be acting for me—it's theatre or nothing at all!

VOICE #1

But, Ira—you're a black man!

IRA

In England that will not matter. Mother, Father, trust me, and you will see. In England, being black does not matter. In England it's only talent—only talent! Wait, you'll see! Mr. Brown said in England color does not matter.

VOICE #2

Listen to me, son: there is no place on this earth where color does not matter, your Mr. Brown notwithstanding. But, if you must—go!

IRA

And Mother—will you give me your blessing?

VOICE #1

Of course I will. Go, my son, go—with God.

IRA

And so, in the year 1825, at the age of eighteen, I landed in London, and—before the year was out I gave my first public performance at the Royal Coburg Theatre.

VOICE #3

Later to be known as the Royal Victoria . . .

VOICE #4

And to us today as the Old Vic.

VOICE #1

For several years thereafter he toured the provinces; working . . .

IRA

For next to nothing in pay . . .

VOICE #2

Watching . . .

IRA

To learn everything I could possibly learn about acting . . .

VOICE #3

And waiting . . .

IRA

For the golden opportunity that would carry me back to London, where I could make a name for myself, not only as an actor, but as a Negro. It was not easy, working in the provinces—but the audiences were warm and wonderful. Except—that is—at the Theatre Royal in Dublin: they wouldn't even let me in! This was one of the gateways through which an actor had to pass in order to get to London, and every year I wrote and asked for an engagement. And every year I was turned down.

Finally, I took the Irish bull by the horns. I went to Dublin, uninvited, and succeeded in getting a personal interview with Mr. J. W. Calcraft, the manager.

VOICE #4

It's absurd, that's what it is . . . there is something absolutely absurd about it.

IRA

Absurd about what?

VOICE #4

A man of your color, acting in the drama.

IRA

And what's absurd about a man of my color acting in the drama? We live, we eat, we sleep, we breed, we die, like everybody else. "If you prick us, do we not bleed? if you tickle us, do we not laugh? if you poison us, do we not die? And if you wrong us—"

VOICE #4

And, "The devil may quote scripture to his own purposes"! I tell you, it just isn't done. Now if you could sing or dance—it's always a pleasure watching you blackamoors sing and dance—by gad, sir, but you people have a gift for singing and dancing the likes of which a man has never seen!

IRA

But not for acting!

VOICE #4

Not at the Theatre Royal in Dublin!

IRA

But why not? I've played the provinces for six years—I even played in London once. Why not the Theatre Royal in Dublin?

VOICE #4

As I told you—it's absurd!

IRA

Look Mr. Calcraft, you're a sporting man.

VOICE #4

The Irish are not averse to taking a chance now and then.

IRA

I understand that Mr. Edmund Kean is passing through, and plans to visit Theatre Royal very soon. Let me play before him—and if he recommends me—

VOICE #4

You mean to tell me that you, a black man, would have the effrontery, the infernal gall, to parade yourself on a public stage in front of England's greatest actor, and invite his opinion?

IRA

Exactly!

VOICE #4

Young man, if you weren't so black, I would call you an irritating, arrogant, conceited upstart of an Irishman, and it'll be a great pleasure to see the likes of you brought down to his proper station in life! It's a deal!

IRA

We rehearsed and made ready for the opening night which finally came, and finally went; and there we were, all waiting backstage to greet Mr. Edmund Kean. We didn't wait long.

VOICE #1

For heaven's sakes, Edmund, don't be in such a rush. After all, he's colored, you know.

VOICE #3

Exactly, Celia, which makes it all the more astonishing. Ah, here he is. Celia, I want to introduce you to Mr. Ira Aldridge.

VOICE #1

How do you do, Mr. Aldridge.

IRA

I am honored my lady—

VOICE #3

Mr. Aldridge, I have witnessed your performance with great pleasure, and am delighted with your wondrous versatility. You, sir, are the African Roscius!

IRA

I am honored by your high opinion, Mr. Kean.

VOICE #3

And lest you think I hold it lightly, I'm getting off a letter to the manager of the Theatre Royal at Bath, and shall be delighted to tell him as much. Come Celia, let us give Mr. Aldridge a chance to get dressed: all Dublin must be waiting for him.

IRA

Well, Mr. Calcraft?

VOICE #4

It's absurd, that's what it is—absurd. And by the way, Mr. Aldridge—just what is an African Roscius!

IRA

A slave, who became the greatest Roman actor of them all.

VOICE #1

But triumph in Dublin was still not triumph in London.

VOICE #2

London was the city of decision.

VOICE #3

To which all actors in England had some day to come: to try or fail; to live or die.

VOICE #2

And on April 10, 1833, Ira Aldridge, actor and Negro, twenty-six years old, eight years away from America, his home, came at last to London.

VOICE #4

(*Announcing*)

The Theatre Royal at Covent Garden presents Mr. Ira Aldridge, the African Roscius, as Shakespeare's Othello, with Miss Ellen Tree as Desdemona.

IRA

Tonight will tell all, Ira Aldridge; it's all up to you.

VOICE #1

Now in London in those days, only two theatres, Drury Lane and Theatre Royal at Covent Garden, were privileged by the Crown to perform dramas.

VOICE #2

And the appearance of a Negro, playing with a white company, at His Majesty, William IV's own theatre was indeed an epoch-making event!

VOICE #3

So, when the final curtain had fallen, and we stood there backstage listening to the ocean's roar of applause, everybody heaved a great big sigh of grateful relief.

VOICE #1

For, in addition to the normal tensions surrounding this most important day in Ira's life, there had been those who had not hesitated to try and stir up trouble. For after all—

VOICE #4

(*Cockney accent, if possible*)

'E's black, that's wot 'e is, and it hain't fit nor proper for the likes of 'im to be up there on our English stage!

VOICE #2

(*Cockney*)

We'll not have the blackamoor pawing 'is way around over our Henglish womanhood!

VOICE #3

(*Cockney*)

African Roscius indeed! I say 'e is a black fiend from hell!

VOICE #2

(*Cockney*)

And if 'e shows up on that stage Wednesday night, opposite our own Miss Ellen Tree, I say let's send 'im back to hell!

ALL

(*There are general ad-lib noises of threat and abuse, rising to a crescendo.*)

VOICE #4

(*Overriding and gradually subduing them*)

Quiet, quiet, you lame excuses for Englishmen. Quiet!

(*Order is finally restored.*)

This foolish attempt to prevent Mr. Aldridge—yes, our African Roscius!—from appearing as Othello at Covent Garden is both base and unmanly!

ALL

(*Crowd noises and ad libs of protest*)

VOICE #4

(*Overriding*)

What is his known offense?—that he was born black, and though descended from a line of kings, his skin is too dark to enable him to personate the "dusky moor," even though he may have the genius of a Kean, the classic taste of a Kemble, combined with the dramatic experience of a Garrick.

To condemn unheard is contrary to the character, and known liberality of Englishmen. Talent, let it come from what country it may, is worthy of patronage. Therefore, fellow countrymen, as a friend to this meritorious, though modest and intelligent foreigner, whose able delineations of many of the principal characters of our most eminent dramatic authors have been established in the Edinburgh, Dublin, Aberdeen, Bath, Brighton, and other papers in the provinces—I beg to ask of a London audience "fair play" on his behalf when he makes his debut on Wednesday next.

VOICE #1

It was a debut—and a performance I shall never forget!

VOICE #2

Nor any of the other hundreds who jammed the theatre to the rafters!

VOICE #3

And found themselves as caught up, as we were, in the mad and scorching jealousy of Shakespeare's Othello . . .

IRA

"Peace, and be still!"

VOICE #1

"I will so. What's the matter?"

IRA

"That handkerchief which I so lov'd and gave thee
Thou gav'st to Cassio."

VOICE #1

"No, by my life and soul!
Send for the man and ask him."

IRA

"Sweet soul, take heed,
Take heed of perjury. Thou'rt on thy death-bed."

VOICE #1

"Ay, but not yet to die."

IRA

"Yes, presently.
Therefore confess thee freely of thy sin;
For to deny each article with oath
Cannot remove nor choke the strong conception
That I do groan withal. Thou art to die."

VOICE

"Then Lord have mercy on me!"

IRA

"I say, amen."

VOICE #1

"And have you mercy too! I never did
Offend you in my life; never lov'd Cassio
. . . I never gave him token."

IRA

"By heaven, I saw my handkerchief in his hand.
O perjur'd woman! thou dost stone my heart,
And mak'st me call what I intend to do
A murder, which I thought a sacrifice.
I saw the handkerchief. . . . He hath confessed."

VOICE #1

"What, my lord?"

IRA

"That he hath used thee."

VOICE #1

"How? unlawfully?"

IRA

"Ay."

VOICE #1

"He will not say so."

IRA

"No; his mouth is stopp'd.
Honest Iago hath ta'en order for't."

VOICE #1

"O! my fear interprets. What! is he dead?"

IRA

"Had all his hairs been lives, my great revenge
Had stomach for them all."

(*The sound of applause—then a silence. Then*)

VOICE #2

". . . In the name of propriety and decency we protest
against a talented actress and a decent girl like Miss Ellen
Tree being subjected by the manager of a theatre to the
indignity of being pawed about by Mr. Wallack's black
servant."

IRA

Which review was that?

VOICE #1

That was the drama critic for the most aristocratic of them
all, *The Athenaeum* . . .

VOICE #3

". . . The part of the Moor was played by an individual

of Negro origin, as his features sufficiently testify, who calls himself Aldridge, and who has been facetiously nicknamed, "The African Roscius." Such an exhibition is well enough at Sadler's Wells, or at Bartholomew Fair, but it certainly is not creditable at a great national establishment. We could not perceive any fitness which Mr. Aldridge possessed for the assumption of one of the finest parts that was ever imagined by Shakespeare, except indeed, that instead of having to rely on pomatum and lampblack, he could play the part in his own native hue."

IRA

And who was that one?

VOICE #3

The critic from the *London Times.* But listen to what he closes with: "It is, however, our duty to state that Mr. Aldridge was extremely well received."

VOICE #1

And what about this: "We had the pleasure last night of being present at the representation of *Othello,* by the celebrated African Roscius and were at once surprised and delighted with the originality and beauty of his reading of the jealous Moor. He reminded us of Kean in many of his best passages, and showed a command over the sympathies of his auditors, which none but an actor of the first order is possessed of. He was loudly applauded in all his points by a crowded and very fashionable audience, among whom we perceived many of the most eminent literary and professional characters of the city"—*The Caledonia Mercury.*

VOICE #4

And what about this? "We witnessed the performance of that singularly gifted actor, the African Roscius, who is the first performer of color that ever appeared on the boards of any theatre in Britain, and we at once gladly express our unqualified delight with his delineation of this masterpiece of the divine Shakespeare. He succeeded in deeply affecting the feelings of his audience, and the representation all through was watched with an intense stillness, almost approaching to awe. At the conclusion he was called for by the unanimous acclamation of the whole house, who, upon his appearance, rose en masse to receive him with bursts of applause, waving of hats and of handkerchiefs!"

IRA

And who was that from?

VOICE #4

That was from *The Standard*. Well, Ira Aldridge, what do you say?

IRA

Let's see: two for Ira Aldridge, and two against—I'd say that was a draw.

VOICE #1

No, Ira, it was no draw—it was a victory. For talent over prejudice for bravery over bigotry, for ambition—and faith —over all the limitations that might be imposed upon a man by a foolish world because of his color.

VOICE #2

From the time of his arrival in 1825, until his departure for the Continent in 1852, he played in almost every important theatre in the United Kingdom.

VOICE #3

Classics, tragedy, comedy, farce, and operettas—

VOICE #4

Titus Andronicus, Macbeth, King Lear, Richard III, and a totally new and unheard of kind of Shylock, in *The Merchant of Venice*.

VOICE #1

Whatever her first feelings about Ira Aldridge at the beginning, by the time he came to leave, England was in love with this magnificent actor.

VOICE #2

And he was in love with England. It was with deep emotion that he took his leave with a poem he himself had written for the occasion:

IRA

"Othello's occupations gone—'tis o'er,
The mask is fallen, I'm actor here no more,
But still your pupil, protégé, whate'er
Your kindness made me, and your fostering care. . . .

You who have long loved liberty so well,
The strange emotions of my soul can tell,
You, who espousing injured Africa's cause
First cheered my efforts by your kind applause,

O'erlooked my errors, taught my mind to soar
And opened my path to England's genial shore.
Though we must part, my best protectors, still
My heart will cherish till its fount is chill,
That proudest record—the fresh memory
That here the sable African was free
From every bound, save those which kindness threw
Around his heart, and bound it fast to you!

VOICE #3

In 1852 he went to Europe, playing in Germany, Switzerland, France, Austria, Hungary, Poland, and Czechoslovakia.

VOICE #4

And in 1858 Ira Aldridge reached Russia—

IRA

I think I can honestly say, that my stay in Russia was the jeweled crown of my career.

VOICE #2

The critics were delighted!—but also astounded at the totally unexpected realism of his acting style.

VOICE #3

"As for the playing of the African tragedian, we find ourselves in a dead alley to understand it. There is so much in it we are completely unaccustomed to. . . . In the role of Othello, he is a real tiger and you become frightened for the actors who play the roles of Desdemona and Iago. It seems to you that they really won't get away from him, and after the curtain you feel like making a special curtain call for them just to see if any are still alive."

IRA

I remember one young Russian actress with whom I was to play Othello, quite seriously asking me about the rumor she had heard, that I had crippled several Iagos, and had smothered a few Desdemonas. "It's all exaggerated," I told her, "I have played Othello more than three hundred times in my life and during this time I have smothered only two, maybe three Desdemonas, and stabbed, I believe, only one Iago. You must agree that for three hundred performances that's quite a small percentage, so I don't see what you Moscow Desdemonas have to worry about!"

VOICE #3

Now that it's over, Ira Aldridge; now that you can look back and see it as a whole, what was it about those last glorious golden days in Russia, thousands of miles from your native land—what was it that impressed you most?

VOICE #1

Was it that Czar Alexander II himself decorated you, with the cross of St. Leopold?

IRA

I was most honored, of course—

VOICE #2

Or was it the warm friendship that sprang up between you and Tolstoy?

IRA

He was a man of compassion and of genius, but—

VOICE #3

Was it the portrait Taras Shevchenko drew of you, and which even now is hanging in the Hermitage Museum in Leningrad?

IRA

It was a wonderful likeness . . .

VOICE #4

Or perhaps the scroll presented to you, written in Russian and English: "To Ira Aldridge," it said, "the great interpreter of the ever-living Shakespeare, from the Russian actors, St. Petersburg, 1859." Signed by all the actors of the Imperial Alexandrinsky Theatre. Surely nothing in an actor's career can have surpassed that moment?

IRA

The sincere esteem of one's fellow performers must rank above all other honors, true. And yet—well, you must remember that at that time all Russia was violently anti-Semitic and hostile to the Jews. But one day, after my performance as Shylock in *The Merchant of Venice* in the Ukraine, the Jewish people did a very brave thing. They came, their whole community, headed by the chief Rabbi, to thank me for showing, in my performance of Shylock, so deep an understanding of the Jewish plight.

VOICE #2

Extraordinary!

IRA

No. For am I not a Negro? And were not my people in

America still enslaved. So that when I came to that magnificent speech—"If you prick us, do we not bleed? If you tickle us do we not laugh? If you poison us do we not die? And if you wrong us, shall we not revenge?" Not my voice only, but the voices of four million of my black brethren, were in those lines. I could not have been so much a Jew had I not remained so much a Negro. And I consider it the glory of the art of acting that it can embody the brotherhood of all suffering humanity, not only in the idea, but in the flesh! And when the Rabbi of the Ukraine embraced me, he embraced his brother! and through me, all my brothers, bound and free; and as for me, I became at one with the ghetto.

He found in me, and I in him, that kinship of the spirit which maketh all men one. And it was Shakespeare who had brought us together. That was the greatest and most noble moment, not only of my stay in Russia, but of my life!

VOICE #2

Ira Aldridge lived to see the emancipation of his black brothers, but was never himself to set foot in America again.

VOICE #1

In August, 1867, in Lodz, Poland, the following poster was distributed far and wide:

VOICE #2

Theatrical Announcement: The Famous Tragic Cavalier of Europe, Ira Aldridge, Negro, son of the wealthy king of an African tribe, born on the shores of the Senegal, Court Artist of Her Majesty, decorated with many orders of foreign places, and declared by all the foreign newspapers to be the only one who can portray in all its full beauty and strength the most difficult role of the great Shakespeare, Othello, for which he has received from the hands of His Highness the King of Prussia and from the hands of His Highness the Emperor of Austria, awards which are only presented to those of the highest talent in all Germany, on his way from Paris to Petersburgh, has consented to make appearances.

VOICE #3

But he never played the engagement. On August 7, 1867, one day before the opening at Lodz, Ira Aldridge died.

VOICE #2

He was laid to rest in the Evangelical Cemetery.

VOICE #3

And to this day his tomb is given special attention by the Society of Polish Artists of Film and Theatre.

VOICE #4

At the time of his death, Ira Aldridge was in correspondence with theatrical agents in New York. His plan was to come back, and tour the United States.

VOICE #1

Ira Aldridge, the man nobody knows . . . Why?

IRA

". . . O good Horatio, what a wounded name,
Things standing thus unknown, shall live behind me.
If thou didst ever hold me in thy heart,
Absent thee from felicity awhile,
And in this harsh world draw thy breath in pain,
To tell my story."

VOICE #4

"Good night, sweet prince,
And flights of angels sing thee to thy rest!"

The End

Tell
Pharaoh

by Loften
Mitchell

characters

MISS BLACK: A woman in her twenties or thirties, a singer

MRS. BLACK: A woman in her forties

MR. BLACK, SENIOR: A man in his forties

MR. BLACK, JUNIOR: A man in his twenties or thirties, a singer-guitarist

Note: In the event Miss Black and Mr. Black, Junior, are to be played by actors who do not sing, it is suggested that a female singer and a male singer perform all the songs. The songs may be delivered with guitar accompaniment or rendered without accompaniment.

notes

Tell Pharaoh is the type of work that makes a playwright have insomnia plus all kinds of psychosomatic pains. It is that type of work a playwright creates accidentally, and it develops a life of its own while other works sit on shelves—works that have been created over a period of years.

Tell Pharaoh is in all honesty an accident beyond all theatrical accidents. If I put it in a play, no one would believe it. In fact, critics would yell: "Contrived! Contrived!" This, therefore, is the reason for this preface.

I had just completed my book, *Black Drama,* when the Jamaica National Association for the Advancement of Colored People had a Mr. Peter Saltz telephone me. He told me there was to be a big Negro History-Brotherhood affair at Queens College Colden Auditorium on February 19, 1967 and the Association members wondered if I would serve as a consultant. Since this involved no *real* work on my part, I readily agreed. Mr. Saltz spoke of the actors the association planned to invite, and I told him I admired the lot.

Well, a few days later Mr. Frederick O'Neal telephoned me and wanted to know what I was writing for him to read on February 19th. When I recovered from shock, I told him he could read anything he liked. The next day Mr. Louis Gossett telephoned me and he wanted to know what I was writing for him to read. I stalled for a moment, then told him I would get back to him. Two days later Miss Ruby Dee called and asked what I was writing for her to read on February 19th. And right after that I heard from Miss Micki Grant and she wanted to know what I planned to write for her. What I later learned is that one of the NAACP workers had, in calling the actors for their approval to appear, mentioned that I was writing a special play for the occasion. I knew then it was too late to turn back and I had to write something, so I decided to take a few pages from *Black Drama,* have the actors read these, and work in a narration.

That simply did not work, so I sat down and wrote the first version of what came to be known as *Tell Pharaoh.* There followed more rewrite and yet more rewrite. On February 19, 1967, we had the following professionals do the show: Ruby Dee, Micki Grant, Louis Gossett, Frederick O'Neal, Gloria Daniel, and Mary Alyce Glenn, assisted by singers Robert Alexander and Lucille Burney and the St. Albans Children's Choir. More than twenty-three thousand people jammed Queens College Colden Auditorium that Sunday afternoon. They were dignitaries and common folks, old folks and young folks, and they gave the cast a standing ovation.

I thought that was the end of *Tell Pharaoh*, but backstage the cast spoke of the "next time we do it." All kinds of plans and suggestions reached my ears, but in theatre—as in all of American life—plans and suggestions are abundant, and sometimes talk takes the place of action.

This time it didn't. My wife, Marjorie, spoke to two relatives, Jo and Milton Coulthurst and their in-laws, Virginia and James Glass. They decided to revive *Tell Pharaoh* at the National Maritime Union Theatre on May 7, 1967, as a benefit for the Schomburg Collection on Negro History and Culture. Albert Grant was engaged to direct the production.

That offering was exciting offstage as well as on. Ruby Dee, who lives in New Rochelle, had no car that day, and she asked for someone to pick her up. It was a day of continuous and cold rain and, when I told the producers to arrange to pick her up, each one pointed out some very important dignitary that had to be given a ride to the theatre. Finally, I turned to my wife and laughed in spite of my annoyance: "My God!" I said. "The star of the show is up there in New Rochelle and can't get to the show, yet people are all running around picking up other people to come to see her! It just goes to prove one thing: When you go into the theatre, you may be an amateur, but you'd better act like a professional."

"Then," said my wife, "let's be professional and send a taxi for Ruby Dee and bill the producers."

We did just that.

Again the show received a standing ovation from a packed house. There followed an invitation to perform in Brooklyn at the Concord Baptist Church and again it was a cold, rainy day. And again there was standing room only.

There exist at present six other possible engagements of the "accident" known as *Tell Pharaoh*. The work has certainly had the very best of performers. In addition to those named previously, Miss Hilda Simms and Mr. Ossie Davis have appeared in the work, and Mr. McKinley Johnson did all the singing in Brooklyn.

I cannot explain the amazing reception accorded this work, but I certainly am gratified over it. And I am eternally indebted to those splendid artists who did more for *Tell Pharaoh* than it could possibly do for them.

LOFTEN MITCHELL

Act One

THERE IS NO SCENERY. *Four lecterns are onstage, two at stage left and two at stage right. There is a microphone in center stage.*

Four actors take their places at the lectern after the house-lights dim. They are: Miss Black, a woman in her twenties or thirties, Mrs. Black, a woman in her forties, Mr. Black, Junior, a man in his twenties or thirties, and Mr. Black, Senior, a man in his forties or fifties.

A strong, stirring note is heard on the guitar, playing the theme song of the play. Out of the darkness we hear Miss Black singing from center stage as the lights fade in:

> MISS BLACK
> (*Singing*)
> When Israel was in Egypt's lan',
> "Let my people go!"
> Oppressed so hard they could not stan',
> "Let my people go!"
> "Go down, Moses,
> Way down in Egypt's lan',
> Tell ole Pharaoh
> To let my people go!"
> > (*The lights on her now dim as the music carries under. Lights come up on Mrs. Black as she stands at a lectern, stage right.*)
> > MRS. BLACK

There is a beautiful hill at the northern end of Central Park. This hill is grass-covered in the spring and summer, bare and brown in the autumn, and cold and foreboding in the winter. But—even in the winter when the earth is dark and cracked, you can look at that hill and know somehow that spring will come to it again and again and the grass will be green. And, as you look, you know that spring will come again and again.

261

MR. BLACK, SR.
(*At lectern*)

From the hilltop you can see all of Harlem. You look directly down on 110th Street and Seventh Avenue. Then—as your eyes gaze westward—you can see the Cathedral of St. John the Divine, Columbia University, and Morningside Heights. You look straight up Seventh Avenue, and on a clear day you can see 125th Street, 135th Street, and 145th Street and on to where the Avenue runs into the Harlem River. As your eyes gaze eastward they pick out the Triboro Bridge spanning the East River, connecting Manhattan, the Bronx, and Queens. As your eyes move downtown again, you see Fifth Avenue, then Lenox Avenue at 110th Street.

MR. BLACK, JR.
(*At lectern*)

All of Harlem is before you. Harlem with its swank apartment buildings, its monuments, its slums, its numerous buildings and its proud history. For Harlem is many things to many people. Each time I read something about Harlem, I am reminded of a story my father used to tell:

SENIOR

A cruel slave master died. Now at his funeral the preacher raved and he ranted. He cried and he moaned. He talked about what a gentle soul the slave master was, about how kind he was, about the way he loved all mankind. Well, an old Negro slave woman sat there in the back of the church and she listened and she listened. Finally, she got up and ambled on out of that church. Back at the slave quarters she saw the other slaves singing and rejoicing and celebrating old master's death. The slave woman told them:

MRS. BLACK

You all better get them grins off'n your faces. You think old master's dead, but he just liable not to be. That sure wasn't him that man's in church preaching about!

MISS BLACK
(*At lectern*)

Harlem certainly isn't analogous to a slave master, but the lies told about the community are as bizarre as those the minister told about the old master. These lies are products

of the same structure which idolizes the slave owner and
decries the enslaved!

SENIOR

Harlem! Big, broad-backed, large-shouldered target for
thousands of lies, cruel epithets, verbal assaults!

MRS. BLACK

Harlem. A gentle land, fertile with dreams,
Yet writhing in nightmarish pain.

JUNIOR

Harlem. The modern slaver's whip lashes your young,
Your teen-agers, middle-agers, and your very old,
Sentencing them to abject poverty in the midst of plenty,
To hopelessness in a world of euphoria,
To powerlessness in a power-mad world!

MISS BLACK

Harlem. A defiant land, laughing at hostility,
Challenging it, demanding universal manhood rights,
Demanding freedom now!

MRS. BLACK

This land has been called evil,
But no lynch mobs mar its history.
It has been called a jungle,
But the snakes of Mississippi are more venomous.

SENIOR

It has been called a swampland,
But the Bowery and Forty-second Street devour more hu-
    manity.
It has been called a No Man's Land for whites,
But what are Palm Beach and Westchester and Roslyn
    Heights
For black people?

MISS BLACK

Harlem has been called middle-class, yet
It could never be as much in the middle,
Signifying nonalignment and decadence as
Park Avenue and Madison Avenue and Fifth Avenue.

MRS. BLACK

Beautiful, black Harlem. A black woman.
An innocent child.

JUNIOR

A garrulous youth crying out
For his identity!

SENIOR

A nationalist leader exhorting his people:
"Buy Black!"

MISS BLACK

And young people,
Old people,
Seeking leadership, demanding answers
To questions raised long, long ago.

SENIOR

Wise, black Harlem. Patient.
Repositor of a black nation's wisdom.
The very heart and pulse of that nation.

JUNIOR

Much studied, rarely understood Harlem.

MRS. BLACK

Amused. Bemused. Refused.
Talked about, written about.
Purveyed. Surveyed.
Yet the truth lies hidden,
Hidden behind stacks of lies.
What is the truth about you, Harlem?
The truth is that you are what you are because
White America has never been honest in
Its treatment of black people!

MISS BLACK

That's the truth!

JUNIOR

The whole truth!

SENIOR

Nothing but the truth!

MRS. BLACK

White America, get off Harlem's back!
Get off every black man and woman's back!
Get off! Get off!
And if you don't,
We're going to push you off!

> (*A stirring note is heard as the lights begin to dim.
> Led by Miss Black, the group sings.*)

ALL

Ohh, Freedom! Ohh, Freedom!
Oh, Freedom over me—
And before I'll be a slave,

I'll be buried in my grave
And go home to my Lord and be free!
>   (*The lights are down completely. Now a spotlight
>   comes up on Mrs. Black at lectern.*)

MRS. BLACK

The history of Harlem is rooted in the birth of this nation.
Africa's children contributed to that birth. . . . While Europe was a land peopled by what we today call barbar-
ians, Africa had advanced civilizations that could build
Pyramids, a Sphinx, smelt iron, and record human history.
Later, too, there appeared the Songhay Empire, early
Ghana, and the world's oldest university at Timbuktu. Its
learned scholars had advanced knowledge of mathematics,
astronomy, and other sciences. One such man, Ahmed
Baba, wrote forty-seven books on forty-seven different
subjects. His personal library of 1,600 books was destroyed
when the Moors invaded Timbuktu.

MISS BLACK

Restless is the child of the African mother—
Community-minded, generous to a fault,
Believing that the land belongs to all,
And all to the land.
Restless, indeed, is the child of the African mother,
Seeking to share his wealth in the midst of impoverish-
    ment,
Seeking to share the sunlight of his experience with those
    away from the sun.

MRS. BLACK

Restless, indeed, is the child of the African mother—
He was Solomon and Sheba, Moses and Pharaoh—
He was Hannibal of Carthage invading Rome,
And he overran Spain—
He walked with the Christ,
And he fought the Caesars.
Restless, indeed, is the child of African mother,
And many a professor and many an artisan journeyed
    north
To Crete,
To Phoenicia,
Greece and Rome,
To civilize barbaric Europe,
To bring it human knowledge.

MISS BLACK

Middle-aged Europe: Impoverished land,
Wartorn, tradeless,
Going nowhere for it had nowhere to go—
Then—
Marco Polo and his adventures
Set tongues to wagging with lurid tales
Of endless Oriental wealth,
And it is said that Christopher Columbus heard
Of a land to the west from his contact with Africans.

MRS. BLACK

The Africanesque features of ancient Latin works
Suggest that Africa touched America
Long, long before Europe.
A man of African origin named Pietro captained one of
Columbus' ships.

MRS. BLACK

There was a black man with Ponce De León when he
reached Florida in 1512.
And one with Balboa when he discovered the Pacific,
And a man named Estevanico led an expedition from
Mexico City
Into what is now Arizona and New Mexico.
Let the record be read and read well,
For we helped to discover—or discovered
San Francisco,
Los Angeles,
Chicago,
Wisconsin,
Denver,
Pike's Peak,
And we brought the dawn to sleeping America.

MISS BLACK

Let the record be read and read well:
This New World that Columbus allegedly discovered—
This Eldorado of the West was a vast wilderness,
A harsh, hideous world.
Forty-four Pilgrim fathers died their first winter here—
Only six or seven remained sound persons.

MRS. BLACK

Neither the first white men here nor the red men

Could fell the forests,
Plant the crops
Nor build the cities
For this New World.
Senseless wars had wasted European men,
And there was only one place to turn for labor:
That place was Africa!

    (*Music under, then it rises.*)

    ALL

    (*Singing*)

I'm gonna tell God all my troubles when I get home—
I'm gonna tell God all my troubles when I get home—
I'm gonna fall down on my knees and pray
'Cause I'm gonna meet Him on that Judgment Day—
I'm gonna tell God all my troubles when I get home!

    MRS. BLACK

    (*As music carries under*)

Turn to Africa the Europeans did, and they wrote in blood that savage crime known as chattel slavery. They dumped chained black Africans into slave ship holds, transplanted them from the dark beauty of their motherland, and denied them their family ties, traditions, and cultural continuity. Black people were sold into southern and northern areas of the New World.

    MISS BLACK

I was in my own land and the white man came for me—
I was home under the moon and stars, completely free!

I danced there on a thousand moonlit nights,
My black soul sailed on a thousand flights—

The sun seemed to glow for just my people and me—
I was warmed by that sun in the land of the free.

The need for free labor made me into a slave—
The world forgot all—all that to it I gave.

They dumped black men and women into the slave
    ship hold,
And we sailed away from the sun to the New World's
    cold.

Don't think we took it calmly, for we did not—
No! We left our own brand of forget-me-not!

The truth about the slave trade remains yet untold,
Of our warriors battling, brave and bold—

Of black men who arrived across a wild sea
And pledged openly that they'd always be free!

JUNIOR

(*Steps into center stage with others*)

Brother and sister Africans, there are five hundred of us
here—five hundred that they would doom to a life of slavery. We are chained together here, ready to be sold on
their auction block. But, I ask you—would you live as
slaves or die as free men?

ALL

Die, die, die!

JUNIOR

There is the mighty sea, beckoning to us. Across it lies
Mother Africa. Let us walk into the sea, walking back
across it toward Africa. And if we should drown, we do so
as free men and women, eternally free! And the world will
know that the people of Africa love freedom so much that
they will destroy themselves for that freedom! Let us
march!

ALL

Let us march!
March!
March toward freedom!
What can the sea do to us?
Kill us?
We've died before!
We'll die again!
March, brother!
March, sister!
Mother!
Brother!
March!
March into the sea!

(*Music rises, loud, pulsating, then carries under as
Mrs. Black speaks.*)

MRS. BLACK

Only the ocean floor knows how many black men and

women lie in the graves beneath it. The silly songs of Stephen Foster become even sillier when we face the truth that slaves burned down plantations, put spiders in old master's soup, and sometimes killed him while he was a-sleep. Anyone who thinks that slavery represented the "good old days" ought to look at the record! Let the record be read and read well!

MISS BLACK

Yes, they killed me and they raped me.
They sold my man far-off, away from me.
They put a badge on color, decried being black—
They made it symbolic of the mighty slaver's track.
Their standard said whites could be swarthy or blond,
For this was the complexion of which whites were fond—
Their standard said: Chain Negroes in the slaver's track—
Never admitting you could be many colors, yet *black!*

Their standard reduced poor black folks into a search for hair—
Their standard made some black folks search for what they called "good hair"—
Their standard made many start to search for something else again,
Forgetting divide-and-conquer is an old, old refrain!

They sold my mother's body into a town called New Orleans—
They sold my father into Georgia with all his dreams!
White scoundrels raped my family in a manner yet unseen,
Yet cursed me because I was born "in-between."

I been 'buked and I been scorned—
I been talked about sure as you borned!

I been 'buked and I been scorned!
I been talked about sure as you born!
I been 'buked and I been scorned!
I been talked about sure as you born!
I ain't gon' lay religion down—
I been 'buked and I been scorned—
I been talked about sure as you born!

MRS. BLACK
(*As music carries under*)

While I was being 'buked and scorned, Truth was being torn from the history books—

One such truth was that I was in the New World before it was born.

Let the record be read and read well—

In 1626 when New York City was a Dutch outpost called New Amsterdam

Eleven African slaves were imported.

They lived on the fringe of what is now The Bowery.

These Africans built a wagon road to the upper part of the Settlement—

To a place the Dutch called Haarlem, spelled with two "a's."

Yes! Let the record be read and read well—

Eighteen years later these Africans were supported by rank-and-file white colonists

When they petitioned the Dutch for freedom.

They received it, and they settled in a swampland which they built into a prosperous community.

That community is today known as Greenwich Village.

And all you black children in the world out there—

When you think about Third Avenue

Think about those eleven Africans!

When you see Greenwich Village,

Remember those eleven Africans!

Race relations in New Amsterdam?

They were relatively cordial.

Black men were artisans, craftsmen, executioners, doctors.

Many well-to-do Negroes owned slaves—

Black slaves and white slaves—

Among the prominent Negroes were Domingo Antony, who owned land on Canal Street,

And Catalina Anthony, who owned land on what is now Pell Street,

And Annie d'Angelo, who owned the site of the original Madison Square Garden,

And Solomon Pieters, who owned thirty acres of land at Twenty-third Street and Fifth Avenue

Where the Flatiron Building now stands.

And Negroes owned much of the land that is now around Astor Place, City Hall Park and the site of the Woolworth Building!

Let the record be read and read well.
For little color discrimination existed in seventeenth-century New York.
People of different races attended the same churches, drank in the same taverns.
Peter Stuyvesant said everything was in God's blessing as a result of the employment of Negroes.
He said in 1660: "Let the free and the company's Negroes Keep good watch on my Bowery."

Discrimination in seventeenth-century New York was integrated.
It was a matter of caste and class. Then—
The British came. They seized New Amsterdam and named it New York.
They instituted chattel slavery and brought rigid slave codes.
Color discrimination became a reality,
And the Rights of Man were denied black people. . . .

> JUNIOR
> (*Singing*)
> And I couldn't hear nobody pray,
> Couldn't hear nobody pray,
> O way down yonder by myself
> And I couldn't hear nobody pray!

> MRS. BLACK
> (*As music carries under*)

In 1682 an edict was passed stating Negroes could no longer be buried in Trinity Church cemetery. The land owned by Negroes was willed to the British Crown. The manumission of slaves became increasingly difficult.
The doctrine of nonviolence was then nonexistent. Black people struck back, helped by poor whites and Indians. One insurrection followed another. Fire was the black people's chief weapon, and they nearly burned the city to the ground. It was during that period that the New York City Fire Department came into existence. But, you don't

read that in the history books or see that on television or
movie screens. . . .
(*Music: A defiant chord, then—*)
MISS BLACK
Tell Pharaoh
To let my story be told!
My story about Crispus Attucks.
The first man to fall in the American Revolution—
Pharaoh!
Let my story be told!
Let my story be told!
About the black women who fought the Revolution,
About the five thousand black men who fought then
As black Africa saved white America!
Tell Pharaoh
To talk about Peter Salem
And Salem Poor
And tavern-owner Sam Fraunces—
His daughter saved George Washington's life!

Let my story be told
Of the way I was 'buked and scorned,
The way I was talked about sure as you're born—
Let my story be told
Of white America turning on black Africa
When Africa had saved it!

Let my story be told
Of the way America stereotyped me,
Villified me when it knew my deeds!
This was no accident!
This inglorious, infamous act was to destroy black people,
To make proud people beggars in the American drama!
SENIOR
Yes! Let my story be told—
Of the African Free School,
Of James Hewlett and the African Grove Theatre
Who performed Shakespeare in 1821.
Let my story be told
Of hoodlums wrecking it,
Of the great Ira Aldridge going abroad,
Playing before royalty because he couldn't play here!
Yes, Pharaoh!

Let my story be told
Of the way you ignored my heroism during the Civil War,
Of the way the slave walked off the plantation and joined
    the Union Army
And broke the Confederacy's economic back!
Let my story be told
Of the way I created minstrelsy,
Yet you stole it and used it against me!
Let my story be told
Of the way I paraded through our history
For we'd have no history without me,
Black me!

MISS BLACK
(*Singing*)
I am a poor pilgrim of sorrow,
I'm left in this wide world to roam,
No thoughts have I of tomorrow
Except to make heaven my home.
Sometimes I am tossed and driven,
Sometimes I don't know where to roam,
But, I heard of a city called heaven,
I'm trying to make it my home!
My mother done reached that poor glory,
My father's still walking in sin—
My brothers and sisters won't own me
Because I'm trying to get in!
Sometimes I am tossed and driven,
Sometimes I don't know where to roam—
I've heard of a city called heaven,
I'm trying to make it my home!

MISS BLACK
(*As music carries under*)
Harlem lay dormant until the mid-nineteenth century . . .
Mid-nineteenth century Harlem was peopled by crude
    squatters who lived in cottages.
Industrial development, business expansion, improved
    transportation,
And the arrival of the so-called foreign-born transformed
    Harlem.
By 1886 three elevated lines reached the community.
Fashionable New Yorkers fled from Lower Manhattan
To build New York's first suburb: Harlem!

MISS BLACK
> (*As a wealthy white dowager*)

I remember Harlem. We built our house there in 1888 and, oh, it was swank, high-fashion, with carriages, mansions, and the very best people. We were careful to tell people we lived in Harlem, not New York City. The city was for foreigners! Why, in 1893 the *Harlem Monthly Magazine* wrote that Harlem was the future center of fashion, culture, and intelligence. But, in the early 1900s something happened: The news got out that they were opening a Lenox Avenue subway. By 1904 all of Harlem's vacant land had been sold. Wild speculation raged. And the bust followed the boom. Houses stood vacant, waiting to be rented. But, the high rents scared off the general population and—this is what happened.

JUNIOR
> (*To Senior, who plays a white realtor*)

Mr. Man, my name is Philip Payton. My friend Solomon Riley and I have been talking about Harlem. We figured that if Negroes moved in there you could get twice and maybe three times the rent that white folks would pay.

SENIOR
> (*As a white realtor*)

Rent to colored folks? In Harlem? Boy, you've got to be kidding—

JUNIOR

No, sir. Colored folks living downtown, getting beat up when they come home. Menfolks have to meet one another on corners and walk home together to keep from getting beat up. Gangs are going into colored homes, beating women and children. Colored folks would just love to have a place all their own so they wouldn't be bothering white folks. And they'll pay. That means money for you. And some for me.

SENIOR

Money? . . . Well, now, boy, you all do love to sing and dance and pray and be off to yourselves, don't you? Now, I ain't thinking about money alone, but this is my chance to help you all out. So—you rent these apartments to your folks, for that's a real Christian act—especially if you can rent to colored folks at *three* times what white folks would pay.

JUNIOR

Boss, you and me—we sure ain't going to die poor!

SENIOR

Dying poor ain't Christian.

JUNIOR

Sure ain't, boss! You know what I think was the meaning of Moses not making the Promised Land and Jesus dying like He did? It was to show folks how *not* to act!

SENIOR

Boy, we'll talk all that religion after you rent to colored folks for three times what white folks would pay!

MRS. BLACK

(*From lectern, narrating*)

Rent to colored folks for three times what white folks would pay. It wasn't difficult, for this is what went on in too many homes—

MISS BLACK

(*Appears in center stage as a teen-ager*)

Mama! Mama!

MRS. BLACK

(*Appears as her mother*)

What is it?

(*Then*)

Lord, my child been beat up again! Lemme look at you, girl.

MISS BLACK

Mama, I ain't hurt bad. Not as bad as one of them. I took off my shoe when them two boys come up to me and said something nasty. And I parted his hair with the heel of my shoe.

MRS. BLACK

(*Happily*)

You did?

(*Then*)

But, child, the Lord says you got to turn the other cheek.

MISS BLACK

I turned the other cheek, Mama—after I hit the other one with my fist and bloodied his nose.

MRS. BLACK

You did? That's good!

(*Then*)

No! That's bad! . . . Lord, I ain't never gonna get used to this North. I couldn't get used to down home, either. The Bible says you is supposed to love your neighbor, but they beat us down there and up here they come in your house and beat on you! Lord, what we gonna do?

MISS BLACK

Mama, stop calling on the Lord, 'cause He can get all confused if these white folks calling on Him to get rid of us while you calling on Him to help us!

MRS. BLACK

Girl, you shut your mouth! We already got white folks down on us, so don't go getting the Lord down on us, too!

MISS BLACK

I don't mind the Lord being down on us, 'cause He ain't beating on us like white folks is.

MRS. BLACK

He ain't gonna get a chance to beat on you 'cause if you keep on blaspheming His name, I'm gonna work on your backside 'fore He reaches you. I sure wish your Pa had a lived.

MISS BLACK

They'd a beat on him, too! How many nights did he come in here and knock over a chair or bang the wall? I used to lay in my bed and hear you all arguing about any little thing, and one night I heard you tell him: "Go fight where you got mad!" And he told you: "If I did, you'd be a widow before you could bat an eye!"

(*Then*)

Mama, I don't wanta stay here no more. I'm tired—tired of fighting to get in the front door, tired of walking the street and having men grab at me! This ain't what you and Papa walked all the way north for! If I don't do something about it, I ain't gonna be able to look you in the face or to even remember Papa for the man he really was!

MRS. BLACK

Yes, child! Yes! We going from here. A man come round the church the other day and he told us about apartments in Harlem, renting to colored folks. Six-room apartments for thirty-four dollars a month, with all modern conveniences except steam heat and bathroom. Lots of colored folks talking about moving there. You think you'd like it?

MISS BLACK

Like it? Oh, Mama, please! Let's move. Move to where we can live like people and not be afraid. You can go out to your church groups, and I won't have to meet you after, and maybe boys can come down to see me one at a time and not have to bring their friends to keep from getting jumped on the way home. Mama, let's move. . . .

(*Music rises, then*)

JUNIOR

(*Singing*)

On that great-getting-up morning,
Fare thee well, fare thee well!
On that great-getting-up-morning,
Fare thee well, fare thee well!
There's a better day a-coming
Fare thee well, fare thee well!

MRS. BLACK

(*As the music carries under*)

And so the first Negro families moved into Harlem. And the whites resisted. And Negroes kept moving in, and the whites kept fighting back.

To the land north of 110th Street came southern Negroes escaping from physical lynchings, West Indians escaping from economic lynchings and northern Negroes escaping the terror they knew in Lower Manhattan. They met in the land north of 110th Street and they brought with them their folkways, their mores, their religiosity, and their dogged determination.

There was a subway stop at 135th Street and Lenox Avenue—a stop known as the Pearly Gates. It was also known as one of the stops on the Underground Railroad. Black people milled around that subway stop daily, waiting to meet newly arrived relatives from the South, the West Indies, or Lower Manhattan. There a drama as magnificent as the Exodus was played daily. A southern Negro laborer appeared and looked out at the crowd of people. . . .

SENIOR

(*In center stage*)

Lord, I ain't never seen so many colored folks since you sent the Word! . . . Why, this ground here is hard—real hard, real *concrete!* Wonder how a body plants corn in these parts?. . . Look at them buildings! One, two, three, four stories high! They mighty high for chicken coops! . . . Ummm. Kinda cold. The sun ain't warm like it is down home. Mary Belle and the young'uns ain't gonna like this a speck. . . . Everybody here wearing shoes, too! Must cost a heap of money to be staying up here . . . I sure wish I was back home with Mary Belle and my children right now . . . Well, I can't be back 'cause the land ain't fallow and ain't nothing growing. Schoolhouse is six miles away and the young'uns can't learn nothing. I got to rassle with this here concrete and tear it up so's something can grow for my wife and kids. Yeah, old concrete! You and me is gonna have one jim-dandy fight and I'm gonna win!

(*He returns to lectern.*)

MISS BLACK

(*Appears as a teen-ager*)

Lenox Avenue and 135th Street! That's what the sign says. What're all these folks looking at? . . . Mama, I sure wish you coulda come with me. It's lonesome and I'm scared. Lord, I wish I had the fare! I'd take the next thing smoking right on outa this city! . . . But, what would I do if I did? Ain't no work down home for a colored girl, 'cept cleaning up after white folks and having their men trying to flirt with you. I got to stay here where colored folks is free! . . . Mama, I'm scared—scared of this place and its people. It's big. And everybody's looking at me, but nobody sees me. . . . I'm gonna work real hard up here, Mama, then I'm coming back home to stay. You hear me, Mama? . . . Oh, who'm I lying to? I can't go home no more 'cause home ain't got nothing for me!

(*She returns to her lectern.*)

JUNIOR

(*Appears as a West Indian youth*)

This is New York. A strange place. No palm trees swaying. And the sun is not friendly. My people do not look like they do on the island. There is no warmth here in the people nor in the climate. . . . If I were home now, I'd be on the island shore, casting my net and the sun would be kissing my face. But, who can earn a living casting a net and having his face kissed by the sun? What hope is there at home except for tomorrow when I must live today? . . . New York, you shall not defeat me as you have so many of my people. You shall not send me running back to the island to drown your memories in rum. I shall love you, big city, if you love me—and fight you if you mistreat me!

(*And he returns to his lectern.*)

MRS. BLACK

(*Appears as a mother with children.*)

Come on now, children. We at 135th Street and Lenox Avenue. Ohhhh! Look at the buildings! You reckon folks live that high off the ground? . . . Joseph, Junior, you stop that! We ain't down home now. We in the big city! . . . Lord, I sure wish my man was here with me 'cause I'm scared. Joseph, Senior, why you got to be off working in Atlantic City when I needs for you to be in New York with me and our children? . . . I know. I know. You work where there is work. But this town is so *big*. Ain't right for a woman to be alone in it, much less with children. . . . What am I gonna do here where I don't know a living soul? Who gonna help me tend the children when they gets sick? Who gonna be my friends now? . . . Lord, I wish I was back home! . . . But, I can't go back home. No sir! These young'uns got to grow up not being scared to walk into town! They got to get some learning and be somebody when they grows up. They got to have what I ain't never had! And they gonna get it! They gonna get it, else I'm gonna go to my grave trying to see that they do! Yes, Lord, they gonna get it!

(*And she returns to her lectern.*)

MISS BLACK

(*Singing*)

Tramping, tramping,
 Trying to make heaven my home—
I'm tramping, tramping,
Trying to make heaven my home!

(*The music carries under as the lights pick out Mrs. Black at her lectern.*)

MRS. BLACK

Harlem life was difficult, but it was fun. There were churches and lodges and clubs and there was friendship on every block. There were such institutions as the Schomburg Collection where Negro history and culture were

housed. And there was the Old Dutch Bell on Mt. Morris
Park Hill and the Jumel Mansion and the 135th Street Library and the Savoy Ballroom and the Renaissance Ca-
sino. And there were legitimate theatres—first the Crescent
on 135th Street, then the Lincoln, the Lafayette, and the
Alhambra where sometimes you could see vaudeville skits
such as this—

JUNIOR

(*Meets Senior in center stage*)

Hey, man! I didn't know that was you!

SENIOR

I didn't know that was you, either! I sure am glad to see
you. I just run into—

JUNIOR

I saw him yesterday and he said—

SENIOR

That ain't what he told me. He told me—

JUNIOR

Oh, he told me that, too. But, he told that woman next
door to him—

SENIOR

I didn't know that about her. I thought she was—

JUNIOR

I thought so, too, until the other day when her doctor told
me—

SENIOR

He said *that* about her? Last week he told me—

JUNIOR

He told me that, too, but you know what I think? I think—

SENIOR

You've got to be kidding! I thought—

JUNIOR

I thought so, too! I ain't never heard of a doctor's wife telling him *not* to charge another woman unless—

SENIOR

That's what I thought, too! But, she's a good girl. A real
good girl. She goes to bed every night at nine P.M.

JUNIOR AND SENIOR

(*In unison*)

Then she gets up at three A.M. and goes home!

JUNIOR

You know something, man? The thing I like about running

into you is—a man can always get into a *good* conversation!

> (*And they go off together to their respective lecterns.*)

MRS. BLACK

One of the grave problems of being a Negro in America is that each generation must discover you. This is part and parcel of America's attempt to destroy black people. It states, in effect, that it was all right to lynch, cheat, and kill the so-called old Negro, and it justifies many a guilt complex. The reality is there has never been an "old Negro."

Whites discovered the so-called New Negro in the nineteen-twenties and there flowered in Harlem what came to be known as the Black Renaissance. The arts flourished. Many thought this was the millennium. Columbia's students ran around Harlem, measuring Negroes' heads. Rich whites invaded Harlem night spots and many found Negroes exotic.

The Depression of 1929 flooded the nation and drowned the Black Renaissance. Grown men, able-bodied, stood on 125th Street with apples for sale. They wore signs: "Unemployed. Please buy apples." America trembled. Unemployed workers searched garbage cans for food. Many milled together into communities of hungry, homeless men who squatted along riverfronts in crude cottages that became known as Hoovervilles. The nation cried, and Harlem cried with it, for both had the blues and this is the way poet James C. Morris described them:

> These are the Blues;
> a longing beyond control
> Left on an unwelcome doorstep,
> slipping in when the door is opened.

> These are the Blues:
> a lonely woman crouched at a bar,
> gulping a blaze of Scotch and rye,
> using a tear for a chaser.

The Blues are fears that
blossom like ragweeds
in a well-kept bed of roses.

Nobody knows how tired I am.
And there ain't a soul who gives a damn!

(*A strong musical note, then she continues.*)
The election of Franklin Delano Roosevelt stopped America from searching for the Good Old Days. The nation began to dig its way out of the Depression, and Harlem dug, too. The Federal Theatre, the Rose McClendon Players, and later the American Negro Theatre attempted to build black theatres in Harlem and, in so doing, they launched many theatrical careers.

The child of Harlem had the will to live, to survive, to make it. He knew his black identity and, in the nineteen-thirties he made up his own language which he threw into the faces of whites much as they resorted to Yiddish, Italian, or Spanish.

JUNIOR
(*Meets Senior in center stage*)
Man! What you putting down?

SENIOR
I'm putting down all skunks, punks, and a hard hustle!

JUNIOR
Dad, I ain't dead, but I'm looking for some bread. I am like the beat. I ain't nowhere. I'm like the bear's brother. I ain't gonna get no further. In other words, I'm like the black night facing the white day. I am up tight and I don't want to stay that 'way!

SENIOR
You beating a dead horse to death 'cause I ain't no man of great wealth. If I'm lying, I'm flying. In fact, Jack, if I'm lying, God's gone to Jackson, Mississippi, and you know He wouldn't be hanging around in *that* place!

JUNIOR
You done come up crummy when I need you, Sonny. You have been a social hanger when I need a banger. You have low-rated me, ill-fated me, disgraced me and abraced me.

I thought you were my main man and you have showed your can. You have been a drag and darn near a hag. You have brought me down, clown. You are supposed to be hip as a whip, but you are a crum, chum, and if I could afford a broom, I would sweep you off the scene, Gene!

SENIOR

You may be a poet and not know it. Go on, Gates, and solid swing, but I am forced to tell you just one thing: Your eyes may flash fire and you may spit, but none of my green bread will you git!

(*They walk away from each other.*)

MRS. BLACK

Translation? One Harlemite was trying to borrow money from another, was rejected, hence the retort. . . . There were other things in Harlem. We partied. We dug Joe Louis and the Yankees before they became pompous. And we strolled. . . .

JUNIOR

(*In center stage*)

Seventh Avenue was once a fashionable, tree-lined boulevard, sometimes called Colored Folks' Broadway. City authorities fined building superintendents for allowing rubbish to accumulate. People glared you out of existence if you were seen improperly dressed or misbehaving there. And you got tongue-lashed at home for shaming the family and the neighborhood. Besides, Negro policemen like Brisbane, Brown, Pendleton, and Lacey kept Seventh Avenue orderly. They would go upside your head in a minute, then—since they knew all families around—they'd tell your Dad and he'd go upside the rest of your anatomy.

Seventh Avenue was where you strolled those exciting Sunday afternoons. No one who knew Harlem from the 1920s through the 1940s can forget strolling.

We youngsters had suits issued by the WPA. That's the Works Progress Administration, or—for you youngsters—the granddaddy of the Anti-Poverty Program. We had tailors "drape" these suits, then we put on our shirts, ties, and hats and called on our young ladies.

Strolling was seemingly casual, but it was exacting, with a

point and a purpose. You had to walk with your right leg dipping a bit, resembling a limp. You and your young lady started just below 116th Street, moving north on the west side of the avenue. In front of the Regent Theatre you met a couple. The male tipped his hat to your young lady and you responded, smartly, in an almost military manner. Invariably, the couple invited you to a "function" or a party. You told them: "Lay the pad number on us and we'll pick up that action later. You dug your stroll. We got to dig ours."

On you moved, meeting and greeting folks. You reached 125th Street one hour and a half later. At the Theresa you saw Bill Robinson, George Wiltshire, Ralph Cooper, Pigmeat Markham, Dick Campbell, or Joe Louis, waving at you, acting like they knew you even if they didn't. They had less ego than many of our present-day celebrities.

Scores of other strollers brought new from all parts of Harlem to 125th Street. Then—replenished and recognized —you strolled north again, knowing you had the "sharpest chick" in the world and that you were the "sharpest cat" that ever strolled!

Three hours after the start of your stroll, you "fell" into Henry's Sugar Bowl at 134th Street and Seventh Avenue. You had a malted, met other friends, then started downtown again. You told the world: "This is black me in my Harlem. I belong here and I'm somebody!"

Man we strolled!

Strolling is gone from Harlem, possibly never to return. The Establishment's standards claw at our culture, malign our community and its beautiful people. Somehow, some way, as we move toward the mainstream, I wish we could stroll with our true Black Identities, telling the world: "This is Beautiful Me in my Beautiful Black Harlem. Dig me! If you really dig, you can reap a great harvest!"

MISS BLACK

(*As Junior returns to lectern*)

While we were strolling, a second Dred Scott decision was being written in New York City—a decision that was to enslave Harlem, Bedford-Stuyvesant, South Jamaica, and the

South Bronx. The slaveholders now sat in big offices behind fat cigars, directing bank operations. In the 1930s
these banks foreclosed on loans and mortgages in Harlem.
They noted the high rents being paid there and they
established the Savings Trust Company. Reporter Ted Pos-
ton states that in the very next year they formed the Mort-
gage Conference of New York. They confined Negroes and
Spanish-speaking people to definite areas. They induced
realtors to refuse minority groups space in certain areas.
They denied mortgage-financing for maintaining homes in
habitable conditions. They made successful operations at
reasonable rent levels impossible. The United States Justice Department proved all of this in 1946. The court issued a decree forbidding such practices. But, the court
could not prevent banks from doing *individually* what
they were forbidden to do *collectively*.

MRS. BLACK

This action, written in infamy, boxed in the black American's community and allowed it to deteriorate because his
misery made others rich! Physical lynchings were no
longer needed. Profits could be made by maiming families
through poverty, disease, disillusionment, and death. This
conspiracy could destroy family structures in ways never
dreamed of by ex-convicts and rogues. This conspiracy
chased those aggressive, stubborn Harlem children from
the land of their birth while the white hoodlum reaped
untold wealth from drugs, defective buildings, graft, and
human misery. With the stubborn Harlem children out of
the community there was no need to spend money for essential services, to meet legitimate human demands or to
recognize the people of Harlem as human beings! The battle of the Harlem child against the white hoodlum had, in
the last analysis, been won by the hoodlum! That hoodlum
had placed every allegedly antisocial act committed by
oppressed Negroes squarely on the table where black
leadership would have to cringe and apologize for its existence!

The rape of the black American was complete!

MISS BLACK

(*Singing*)
I'm so glad trouble don't last always—

I'm so glad trouble don't last always—
Oh, my Lord,
Oh, my Lord
What shall I do? . . .

MRS. BLACK
(*As music carries under*)

The strength of power lies in its manipulation. While the world battled poverty, its power structures conspired. There arose in Germany conspirators financed by people outside and inside that nation. Stories seeped out about Jews being burned in gas chambers. No one cared to believe it because the Nazi army had been built to destroy communism, not us. . . . The world went up in flames in 1939 and once again it became a battle for democracy. People in Harlem wondered how America could fight for democracy abroad when it didn't exist at home.

Something called Selective Service came into existence—and this was after all America had piously shouted about "No More War"—shouted this while fascist Italy raped Ethiopia and Franco destroyed the Spanish Republic. . . . Yet, the draft became a reality. And the "Cats" everywhere worried. You could hear them up and down the streets of Harlem. . . .

JUNIOR
(*As he meets Senior in center stage*)

Man, this draft is giving me a *cold!*

SENIOR

You? For years I been trying to get a government job, and now I'm liable to get exactly the one I don't want!

JUNIOR

I hope that after this action I don't face no *inaction.*

SENIOR

Things is bad! I hear that cats are jumping off closets, barefooted, trying to get flat feet so they can beat this jive. Me—I am going to be 4F from heart failure, which I get every time I go to my mailbox.

JUNIOR

Man, don't you sing the blues to me when I got 'em. You married and supporting a family.

SENIOR

Let me take you to school, fool! I been trying to get that

wife of mine to go to work for years. Soon as I fall down to the draft board and get a deferment 'cause I'm supporting her, that woman goes out and gets a job. I told her: "You better get on down there and quit that job fast—like yesterday!" I said: "Baby, I'm working on keeping this deferment."

JUNIOR

Deferment? Man, they have taken that word out of the dictionary. I know a cat who has no arms. They drafted him into the army and he asked the man: "What am I going to do here with no arms?" The man told him: "You see that fellow over there drawing a pail of water? Well, he's blind. You tell him where to put the water!"

(*And they walk off, shaking their heads*)

MRS. BLACK

Despite all the objections and protestations, black men did what they have done since the founding of this nation: They went off and fought the war.

Suddenly it became possible to walk from 116th Street to 125th Street in less than an hour and a half. For the young men were all away, and the people you met had their hearts and minds with those who were away. . . . And the streets lay crying, lay crying alone, for their youth had deserted them. Some were to die on alien soil. Others were to return and move to suburbia. The streets probably knew this before anyone else, and so they lay crying, lay crying alone, for their children—their children had been taken from them. . . .

MISS BLACK

(*Singing*)

Sometimes I feel like a motherless chile,
Sometimes I feel like a motherless chile,
Sometimes I feel like a motherless chile,
Far, far away from home.
A long, long ways from home!

(*The lights have begun to dim and now the entire Company is singing as the curtain falls.*)

Curtain
End Act I

Act Two

The lights fade in around the cast. Its members have returned to respective lecterns. Miss Black is in center stage, singing:

MISS BLACK

(*Singing*)

Sometimes I feel like a motherless chile,
Sometimes I feel like a motherless chile,
Sometimes I feel like a motherless chile,
Far, far away from home.
A long, long ways from home!

MRS. BLACK

(*As music carries under*)

Freedom is anything but free.
Its cost is human lives and sacrifices,
And time, unpaid-for time.
Freedom's cost is a mother's tears,
An agonizing shriek in the night for a son
Digging a foxhole on foreign soil
As bullets spit death!

MISS BLACK

(*As a war mother*)

Telegram from the War Department. My son died a hero's death. They gonna send me a big check for his insurance. Money I ain't never seen before. Gonna be able to stack all that cash up in a row bigger'n me. Gonna have a big medal, too, pinned on me by the government. Gonna take a day off from scrubbing floors and go on down to Washington and get myself all honored. Yes, indeed! Gonna take that medal and put it right beside my husband's medal! I got no husband now. I got no son. I got nothing but heartaches and medals!

MRS. BLACK

(*As a war wife*)

Telegram from the War Department. My husband died a hero's death. I'm going to Washington, D.C., and get myself a medal and I'll get his insurance. I'll have my picture in the papers and people will sing their praises. But, when my child cries out for his father, what will I say? Whose hand will I reach for in the lonely hours of the night? . . .

288

I swear to God that governments ought to be run by women! They'd never send sons out to die!

SENIOR

(*As a war father*)

Telegram from the War Department. My son is dead. Lord, it seems like I'm dead, too. I done mopped floors and washed dishes and lifted concrete and shoveled coal and lugged ice and cleaned slime from spittoons so that boy could grow up and get some learning. I recollect when he graduated, he said to me, says: "Dad, you gonna retire now. I'm gonna take good care of you." Well, he took care of me all right—out there fighting for something he ain't got at home. Out there dying so folks can kill his brothers!

MISS BLACK

(*Singing*)

Nobody knows de trouble I see—
Nobody knows my sorrow—
Nobody knows de trouble I see—
Glory, hallelujah!
Sometimes I'm up, sometimes I'm down—
Oh, yes, Lord!
Sometimes I'm almost to the ground,
Oh, yes, Lord!
Nobody knows de trouble I see—
Nobody knows my sorrow—
Nobody knows de trouble I see—
Glory, hallelujah!

MRS. BLACK

(*As music carries under*)

Peace came to the world in 1945. But—
Peace is an interlude between wars,
A time out, an intermission for the mighty to regroup their
    forces
And prepare to cut down another generation.
Peace is a nightmare to the mighty,
A threat to their power and position.
The Cold War replaced the hot war during this intermis-
    sion,
And the world's powers raved and ranted at each other,
And hysteria reigned!
The fearful fifties saw America in flight,

From self, into self.
Hysterical lies wrecked careers and human lives
And we laid to waste the Bill of Rights
To prove we were not Reds.
McCarthyism struck terror into the hearts and minds of
  people everywhere
As bestiality displaced humanity,
And dissent was silenced,
A silence that made Korea a reality
That we buried yesterday, yet festers today
And becomes a running sore throughout our history!
America sought suburbia in the nineteen-fifties,
Leaving the cities for the impoverished and downtrodden,
The displaced and the disadvantaged.
A new stereotype spread its wings and did to Harlem
What black faced comics had done to black people long
  ago.
And black communities became places from which one
  had to flee
As though one had the plague!

But, stubborn is the child of the African mother,
The most avid seeker of the American dream,
Reaching, reaching,
Believing always in tomorrow,
And the Black Revolution thrust itself upon the scene,
A Revolution as old as the nation.
In a small parish in Clarendon County, South Carolina
The Reverend J. A. DeLaine exhorted his followers:

SENIOR

The Voice of God has roared in my ears this terrible day,
charging us with the duty of saving white children that
they may grow up to be our brothers, of saving the souls
of all those who have been taught hate instead of love. In
the words of St. Paul: "When I was a child, I spake as a
child, I understood as a child, I thought as a child: but
when I became a man I put away childish things. Now
abideth faith, hope and love, and the greatest of these is
love!"

MISS BLACK

Yes, love!

SENIOR

Oh, yes! The Voice of God has roared in my ears, testing my faith by letting them kill my beloved wife—testing me as Job was tested, as the Children of Israel were tested—as our people have been tested through nearly three hundred years of slavery! Testing to see if God's work can be done on earth as it is in heaven! And, oh, my friends, it will be done!

MISS BLACK

God's work will be done!

SENIOR

For even when the Law has been read and the signs that read "This is for white" and "This is for black" have been burned, still shall there be lynch mobs, still shall there be deaths! There will be more testing, more suffering!

MISS BLACK

Preach to 'em!

SENIOR

But, let not your heart be troubled, for the Seventh Seal shall be opened and they cannot hide! They cannot hide!

MISS BLACK

Ain't no hiding place down here!

SENIOR

And *we* cannot hide! We cannot hide by trying to kill the killers! For us to be worthy of our Great Duty is for us to teach them love on earth. And how's that done?

JUNIOR

Through love!

SENIOR

Yes, brother! Through love! And where's that taught? In the home, in the church, and in the school. Now, we started this thing up for buses and then we switched to suing for separate but equal schools. Some of us didn't think we'd get that and some of us didn't much care! But, I care now! For there's no such thing as being separate and equal! The only thing a man learns when he's separate is that he's not equal!

JUNIOR

That's right!

SENIOR

Now, they beat on this child and called him an ugly ape. Well, son, that black in your skin was given to you by God and it's a mark of your heritage from Great Africa. Son, all nations and lands have their beauty standards and no one standard is better than any other. In my Father's house are many mansions. If it were not so I would not have told you so. . . . And that means there's room for all—not up yonder in the sky, but here on earth! I'm not going to be a traitor to the little child that would lead me! I'm going on with this case to the highest court in the land! Before I turn back now, may I go rotting to my grave!

ALL
Amen! Amen!

MRS. BLACK
To the highest court he went with five other cases,
And on May 17, 1954 the Supreme Court said:

JUNIOR
"In *Sweat* v. *Painter, supra,* in finding that a segregated law school for Negroes could not provide them with equal educational opportunities, this Court relied in large part on 'those qualities which are incapable of objective measurement but which make for greatness in a law school.' In *McLaurin* v. *Oklahoma State Regents, supra,* the Court, in requiring that a Negro admitted to a white graduate school be treated like all other students, again resorted to tangible considerations . . . 'his ability to study, to engage in discussions and exchange views with other students, and, in general, to learn his profession.' Such considerations apply with added force to children in grade school. To separate them from others of similar age and qualifications solely because of their race generates a feeling of inferiority as to their status in the community that may affect their hearts and minds in a way unlikely to ever be undone. . . ."

MRS. BLACK
The law was read but not obeyed,
And vicious forces sought to evade it,
To drive deep despair into the hearts and minds of little children.
Reigns of terror were unleashed,
Striving to push back into the soil the seeds of truth
That refused to remain hidden there.

Flaming seeds scorched the soils of Alabama
And Little Rock, Arkansas,
And Florida,
And Louisiana,
And North Carolina,
And South Carolina,
And smeared the cities of Baltimore and Cambridge,
And Louisville and Atlanta,
And Clinton, Tennessee, and Albany, Georgia,
And blazed into the Mississippi night.
The truth thrust its way upward, out of the soil,
Defying the cruel planter's land, reaching toward
The rays of the sun!
The hearts and minds of little children erupted!
They erupted, breaking through concrete and stone.
They erupted, overflowing city streets,
Defying mad dogs and madmen who once struck terror
Into the hearts and minds of children!

Southern cities, northern cities,
Small towns and large towns and villages and hamlets
Shut their eyes to the cry: "We shall overcome!"

Latrine legalism, moderation, gentility, and patience
And long lines of crooked thought sought to delay
The march toward the sunlight.

What price the right to protest
Guaranteed nearly two hundred years ago?
Vicious dogs, fire hoses, cruel epithets
To claw at the hearts and minds of little children. . . .

The world looked on, awestricken,
In wild disbelief, yet this was no new page
In the nation's history! No!
This was the result of three centuries' attempt to destroy
The hearts and minds of *people!*

But, volcanic truth
Soared inexorable from the soil,
Hurling challenges to those who had planted,
To plow, to cultivate—

It challenged them in a way they had never known before,
Challenged them before a World Assembly dominated by
   adults
Whose minds the planters had tried to twist years ago!

Twist some they did,
Black and brown and white,
Into vineyards of impoverishment
Where hope is an unknown word
And yesterday dark despair, and tomorrow is
A fleeting stillborn moment.

And Skid Row?
This is not Birmingham, Alabama, nor Montgomery,
Nor Atlanta, nor any southern town—
This is New York
And Philadelphia
And Chicago,
Skid Rows where black men and white men
Scrounge side by side in the gutter,
Playing out their last hopes together,
Playing them out because they could not train together!

This, too, is challenged by the children and their parents!
This shall not last!
Nor shall resistance to the law!

Innocent, indeed, are the hearts and minds of children,
But, searching, too,
Expressive,
Demanding when denied,
Presenting new challenges that must be met,
Or chaos faced!

>   MISS BLACK AND JUNIOR
>   (*Singing*)
>   Ohh, Freedom! Ohh, Freedom!
>   Oh, Freedom over me!
>   And before I'll be a slave,
>   I'll be buried in my grave
>   And go home to my Lord and be free!
>   MRS. BLACK

The nineteen-fifties brought something else: In Montgom-

ery, Alabama, a woman named Rosa Parks got on a jim-
crow bus and sat down up front. The driver ordered her
to move to the rear and she said:

MISS BLACK

I moved yesterday, I'm too tired to move today!

MRS. BLACK

Tired. We're all tired.

MISS BLACK

Yes, tired. Tired of the aggravation and irritation.

MRS. BLACK

Tired of frustration and worriation.

MISS BLACK

Tired of being misused and abused.

MRS. BLACK

Tired of being used and confused.

TOGETHER

Tired. Tired! Tired!

JUNIOR

And all Montgomery walked. In the classic words of Martin Luther King, Junior, "We substituted tired feet for
tired souls."

MRS. BLACK

Freedom's fires burned throughout the South,
And the blaze spread northward,
Searing the urban centers.
The voice of Malcolm X roared from Harlem,
And black voices everywhere shouted at Pharaoh,
Telling him to let my people go now!
Insidious Pharaoh, venomous hate-spreader,
Created the backlash which is really a frontlash,
Created it and made black people beggars in the Ameri-
    can dream,
Insisting upon God-given rights, yet being told:
"Be good, you Negroes, or we won't give you
What we have no right to keep from you in the first
    place!"
God, said Pharaoh, is white
And white is right!
But, stubborn is the child of the African mother,
Challenging, continuing to fight!
Cries of freedom rang out from everywhere:

ALL

(*Singing*)

Good news! The chariot's coming!
Good news! The chariot's coming!
Good news! The chariot's coming!

MRS. BLACK

(*As the music carries under*)

The 1960s were the destroying years,
The death years, the violent years, the murderous years.
Assassination aborted the lives of
Patrice Lumumba, John Fitzgerald Kennedy, Malcolm X,
Martin Luther King, Medgar Evers, and Robert Kennedy.
Plunging them into the earth in a downpour of discontent.
The pollution of our soils spread to the sea and sky,
And God cried for humanity!
But, stubborn is the child of the African mother,
And onward he went, claiming his birthright,
His heritage, which Pharaoh had denied him.
And Pharaoh knew that in denying him his heritage
The child of the African mother would seek just that
And become involved in semantics about whether he is
    black,
Or Afro-American or Negro, or truly integrated
While Pharaoh had his foot upon his neck,
Stealing gold from South Africa,
And all the wealth of Africa and Asia,
Knowing always how to deal with latrine legalism
By uttering pious phrases—
And Pharaoh knew, too, he was a genius at creating family
    fights,
And he could get the American child of Africa to fight
    over petty things
While he stole from him the right to Harlem bought long
    ago
From the blood spilled in its streets!

Patient, indeed, are Pharaoh and his followers,
Ready to wait one hundred years to reassert his mastery,
Ready to offer New Deals and Fair Deals and New Fron-
    tiers and Great Societies,
Waiting, waiting for the day when he can send the bull-
    dozers

Into the Harlem he did not mean to lose at the beginning
   of the twentieth century,
Seeing the land for what it really is,
A choice location, a seat of black power that must be integrated
To keep black people subjected to the whims of their enemies!

Yet, Pharaoh, sly snake that he is,
Kept black people suddenly learning things about them-
   selves
And reveling in their newfound knowledge.
They learned that fifteen percent of America's cowboys
   had been black,
And they reveled in these stories untold by movies or tele-
   vision.
They told the story of Black Sam as though it had major
   significance
And all America loved it at a time when it had outlived
   what it meant to say:

JUNIOR
(*In center stage*)
Somehow or other folks are just catching up to the fact
that there was a Negro cowboy. If they'd bothered to look,
they'd know that fifteen percent of America's cowboys
were black men. The baddest cowboy in the Old West
was Black Sam. He was so bad that Webster had to look
at him twice before he put the word "bad" in the dictionary.

Well, this western town was quiet one Sunday morning.
You could smell the coffee brewing and the bacon frying,
and from every house you could hear the chatter of folks
as they put on their Sunday-go-to-meeting clothes for
church. Suddenly, on the top of the hill outside of town
there rode up this big black cowboy. He was riding a
bear. He rode that bear right into town and stirred up so
much dust that the town got quiet. The coffee stopped
brewing, the bacon stopped frying, and houses got quiet
because everybody and his brother got out of that town. It
was so deserted that tumbleweeds flew up and down that
town's street, crying about being so lonely.

This black cowboy rode that bear right up in front of the town saloon. He told the bear to "Whoa!" and he got off it, wrapped his big hands around the bear's neck, choked it, then flung it across the street. Then, he started into the saloon. He was so big he couldn't get into the door. He was seven feet tall and he weighed 475 pounds. He walked right on through the door, pulling off half the wall and half the ceiling. He brushed the dust from his shirt and he walked up to the bar. The bartender and the sheriff were the only two people who hadn't run out of town. Both stood there, trembling, 'cause they knew this was Black Sam, the baddest cowboy in the Old West. The black cowboy ordered a bottle of red-eye and he broke the top of the bottle and poured down the liquor. He ordered another and he broke the top of that bottle, too, and he poured the liquor down again. He wiped his mouth and the sheriff trembled and decided he'd better get on the good side of Black Sam. He looked up at the black cowboy and said:

"What about another bottle of red-eye on me?"

The black cowboy shook his head and wiped some more liquor from his mouth and said:

"No, thanks. I got to get out of town before Black Sam gets here!"

MRS. BLACK

All of this Pharaoh has denied us,
And we search for it and our identity
While he seeks untold wealth in undreamed-of forms.
We seek yet the story of Long Island and Brooklyn and
   the Bronx,
And Westchester,
And the heroic souls who built these communities.
We seek yet to plant our feet on this earth,
To discover it, when this earth no longer has a meaning,
For Pharaoh is reaching toward the stars!

MISS BLACK
(*Crying out*)

Pharaoh!
Who is he?

MRS. BLACK

The oppressor of black people, brown people and, yes,
white people!
Pharaoh, let my people go!

MISS BLACK

She's telling you, Pharaoh,
And I'm telling you, Pharaoh,
You'd better let us go!
Yes, old Pharaoh—
Let black Africa go!
Let the islands of the sea go!

JUNIOR

Pharaoh!
Let the children of Israel go!
Let there be brotherhood among the Arabs and Jews,
And let peace reign in Asia and everywhere!

MRS. BLACK

We're telling you, Pharaoh—
Free the Latins,
The Indians here and those over there!
Pharaoh, Pharaoh! Let all people go!

SENIOR

Let all people go!
Let there be peace on this earth,
And freedom to build a tomorrow of brotherhood
Where we can plant the crops of goodness
And reap its harvest.
And God can then look down from His heaven
And smile because the brethren dwell together!

MRS. BLACK

Yes! Let all people go! When? When?

ALL

Now. Now! Now!
   (*Music rises and they all sing.*)
   "Go down, Moses
   Way down in Egypt's lan',
   Tell ole Pharaoh
   To let my people go!
   Tell ole Pharaoh
   To let my people go!"
      (*This rises to a crescendo and the lights fade out.*)
               Curtain
               The End

A Land Beyond the River

a play in
three acts by
Loften
Mitchell

characters

(All members of the cast are Negroes unless otherwise designated.)

GLENN RAIGEN: A brownskinned boy of approximately nine or ten, tall for his age, thin but wiry, intelligent.

WILLIE LEE WATERS: A squat, chubby, dark-complexioned boy of about nine or ten, somewhat slow-moving.

LAURA TURNHAM: An attractive woman, approximately twenty-three, neat in appearance, somewhat naive and unsophisticated.

BEN ELLIS: A tall, thin, intelligent man in his early thirties, well-dressed, impatient, somewhat single-minded of purpose.

PHILIP TURNHAM: A gray-haired, humorless, fair-complexioned man between forty-five and fifty.

JOSEPH LAYNE: A tall, thin, bespectacled man with prematurely gray hair, not quite forty, homespun, stubborn.

DR. WILLIS: A stocky white man, over fifty, slow-moving, carelessly dressed, loud-voiced.

MARTHA LAYNE: A pleasant, soft-voiced woman between thirty-five and forty, of medium height and weight, composed but determined.

THE REVEREND MR. CLOUD: A short, thin, white man of about fifty, immaculately dressed, polished, volatile.

BILL RAIGEN: A tall husky, dark-complexioned man of about thirty-five, good-humored, but quick-tempered.

MARY RAIGEN: An attractive, quiet, sincere brownskinned woman of about thirty.

DUFF WATERS: A tall, heavy-set, brownskinned man of about forty, loud-voiced, opinionated.

J. C. LANGSTON: A short, thin man in his forties, pleasant, mischievous.

THE REVEREND MR. SHELL: A stocky man of medium height, somewhat stooped, more than sixty years of age.

RUBY WATERS: A loud-voiced, strong, aggressive woman, not quite forty.

MRS. SIMMS: An elderly, black woman, gray-haired, direct, who walks with a cane and uses it for emphasis.

Act One

The scene is a rural county in South Carolina. The time is an afternoon in March, the recent past.

The curtain rises upon what might be described as a cross section of a panoramic view of the entire country. At the extreme right, downstage, is the rear part of the Raigen home. There is a back porch and the backyard of this house extends toward the footlights. To the right of the house is a road. This road runs from behind the house, down toward the stage apron, center, then in a straight line toward a huge rock and tree at extreme left. This rock and tree may slide away and be replaced by a desk, chair, and part of Mr. Layne's study.

Downstage, center, just off the road, on the stage apron, is in turn a schoolroom or a church room. The benches and chairs used in these scenes are, in other scenes, a part of the Raigen backyard. In center stage, just off the road, there is another rock. Upstage, center, rear, elevated is a courthouse. A flag flies from its top.

Music rises, then carries under as the lights fade in on the road. Glenn Raigen and Willie Lee Waters, two boys of nine, enter from the extreme left. Willie Lee flops on the ground, throws head back on the rock, center, and declares:

WILLIE LEE
I ain't walking another step!

GLENN
Aw, come on!

WILLIE LEE
I ain't moving. My rear end's dragging in the dust.

GLENN
Be real trouble if we don't find Reverend Layne, Willie Lee.

WILLIE LEE

He ain't home, ain't in church, ain't in school. Ain't under my little fingernail. Where we gonna find him? I think we oughta go fishing.

GLENN

(*Sits, thinks about this . . . then*)

I think we oughta, too. Only thing is—like teacher said— can't have no more school till Rev gets the floor fixed.

WILLIE LEE

That's exactly why I say, let's go fishing. (*Glenn looks at him.*) Don't go looking at me like I'm no fool, Glenn Rai- gen. If we find Rev he's gonna be down the schoolhouse with our daddies, banging on that floor—and first news you know we be sitting up in school again.

GLENN

Reckon you right. (*Leans back lazily.*)

WILLIE LEE

So. Let's go fishing, boy.

GLENN

Yep! (*He starts to rise, reaches, grabs a weed and chews it. Stops as he remembers.*) My Pa always says he wishes he coulda gone to any kinda old school, 'cause he coulda been flying airplanes in the Navy instead of lifting boxes.

WILLIE LEE

That ain't no reason to pee tears, boy. Airplanes break down, you gotta get in one of them parachutes and if it don't open up—Wow!

GLENN

Sure right. (*Sits down.*) That sure is high up for me. Ain't never going no higher'n the second story of my house.

WILLIE LEE

(*Sprawls lazily enjoying the sun's rays as they pour down upon him. Glenn's words suddenly reach his ears. He leans forward.*)

You got rocks in your head?

GLENN

What are you talking about?

WILLIE LEE

What you talking about? I know what kinda house you live in, and it sure ain't got no two stories.

GLENN

Ain't talking about that house. Talking about the one I'm

gonna build when I grow up. (*Lapses into his favorite dream.*) Brick houses right along the road and pavement down here like instead of all this dust and sand. Gonna have a bathroom on every floor, too . . .

WILLIE LEE

(*Taps his shoulder.*) Hey, boy . . .

GLENN

Ain't gonna live in them houses myself. Gonna have a three-story house up yonder on the hill like Phil Turnham's got . . .

WILLIE LEE

Hey . . .

GLENN

Umm . . . umm!

WILLIE LEE

(*Shakes him.*) Wake up there! (*Then*) You better take a look in the mirror and stop listening to your Pa . . . (*He waves his hand, indicating the color of his skin. Glen jumps up.*)

GLENN

Come on! We gotta find Rev. Layne!

WILLIE LEE

(*Grabs Glenn's arm.*) Boy, you colored! Houses with two stories made outa brick, and living on hills! That's for white folks!

GLENN

Who told you that?

WILLIE LEE

Who told me? My Pa told me!

GLENN

Mr. Duff Waters said that?

WILLIE LEE

That's who I said said that.

GLENN

Ma was wrong when she told Pa not to call Mr. Duff simple.

WILLIE LEE

What you say?

GLENN

I said . . . sounds simple.

WILLIE LEE

Glenn, don't you go putting me in no dozens!

GLENN

Ain't playing no dozens. Anybody tell you something like
that don't know from nothing!

WILLIE LEE

(*Angrily*) You gonna take that back right now or I'm
gonna beat your little hiney!

GLENN

You and which army gonna beat me?

WILLIE LEE

(*Holding up fists*) Me and these armies! (*Puts up guard.*)
You gonna take that back—

GLENN

Nope.

> (*Willie Lee leaps at Glenn. They wrestle.*) (*Laura
> Turnham enters from right. Laura is an attractive,
> fair-complexioned Negro woman of twenty-three
> who speaks with just a trace of a drawl. She is a
> small woman who dresses neatly, but somehow the
> way she dresses spells out that she is a country girl.
> She does not know what to do with her hair, and
> one lock of it is constantly falling across her fore-
> head. She wears low-heeled shoes when high heels
> would set off her well-developed legs to advantage.
> She is a nervous person who gives the impression of
> being quite timid or shy. In a sense she belongs in a
> classroom, for there she can relate to children. In-
> deed, she gives the impression of being somewhat
> childlike when she mingles with adults. There are
> few people at whom she will look directly. Rather,
> she gives one a sideward glance through her large
> eyes.*)
> (*She sees the boys fighting and rushes toward
> them.*)

LAURA

Stop it! Stop it now! (*She pulls them apart.*)

GLENN

He started it, Miss Turnham!

WILLIE LEE

You liar! You started it!

LAURA

That's enough! I don't care who started it! I sent you out
looking for Mr. Layne! I did not send you out to fight!
Didn't we have a lesson this morning about fighting? (*An-*

noyed) You ought to be ashamed of yourselves! Now, shake hands and apologize. (*They hesitate.*) I said, shake hands. (*They do so, reluctantly.*) Say you're sorry.

WILLIE LEE

Sorry.

GLENN

I'm sorry too. About fighting you. I still think you're simple. (*This is too much for Willie Lee. He sails into Glenn and they go at it again.*)

LAURA

Stop! Stop! (*She struggles to pull them apart.*)

(*While this is going on, a car door is heard slamming. Ben Ellis appears from the left. Ben is in his thirties. He is tall, thin, bespectacled, neatly dressed. At the first glance it is apparent that he does not belong here. His clothes, his manner, and his speech spell big city. Yet, though he is not quite a part of the landscape, he is very much a part of it by virtue of his sincere and passionate interest in people. In spite of his poise and reserve, he could never be accused of intellectual checker-playing because of his singleness of interest and purpose.*)

(*Ben steps between the two boys as Laura manages to pull them apart.*)

BEN

Hey! Hey! Break it up! . . . Hi, Laura!

LAURA

(*As he holds boys apart*) Hello, Ben.

BEN

Now, come on, boys. Shake hands and be friends.

LAURA

(*Quickly*) No. I don't think they'd better shake hands again!

BEN

Oh, they'll be all right. Won't you, fellows? (*To Laura*) What'd you do, Laura? Give them too much homework?

LAURA

This is serious. We had trouble at school. I sent them looking for Mr. Layne . . .

BEN

I'm heading for his house. I'll run you folks over.

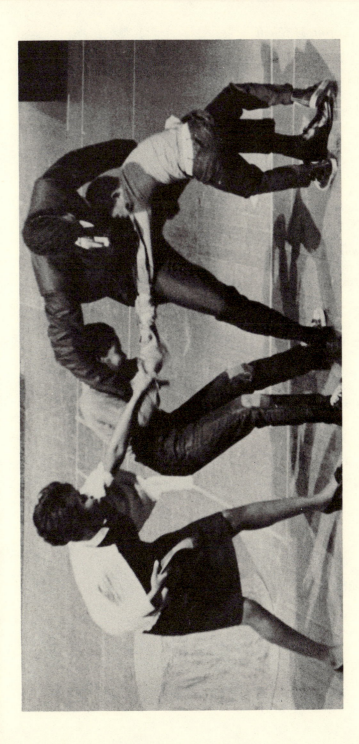

Ben and Laura breaking up a fight between Willie Lee and Glenn

GLENN

He ain't home.

WILLIE LEE

(*Corrects him with relish.*) Isn't!

LAURA

Boys, there's going to be real trouble for Mr. Layne if the School Board finds he wasn't around this afternoon.

WILLIE LEE

Board ain't gonna find out less'n somebody tells your Pa. (*Glenn motions to silence Willie Lee.*) What you making faces at me for?

BEN

(*Laura is momentarily stopped by this. Ben steps forward.*) You fellows wouldn't want to see the Reverend in trouble, would you?

GLENN

Oh, no, sir!

WILLIE LEE

Sure wouldn't!

BEN

Then, maybe you ought to do like Miss Turnham says.

GLENN

Yes, sir!

WILLIE LEE

Sure will!

BEN

(*Calls after them as they start out.*) Without taking time out to fight!

> (*The boys are gone. He looks after them smiling. Laura draws a deep breath, sits on the rock, steals a glance at Ben, then deliberately makes conversation as she sees him turn toward her.*)

LAURA

I . . . I think maybe Mr. Layne's going to have to decide whether he's a school principal, preacher, or agitator.

BEN

Around here he has to do all three to make a living. (*Going to her*) Hi, Laura (*As he tries to kiss her*)

LAURA

I don't think you ought to be kissing me out here on the road. In broad daylight.

BEN

I couldn't wait for the sun to go down!

LAURA

Besides, I'm mad at you! Three letters in three months! You should've heard what my father said!

BEN

I wasn't writing to him. I thought about you every day. I even missed arguing with you.

LAURA

Well, you were just argued out of kissing me pretty easily. (*Suddenly they are in each other's arms and they kiss. And a moment later she is apprehensive and he recognizes it, though she remains in his arms.*) My father wouldn't like this.

BEN

You mean kissing on the road? I guess he wouldn't.

LAURA

Not just that. Know what he said? "Run after your own kind, Laura Turnham. Somebody whose folks were something".

BEN

My father was something. When they chased him from around here for trying to start a union, his picture was in every sheriff's office within a hundred-mile radius. (*He laughs at this, but it becomes a bitter laugh. Laura senses this, glances at him, then looks away.*)

LAURA

Ben . . .

BEN

Yes?

LAURA

Know what some gossips tried to put out? (*He waits expectantly.*) They said if it hadn't been for Papa and me, you'd have stayed on here and fought the bus case, and the children would have school buses now.

BEN

That's nonsense.

LAURA

That's what they say.

BEN

You know better. I withdrew from that case because the School Board proved my client paid taxes in one district and sent his kid to school in another. On legal grounds, he couldn't sue for his kid. It was a bad test case! (*Then*) In a way, it was. In another way, it put this county on the map. For years guys in Harlem have been standing up on 125th Street and Seventh Avenue, bragging about being born and raised in New York City. After that test case, every Negro and his brother was bragging that his ancestors came from right down here in this county! (*He is laughing and so is Laura. Now, again, she becomes sober.*)

LAURA

I'm sorry. I fought you about suing for school buses, Ben. I think now . . . (*Stops, then*) Ben, my father feels it's a mistake to get folks riled up and going into court. And because he does, those people resent him—and me. They ought to forget that stuff and remember a school floor that caves in, and windows that won't open in the summer or close in the winter.

BEN

Please don't feel . . .

LAURA

I haven't finished, Mr. Ellis.

BEN

I beg your pardon.

LAURA

I was wrong, Ben. I wish you'd won that case.

BEN

I know. I know.

> (*Philip Turnham appears on the road. Laura freezes. Ben senses something is wrong, then sees Turnham. Impulsively, Ben lifts his hand to greet Turnham. Philip Turnham is a large, fair-complexioned Negro of about fifty. He is completely gray, with steely gray eyes. He is a humorless man and he seldom smiles. His lips are tightly pressed together, his jaw squared. Turnham is a well-dressed man with a deep sense of self-respect. He peers at Laura and Ben. When Ben lifts his hand to greet Turnham, Turnham does not respond. Ben finds himself hand in air, and he brings hand to forehead, scratches it.*)

TURNHAM

Laura . . . did I hear right? Your school was dismissed early today?

LAURA

Yes, Papa.

BEN

(*Offers hand.*) How do you do, Mr. Turnham. (*Turnham ignores him, turns, walks offstage. Laura calls after him.*)

LAURA

Papa! Papa!

BEN

Well! Your father still isn't speaking to me.

LAURA

I'm sorry, Ben.

BEN

It's all right. If I had a dollar for everyone who doesn't speak to me, I'd be a millionaire. (*Then*) Well, I guess the whole county'll know I'm back in another half hour. Come on . . . I want to catch Martha Layne at her school. We'll drop off at the barbecue shack later.

LAURA

All right. (*They start out. He reaches, takes her hand. He stops, draws a deep breath.*)

BEN

Ummm. What's that? (*He drops her hand.*)

LAURA

Honeysuckle. The wind from the swamp over there's blowing the smell clear across the whole country. In a minute it'll blow the dust and sand off this road right into your face. (*She shudders.*)

BEN

What's wrong?

LAURA

I was just thinking. Early moon's rising. When I was a little girl, I used to think it was a big something pulling evil things out of the swamp so the wind could send them to our house. (*The memory disturbs her. He takes her hand again, and they start out.*)

(*As they do, the Reverend Mr. Layne appears on the road, coming from beyond the Raigen home.*

The sun has slipped from sight by now. The crickets begin to sing, and we can hear a toad croaking from the creek. The stage darkens and the moon's rays pour onto the road.)

(*Joseph Layne is a tall, thin, bespectacled Negro of average height. He wears a brown hat cocked on the back of his head and a brown suit, white shirt, and brown tie. He is not an untidy person, but it is quite obvious that he has no time to waste standing before a mirror making certain he is carefully dressed. Probably the most important thing when he is dressing is for him to be certain his clothes are clean and that his pipe is in his breast pocket. Prematurely gray hair frames an otherwise youthful face. This face is at times pleasant and humorous, then it becomes quite sober and serious. He is a man who is never quite constant, moving easily, rapidly, from the homespun to the intellectual, from the slow-talking, slow-moving country preacher to the sharp, stubborn, dogmatic individual that he often is.*)

(*Mr. Layne is wiping perspiration from his forehead. We hear Glenn's voice offstage.*)

GLENN

Mr. Layne! Reverend Layne! (*He and Willie Lee appear.*)

LAYNE

You, boy! You calling me?

GLENN

Yes, sir. Been looking every which way for you!

LAYNE

It's Wednesday, son. My afternoon to go up in the hills and pray with Grandma Simms. (*Looks at Willie Lee.*) She's a mite too old to get down to church Sunday. Of course, there are folks no place near ninety who don't get to church, either.

WILLIE LEE

Pa wasn't feeling so good last Sunday, Reverend.

LAYNE

He's been sick a mess of Sundays, ain't he? (*Then*) What's on your mind, boys?

GLENN

School floor done caved in again.

LAYNE

School floor done caved in again! Well, I figured it was about time. Nothing's happened down there in two weeks.

GLENN

Can't have no more school till it's fixed.

LAYNE

We'll fix it tonight. (*Willie Lee groans.*) Won't be no vacation for you this time, boy. You boys get on home and tell your Daddies to meet me at the schoolhouse after supper . . . with their hammers and saws.

GLENN

Yes, sir! 'Bye now.

WILLIE LEE

'Bye.

LAYNE

'Bye, boys! (*The boys run off. He starts on down the road singing "Nobody Knows the Troubles I've Seen!" He stops, catches his breath.*) Lord, I'm not complaining, but it's mighty hard to be principal of a school, preacher, and general repairman. Fact is, if I wasn't a man of God, I'd say it's mighty damn hard! (*During the preceding scene the tree at extreme left has been moved away and in its place we find a section of the Layne home.*)

(*Dr. George Willis appears. He is a tall, stocky white man of about fifty, although he looks much older. He is slow-moving, stoop-shouldered, and carelessly dressed. He is a humorless man who speaks in a loud rasping voice. This voice can be heard any place and it makes people tremble for, ostensibly, he is a cantankerous old man. His thoughts are exacting, biting. Those who know him and like him realize that this is just his way and that he is a kind, considerate man. Still, they fear embarrassment when he opens his mouth, for he will bark at anyone. Those who dislike him have long ago decided the best way to get along with him is to ignore him. Dr. Willis is no social scientist. He has simply discovered through science that people are alike, and he does not have time to*

waste treating them as though they were different.)
(*Layne reacts at the sight of the doctor and starts
to move, hurriedly.*)

LAYNE

Doc! What's wrong? How's Martha? (*He has grabbed Willis, anxiously, trying to pull an answer from him, yet not
quite wanting to hear what the doctor might say.*)

WILLIS

(*Removing, Layne's hands*) Now, just a minute! Ain't a
thing wrong . . . except maybe you better stop running
your blood pressure up every time you see me . . . or
else I'm going to have two patients in your house.

LAYNE

Never mind all that, Doc. Is Martha all right?

WILLIS

Well enough to be walking back from town. I picked her
up and drove her on home. And she fixed me the best
meal I had since Mrs. Willis passed on.

LAYNE

Oh! . . . How are you, Doc? Come inside and get some
more coffee.

WILLIS

Nope. Wouldn't put another thing on top of that supper.
Besides, I got patients waiting. I'm still the only doctor in
this county . . . (*Stops*) Rev, I want to have a serious talk
with you.

LAYNE

Yeah?

WILLIS

Can you get Martha to slow down a little?

LAYNE

Doc, I'm a man of God, not God himself.

WILLIS

That's what I figured. That examination last week didn't
make me happy about her heart. She's a sick woman, Reverend.

LAYNE

I know.

WILLIS

She ought to give up teaching. And all this fuss you're
carrying on around here ain't helping her a bit . . .

LAYNE

You want me to give it up?

WILLIS

You know durn well I never said a word like that.

LAYNE

No. You didn't.

WILLIS

What you do in the schools is your business. Mine's to make folks well. And I think you'd both be helping my business if you got out of this county for a spell.

LAYNE

I'm not budging an inch.

WILLIS

Well, that's about the answer I expected to get. Don't reckon my heart could stand up under the shock of you acting any different. (*Starts out.*) I'm going on down here and treat some folks who *want* to live. 'Night, Rev . . .

LAYNE

'Night, Doc. (*Dr. Willis goes off around the Layne home. Layne goes inside the house as the lights come up there.*)

(*We see a desk at the rear, a map of the county above the desk, a briefcase on top of the desk. Martha Layne is sitting at the desk. She is an attractive Negro woman of thirty-five, who speaks in a soft gentle manner. There is nothing about her that gives one the impression that she is sick. She is of medium height and build, extremely neat, with a degree of patience and understanding that can be annoying. Hers is a compressed manner, but beneath this gentility is a strong, stubborn interior.*) (*Layne greets her, warmly, goes over to her, kisses her.*)

MARTHA

Well, you and Grandma Simms must've prayed enough to last for a couple of years.

LAYNE

We talked some, too. Poor old soul gets mighty lonely up there with all her kinfolks gone on. Reverend Shell was there today, too. How he gets up there so often at his age is beyond me. His legs are better than mine.

MARTHA

You do enjoy spending time with Grandma Simms, don't you?

LAYNE

Oh, yes, Martha! The past becomes alive up there! Why, just today she and Reverend Shell were singing a spiritual I'd never heard. . . . How was school today? That Jones boy learned how to spell yet?

MARTHA

Oh, he's making progress since his father stopped doing his homework for him.

LAYNE

Ummm . . . Martha, are you all right?

MARTHA

Why, I'm fine.

LAYNE

Doc Willis didn't think so.

MARTHA

Oh, George Willis wouldn't be well himself if he wasn't always arguing about somebody else's health.

LAYNE

I know somebody else like that.

MARTHA

Who?

LAYNE

You. (*Crosses to desk to fill pipe. Sees briefcase. Lifts it.*) What's this?

MARTHA

Looks like a briefcase.

LAYNE

Umm. Pretty.

MARTHA

Well, maybe it'll keep you from leaving your things all over the countryside.

LAYNE

For me? Thanks! (*Suddenly*) I forgot and left my school-books up at Grandma Simm's! (*Then*) Thanks, Martha. Thanks.

MARTHA

You're welcome. Happy anniversary! (*He stops short. Obviously, he has forgotten this day. He tries to lie, but he is not successful.*)

LAYNE

I . . . I didn't forget, Martha. I've got a present coming for you. Takes these mail-order houses ages to deliver things.

MARTHA

Hope it won't take them as long as it'll take you to learn to lie, Joe Layne.

LAYNE

I do have a present for you, Martha. (*She looks up at him, questioningly. He goes to her, kisses her. She is pleased.*)

MARTHA

Thanks. I'll get your dinner.

LAYNE

I had a bite with Grandma Simms. (*Unhappily*) You had to eat alone on a day like this.

MARTHA

Doc was here.

LAYNE

It's lonely for you here with me gone all the time.

MARTHA

I'm not complaining.

LAYNE

Maybe you should.

MARTHA

Why should I? Ben Ellis is back. He and Laura wanted me to eat with them at the barbecue shack.

LAYNE

But you said no. You were sure I'd be home tonight.

MARTHA

No, I was not sure of any such thing.

LAYNE

Martha, please don't be sharp.

MARTHA

I'm not.

LAYNE

Yes, you are!

MARTHA

What on earth are you yelling about?

LAYNE

You yelled at me!

MARTHA

I haven't raised my voice!

LAYNE

(*Blurts out*) Well, why don't you sometimes? (*She laughs at this. He, too, realizes he has been ridiculous and he grins.*) Pay me no mind. I'm just upset. Your health. Then, slipping up on the anniversary.

MARTHA

There are more important things to worry about.

LAYNE

Yes?

MARTHA

I don't have a list.

LAYNE

Good.

MARTHA

Joe . . . I thought about having some folks in for our anniversary, but Ben and Laura told me about the school floor, and I knew you'd be going down there tonight . . . (*She stops.*) Have you ever thought of expanding this fight beyond just buses? (*This is a touchy subject. He leans forward in his seat.*)

LAYNE

We need buses. Now, how many nights do you come in here, tired out from washing off the kids who walk through sand and mud to your class. (*Rises*) A school bus fight is big enough. Do you remember when we taught up in Santee River Houses, the way the little children came to school barefoot, muddy, sometimes feverish? Do you remember the flu epidemic that killed three of them? (*Points to map.*) Look at this map! Shell's school's here. Mine here. Yours here. Not a single house within two and a half miles of a single school! What kind of expanding are you talking about?

MARTHA

Joe, I've seen that map every day for the last year . . .

LAYNE

Then why ask questions like that?

MARTHA

It's getting so I can't ask a question without bothering you . . .

LAYNE

It's because of the way you ask.

MARTHA

I'm sorry. I didn't mean to get you all upset.

LAYNE

Martha, I am not upset!

MARTHA

Joe!

LAYNE

When we started this thing you were eager as a bird setter . . .

MARTHA

I didn't figure we'd settle on just one bird.

LAYNE

(*Thinks about this, then*) No. I'm going on, bit by bit. My bit is to get school buses. It's up to someone else to get other things.

MARTHA

That's just it. You're the someone else. I remember, too, a young Joe Layne on a college campus. Son of a country preacher. Big, strong, fearless, believing people in the country needed preachers and teachers, on fire to set the world right . . . setting me on fire . . .

LAYNE

You know some of our own people think even this bus fight is too much . . .

MARTHA

The young Joe Layne . . . that was a boy who was shouting, not whispering . . . one who was leading a fight, not dancing on the edges of one.

LAYNE

Yes, that's what he was. A boy. A boy who led ten Negroes in a picket line against a Jim Crow movie house. A boy who cried out in horror as the police tore into the line, swinging clubs and fists. The sight of the blood they spilled still sickens me. And when we went to jail, our wounds still bleeding, the others stared at me, not speaking, but their eyes judged me guilty. That's when I learned there's something wrong with a man who gets ahead of the people . . .

MARTHA

That was years ago, Joe. Those pages aren't on the calendar today.

CLOUD'S VOICE
(*As a car door is heard closing*) Joseph!

MARTHA
I'm sorry. I just don't feel well enough to take those two tonight. (*She goes out of the room. The Reverend Mr. Cloud appears with Philip Turnham. John Cloud is a short, thin, white man of about fifty. He is immaculately dressed, polished, volatile.*)

LAYNE
'Evening, Superintendent. 'Evening, Phil.

CLOUD
Layne, we want to talk to you.

TURNHAM
We sure do.

CLOUD
The School Board Chairman called me up. Your school was dismissed early today. I've told you a hundred times . . . if you want me on your side, stop pulling these idiotic stunts!

LAYNE
What stunts?

CLOUD
Look, don't play dumb with me! I've known you too long, Joseph Layne! (*Angrily*) You ought to know better than to close down school so you can run off agitating! How do you think you are still principal there? If any other white man in the county knew you were in back of this bus business, you wouldn't be allowed in the front door of a school, much less work in one!

LAYNE
Well, now . . .

CLOUD
Well, nothing! I've gone along with you because I'm an ordained minister myself! And I've done things to prove it, too . . .

TURNHAM
He sure has. We only had four months' schooling a year until Mr. Cloud got to be District Superintendant. Now we've got six.

CLOUD
One more crazy trick like today, Layne, and I'm getting off your side fast. I've got my own job to look out for . . .

TURNHAM

I've tried to tell you before, Reverend Layne. When you neglect your duties you make things hard for everybody . . .

LAYNE

Could I say a word now?

CLOUD

You need to say more than just one word.

LAYNE

School was dismissed early today because part of the floor caved in . . .

CLOUD

Again?

LAYNE

Again!

CLOUD

Why the devil didn't you say so?

LAYNE

I didn't get a chance. We can't have any more school till something's done about it.

CLOUD

The School Board'll deliberate two years over that. We've got it sweating over buses now. We can only fight one battle at a time . . .

LAYNE

This is no battle. The floor's rotten. We need a new one.

CLOUD

I know that. I know, too, that we've got to go slowly. But, the day will come when we'll lead the colored people forward. As ordained ministers and school workers, that's our Christian duty.

LAYNE

I believe you believe that.

TURNHAM

Reverend Layne, Laura told me one time you and some of the boys fixed the floor. Can't you do that again?

LAYNE

Maybe you'd like to try that at your school.

TURNHAM

Your wife can tell you: The children at my school don't wreck floors.

LAYNE

What are you trying to say?

TURNHAM

I'm saying, when you let children run wild, they'll wreck anything!

LAYNE

Are you blaming me because that shack's tumbling down? You better go learn something about running a school before you give me advice.

CLOUD

Joseph! That wasn't called for. You ought to apologize to Phil!

LAYNE

Apologize to him? In two seconds I'll put my religion in my pocket and curse him from the day he was born till the day he's going to die!

CLOUD

Why do people always have to fight each other?

LAYNE

I don't like that!

CLOUD

That's too bad! (*He and Layne face each other. Cloud lowers his voice, then*) You don't know what it is to be a Negro down here, Joseph.

LAYNE

I don't, huh?

TURNHAM

No, you don't! Your Daddy brought you up in a big parish house, away from us. You didn't have to go into the mills at fourteen and cut logs till your hands blistered! You don't know what it's like to do something you hate just so you can stay alive.

LAYNE

You mean, things like being extra helpful and getting a nickel more an hour?

TURNHAM

I worked for everything I ever got!

CLOUD

(*To Turnham*) Be quiet! (*To Layne*) You don't know what happens to colored people down here when they stand up there with the kind of look you've got on your face!

LAYNE

I know what happens all right. It happened to old Jim Brown. I remember the night they pulled him out of jail and flogged him to death. (*Looks straight at Cloud.*) I remember too—there was a white boy who could have kept him out of jail by testifying in court—

CLOUD

The boy's family wouldn't let him.

LAYNE

How do you know?

CLOUD

I know.

LAYNE

There were other floggings too—like a ten-year-old one Christmas Day, fired up over getting a bicycle, being taken by his preacher-father to house after house, giving out bundles—in houses with no floors—with just the good Lord's earth staring up at you, and little colored kids eating off it, while the wind ripped through the boards of the shacks. I stopped worrying about a bicycle then. I made myself a promise—a little child's promise—(*Turns to them.*) No. No, I don't know much about being a Negro around here.

CLOUD

You know I didn't mean it like that. I've made promises too, Joseph. To myself and to my God. (*He turns, starts out.*)

TURNHAM

Mr. Cloud—you forgot to tell him about that lawyer man being in town.

CLOUD

Yes, Joseph, I don't think we'd have had as much trouble with that bus case if we'd used a lawyer from home here.

LAYNE

When a person's drowning, it's a mighty good idea for the fellow who's throwing the lifeline to be standing on the shore. You and I can't go into court and fight these cases—

CLOUD

No. But we'll have to keep our eyes on that fellow. Another thing, Joseph, isn't it just as easy for you to call me "Mr. Cloud" instead of "Superintendent."

LAYNE

I hadn't thought about it.

CLOUD

Some folks think you do that just to keep from calling me "Mister."

LAYNE

(*Looking at Turnham*) Do they think that?

CLOUD

Lots of people are thinking lots of things about you. That's why I'm saying—be careful!

LAYNE

Good night, Superintendent.

TURNHAM

Good night, Layne.

LAYNE

Turnham! Be careful you don't butt your head going out that door. Oh, but I guess you're bent over enough not to— (*Turnham glares at Layne, then follows Cloud out. A car door is heard slamming. The motor starts, then dies away in the distance. Layne stands, looking after them. He turns, angrily, toward the map on the wall. Martha appears in the doorway.*)

MARTHA

Seems like those two think the whispering is too loud as it is. (*Quietly*) There is a whispering, Joe—a stirring, like the leaves being torn by the wind when a storm's coming up. Joe, somebody's got to listen to it . . . (*The lights fade out on them.*)

(*The lights now come up on the Raigen home. William Raigen, a tall, husky, dark-complexioned Negro man of thirty-five, comes through the doorway. He is powerfully built, hard-working, good-humored, but quick-tempered. He is dressed in an open collar shirt and a pair of dungarees. He steps out on the porch, speaks over his shoulder to his wife, who is inside the house.*)

BILL

Forget them dishes, Mary, and come on out here and get some fresh air.

MARY'S VOICE

In a second. (*Bill leans over the railing, looks out toward the audience.*)

(*Mary comes from the kitchen, stands beside him. She is thirty-one, appears to be considerably younger. She is strikingly attractive, quiet, likable. There is about her a dreamy-eyed contentment.*) (*Mary goes to her husband, takes his arm, as he points.*)

BILL

Purty as a picture, ain't it? Purtiest land in the world. All yourn and mine.

MARY

(*Rests head on his shoulder. Glenn slips out of the house, unseen by them.*) Yep.

BILL

(*Still looking at the land*) 'Course that rock yonder's got to be moved so she'll slope off right and be level from the brook clear on out to the road. And if the corn comes high this year, gonna have a purty picture with it levelin' off against the trees back yonder. Don't you think so?

MARY

Yep.

GLENN

That all you got say, Mom? Yep?

MARY

(*Sees him.*) Boy, you better get to bed!

BILL

Sure had! But, he's telling the truth—

MARY

William, I done said the land was purty every night this month!

BILL

It's more'n purty! Dreaming about all this is what made them ammunition boxes I had to lift in the Navy seem light as feathers. Payday used to come around and the other boys would run off and get drunk. Not me! Saved my money, Mary—'cause I knowed I wasn't gonna be a sharecropper all my life. Knowed someday I was gonna own my own land and—there it is! Just name one of our folks got land like this—'cepting Reverend Layne.

MARY

And Phil Turnham—

BILL

Aw, he ain't one of our folks! Besides, that no-good, hincty something didn't do a dad-blamed thing to get that land— 'cept be borned into the right family!

GLENN

Pa, why you so down on Mr. Turnham? Ain't he colored, too?

BILL

Son, he's colored all right, but sometimes he don't know it. (*Looks at Mary. She laughs.*) What I mean is, well, this is gonna go off into deep points. (*To Mary*) I don't see nothing funny.

MARY

You always said we got to tell the child the truth—

BILL

Didn't I just tell him the truth?

MARY

Part of it.

BILL

Well, son—used to be a slave owner named Turnham. He had hisself some kids by a slave woman—

MARY

William, that's too much—

BILL

It's the truth, Mary! Phil Turnham's family did come from that! They got that big house handed down to 'em from the old slave master. Only, none of 'em ever kept it up, 'cause they was so busy bragging about being half-white. When our folks get to thinking like that, they in trouble. Well, they let the land and the house get all run-down, and Phil wound up having to go into the sawmill to eat regular. Like to killed him, too, till he found out he could make money by bowing and scraping. That's how come he don't know he's colored sometimes.

GLENN

Does that mean I can't marry Laura Turnham if I wants to?

BILL

Boy, you can't even pee straight, and you talkin' about marrying.

MARY

William!

GLENN

I'm growing up fast, Pa! Look! I'm growing a moustache! Look!

BILL

Boy, that ain't nothing but an evening shadow! Now—getting on past your bedtime. You got school in the morning.

GLENN

No sir. Not less'n—

MARY

(*Quickly*) Glenn!

BILL

Not less'n what!

GLENN

Oh, that's right. I promised Mom I'd let her tell you about it! She didn't want you getting riled up whilst you was eating.

BILL

What you talking about, boy?

LAYNE

(*Appears on road, calls to them.*) Evening, folks. Enjoying the night air?

BILL

Hey, Rev! What are you doing out?

LAYNE

Didn't Glenn tell you?

GLENN

(*Getting out of there*) Think I'd better get to bed. 'Night everybody! (*He kisses his mother, quickly, turns and runs into the house. Bill turns to Mary.*)

BILL

What's going on around here?

MARY

Tell you in a minute. Reverend, come on up and lemme get you some of that dandelion wine.

LAYNE

Ummm. No, better not, thanks. Some of the folks we'll be working with may not realize the Good Master Himself offered wine at his Last Supper. Got a little job tonight, Bill.

BILL

What you talking about, Rev? (*Layne produces his hammer. Bill realizes what this means, becomes annoyed.*) I knowed it! I knowed things was going too good!

LAYNE

We'll try to get in early this time—

MARY

Tell you what—I'll get Martha and the girls and we'll bring you down a little snack.

BILL

Well, don't bring nothing for me.

MARY

Much as you like to eat?

BILL

Oh! I'll be eating some. But it won't be down there. 'Cause I ain't going.

MARY

William—

BILL

Be danged if I am! I work hard each and every day the Good Lord sends—and when I get through, I don't feel like nailing up boards on no shack!

MARY

William, it won't be the first time.

BILL

No, but I done put in my last time! It's that School Board's job to fix up the place! Let 'em try it for a while and maybe they'll give us a new schoolhouse!

MARY

All right, but meantime, Glenn ain't gonna have no school to go to whilst we waiting on the School Board to move!

BILL

Mary, I'm tired of being a mule! First it was the chimney, then the windows, then the roof! Now it's—I don't know what! They oughta burn down the whole shebang and build a new one!

MARY

Please stop shouting!

BILL

It's time for some shouting! When it comes time for taxes, the man comes looking smack in my face. And he takes my money. And he don't put it in no back drawer, either. He integrates it.

MARY

Reverend Layne, you got to excuse William. He just ain't feeling good tonight.

BILL

I do feel good! I was feeling fine—till just now! (*Looks out on land, angrily.*) The dad-blamed land's done got so it ain't purty!

MARY

What's wrong with it now?

BILL

It's in the wrong part of the country! (*Then*) Rev, ain't no sense in waiting on me, I ain't going.

LAYNE

Can't say I blame you much, Bill. This repair work certainly isn't the answer.

BILL

You ain't acting like it.

LAYNE

I'm not?

BILL

No, you ain't.

LAYNE

Sister, I believe I will have a little of that wine.
(*He sits. Mary looks at Bill then goes into the house. Bill turns to Layne.*)

BILL

Rev, you going at this thing ass backwards! You got to get in there and pitch and let folks know you're leading them!

LAYNE

What do you think I'm trying to do, Bill?

BILL

To tell the truth—nothing! (*Layne is silent. Mary comes out of the house, gives him the wine. He takes it, hands trembling.*)

LAYNE

Thank you. What is it you want, Bill?

BILL

I want a new school! (*Then*) Listen, Rev—during the war I was with the Amphibs, delivering supplies to a bunch of Marines on a beachhead. When we got there, weren't no Marines around. They was all shot up. We had to do a heap of shooting ourselves—I'll never forget that. Delivering supplies to Marines who weren't even there. Like putting our kids on buses to get to schoolhouses that ain't even there.

LAYNE

Ummm. Why didn't you bring all this up before?

BILL

I just got to remembering it.

LAYNE

Seems like now that I've started up one thing, everybody and his brother wishes I'd started something else. Big thing on my mind was getting kids to school where I could teach them.

BILL

Big thing on our minds when we got to that island was dumping supplies—

MARY

William . . .

LAYNE

You've got a point, Bill. I'll have to think about it . . . Had a lot of meetings. Wish you'd come and spoke up then.

BILL

I work hard. I been busy.

LAYNE

Everybody's busy! Lord knows, buses and even new schools are just a little bit of what's needed. But—for right now—I can tell you this: We can have six brick schoolhouses and still have illiterate children if they can't get to the schools! (*He starts to drink the wine, changes his mind, gives glass to Mary.*) Thanks for the wine, Sister, I've got to be going. . .

MARY

Reverend Layne, wait . . . (*Layne stops.*) I think you'd better go along, William.

BILL

I will not!

MARY

You got to!

BILL

Why've I got to? Just give me one good reason why!

MARY

Glenn! (*Bill is not prepared for this.*) He ain't gonna have no school to go to less'n you do. And I don't want my child missing one single solitary day of school, you hear me? 'Cause it's real easy to miss one day, then another, and another! I ain't having him growing up, not knowing nothing, and having to work like a mule! I ain't having him going in no Navy and being laughed at 'cause he can't read and write good! I ain't having him abused every single hour of the day 'cause he's ignorant! He's got to learn he's just as good as everybody else, and I want him to learn it good!

(*She is near tears. She turns, runs into the house. Bill stands there. His shoulders sag. Layne looks at him, then turns to go on. Bill calls.*)

BILL

Oh, wait a minute. Wait'll I get my dad-blamed hammer!

(*He goes inside the house as the lights fade.*)

(*Music rises through the darkness, then carries under.*)

(*Now we hear hammers banging against a floor and a group of male voices singing.*)

THE MEN

I'm going to tell God all my troubles when I get home.
I'm going to tell God all my troubles when I get home.
I'm going to fall down on my knees and pray
'Cause I wanta meet Him on the Judgment Day.
I'm going to tell God all my troubles when I get home.

I'm going to tell God how you been a-treating me
when I get home.
I'm going to tell God how you been a-treating me
when I get home.
I'm going to set down beside my mother—
Yes, I'm going to tell it to my sister and brother—
I'm going to tell 'em about my troubles when I get home.

(*The lights come up on the apron of the stage. The Reverend Mr. Shell, Layne, Bill, Duff Waters and J. C. Langston are on their knees, pounding on the floor and singing. Shell is a man of medium height, heavily built, stopped from the weight of more than sixty years. Duff Waters is forty-five, tall, heavy-set, loud-voiced. J. C. is forty, small, thin, and pleasant.*)

(*The song ends and the men continue hammering and humming. Suddenly, Bill brings his hammer*) *down and the wood splits. He slams down his hammer, springs to his feet.*)

BILL

I'm sick of this! Plain sick!

DUFF

What's ailing you, boy?

BILL

We getting no place. Fast as you hits over yonder, the wood flies up in my face.

J. C.

So you get even. You nail your'n down and it'll fly up in his face.

BILL

That ain't no joke, J. C. This floor's rotten! Some of the wood they built it musta been on Noah's ark!

J. C.

If you ask me, the Lord wouldn't let Noah use this wood for his ark! 'Scuse me, Reverend Layne. 'Scuse me, Reverend Shell—but if I had this wood around my outhouse it wouldn't keep a smell inside!

DUFF

Negro, you sure talk simple! You expect wood to do things God Himself can't do.

SHELL

Boys, the name of the Lord, thy God—

LAYNE

I think we oughta work more and talk less.

SHELL

I'm thinking we need some new wood down here, Joe.

(*Duff turns over, flops on the floor in a sitting position. J. C. yells.*)

J. C.

Watch out 'fore you go through the floor!

DUFF

Man, I ain't that heavy!

J. C.

Damn it, I nailed up that part, and I ain't nailing it up no more tonight. It fall down again and you got to point your big behind at the ceiling and nail it up this time!

DUFF

You just forget the size of my behind.

J. C.

Who the hell can when it sticks out all over you?

DUFF

Looks better 'n your face, else I'd be shamed to stand up!

SHELL

Boys, please! Show some respect!

DUFF

Too tired to be showing anything, Reverend Shell. (*Leans back.*) Man, I can see me getting to work in the morning. Old Boss Man gonna say: "Duff, you looks bad. Been drinking corn last night, ain't you?" I'm gonna say: "Wish I was, Boss Man, sir, 'cause then I'd have a headache instead of a backache."

J. C.

They tells me you got to have something in your head for it to ache.

DUFF

You shut up, J. C. (*Then*) Come to think of it, I better tell Old Boss Man I was drinking, 'cause if he ever hears who I was working with, it'll be my job for sure.

SHELL

Meaning Layne and me?

DUFF

Ain't calling no names or signifying, Reverend Shell, but all I know is—when I asked for a bank loan last year to fix up my house, the man told me I wasn't getting a Am-I-born-to-die 'cause I belongs to Reverend Layne's church.

J. C.

Ain't no danger of that happening this year 'cause you ain't been to church in so long you'd walk up and knock on the door to get in.

LAYNE

Why didn't you tell us about this before, Duff?

J. C.

Yea, you coulda borrowed off Rev like everybody else did.

DUFF

Them white folks be down on me for sure for borrowing off him. He and Reverend Shell ain't worshiped by white folks in these parts—

SHELL

That's the best compliment I've ever been paid.

DUFF

Ain't no compliment. Folks can get real nasty around here. You and Reverend Layne don't hafta count on white folks for your daily bread. You-all done burnt the mortgages on your churches.

BILL

All right, boys! What we gonna do?

DUFF

Rest up some.

BILL

I mean, we got to do more 'n we doing.

J. C.

Yeah. Let's get started or the roosters'll be crowing 'fore we finish up this floor.

BILL

Sometimes you gets mighty funny when there ain't no joke, J. C.

J. C.

We the joke, arguing when we oughta be working together.

LAYNE

All right, all right. Let's get back to work.

(*He starts singing, bangs his hammer to the floor, then notices that no one is singing with him. Duff hits his finger with the hammer, stops, sticks his finger in his mouth. The men all stop working at the same time.*)

SHELL

It's no use—

LAYNE

Rotten through and through.

J. C.

What we gonna do?

LAYNE

We've got to fix this floor tonight.

BILL

Why?

LAYNE

Why? Because these children can't be missing one single day of school—that's why.

BILL

Rev, this floor's rotten. Unless we get some new wood

down here, somebody's gonna get hurt sure.

J. C.

Where you gonna get the lumber? School Board sure ain't gonna buy none.

DUFF

There's a whole heap of trees outside.

BILL

You being smart?

LAYNE

Let's try it! At least there'd be something solid down here for tomorrow, and comes Saturday we can put down some real lumber.

BILL

You got to be fooling, Reverend.

LAYNE

I'm not! Get your saws and an axe and come on! (*The men look at one another.*) Come on, I said! (*The men pick up their saws, look at them, then at one another.*)

BILL

Talk sense, Reverend! Only thing that'll get them trees down is a electric saw.

SHELL

Anybody know where we can get one?

DUFF

And where we gonna get the electricity after we gets the saw?

J. C.

Yeah. (*They are silent.*) What you gonna do, Reverend Layne?

LAYNE

I don't know. I don't know. (*One by one the men flop on benches or on the floor.*) Guess that wasn't such a good idea.

BILL

What kinda fools are we anyway? Talking about going out there in the night to cut down trees? Don't we pay our taxes for our kids to go to—

LAYNE

Bill, please! Just let me think a minute!

DUFF

Oh, no! Don't do no more thinking if you gonna come up with another idea like that!

LAYNE

You got any better ones? (*He is sharp, and, almost instantly he is sorry for his words. He turns away. Shell goes to him, puts his hand on his shoulder. Bill stands looking at this. J.C. goes to Duff.*)

J. C.

You oughta be shamed of yourself, Duff Waters!

DUFF

Didn't mean no harm, Reverend. Honest—

J. C.

You did so!

DUFF

Don't tell me what I meant!

J. C.

You just trying to get outa doing any more work around here. Work is your father's name and you don't believe in hitting him a lick!

DUFF

You a dirty liar!

J. C.

I don't wanta tell you who learn't me to lie!

DUFF

I don't play that stuff!

J. C.

Pat your foot while I play it! (*Angrily*) Pick on me, you big ox! Betcha I'll take you down a buttonhole lower! (*Duff grabs J. C. by the collar, lifts him into the air. Bill rushes between them, pulls them apart.*)

BILL

Oh, shut up, both of you!

DUFF

(*To Bill*) Who you shoving?

BILL

You, damn it!

SHELL

Boys, for heaven's sake!

J. C.

(*Steps between Bill and Duff.*) Yeah. Break it up! (*As he steps between them, J. C. steps on Duff's foot. Duff lets out a yell, grabs his foot.*)

DUFF

You stepped on my toe, you little son-of-a—

(Before Duff can finish, J. C. has rushed into him and hit him. They clench and Duff wrestles J. C. to the floor. Bill stands off at one side and begins to laugh at them. Shell and Layne rush to try to pull Duff off J. C.)

LAYNE

Bill! Bill! *(Bill feigns ignorance.)*

(While Layne is talking, Duff continues working on J. C. Bill finally pulls Duff off J. C. As Bill does, Duff strikes him accidentally. Bill loses his temper, strikes Duff back. Shell and Layne are busy trying to break up this free-for-all.)

RUBY'S VOICE

Y'all in there? *(Layne has grabbed Bill by now and Shell is holding J. C. Duff turns on J. C. and declares:)*

DUFF

You started this, you—*(And Duff draws back, swings at J. C. J. C. ducks and Duff strikes Shell. Shell loses his temper, yells.)*

SHELL

You damn fool! *(He raises his hand to strike back, then he remembers his religion.)* Lord, forgive me!

(Duff is shocked over hearing the old preacher curse. He stands there with both hands in the air. J. C. seizes the opportunity. He springs into Duff, strikes him in the belly. Duff doesn't budge. Now, Duff throws a wild haymaker. J. C. ducks again. The momentum of Duff's swing carries him to the floor. He lands on both knees with his buttocks in the air. The fall stuns him. J. C. stands, looking at Duff's buttocks as they protrude. J. C. is tempted. He pats Duff's rear end, then stands back, readying himself. He rushes forward, foot raised, as he prepares to kick Duff. At this very moment, Ruby Waters, Martha, and Mary appear with a basket of food. Ruby is a loud-voiced woman of about forty, quite positive, quite aggressive. She stops short as she sees Duff on the floor.)

RUBY

Lord!

MARTHA

What's going on here? (*The men remain frozen and embarrassed. They do not answer.*)

MARY

William, you been fighting again?

BILL

Aw, Mary, why you got to ask me somethin' like that?

MARY

Well, what's Duff doing like that?

BILL

Like what?

MARY

On his knees.

BILL

Oh! (*He turns, looks at Duff as though he has just discovered him on his knees. He turns back to Mary.*) Why don't you ask Duff?

J. C.

I think he's trying to show Reverend Layne and Reverend Shell a new way to kneel down and say their prayers. Yeah—that's all he was doing.

DUFF

(*Rising*) Yeah, and I'm gonna show you a new way, too—first chance I get!

RUBY

We been rushing to fix y'all some food and here y'all down here praying or playing.

SHELL

We sure ain't been playing. I can guarantee that.

RUBY

(*As Martha and Mary begin to place food on benches*) Well, just stop working or what-in-ever y'all been doing and come on and eat something.

MARTHA

Doesn't look to me like this floor's close to being fixed.

LAYNE

No. Whole thing's rotten.

(*There is a deep silence as his words register. The women spread a cloth over the bench, then place sandwiches, wrapped in wax paper, on the top of*

*the bench, along with a thermos bottle of coffee.
Not a word is spoken. The men and women sit
around the bench. Slowly, Duff reaches for a
sandwich. As he picks it up, he hurts his finger
again—the same finger he injured during the repair
work. He makes a soft sound—unusually soft for
Duff. Mary trembles a bit from the cold. Bill takes
his jacket, puts it around her.)*

MARY

It's cold in here.

BILL

Here.

MARTHA

Drink some coffee. Warm you up some. (*She gives Mary
coffee. Mary lifts it, then looks at a despondent Layne.*)

MARY

You—want to bless the table, Reverend?

LAYNE

Yes. (*Slowly*) (*They bow their heads.*) Almighty God,
Maker of all things, we humbly thank Thee for—(*He stops
then.*) for—(*His eyes wander to the school floor, up to
the walls of the building, and to the faces of the people*)
for—(*He is unable to finish. He sinks his face into his
palms.*)

MARTHA

Joe—(*She too is unable to speak. The others simply sit
there, looking. Layne cries out.*)

LAYNE

Jesus, God! It's wrong—wrong!

SHELL

Layne—

LAYNE

It is wrong, I tell you—to have you here at this hour of the
night, away from your kids, freezing in this shack—working on floors that aren't floors. Spilling your blood over
them for nothing! God knows it's a sin!

SHELL

Joe, please . . .

BILL

He's right. It is a sin and a shame, Reverend Shell. I'm
saying we oughta burn down the whole shebang!

J. C.

Sure right! That's one way of getting a new schoolhouse!

DUFF

I'll sure give you a match!

LAYNE

And I'll strike it!

SHELL

Now, just a minute! You know better than this, Joe! Getting these folks all riled up like this. Getting them ready to start rioting. What's gotten into you, man?

BILL

(*To Shell*) Well, we better do something, else I'm gonna be right down here banging on this floor till I get your age!

MARY

Stop all this hollering and yelling. All I want is for my child to get some learning. Do you folks have to yell and fight for that?

LAYNE

Yes! Yes, they do—for I will not have you down here another night like this! May I go to my grave this moment if I do!

BILL

Well, you better start going, 'cause this is where we gonna be every night unless we get a new schoolhouse.

LAYNE

We will not, I tell you!

MARTHA

Then we've got to do more! This bus fight isn't big enough. We've got to haul these folks into court and make them give us decent schools! The state laws say separate but equal schools shall be provided for both races.

RUBY

Now, Martha, how you gonna be separate and equal at the same time?

MARTHA

I don't know that. But I know the state law.

RUBY

This school is separate, all right, but it sure ain't equal.

BILL

Dad-blame it, I pay my taxes to keep that law in business. We oughta sue 'em to make it work!

SHELL

Now, you're using your head!

J. C.

Man, you a suing fool. (*Suddenly*) We gonna catch these white folks with their pants down! Ain't a thing they can do to us for suing them to make *their* laws work!

LAYNE

They'll do something, all right—but can it be any worse than sticking us out here in this shack all night?

SHELL

Sure can't!

BILL

Let's start suing! Get hold of that lawyer man! (*Sees Duff packing tools.*) What you say, Duff?

DUFF

My name is Fess. I ain't in this mess.

LAYNE

What does that mean?

DUFF

It means, I got to live out yonder with them white folks, and I aims to live!

RUBY

What you doing?

DUFF

Getting ready to get on home and let these colored folks go on fighting like they doing.

RUBY

You mean—you walking out?

DUFF

Fast as I can walk! You heard them talking about suing to be equal with white folks? And these colored folks here been fighting even 'fore they get to suing. If they acting like that now, I know good and well soon as old white man says "Boo" to 'em they gonna start backing up! And I ain't gonna have my toes around for them to back up on!

RUBY

You just better sit down over there and quit hollering.

DUFF

Get ready if you going home with me.

RUBY

I ain't going home with you. (*He looks at her.*) You heard what I said!

DUFF

Woman, you gone crazy?

RUBY

No, sir, I ain't. You walk outa here now, and I ain't putting myself in your bed no more!

DUFF

Ruby, get some sense!

RUBY

I got some! That's why I ain't letting Willie Lee go to no shack if I can do something about it. So, I don't care how much fighting these folks doing, 'long as they fighting. If you wanta stay married to me, you just sit over there and be quiet! (*Duff starts to move away. She stops him with her voice.*) Man, you heard me talk to you!

(*Duff turns, suddenly. He is beaten and he knows it. The others laugh. Duff sits.*)

RUBY

(*Continues*) Reverend, y'all was talking. 'Scuse me for butting in. Y'll talk on.

LAYNE

All right! If this is the kind of fight you want, let's face this: It won't be just one or two of us suing. We're going to have to get a whole heap of names on some kind of a petition, authorizing Ben Ellis and his organization to represent us in court.

RUBY

Then, we'll get them!

SHELL

For the bus case, we only needed one.

LAYNE

This is different. If it's only one or two, somebody might move away or withdraw—

DUFF

Or get killed.

LAYNE

Or get killed.

RUBY

Oh, look. Ain't no sense in going into a whole lot of Who-Struck-John and Why! Start up that petition, or what-in-ever you call it!

BILL

Yeah!

RUBY

Ain't nobody here looking for no picnic!

J. C.

We can take all the hell they wanta give us!

RUBY

A body can die but once, and it might as well be for something like this! (*She nudges Duff.*)

DUFF

I ain't said a word against it.

LAYNE

(*Looks up.*) "Out of darkness have I cried unto Thee, O Lord! Lord, hear my prayer." If any soul has to die in this, let it be me! Let it be me!

MARTHA

It won't be just you, Joe. It'll be all of us! Now is the time! Now is the time to shout in righteous indignation!

BILL

Every last one of us.

RUBY

You tell'em! We gonna shout till they lets us go free, or we gonna drive 'em deef!

> (*Shell has begun to hum "Oh, Freedom!" The others pick it up*)

SHELL

"Oh, Freedom! Oh, Freedom!"

THE OTHERS

"Oh, Freedom over me!
And before I'll be a slave,
I'll be buried in my grave,
And go home to my Lord and be free!"

> (*They are singing courageously. They continue to sing as they get their things and start for home.*)

Curtain

Act Two

When the curtain rises, the stage is in darkness. The lights come up on the Reverend Mr. Layne's study. The time is two months later. Evening.

Before the lights fade in, we hear the persistent ringing of the telephone. Layne appears, a piece of bread in his hand. He lifts receiver.

LAYNE

(*In telephone*) Hello? . . . Hello? (*Then*) Well, just call all you want to! Only you're wasting your time, for I sure ain't frightened! (*He hangs up.*)

MARTHA'S VOICE

Who was that?

LAYNE

Same people.

WILLIS'S VOICE

Take the receiver off the damn hook! You'll never finish your supper if you don't!

> (*Layne goes to telephone to lift receiver. Telephone rings again. He lifts receiver.*)

LAYNE

Now look . . . (*Stops*) Oh, Bishop Jones! I thought you were . . . (*Listens*) No, I don't want to be transferred to Lake City. Why should I? (*Firmly*) Bishop, you can order me if you want to! I'm not leaving here until God tells me to leave!

> (*He hangs up, then sits, silently. He is about to reach to remove the receiver when, from offstage, we hear a car motor, wild screams, and jeers. The sound of gunfire pierces the air. He springs to his feet. Martha rushes into the room, hurries into his arms. Willis follows her into room, followed by Mrs. Simms.*)

(*Mrs. Simms is an elderly woman who walks with a cane. In spite of this she is surprisingly agile. She is a stubborn blunt woman who has never known anything but directness. Her hair is completely white and frames a lined, strong black face. She has a habit of banging her cane for emphasis, and just now she is bringing it down with full force as she enters.*)

MARTHA

Some men in a car just shot at the house!

LAYNE

Easy now, honey!

WILLIS

Nothing to get excited over, Martha . . .

MRS. SIMMS

Doc Willis I spilled my dessert all over the table.

WILLIS

Probably just a few wild kids.

MRS. SIMMS

I'd sure like to raise a couple of them! Lord, it seemed like it was so good to get invited down here for dinner, out of them hills where it's so quiet you can hear the ants crawling on the cotton.

(*The sound of a car motor is heard. They all stop, holding their breaths. The car moves on into the distance.*)

MARTHA

It's enough to scare a dead man silly. Phone calls, threatening letters, now this . . .

MRS. SIMMS

Y'all gonna have to do like we used to do: sleep with your britch-loader under your pillow.

LAYNE

Please, Grandma Simms!

WILLIS

Oh, it's nothing to get all worried about. Probably just a few ignorant folks. They got to learn.

MRS. SIMMS

When they gonna start?

WILLIS

Some start young. Some later. Me? I was lucky. (*He sits back in his chair now.*) When I first started practicing

around here, I didn't like being around colored folks a bit.
Well, one night old Sam Smith got sick up yonder in the
hills. Well, no matter what I thought of folks, I couldn't
let 'em die. So I drove all the way up in the hills and doc-
tored on old Sam. Wild storm come up and blowed trees
all over the road. Was no way of getting out of there
till morning. Sam told me I'd better stay all night. He
didn't have but one bed, though, and I sure wasn't going
to sleep with no colored man! I tried sitting up in a chair
all night, but the wind came howling through the boards,
the fire went out, and pretty soon I got cold! Long about
three A.M. I crawled on in that bed beside old Sam and
covered up, nice and warm. Next morning I woke up the
same man. Hadn't been tarnished a bit! I always figured,
though, that if I'd started off knowing something about
colored folks, I'd have gotten me a full night's sleep up
at old Sam's.

(*The noise of a car motor is heard. Layne starts out.*)
LAYNE
The only trouble is, Doc . . . most folks never get up to
old Sam's . . .

WILLIS
(*To Layne, who has gone offstage.*) Stop worrying, I tell
you! These new fangled psychology books say that folks
who make threats are just letting off steam and they won't
hurt you a bit. (*Car motor is heard again. The brakes
screech. Wild screams. Willis turns to the window. A shot
pierces the air and we hear the shattering of glass. Willis
ducks to the floor.*) The psychology books told a God-
damned lie! (*Rises, shouts out window.*) You dirty trash!
I'll come out there and horsewhip the bunch of you!
LAYNE
(*Appears with a rifle.*) Move over, Doc. I'm going to put a
stop to this nonsense!
VOICE FROM OUTSIDE
Come on out, Layne! Next time we ain't gonna shoot at
plain air!
LAYNE
All right! You're on my property! Get moving!
A VOICE
Make us, damn you!

WILLIS

Lend me that gun! (*Layne has raised rifle, points it. We hear Cloud's voice.*)

CLOUD

Wait a minute! Get going, you tramps! Get going before you have real trouble on your hands!

VOICES

Aw, we was just fooling a little, Mr. Cloud. Just wanted to scare him some!

CLOUD

Just get going! (*A car is heard moving away. Cloud and Turnham approach the house. Willis groans.*)

WILLIS

Get rid of the devil and his disciples appear.

LAYNE

Doc . . . you and Grandma Simms go in the back room.

WILLIS

I will not!

LAYNE

Please!

MRS. SIMMS

Come on, Doc. Seeing folks like that ain't no great help to a body's digestion.

> (*They go out. A moment later Cloud and Turnham step into the room. Layne still has the gun in his hand. Cloud speaks directly to him.*)

CLOUD

Put that gun away! You want to be in more trouble than you're already in?

LAYNE

When the Good Book mentioned turning the other cheek, gunpowder wasn't invented.

CLOUD

What's gotten into you? Pointing guns at people! And putting out fool things like this! (*Cloud is waving a petition in the air.*)

LAYNE

I figured it was time for a visit from you. I got my dismissal notice today.

CLOUD
What did you expect?

LAYNE
Exactly what I got.

TURNHAM
That petition lied about me! What do you mean, the schools are in the hands of incompetent people?

LAYNE
Does the shoe fit, Phil?

TURNHAM
Ever since they made me a principal, you been down on me . . .

CLOUD
That's right! It shows exactly what you think of your own people! (*Layne walks away, refuses to answer.*) The School Board isn't happy about this petition, Joseph.

LAYNE
Seems like I've already heard of their displeasure.

TURNHAM
That ain't the half of it! You're in real trouble, Joe Layne. I'm going to see to that!

CLOUD
(*To Turnham*) Will you let me handle this? (*To Layne*) I was on your side. We were fighting for school buses . . . but you acted without consulting me . . .

MARTHA
He didn't have to! He consulted me—and some others! (*Cloud is furious but fights to control himself.*)

CLOUD
Now look, I didn't come here to argue. You need that principal's job, don't you! I happen to know your church doesn't bring you in enough for you to live on. (*Weighing his words carefully*) I told the Board I might work out a little something. How'd you like to work over at Scott's Branch school? Right in the same school where your wife teaches?

LAYNE
That's ridiculous—

CLOUD
An arrangement can be made. Suppose you were offered the principal's job at Scott's Branch . . .

LAYNE

You must be joking.

CLOUD

No. We'll move Phil over to your school. (*Then*) Look, Joseph—I'm going to lay my cards on the table. These people are doing what you tell them and we want you to stop them. You owe it to them to give them better leadership.

LAYNE

That's exactly what I'm trying to give them—(*Slowly*) You'd better learn—there are Negroes who can't be bought.

CLOUD

Suppose we draft your wife for principal? (*This is his trump card and he sits back, waiting.*)

MARTHA

You've got a lot of nerve! Expect my resignation in the morning.

CLOUD

I counted on you having some sense.

TURNHAM

You see that, Mr. Cloud? I told you so! You get no thanks for trying to help these folks out! Give them one pork chop and they want the whole hog!

CLOUD

Oh, shut up! (*Then after thinking about it*) Phil's right! I'm through giving breaks that aren't appreciated.

LAYNE

This ought to make you feel a little less guilty about old Jim Brown.

CLOUD

Oh, you're not going to be lynched. But when we get through, you'll wish for something that easy!

(*Willis appears in the doorway.*)

WILLIS

Hold on, now! I didn't get into this before because it wasn't my business. But when you get to yelling and upsetting my patient, it gets to be my business!

CLOUD

Seems like you need to study up some on how to improve your business relationships, Doctor.

WILLIS
Seems like you need to be told just who in the hell you're talking to! I know every gallstone in your bladder!

LAYNE
I think maybe you've said enough, Superintendent.

CLOUD
You're pretty damn big, aren't you?

LAYNE
Bigger than any price you can pay.

CLOUD
This is the end for you, Layne! You're going to be caught out on that limb alone, for you'll never get this petition signed around here.

LAYNE
I thought I ended this conversation! (*Cloud is furious. Layne continues.*) One thing you don't understand. I'm responsible to my God and to my congregation. Neither of them is white—

TURNHAM
Well, let God and your congregation haul you out of the mess I'm going to get you into! I'm going to fix you good, Joe Layne! I'm going to haul you into court and sue you for slander over this petition.

(*He turns, stalks out behind Cloud. Martha, Layne, and Willis look at one another.*)

WILLIS
If you both took my advice and went off for a vacation, you wouldn't have to put up with that . . .

(*Martha and Layne look at him. He shrugs, says no more.*)

MARTHA
Joe, we're in trouble. These shootings. And that slander suit. In a Jim Crow court. We'll lose everything we own.

LAYNE
Easy, honey. (*Mrs. Simms appears in doorway.*)

MRS. SIMMS
I told you. You gonna have to sleep with a britch-loader under your pillow.

LAYNE
Grandma Simms, please. (*To Willis*) Doc, will you see that Grandma Simms gets back up to the hills?

WILLIS

Sure will. (*He starts out with her.*)

MRS. SIMMS

(*As she starts out*) Don't need nobody to see that I get up to no hills! I been getting up to them hills by myself for umpteen years.

> (*She and Willis have gone out by now. Layne crosses, takes telephone, speaks into it.*)

LAYNE

Three-four-six, please. (*To Martha*) Seems like the night of the Crucifixion is here! (*Then into phone*) Hello, Ben? Ben, I want you to meet me at the Raigen house as fast as you can . . . Well, drop the barbecue sandwich, man. Yes, Ben, there's trouble!

> (*The lights are down now. Through the darkness the sound of the howling wind is heard. The lights now come up on the Raigen home. Bill appears, a lantern in his hand.*)

BILL

Anybody out there?

MARY

(*Steps out on porch.*) Umm. It's a black night, ain't it? Clouds over yonder look like they gonna bust loose any minute.

BILL

Yeah. Listen to that wind, will you? There's something heavy and powerful out yonder, pushing down against the trees—like something wants to tear them loose and there ain't nothing in the world can stop it.

MARY

William, I'm scared.

BILL

About a little rain, Mary. Naw—that's when the dust becomes part of the earth and you can smell it, and it won't choke you up—

MARY

Ain't talking about no rain and dust. I'm scared about what's coming. I can see why folks is scared to sign that petition.

BILL

Oh, what they got to lose?

MARY

William, you born and raised right down here! You know what they got to lose: Their lives! (*The wind continues to howl. Ben and Laura are seen on the road walking against the wind. They step into the Raigen backyard.*)

BEN

Hi, folks.

BILL

Hey, Ben, Laura. What you folks doing out this way?

MARY

Come on up and get outa the wind.

(*Laura goes up on porch. Ben is about to follow her when Layne and Martha appear on the road. Ben speaks to them.*)

BEN

We beat you here. Looks like a storm's blowing up for sure.

LAYNE

In more ways than one. I've got to talk to you folks.

BILL

Something wrong, Rev.

LAYNE

Plenty. They shot at my house tonight.

BILL

Who was it?

LAYNE

Same trash that's been making the telephone calls, I guess. Nobody hurt. I hope those folks don't miss heaven like they missed me. Got another problem, too. Phil Turnham's suing me for slander. (*There is silence. Inadvertently, every eye in the place rests upon Laura's face. She braces herself, asks:*)

LAURA

Slander? Why?

LAYNE

Something on that petition.

LAURA

It doesn't even mention Papa's name.

BILL

I been slandering old Phil for years and he ain't never

sued me! (*Layne nudges Bill. Laura turns quickly, starts out. Ben reaches for her.*)

BEN

Laura—

MARTHA

Where're you going?

LAURA

Home. Maybe I can talk to him.

BEN

You've tried that before.

LAURA

I'm still going. So you folks can talk.

MARTHA

We can talk with you right here. Honey, if we don't know how you feel by now, we're not fit for what we've got to do. (*Laura looks up into her face. Suddenly, Laura throws her arms about Martha.*) Now, you get yourself together. We've got work to do. Tell them about the plan, Joe—

LAYNE

I want to put half my property—the land—in your name, Bill. The house I'm putting in Doc's name. I'm sure it'll be all right with him. How about you, Bill?

BILL

You don't even have to ask, Rev . . .

BEN

I'll start drawing up the papers tonight. Of course, you folks know this isn't exactly legal.

MARTHA

What's not legal up north is legal down here, Mr. Ellis.

BEN

Don't get me wrong. I'm talking about legality, not about what's right. Come on, Laura.

LAYNE

And I don't want this news spreading around. It'll be just enough to scare folks off that petition. These people are riled up!

BILL

Man, you'd think we was trying to send our kids down to their schools!

LAYNE

They sure couldn't act much worse.

BILL

Bunch of heathens!

MARY

Not all of them.

BILL

Most of them! They make bombs and drop 'em on top of one another, don't they? What you expect 'em to do to us if they do that to theirselves?

(*Layne, Martha, Ben, and Laura have been preparing to leave. Duff's voice is heard offstage. He rushes down the road, now, and into the backyard.*)

DUFF

Reverend, Reverend Layne!

LAYNE

Here, Duff—

DUFF

I been looking every which way for you.

LAYNE

What is it?

DUFF

Reverend, is her Pa suing you? (*He points to Laura.*)

LAYNE

Yes, Duff. Who told you?

DUFF

It's all over the county.

LAYNE

May I never be caught breaking one of the Commandments around here!

DUFF

Folks also saying you getting threats and phone calls and your house being shot at!

BILL

So, what you shaking about, Duff? Ain't *you,* so don't go crossing no bridges till they built!

DUFF

I'm talking to the Reverend.

BILL

I'm talking to you!

DUFF

I get sick and tired of folks all the time signifying!

BILL

I ain't signifying! I'm telling you!

DUFF

Oh, tie something to your lip so's I can finish talking! . . . Rev, I been asking you them questions 'cause J.C. sent me for you. His brother done left us flat!

LAYNE

What?

DUFF

Went to buy some goods for his store today and the wholesale folks told him, "Nothing doing," 'cause they'd be boycotted by white folks if they sells to him. I tell you, they up there in the back of the store right now, with a whole heap of folks, being showed deep points about getting their names off that petition.

LAYNE

No . . .

DUFF

You better come along with me and do some fast talking!

LAYNE

Yes. Bill, you folks get your things and get on over to the Church. Martha, I want you to go along with them.

BILL

I'm going on up there with you.

LAYNE

No, sir! This is going to take some slow, all-night talking, and I don't want your hot head getting in the way . . .

BILL

Well, I ain't gonna sit up in no church till . . .

LAYNE

You do like I'm telling you! They've already shot at my house! Your name's second on that petition, and if they shoot at this place, I know what's going to happen. I'll meet you at the church later . . .

MARTHA

Joe, be careful . . .

LAYNE

No time to worry about that now . . .

BEN

Anything I can do, Mr. Layne? You want me to drive you up there?

LAYNE

Not a car in the world can get up that hill with this storm blowing up. You get moving on those papers.

DUFF

Come on, Rev!

BILL

Duff, I wanta apologize.

LAYNE

Apologize tomorrow! (*To Ben*) Get moving like I told you. (*Layne and Duff go out onto road. Ben and Laura start out.*)

LAURA

Drive me home first, Ben. I'll be packed by the time you finish with those papers—(*They, too, go out.*)

(*The wind rises as the lights go down. A roar of thunder crashes through the night. The lights pick up Layne and Duff on the road. Repeated crashes of thunder are heard, followed by streaks of lightning. Layne trips, nearly falls. Duff grabs hold of him. Repeated crashes of thunder are heard, followed by streaks of lightning.*)

DUFF

Reverend—you all right? You reckon we oughta go back?

LAYNE

No! No, we can't go back!

DUFF

This storm is something fierce!

LAYNE

Let it be fierce, Duff! It can't stop us. (*Turns, yells out at the storm.*) Cry out, O God, in your anguish! Send the thunder to jar us awake! (*Thunder roars.*) Send more and more and more! And lightning to light our way! (*Thunder roars, lightning flashes.*) Your Voice will be heard, and the rain shall make us clean! (*Another roar of thunder*) The right is with us, Duff! We won't be stopped! We won't!

(*He and Duff are swallowed up by the night and the fury of the storm.*)

(*The lights are down now and the raindrops are heard. These gradually begin to lessen and finally there is complete silence. The lights fade in on the church. Bill enters with a blanket and his lantern. He is followed by Martha, Mary, and Glenn.*)

BILL

I don't see why we got to be coming here.

MARY

William, don't. The Reverend tried to tell you . . .

BILL

I done worked like a mule half my life so I could have my own home to sleep in, and I got to come to church instead of laying up in my bed!

GLENN

Pa, why we gonna stay here all night?

BILL

You hear that, Mary? Now, you try telling him the truth for a while.

MARTHA

Reverend Layne wants us all to meet him here later, Glenn. We're going to talk a little, then we're going on in the back room and light the stove. And there's a bed there, and you can say your prayers and go right to sleep—just like you would if you were at home—

GLENN

Why?

MARY

Sometimes you acts just like your Pa! (*Before Bill can answer, the sound of gunfire is heard in the distance. Glenn is frightened, rushes into his mother's arms.*)

GLENN

Mom! Mom!

MARY

Don't, honey! Don't!

BILL

It's from back up yonder, son—near the valley—

GLENN

Mom! Pa! They gonna shoot us! They gonna kill us!

BILL

No they ain't, son! No they ain't!

MARTHA

Glenn, don't you worry a bit. You're going to be all right here.

MARY

They didn't shoot at us, honey—or at our house . . .

BILL

They know better than that! They know I'll blow their heads off'n their shoulders if they do!

MARTHA

Bill, don't! You'll just upset the child more, and that's one thing we don't want to do—upset the children.

BILL

The child can't be any more upset, Martha. I'd sure like to have my gun—

MARTHA

That's exactly why Joe doesn't want you at home. Because he knows what you'll do. And that's what they want—to rile us up so much we'll strike back. And when we do that, Bill, we've lost. (*Then*) Grow up, Bill! And get used to this—for there's more coming. More shooting and slander and spitting in faces. Lots more before the end. (*She stops then.*) Now, you take Glenn on in the back room. I'll light a fire in the stove. We're going to cover you up nice and warm, Glenn and we're going to sit right there beside you . . .

> (*She goes out. Mary and Glenn follow her. Then Bill starts out, too. The sound of gunfire is heard again. The roar of a car motor is also heard. Bill stops, looks toward the direction of the sounds, then goes out.*)

> (*The stage darkens. Once again there is gunfire. Then the roar of a car motor. Ruby and Willie Lee appear in the doorway of the church. She speaks to him in hushed tones.*)

RUBY

In here, baby. In here!

WILLIE LEE

Ma—why they shoot at our house? Why?

RUBY

Hush, child! You forget about that. We gonna be safe here. Ain't nobody gonna bother us—

WILLIE LEE

Why they wanta shoot at our house?

RUBY

I don't know that, baby. But I sure wish Ruby Waters coulda just got her hands on one of 'em! (*She has been removing his raincoat.*) Baby, I know you tired. Sit down a minute . . .

WILLIE LEE

Ma—I'm scared . . .

RUBY

(*Sitting him on bench. Holds him close.*) Honey, ain't I told you—no need to be scared. We gonna sit right here and this old night's gonna lift its ugly head. Gonna be sunshine all over the road soon. And your Pa's gonna come stumbling in here with a whole lot of excuses about where he was last night.

WILLIE LEE

You sure he's coming here?

RUBY

Oh, he'll be here all right. Now, just be still. Nothing in the world gonna bother you with your Ma sitting here side of you. This ain't gonna last always. No, sir—ain't gonna last always, baby—

> (*She begins to sing, not only for the child's benefit but for her own.*)

"I'm so glad trouble don't last always—
I'm so glad trouble don't last always—
Oh my Lord, Oh my Lord, What shall I do?"

> (*Her voice rises as she sings. Suddenly she chokes and tears fill her eyes. She is unable to continue. Bill's voice is heard offstage.*)

BILL'S VOICE

Who's that?

> (*He comes in, raises light, and peers into the faces of Ruby and Willie Lee. Martha follows Bill into the room.*)

MARTHA

Good Lord!

BILL

Ruby, what y'all doing here?

RUBY

They shot at my house tonight.

MARTHA

Your house, too? Give me this child . . .

RUBY

Duff wasn't home, so we come over your place . . .

MARTHA

(*Holding Willie Lee in her arms*) And we weren't home, either . . .

BILL

Duff's up in the hills with Rev, Ruby . . .

RUBY

I sure am glad you told me. I was getting ready to turn him every way but loose!

MARTHA

Willie Lee, there's nothing to be frightened about. We—we're just playing a game. Like you play in school. Hide and seek. Remember the song that goes with it . . . (*She holds him, sings.*)
   "Last night, night before—
   Twenty-four robbers at my door,
   I got up, let them in,
   Hit them in the head with a rolling pin—
   Look out—I'm peeping—"
(*Willie Lee dozes off. She looks at him.*) Fast asleep.

RUBY

Martha, you got a way with children.

MARTHA

I had to raise a grown-up child myself . . . Mary and Glenn are in the back room, Ruby. Bill—put this child in there, please . . .

RUBY

(*As Bill starts to lift Willie Lee*) You sure we gonna be all right here, Martha?

MARTHA

There's got to be someplace where they draw the line. Maybe it's here in the church . . .

RUBY

Lord knows I hope so. Sure better be.

   (*They hear Layne's footsteps. Then turn quickly. He steps into the church.*)

LAYNE

I got back as fast as I—(*Stops as he sees Ruby.*) Oh! (*Turns, steps back onto road.*) Duff! Duff! Ruby's in here! (*Duff appears on road, steps into church.*)

DUFF

Ruby—Willie Lee. What y'all doing here?

RUBY

They shot at our house . . .

DUFF

Oh, Lord And I wasn't around. (*Embraces her.*) Honey, you all right?

RUBY

Yes, Duff, I'm all right now.

DUFF

Honey, forgive me! I ain't never gonna leave you and go running off no more!

RUBY

(*To Willie Lee, who is awake by now*) You all right, Big Boy?

WILLIE LEE

Yeah, Pa. You gonna stay here now?

DUFF

Right here, son. Right here with you. Nobody gonna shoot at you no more, either . . .

RUBY

Come on, honey . . .

> (*Duff, Willie Lee and Ruby go out. Bill turns on Layne.*)

BILL

Rev, I got to talk to you. This is got to stop! We can't be having our kids seeing us running around in the night like this! I got to be able to look mine in the face, and I can't if this keeps on! I shot down men in the war for less than this!

> (*He is angry. The sound of his voice brings Mary into the room. Martha goes to Layne.*)

MARTHA

Joe, come. Sit down. You're wet through and through.

LAYNE

I'm all right.

MARTHA

What went on in the hills?

LAYNE

Lot of talking. J. C. had Reverend Shell there by the time we got there. The folks got their backs up after Shell explained to them that we're only trying to get this state to follow its own laws.

MARTHA

Any shooting up there?

LAYNE

No.

MARTHA

There's been some down here. Tired?

LAYNE

I haven't had time to think about it.

(*There is a rumbling in the distance. It is the sound of gunfire, followed by the noise of a car and jeering voices.*)

MARY

What's that?

MARTHA

They're on a rampage.

MARY

I want my baby.

BILL

He's all right, Mary.

MARY

I got to see.

MARTHA

Let him sleep. He's safe, honey. Duff and Ruby are back there.

MARY

I got to see for myself!

BILL

He's better off than he'd be in here, seeing his Pa take low!

MARTHA

Besides, Mary, those shots came from way back yonder at the edge of the hill.

MARY

I don't care where they come from!

MARTHA

Honey, don't go back there and upset those children with that crying look you have on your face.

MARY

Oh, you can talk! You ain't got no child to fret over!

(*This hurts Martha. She drops her head. Mary stops short as she realizes what she has said.*)

Martha—Martha, I didn't mean nothing like that! I didn't mean it the way it came out.

MARTHA

It—it's all right.

(*The sound of gunfire is again heard in the distance, but this time it seems nearer than before. Layne, who has gone to console Martha, turns, looks in the direction of the gunfire. Duff and Ruby come into the room. Duff, too, looks in the direction of the gunfire, then turns, moves down front and sits on the floor. Bill stands next to Mary, saying nothing. Layne, in the meantime, has begun to pace the floor. It is the pacing of a leader who is perplexed, not quite knowing which way to turn, walking, walking, trying to walk out from under the weight on his shoulders, yet trying not to walk out from under this weight.*)

DUFF

Both kids dead asleep. I stuck that big cabinet over in front of the window so's they won't be hearing nothing. (*As Layne continues pacing*) Things sure ain't working out like I figured. (*No answer*) I said—things sure ain't working out like I figured.

RUBY

What you been figuring on, Duff?

DUFF

When we get to suing these folks, I said to myself, "Duff, boy, when these folks gets to lynching, they gonna pick on Reverend Layne first, then on Reverend Shell, and by that time, man, you got yourself a head start!"

RUBY

Head start for where?

DUFF

For up north, where you think? Why you think I been keeping that jalopy full of gas? (*He laughs, but no one joins him. He realizes it is not as funny as he thought.*)

RUBY

Baby, do I hafta start telling you to shut up again? Yappity-yap-yap all the time! Mouth going like a bell clapper in a goose's behind.

DUFF

Mouth better be going some kinda way, Ruby, 'cause if it ever starts saying what's deep down inside my heart, I'd be having to go to church every day for the rest of my life! If I'd a been home tonight, I'd a killed 'em dead!

RUBY

Duff!

BILL

I know what you mean, man. Ain't no other way but to get a gun and shove some bullets in their faces!

DUFF

I'm ready any time you say.

MARTHA

They've got more bullets than we have.

BILL

Then they'll just kill us, and that way we won't hafta be shamed to show our faces!

LAYNE

Bill—Duff—would you shoot down Glenn and Willie Lee if one of them were the Prodigal Son?

DUFF

Come on now, Rev!

BILL

That ain't a fair question and you know it!

DUFF

Them ain't sons out yonder shooting. They grown men!

LAYNE

Answer my question! No. No, you wouldn't. You'd teach them. And that's what we've got to do to all these Prodigal Children.

BILL

Man . . .

DUFF

These folks won't even let us in our homes tonight, and here you talking about going in their schoolhouses and teaching 'em something! (*The sound of gunfire is heard again. This time it is a little nearer. The women flinch.*)

MARY

Lord, it goes all through me!

RUBY

I can't stand much more!

LAYNE

God give us strength to find a way!

BILL

God alone ain't gonna do it, 'cause He's hiding His head in shame! (*Martha breaks down and begins to cry. Layne rushes to her.*)

LAYNE

Martha—Martha!

RUBY

Oh, Lord!

MARY

God, don't let this happen to us! Please don't let this happen to us!

LAYNE

Martha, Martha, please—

MARTHA

I can't stand anymore of this!

LAYNE

Martha, honey . . .

(*The sound of a car motor is heard and then a mocking laugh fills the night. Layne turns to look and sees Bill, who has gone to the door.*)

LAYNE

Get away from that door, Bill!

BILL

(*Yelling out into the night*) Stop it, there, you dirty bastards! Stop it. (*Layne and Duff rush toward Bill. They grab him and pull him away from the door.*)

LAYNE

Bill, in the name of God!

DUFF

Stay away from there, man! Them bullets ain't coming from that far away. (*Pats Bill's back.*) Easy now. Easy, man.

MARY

Honey, please! You gonna make yourself sick.

BILL

I can't be listening to no more gunfire! I can't be letting

folks shoot at me and do nothing about it! I'm going home and get my gun, Rev. I know how to stop these folks. One shot in the night and they'll go running.

LAYNE

Bill, you just can't go out shooting people!

BILL

I been waiting on you to tell me why I can't, but you ain't!

LAYNE

I don't have an answer, Bill. And I can't stop you, either. All I can tell you is, every bit of my body says, "Go with him! Shoot back!" My hands are aching for them! (*Then*) But, there's something else holding me back—telling me that even if a white man walked into this church and stuck a gun in my face, I'd have to get on my knees and pray for him. I'd have to pray for him because he's sick deep down inside his soul! God Almighty, you're calling on me to have the guts to let people kill me! (*Turns to Bill*) So—you go on home if you want to, Bill. I don't know if I've got the right to ask you to turn the other cheek.

> (*Bill is not prepared for Layne's answer. He is moved by Layne's remarks, and impulsively Bill reaches and puts a hand on his friend's shoulder. Mary goes to Bill.*)

MARY

The shooting's stopped a bit, honey. Let's wait. Let's wait and just pray it'll be quiet a minute.

> (*She sits and Bill sits beside her. Layne and Martha are sitting on the bench. Duff and Ruby are behind them. Bill looks out as he speaks.*)

BILL

It's quiet now, all right. Like it was in the war. Only out there you knowed who you was fighting, even when you didn't see them. And their bullets didn't cut your insides up! Them bullets couldn't cut you up 'cause you was all fired up about that United States Constitution and swore to fight for it in the Pacific—and which don't mean a damn thing in the land where you was borned. But it sure sounded good when they read it to me.

DUFF

Sounded all that good, you oughta get 'em to come down here and read a little bit of it.

RUBY
Ain't a thing in it gonna keep these folks from running us raggedy!

BILL
Sure sounded like it had something then. Talking about everybody being citizens that was born here, and about nobody taking it away from them—(*Trying to quote.*) "No state can make no law or force no law bridging up—bridging up—" (*As Bill falters, Layne supplies him with the words.*)

LAYNE
"No state shall make or enforce any law which shall abridge the privileges and immunities of citizens of the United States."

RUBY
I reckon somebody oughta say "Amen"!

DUFF
Honey, stop making out like you know what all them big words mean, 'cause you don't!

MARTHA
They mean that South Carolina, North Carolina, or no other Carolina can make a law cutting off our rights!

DUFF
Seems like South Carolina ain't heard about this. They don't need no law to cut off my rights. They just cuts.

LAYNE
"Nor shall any state deprive any person of life, liberty or property without due process of law."

DUFF
Reverend, I ain't never had them things to be deprived of
. . .

BILL
What little of 'em you had, they sure tried to take away tonight.

LAYNE
"No state shall deny any person within its jurisdiction of the equal protection of the law."

MARTHA
Which means, in the eyes of the law, we're all supposed to be equal—and protected—

BILL

I know damn well I'm equal—and my kid oughta be protected so he can sleep in his own bed!

LAYNE

(*Angrily*) But the South Carolina state constitution says you've got to be separate!

RUBY

Well, who's the boss? South Carolina or the United States?

DUFF

You been living in South Carolina all your life, and you don't know the answer to that?

MARY

Reverend, sounds to me like the United States is saying one thing, and South Carolina's saying something different!

LAYNE

But the 14th Amendment says there's only one law—for everybody! And no state can take it away!

RUBY

How long that 14th Amendment been kicking around?

LAYNE

Since 1868.

DUFF

Man!

RUBY

You mean—these folks down here been busting the law all these years?

LAYNE

Eighty odd years of Jim Crow, and all the time it's been illegal!

MARTHA

Lord, have mercy! All that time! (*The people look at one another. Not a word is spoken. Then*)

DUFF

Going against the Constitution!

RUBY

For eighty odd years!

MARY

Eighty odd years of meanness and aggravation!

DUFF

And busting the law. The Constitution!

BILL

The thing I swore to fight for—they busting it!

RUBY

We caught particular hell tonight, and it was against the law! It's a downright shame!

BILL

Reckon that's the law we oughta be suing 'em about, not all this separate stuff!

RUBY

I ain't gonna let 'em put me through no more of what they put me through tonight!

MARY

Not another minute!

RUBY

Start changing that petition now!

MARY

Tonight!

BILL

Yes, sir, we gonna introduce them to the United States Constitution, and let them go crazy for a while, and let them know that Bill Raigen ain't taking no more shoving around!

DUFF

And Duff Waters, either—(*Reflects on the pronunciation of "Either."*) Eye-ther? (*Then*) Ee-ther? (*Finally he throws up his hands. The others laugh.*)

MARTHA

Let's start shoving!

RUBY

I'm ready this minute!

MARY

I been ready! How do we start?

BILL

We just walk outa here and look them folks square in the face . . .

LAYNE

No. It won't be like that.

BILL

You ain't even let me finish.

LAYNE

I didn't have to. This is gonna take a whole heap of legal

maneuvering and a whole battery of lawyers!

RUBY

Well, we got one! I didn't figure he come all the way down here just to eat barbecue and court Laura Turnham!

LAYNE

Yes, we'll get hold of Ben Ellis and change that petition—and sue, not for separate and equal schools, but for just schools! We'll sue this state because its Jim Crow laws are breaking the United States Constitution!

RUBY

Lord! Hurry up and send the morning so we can start writing!

MARY

Yes, but the morning's coming different from what I thought! (*The sound of a car motor is heard outside. The people stop for a moment.*)

BILL

Y'all done forgot them folks out yonder.

MARY

(*As the car sound dies out in the distance*) Honey, forget them old folks! There's a whole heap of different mornings coming now! I been wondering about that little white boy that comes around to play with Glenn—been wondering what morning he's going to wake up and find out he's white and stop coming. (*Then*) But now I know something: He's gonna come around every day if we don't let them get separated. For we the soil that brings the flowers. Good soil brings good flowers!

RUBY

And I sure ain't never seen no good soil all separated up!

DUFF

Hey! Ain't we done decided on no more of that separate stuff? (*He has asked the question and answered it. Now, he thinks about the whole thing:*) Man, I reckon when I gets to work in the morning—if I still got me a job—Old Boss Man gonna say: "Duff, boy, we give it to y'all down the country last night. Reckon you gonna stay in your place from now on!"

RUBY

You gonna say, "Yes, Sir"?

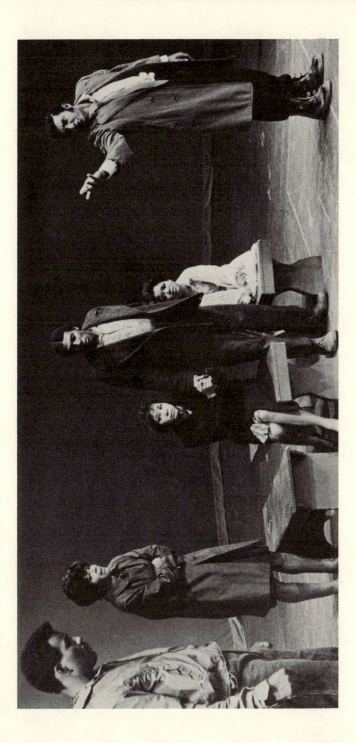

Moment of great decision

DUFF

Sir, my foot! I'm gonna tell him: "Man, where you get that
'Boy' stuff? How big do boys grow where you come from?"

BILL

Don't talk to me! I ain't your boss!

RUBY

Talk on, baby! Talk on!

(*Duff's imagination has suddenly taken wings and
fancy has become fact. He is now talking to his
boss in no uncertain terms.*)

DUFF

Oh, yes! I'm gonna look him smack in his face, and I
gonna say: "Furthermore, you calls me Mister Duff from
now on!"

RUBY

Lord!

DUFF

Then Mr. Duff's gonna take the rest of the day off, 'cause
Mr. Duff's gonna be a bit tired and needing some rest.
Then, I'm gonna take me some more time off and get on
down to that bank and tell the man if he don't give Mr.
Duff a loan to fix up his house, it's against the law. Ain't
that right, Reverend?

LAYNE

Well, not—

DUFF

Right, and when I gets the loan, I'm gonna fix up my
house outa brick—with a bathroom! So when the wind
blows, you won't hafta hold your nose no more!

RUBY

Baby, you talking a blue streak!

MARTHA

Who let him loose?

LAYNE

Well, you figured on more than just one bird, Martha.

MARTHA

Yes, and it looks like they're going to fly, too!

RUBY

(*Flinging her arms around Layne*) Hallelujah!

DUFF

Hey, Rev! Get your hands off'n my wife! (*Then*) 'Course,

when I gets to be the Boss Man myself, I'm gonna have a whole heap of women running after me!

RUBY

Now, hold on, Duff! I ain't heard nothing about that being in this here law!

DUFF

Honey, that law said I'm equal.

MARTHA

There's a law that says women are equal, too.

DUFF

One law at a time, Martha.

(*They are all laughing. From the left side of the stage, we see a red glow. A car is heard coming to a halt. Laura's voice rings through the night.*)

LAURA

Reverend Layne! Reverend Layne! (*She rushes into the church.*) Reverend Layne! Your house! It's on fire!

LAYNE

Merciful Redeemer! (*He runs out, followed by Bill and Duff. Duff calls back to Ruby:*)

DUFF

Ruby, y'all stay here! (*Martha starts to follow them. Mary stops her.*)

MARY

Martha—no! No!

LAURA

You stay here! They'll handle it!

MARTHA

I'm all right! I want to go!

MARY

Ruby!

RUBY

(*Assists them in holding Martha.*) Now you just stay right here, Martha. They gonna get the fire under control.

MARY

Yeah, sit down. Sit down and be still. (*They seat Martha. She struggles to be free.*)

MARTHA

Let me go, please. It's my house. I've got to see about it . . .

MARY

You can't go, Martha . . .

MARTHA

That's my house, Mary. You hear me! It's my house! You just said I don't have chick or child! That's all I have in the world! (*Fire engines are heard, dying away in the distance.*) The engine sounds like it's going the wrong way!

RUBY

No! No, it ain't!

(*Layne is seen on the road with Willis and Ben.*)

WILLIS

Go back! It's no use!

LAYNE

Man move out of my way!

WILLIS

Will you listen to me! The roof caved in!

LAYNE

What was the Fire Department doing?

WILLIS

Ben and I called them. They came and left. They said your house is a half mile outside the city limits!

(*Layne stands, speechless. In the meantime, Martha, inside the church, struggles to free herself.*)

MARTHA

The engine did go the wrong way! I've got to get to my house! (*She breaks away from the women, runs out onto the road. Layne grabs her.*)

WILLIS

Martha—please go back and sit down.

RUBY

(*Follows Martha on road.*) Yes. Come on, honey.

LAYNE

Try to calm yourself, Martha.

MARTHA

Now, I'm all right. I just want to see about my house. I want to make them stop burning it. It's my house. Mine, mine, mine—(*She breaks away from Layne, starts down the road, then stops short as a sudden pain stabs her. She sinks to the ground. The women begin to cry. Willis rushes to Martha, begins working over her. He stops, bows his head, tears stream down his cheeks. Layne sees this, lets out a wild scream as he grabs Martha in his arms.*)

LAYNE

Martha! Martha! No! No! You can't die! I won't let you! I won't let you! (*His voice trails off as he chokes with tears.*) I won't let you! (*He holds her close, then, as he realizes she is dead, he cries out wildly:*) Almighty God, I said, let it be me! Didn't you hear me? I said—let it be me! (*There is nothing said by the others. The fire in the distance continues to burn brightly, then gradually it begins to die out.*)

Curtain

Act Three

Two months later—the day of the trial announcement

    (The low humming of a spiritual fills the darkness. Bill's voice comes offstage as he begins the song.)

    BILL'S VOICE

"There's a land beyond the river
That we call the sweet forever,
And you only reach that shore by faith's decree—

    MARY AND BILL

One by one, we'll gain the portals
There to dwell with the immortals
When they ring them golden bells for you and me!

    ALL

Can't you hear the bells a-ringing?
Don't you hear the angels singing?
It's a Glory Hallelujiah Jubilee!
One by one we'll know our number
Then, in death we'll sweetly slumber
When they ring them golden bells for you and me!

In that far-off, sweet forever,
Just beyond the shining river,
There the king commands the spirit to be free!
There we'll know no grief, no sorrow
In that haven of tomorrow
When they ring them golden bells for you and me!"

    (During the singing the lights fade in completely on the church. Mary, Laura, Duff, J. C., Ruby, Shell, and Mrs. Simms sit in the church humming. They are waiting—waiting. Bill comes into the church. Mrs. Simms turns to him.)

    MRS. SIMMS

Go on out yonder and see if they coming, William. (*Bill*

turns, goes out.) You all get them looks off your faces. Can't nobody here do no smiling?

MARY

Ain't nothing to smile about. Every time I come in this church, I think about Martha lying out yonder in her grave.

MRS. SIMMS

Poor soul been dead two months. Let her rest. Well (*looks around*), if I'd a knowed you all was gonna sit around here like this, I'd a waited on the news up in the hills by my lonesome.

RUBY

Reckon you more used to waiting than we is, Grandma Simms. And dying.

MRS. SIMMS

Sure seen a heap of them go to their glory. May see a heap more, so don't you be numbering my days, Ruby Waters. (*Ruby goes out.*) Now y'all just sit down and wait. (*Bill comes back in, gets ready to sit. She speaks to him sharply.*) Didn't I tell you to get out yonder? (*Bill goes out, mumbling to himself.*) I said, y'all got to wait, so you might just as well smile and sing a little bit so's you can get used to it.

LAURA

You should sing for us, Grandma Simms. My mother used to tell me about you and those slave songs.

MRS. SIMMS

Had to be your Ma telling you. Your Pa sure wouldn't.

LAURA

(*Embarrassed*) Reverend Layne told me, too.

MRS. SIMMS

You ain't like your Pa a bit. Stand over there in the light so's I can get a good look at you. Go ahead! (*Laura rises.*) Mmm. You your Ma's child, all right. That's the best thing coulda happened to you—

SHELL

Grandma Simms . . .

MRS. SIMMS

Reverend Shell, don't be putting your big feet all over my words! St. Peter be trying to show you which way at the Gate, and you'll be butting in, trying to show him deep points. (*Turns back to Laura.*) When you getting married, girl? We could use a little celebrating around here!

DUFF

(*As Bill reenters*) You took the words right outa my mouth.

BILL

And mine, too.

MRS. SIMMS

(*To Bill*) Why ain't you out yonder seeing if Joseph's on the way? Lord, we gonna be all night getting back up yonder in the hills—

SHELL

He'll be here soon, Grandma Simms. Court doesn't last all day. The judges like to get out of there, too—so they can start breaking up the Commandments.

RUBY

(*Enters.*) Well, this waiting is driving me crazy. I been running out to that back house so much, my legs is about to cave into my body!

SHELL

Wait'll you wait as long as I've been waiting!

MRS. SIMMS

And you'll wait'll you wait as long as me! Been saying that to Joseph those two months he been up there with me— walking the floor all night long. Been telling him: Takes a long time for the coming of the Lord!

SHELL

Yes, a long time—wherein a man speaks one word and means another. Brothers and Sisters, it took the good Lord six days to make heaven and earth!

BILL

The only trouble is, them judges down there, figuring on whether or not our kids can go to white schools ain't the good Lord, Reverend Shell, and I'm saying, we oughta gone on down there with Reverend Layne today.

MARY

Oh, William, take one look at your head and you'll know why we ain't there!

J. C.

Sure right! If you didn't go fighting that white man the first day in court, Reverend Layne woulda let us gone down today for the news!

BILL

What you expect me to do when somebody throws a stone at me?

SHELL

Not fight. Return hate with love—

MARY

It might even keep you from being hit in the head!

BILL

Besides that, won't no white man that hit me in the head. It was that old Duff pulling me off'n him!

DUFF

I figured you'd be figuring out a way of blaming me!

MARY

(*As Bill makes a face at Duff*) William, you is behaving just like a child!

BILL

Ain't no such thing!

MARY

Yes, you is! Just like Glenn's behaving when he's needing a good spanking!

BILL

I'd like to see somebody try spanking me.

MARY

Oh, be still before I slap your face for you!

J. C.

Loud-talk him, Mary, girl! Loud-talk him!

BILL

Now, there's my face. Who wants to try slapping it?

> (*He sticks his face out, never dreaming that she will slap him. She raises her hand, brings it down across his face. He is shocked, and so are the others, including Mary. She realizes what she has done and turns away, almost in tears.*)

J. C.

(*Yells.*) Ooooo! Ooooo!

RUBY

Lord, have mercy!

DUFF

Ruby, I declare I believe that little woman can hit harder'n you! (*Bill is wild with anger now. He stands there, looking for someone to attack. He starts at Duff. In the meantime, everyone is talking at once. Mrs. Simms rises.*)

MRS. SIMMS

I heard about enough! Now, all of you, just stop it! (*Bill, turning, starts toward Duff.*) You heard what I said, Bill Raigen! (*He stops short. Mrs. Simms turns on the others.*) You oughta be ashamed of yourselves, carrying on like that! (*Then*) Don't nobody say nary a word till I tells 'em to talk!

SHELL

Amen!

MRS. SIMMS

Not even Amen, Reverend Shell. (*Turns on the others.*) We here waiting on the Lord's message, and carrying on—

SHELL

And right here in the House of the Lord! (*Mrs. Simms glares at him.*)

RUBY

Sure is a shame.

(*Mrs. Simms is about to rebuke her for talking when Ben and Layne appear on the road. They step into the church. The people rise, looking into the faces of the lawyer and minister.*)

BEN

We lost. (*There is silence. He walks into a corner of the room and simply stands there, silently. Laura goes to him.*)

LAYNE

We lost in words. The judges said segregation is legal, but the state has to make the schools equal.

(*There is a pause as they all realize what has happened.*)

RUBY

Equal schools? Then we ain't lost nothing!

DUFF

Man, oh man.

J. C.

We did it! We did it! No more fixing them school floors!

RUBY

And Willie Lee won't be snagging his pants on them wood benches no more!

MARY

I got a notion we didn't get what we oughta got.

J. C.

Aw, don't be a drag!

BILL

I don't know what you talking about, woman. We started off asking for ten bucks and got five. Which is five more'n we had. What more you want?

SHELL

Maybe a lot more.

DUFF

A new brick schoolhouse!

J. C.

How you know it gonna be brick?

DUFF

Fool! You heard the Reverend say the schools gotta be equal! All the white schools made outa brick, so ours gotta be equal! (*Suddenly*) Made outa brick! With a bathroom! Little Willie Lee gonna be running around like a chicken with his head cut off. And Laura's gonna be calling me down the schoolhouse, wondering . . . "Mr. Waters!" That's what you gonna call me, Laura: "Mr. Waters—How come your boy just stands there and gapes at the bathroom all day long?"

J. C.

What you gonna say?

DUFF

Gonna say the truth: "Miss Turnham, my boy ain't never seen no bathroom 'fore and he kinda gotta get used to it!" (*He becomes sober almost to the point of tears.*) Ruby, my boy gonna be able to read and write better'n me. (*Ruby throws her arms around his neck. They remain in an embrace. Bill smiles, self-consciously.*)

BILL

I . . . I don't know what y'all gonna do, but I'm gonna do me a little celebrating—starting right now!

J. C.

Ain't never been one not to cooperate!

BILL

Let's go. Gonna be big doings over to my house.

(*He runs out. J. C. follows him, then Ruby and Duff follow. Duff beckons to Shell as he goes and Shell, too, goes out. Laura remains with Ben. Mary and Mrs. Simms look at Layne.*)

MRS. SIMMS

That all there is to it, son? Ain't we suing no more?

LAYNE

For what?

MARY

For what we want. For schools for just children so they can grow up like they oughta.

LAYNE

We got what we went after.

MARY

The lawyer said we lost.

LAYNE

Well, we don't want that part, anyway! We don't want our kids going to school with their kids, where they can learn how to make bombs and burn homes and lynch folks! We don't want to be with them and their crucifying souls!

(*His words shock them. He turns, bitterly, goes out into the next room. There is a moment of silence— then Mrs. Simms rises.*)

MRS. SIMMS

Reckon I'll have to wait a mite longer. (*Starts out.*) Come on, Mary.

(*She and Mary go out and into the Raigen home. The shadows begin to fall outside. Ben and Laura are now alone in the church. From the distance we can hear music rising faintly.*)

BEN

How can they celebrate?

LAURA

They got what they wanted.

BEN

I didn't.

LAURA

You always put what they wanted first.

BEN

Yes. Till I found out they don't want enough.

LAURA

A person doesn't just start out wanting the whole world. First, it's just a little something, and then suddenly it becomes a mountain or a tree or a piece of land. But, as long as the want is there, it'll grow bigger and bigger—

BEN

Laura, I stood up there today and heard two judges say segregation is legal! It was legal for a mob to chase my father out of the South for trying to organize a union! Legal for him to live in a cold North he never understood! Legal for him to die heartbroken, and my mother to die worrying over him! Legal!

LAURA

Ben! Don't frighten me—

BEN

I'm sorry, I can't celebrate—

LAURA

Then, at least understand—

BEN

Laura, I'm trying, but these people—

LAURA

I'm one of them. (*She goes to him.*) You made me one of them. (*She takes his hand. He looks at her as the full meaning of her words reaches his ears. They sit there silently. Footsteps are heard. Turnham steps into the church. Laura senses his presence, but does not turn.*)

TURNHAM

Laura—I've been looking for you. (*She is silent.*) I want you to come home. You don't belong with these people.

LAURA

For the first time in my life I belong somewhere.

TURNHAM

They'll hurt you, Laura. They're no good. (*Bitterly*) They made me lose my job. Mr. Cloud just fired me. Said I'm no good to him—that I can't make these folks behave! (*Then*) Come home.

LAURA

No.

TURNHAM

It gets dark early up there in the house.

LAURA

It's been dark. It's been dark for many a year. I can't go back, Papa.

TURNHAM

You—you're not talking like Laura. You're talking like somebody different and wrong, and all messed up from hanging around these dirty tramps! (*To Ben*) I've got you and Layne to thank for this, Ellis! You dragged my daughter into the pigpen with these animals! You're no good! You're a devil, that's what you are! You're a devil. You're a devil and somebody ought to kill you! Somebody ought to kill you! (*He charges Ben who takes his arms, holds him. Turnham falls to the floor on both knees, struggling to free himself.*)

LAURA

Papa! Papa! (*Layne rushes into the room.*)

LAYNE

Stop it! (*To Ben*) Leave him alone! (*His words are sharp. Ben turns away.*)

TURNHAM

Devils, that's what you are! Cutting up and messing up your own homes and mine! You don't care about anybody but yourselves! I've got to go back to working in sawmills or cleaning spittoons someplace or mopping floors and grinning at people I could kill!

LAYNE

Go home, Turnham. (*And he helps him to rise.*)

TURNHAM

Home? Where's my home? Where've I got to go now? Where? (*He turns, goes out slowly, his head bent.*)

LAURA

(*Crying out*) Papa—Papa—(*She breaks down, rushes into Layne's arms. Awkwardly he tries to console her.*)

LAYNE

Laura, don't . . . don't.

LAURA

I can't help it. He's my father!

LAYNE

I know. I wanted to cry for him, too!

BEN

(*Sincerely*) I wish I could say I did, too!

LAYNE

You're too young to know how.

BEN

Maybe he should cry as he made me cry today. Then maybe his kind wouldn't give those judges the nerve to turn the law into a mountain of lies!

LAYNE

It's mighty easy for you fellows to sit over cigars in big

offices up north and play checkers with us down here. You don't know what it's like down here in the country with the night settling down on top of us, not knowing what's lurking in that night, or whether we'll live to see a morning! You don't know what it's like when men have to forget their souls so they can live to see a morning!

BEN

You—defending Phil Turnham. The man who sued you for slander on a trumped-up charge—who took the fire insurance from your house to pay off the judgment! (*Somewhat awed*) How can you defend him?

LAYNE

It's a sad day, son, when a man can't try to understand people—when he can't forgive those who trespass against him!

BEN

You can understand an Uncle Tom, but you can't understand your own wife.

LAYNE

What do you mean by that?

BEN

Do you think your wife would have settled for what that court said today? (*Layne is jarred and Ben knows it. Yet Ben will not take advantage of the situation. He turns away, sorry for having spoken. In the distance we can hear music and laughter. Layne speaks, softly.*)

LAYNE

I—think we'd better get on to the celebration.

(*The lights fade out on the church as the music and laughter roar through the darkness. The lights come up on the Raigen backyard. Duff charges through the doorway, pulling Ruby behind him.*)

DUFF

Come on out here to dance, woman! You so big you rocking that floor!

RUBY

You shut your mouth! (*They begin to dance. J. C., Bill, Shell, and Mrs. Simms step out on the porch. Mrs. Simms sits.*)

MRS. SIMMS

Just watching 'em wears me out!

(*Duff and Ruby finish their dance. As they do, the*

others applaud. Layne, Ben, and Laura step into the scene.)

SHELL

You know, Joe, this is not the kind of affair we can preach sermons on!

BILL

Let me get 'em some more wine and you'll see something you can preach against!

DUFF

I'll hafta get the wine, Bill. I hid it so's Reverend Shell wouldn't hafta do a whole heap of explaining to his congregation. (*The others laugh as Duff runs out.*)

MRS. SIMMS

My husband used to say a little nip now and then is good for the soul. Reverend Shell, I recollect you preached a sermon about that.

SHELL

Sure did.

MRS. SIMMS

And then all your deacons come to your house and found a case of licker!

SHELL

Don't recollect recollecting that.

MRS. SIMMS

My husband was one of the deacons. Sure wish he was here tonight. Him and a whole lotta people. Told 'em I had to wait on this day. Now I'm waiting on another . . .

DUFF

(*Comes back in with a jug of wine.*) Hey! Y'all getting too serious. This is a party!

BILL

Yeah! Mary! Mary! (*She appears on the porch.*) Fix something for these folks!

RUBY

I'll go get it. Don't be working Mary to death!

DUFF

You women got to stick together even when you partying?

RUBY

You better stop all this talk about partying and celebrating! First news you know, white folks be coming by here,

seeing you doing just what they expects you to be doing—
raising hell!

BILL

Well, they needs to watch so's they can learn how to enjoy
themselves! That way they won't be so dad-blamed evil
sometimes!

(*Duff starts to go into a dance step as Mary brings
a plate from the house. Duff, who is dancing alone,
stops short as he looks toward the road. The others
follow his gaze. Dr. Willis has appeared on the
road with Glenn in his arms. Glenn's head is ban-
daged. Mary lets out a scream. Bill rushes to Willis
and Glenn.*)

BILL

Glenn! What happened? (*He takes Glenn from Willis.
Mary rushes to Glenn.*)

MARY

Baby! Baby!

WILLIS

He is going to be all right. Nothing serious.

MARY

Give him to me.

BILL

(*Puts boy into his mother's arms. Then*) I want you to tell
me. Who did this to you?

GLENN

Was—coming back from the store. Some white men caught
me on the road, asked me wasn't I gonna look like a ugly
ape sitting up in school side of white kids—

BILL

Damn them!

GLENN

I told 'em I wasn't no ugly ape. They said they was gonna
beat me till I said I was!

BILL

Who?

GLENN

The men! I wouldn't say it, Pa!

BILL

Tell me who they was, son, and they never gonna beat on
nobody else's kid!

GLENN

I don't know!

BILL

You got to know! You must have seen 'em.

WILLIS

It was dark, Bill. I couldn't make out who they were myself. I'll tell you about it later—

BILL

Later? Man, how can you talk about later?

WILLIS

Now, just a minute. (*Then*) I was coming this way when I
heard slaps in the dark. Two white men were slapping
Glenn pretty hard and trying to get him to say he'd look
like an ugly ape sitting in school beside white kids. The
child was yelling: "I won't say it! I won't say it!" Well,
sir, I forgot all about doctoring and saving lives. I took a
wild swing at one of the men—but I missed. The men ran
off in the night. Bill, if I'd connected with that swing, doctoring wouldn't have helped him a bit. Been a job for the
undertaker for sure. Anyway, I took Glenn on home and
patched him up some. (*To Layne*) Reverend, I know this
isn't religious, but it sure felt good swinging—

BILL

Doc, you better go inside and rest up some—

WILLIS

I'm all right. (*He goes over, sits down.*)

BILL

Mary—get Glenn inside. (*She starts out with Glenn.*) I got
some business to take care of.

DUFF

Reckon I have, too.

J. C.

Yep, let's get going! (*J. C., Bill, and Duff have started
out of the backyard. Glenn cries out.*)

GLENN

Pa! Pa! (*The sound of the child's voice causes Bill to
turn.*)

LAYNE

Where do you think you're going to find them, Bill?

BILL

I don't know, but I'll find 'em.

LAYNE

And what's that going to solve?

BILL

A hell of a lot!

SHELL

What? More houses burned! More people mistreated!

BILL

Man, talk sense! (*Bill turns, starts out again. Again Glenn cries out to his father.*)

GLENN

Pa! Pa! (*Duff, J. C., and Ben take hold of Bill. He struggles with them.*)

J. C.

Wait a minute, now! Wait a minute!

BEN

Go back there now! You're not doing yourself or the child any good!

DUFF

Yeah! Gonna get him worked up some more, Bill! Better wait a minute—

BEN

Listen to what the Reverend's trying to tell you!

LAYNE

You sit down there, Bill.

BILL

This ain't no time for sitting!

LAYNE

Sit down, Bill, and listen a minute.

BILL

(*As he is led to a chair by the men*) Reverend, I don't feel up to no sermon!

LAYNE

Well you're going to hear one! For you—and for me! (*He turns, looks at Glenn.*) "A Little Child Shall Lead Them." (*Then*) The voice of God has roared in my ears this terrible day, charging us with the duty of saving the souls of white children that they may grow up to be our brothers —or saving the souls of all those who have been taught hate instead of love! In the words of St. Paul: "When I was a child, I spake as a child, I understood as a child— But when I became a man, I put away childish things . . . And now abideth faith, hope and love, but the greatest of

these is love!" (*A chorus of agreement from the others*)
Oh, yes! The voice of God has roared in my ears, testing
my faith—by letting them burn my house, by letting them
crucify my beloved wife—testing me as Job was tested, as
the children of Israel were tested, as our people were
tested through nearly three hundred years of slavery!

MRS. SIMMS

Yes, Lord!

LAYNE

Testing to see if God's work can be done on earth as it is
in heaven. And, oh, my friends, it will be done!

SHELL

(*As the others chorus agreement*) God's work will be done!

LAYNE

Brothers and Sisters, we have been charged with the duty
of bringing back all the Prodigal Children! May we be
worthy of that great duty!

SHELL

God, make us worthy!

LAYNE

For, even when the Law has been read, and the signs that
read: "This is for black" and "This is for white" have been
burned—still shall there be fires! Still shall there be lynch
mobs! Still shall there be deaths!

MARY

Preach!

LAYNE

There will be more testing! More suffering! But let not
your hearts be troubled—for the Seventh Seal shall be
opened, and they cannot hide!

MRS. SIMMS

Ain't no hiding place!

LAYNE

No, they cannot hide! For the truth shall be a blazing
streak, lighting up the darkness everywhere, and the sins
of each shall sicken the other until those who sin will
themselves be sickened, and they shall seek righteousness!
No! They cannot hide! And we cannot hide! We cannot
hide by trying to kill the killers, Bill. For us to be worthy
of our great duty is for us to teach them Love on earth!
And how? How?

SHELL

Through love!

LAYNE

Yes, Reverend Shell! Through love! And where's that taught? In the homes. In the churches. In the schools. Now we started this thing for buses, then we wanted a brick school—then we asked to go to the same schools. Some of us believed we'd get that, and some of us didn't much care. But I care now!

MRS. SIMMS

I'm glad, son!

LAYNE

For there's no such thing as being separate and equal! The only thing a man learns by being separate is that he's not equal.

J. C.

That's right!

LAYNE

(*To Glenn*) They called you an ugly ape, did they, boy? Well, folks have got to sit side by side in the same schools and learn the true meaning of beauty—that all nations and peoples have their standard of beauty, and no one standard is better than any other.

That color in your skin, boy, was given to you by God, and it's a mark of your heritage from great Africa! But here in this troubled land, Glenn, it's more than a mark of beauty—it's a mark of duty! It's your everlasting badge of dignity and honor. Every house has its standards, son, but there are many houses, many mansions. "In my Father's house are many mansions. If it were not so—I would have told you!" (*Glenn now runs into Bill's arms. Layne turns to the others.*) And that means there is room for all—white, black, blue, or green! Not up yonder in the sky, but here on earth!

RUBY

Yes, Reverend!

SHELL

Yes, indeed!

LAYNE

And I'm not going to be a traitor to the Little Child that would lead me! I'm going on with this thing to the Highest Court in the World! Before I turn back now, may I go rotting to my grave!

SHELL

Amen! Amen!

MRS. SIMMS

I been waiting on this sermon!

SHELL

It was worth waiting on!

RUBY

Rev, you preached one that time! (*They have all gathered around Layne, shaking his hand and patting him on the back. Mary goes to Glenn, who remains in Bill's arms.*)

MARY

Did you hear him, baby? Did you hear what the Reverend said?

LAURA

Let's all hear!

RUBY

Sure right! Now, come on, you-all, and let's get that child that's leading us into the house so we can put some soup into him! (*Glenn clings to his father.*) And some food into the doctor.

WILLIS

I reckon I been fed plenty, Ruby—

RUBY

And Rev. I'm going to fix you the biggest barbecue sandwich you ever et! (*Going out*) Lord, he preached one that time! (*And she goes out followed by Laura, Willis, and Ben.*)

MARY

Come on, William. Better ways of fighting than with fists and guns. We gonna teach that to *some* white folks before Judgment Day rolls around.

BILL

Well, they better start learning, 'cause I ain't gonna keep on waiting. (*Bill rises, takes Glenn into the house. Mary follows them. Duff takes the wine jug—turns to J. C.*)

DUFF

Well, J. C., with us going up to Washington for the Judgment Day, I reckon we better get on in here and fill up whilst we can.

After the trial

J. C.

How you know we going to Washington?

DUFF

Fool! You heard the man say we going to the Highest Court in the world. Where the hell you think that is? In South Carolina? (*He and J. C. go into the house, now. Mrs. Simms rises and speaks to Shell.*)

MRS. SIMMS

Reverend Shell, come here and gimmie your arm. I'm gonna in there, too. I think I need just a little bit more of that dandelion wine and I can get me a real night's rest. I ain't gonna tell no lie about just eating.

SHELL

Well—the truth is what sets you free.

MRS. SIMMS

Yes! (*She turns, ready to go. Shell takes her by the arm, then turns to Layne.*)

SHELL

Coming, Joe?

LAYNE

I'll be along in a minute.

SHELL

Something wrong?

LAYNE

No. I was just thinking about Martha—(*He stops himself, then*) I was thinking, too—I was thinking that I need a little bit of that dandelion wine myself. (*A smile covers his face. He joins them, takes Mrs. Simms by one arm and Shell by the other. Together they start into the house as the lights fade.*)

Curtain

Morning, Noon, and Night

by
Ted
Shine

characters

BEN MARVIN MCDANIELS: A mature little boy, eleven

GUSSIE BLACK: His grandmother, an elderly pseudoreligious busy-body with a wooden leg which she has boldly painted white.

IDA RAY CLARK: The boy's aunt

SISTER SUE WILLIE HOLLIS: A traveling evangelist. She is in her early thirties, plump and energetic.

SCENE 1 *Morning. The lights come up dimly revealing two rooms and the front and back porches of a modest shotgun house in Earth, Texas. The rooms are neat but sparsely furnished. In the kitchen there is a stove, a table and two chairs, a sink, and cabinets. A door leads from the kitchen onto the back porch. A rocking chair is placed on the porch. Another door leads from the kitchen into the front or living room. The room is furnished with a few odds and ends; curtains at the window, simple chairs and a few small tables. There is a fireplace in the wall, stage left, and two doors upstage. One door leading to Ida Ray's room, and the other leading to Gussie's room. A third door leads onto the front porch, which is filled with various kinds of potted plants. Both the front and back yards are visible. There is a well in the backyard and shrubbery, one shrub large enough to conceal an adult, in the front yard.*

At Rise: Ben Marvin McDaniels, a small boy of eleven, is asleep on a pallet in a corner of the living room. Offstage, Gussie Black is heard singing a rousing spiritual, "I'm Callin' Jesus My Rock." She enters from her room dressed for the day. She is seventy-two, but this age is deceiving; she moves about with the gusto of a much younger woman. She has a wooden leg painted white which does not handicap her in the least. She stamps about the room humming and singing, moves over to Ben and jabs him in the side with her stump. The boy mumbles something to himself, then rolls over.

GUSSIE

(*To Ben. Kicks him.*)

Get up from there you lazy rascal and get me some water from the well. Your poor old grandma's dying of thirst. Coffee!

BEN

Cold . . .

GUSSIE

Stir about! Light the kitchen stove. The good Lord didn't put us here to sleep our lives away. Ida Ray, girl! Fix me a cheese omelet. Boy!

BEN

Shoot! It's still dark.

GUSSIE

The days are getting shorter—all of our days are shorter. Get up now in the name of the Lord and serve Him with every breath. (*To Ida's door*) Ida! You're gonna be late for work, child Idoooo!

IDA

(*From within her room*) I hear you! I hear you!

GUSSIE

(*To boy*) Get your butt out of that bed, boy! You ought to have been up hours ago. All them books scattered about you. It's a wonder you can breathe. Boy, I'm waiting on my water. (*She jabs him in the side, then picks up a book.*)

BEN

I've got to put my clothes on. And you put my book down!

GUSSIE

(*Drops book on the boy.*) Ida Ray, this boy's in here yelling at me!

(*Ida Ray Clark enters. She is a firmly built, mature woman in her early thirties.*)

IDA

(*Moving into kitchen*)

Miss Gussie, how many times do I have to tell you that I don't have to be at work until seven o'clock? You keep us up half the night and get us up before . . . Lord, it's only four thirty.

GUSSIE

(*Following Ida*)

My mama always made me get up, and look at the ripe age I've reached. Ida, child, you don't look well this morning!

IDA

How could I at this hour?

GUSSIE

You're sick, child. There no color to your skin at all.

IDA

Miss Gussie—

GUSSIE

Have a cup of coffee with me. And then I want you to get in bed and rest.

IDA

I was never a person to lay and suffer.

GUSSIE

Child, you're sick. I've got as much sense as a cat's got hair, and I know you're sick, child . . . sick.

IDA

Miss Gussie, I know. I have stomach pains, headaches . . . I vomit . . .

GUSSIE

And you've lost your color, child! You're as pale as death itself.

IDA

Miss Gussie, please . . . (*Takes aspirin.*)

GUSSIE

All this suffering is depressing to me.

IDA

You're making it worse talking about it like this.

GUSSIE

Well . . . it's probably nothing but a little female trouble. Put the skillet on, child, and start my breakfast.

IDA

(*Entering living room*)

Does it ever occur to you, Miss Gussie, that I might be tired? I pick up after the Lappas' all day, then come home and pick up after you and Ben.

GUSSIE

(*Following Ida into living room*)

I don't mean to be a burden. I'm just here as a guest.

BEN

(*Now dressed and has his bed put up*)

Miss Lappas' house guest don't stay three months!

IDA

Ben, hush.

BEN

You said so yourself.

IDA

Hush, I told you!!

GUSSIE

I don't suppose this lazy young'un plans to get my water.

IDA

Why don't you make your own coffee when you get up? You know where things are.

GUSSIE

I'm old and sickly, child. Besides I don't want to be messing with that stove of yourn. I'm scaired to death of fire.

IDA

I'm going to start making a big pot of coffee at night just before we go to bed—

GUSSIE

Shoot, I don't want no stale coffee! (*Turns to Ben.*) I'll get my own water since you ain't gonna do it. You sure don't act like my son's boy. It's a pity he didn't live to bring you up. (*She exits out into the backyard.*)

BEN

She makes me sick! Jugging that old stump in my back every morning and yelling in my ear like I'm deaf.

IDA

One of these days she's gonna catch me when my temper is up and I'm gonna let her have it. I told her last night when I come in I didn't feel well.

BEN

You feel any better?

IDA

Worse, if anything. I hardly slept at all.

BEN

Maybe you should stay home today.

IDA

I need the money, Ben, besides—I'll probably feel better if I'm doing something.

GUSSIE

(*From the yard*)

Ben, you get that drum I brought here. We've got to praise Jesus this morning.

IDA

I have no intention of playing church at this hour, honey.

GUSSIE

Playing church? "Playing church?" Why I'm not "playing"

nothing. I'm serving my Jesus. Giving him the respect and devotion that he deserves. Come on out into this wilderness with me, children.

BEN

If you want that coffee you'd better bring that water in here.

GUSSIE

Oh, you're a little sinner all right. Just like your grandfather was.

BEN

I'm not like anybody but me.

IDA

Don't be sassy, Ben.

BEN

She makes me sick comparing me all the time. She ever tell you how grandpa died?

IDA

All I know is what folks say—he died suddenly and mysteriously.

BEN

He probably died from the lack of sleep if she had anything to do with it.

IDA

Folks sort of believed that he was poisoned, but that was a long time ago and there never was any proof.

BEN

Why don't you ask her to go back home?

IDA

What home?

BEN

She always talking about that big place she's got in Forney.

IDA

You like to dream sometimes don't you?

BEN

Yeah.

IDA

Old folks do too—especially when they're practically alone in the world. You're the only blood kin she's got now.

BEN

She don't act like it.

IDA

She loves you in her way, so be patient with her.

GUSSIE

(*Entering with water*)

Boy, this stove ought to have been blazing by now! Ida Ray!

IDA

Just please be quiet, Miss Gussie. I'll fix your coffee and your breakfast if you'll just please be quiet.

GUSSIE

Well, the Lord has a place for the old in His heaven, I guess.

BEN

The way you act He's gonna lock the door and throw the key away when He sees you coming.

IDA

(*Sharply*)

Ben Marvin!

GUSSIE

Cora spared the rod with this child, didn't she Ida? You must be proud I'm here taking some of the burden of raising him off you. You can't leave 'em at home while you're off at work like you used to. It's amazing the juvenile delinquency that goes on in the young folks' minds these days.

IDA

Ben never gave sister any trouble to speak of.

GUSSIE

'Cause she spoiled him that's why. He's just ruined with corruption. (*To Ben*) Stand up, sinner, and be counted in that number! Boy, there's not a trace of my side of the family in you.

BEN

You just said that I was the spitting image of my granddaddy.

GUSSIE

That man wasn't my blood kin, child. He was one of them old McDaniels. I'm a Black from way back. (*She takes her tambourine and begins to sing.*)

IDA

Please, Miss Gussie! (*The old woman ignores her.*)

BEN

Ida Ray wants you to hush up that racket.

GUSSIE

You sinners don't want this poor old dying creature to serve her Jesus?

IDA

Just wait until I get out of the house, then you can do anything you want to do. Your voice is as piercing as a sword. Now sit at the table and eat these eggs.

GUSSIE

(*Takes the food and extends a forkful to Ben.*)

Here, take a bite of this for me.

BEN

I'm not hungry.

GUSSIE

Just a bite to test it.

IDA

Test it for what, Miss Gussie?

GUSSIE

I always test other folks' cooking, child. You never can tell.

IDA

Never can tell what?

GUSSIE

Like they say: Never put all your eggs in one basket— never put all your trust in nobody. People are evil by nature and have to be reborn.

IDA

What's that got to do with this omelet?

GUSSIE

Ida, I'm not saying nothing except that I didn't see you cook it, child.

IDA

Miss Gussie, if I had wanted to get rid of you I could have done that a long time ago, and I wouldn't need poison either.

GUSSIE

(*Pushing food away*)

Poison, huh?

IDA

You've been worrying me to death to cook your breakfast, now you eat those eggs.

GUSSIE

Suddenly I ain't hungry, child. Lost my appetite completely. (*Rises and starts for the back porch.*)

IDA

Miss Gussie, you're trying me.

GUSSIE

(*Singing as she exits*)

BEN

You were the one who pretended to be sooooo happy when she came. I never did like her. Taking my bed and making me sleep on the floor—and no sooner than she got here, Mama died.

IDA

Your mama was real sick, baby. And say what you will the old woman was a lot of help. If it hadn't been for her I couldn't have gone back to work, and Mrs. Lappas said she just couldn't do without me a day longer.

BEN

The day she got here Mama took a turn for the worse.

IDA

Well, she and Cora weren't the best of friends.

GUSSIE

(*From the back porch*)

What're you all talking about in there?

IDA

Oh, nothing much—the heat and all.

BEN

Why don't you tell her to stay out of our business?

IDA

Ben Marvin, none of us is perfect, and she is right pitiful with that leg and all.

BEN

She walks a good twenty miles a day gossiping up and down the road.

IDA

She's lonely, I guess, with me being at work all day. She likes to be around people—and you're certainly no company for her.

BEN

Joe Sedrick said his mama's gonna ask her to stay home. Eating them out of house and home and then talking about what a bad cook Miss Evelyn is behind her back.

IDA

I think she needs responsibilities, Ben. Chores to do.

BEN

That old soul ain't gonna do a thing except eat and walk and go into those trances.

IDA

What trances?

BEN

Oh, I told you how she dances about and sings until she goes right crazy. Her eyes get as big as golf balls and she shakes herself like she's having a fit. She says the Lord touches her and she gets that way.

IDA

Don't you get too close to her when she's like that, hear? No telling what she might do.

BEN

You don't have to worry.

IDA

I think I'll turn the house over to her.

BEN

She's took it already.

IDA

I mean let her cook and clean up for us. Old folks like to be kept active. Miss Gussie. Miss Gussie?

GUSSIE

I'm just sitting out here in the cool of the morning trying to mind my own business and keep out of folks way when I ain't wanted. The meek shall inherit the earth, you know.

IDA

(To Ben)

Go out and talk to her while I get dressed.

BEN

Shoot! All she ever talks about is me being a preacher.

IDA

Her feelings are hurt, honey, and—

BEN

My feelings and my back hurt—sleeping on that hard floor!

IDA

You mind me, Ben Marvin!

BEN

Shoot!

IDA

Go on out there now—and you be nice to her.

BEN

Ah, Ida Ray! (*Reluctantly he exits onto the porch. Ida Ray exits into her room. Miss Gussie sits rocking back and forth.*)

(*After an awkward moment*)
Daylight ain't even come up yet!

GUSSIE

This is when the air is the purest. People ain't rambling about spreading germs. Look up in the sky and say good morning to my Jesus. Say it, boy!

BEN

Good morning, Jesus.

GUSSIE

Now He'll keep His good eye on you for the rest of the day.

BEN

Shoot!

GUSSIE

When I was your age I would have had me a day's work done by now. We got up early to beat the heat. Folks used to say that the heat was the anger of the Lord. If there's any truth to that He sure must be angry with you young folks today. It gets hotter and hotter each summer. The world's to end by fire, you know. That's in the Bible which you ought to read each and every day. You're steeped in sin, I do hate to say.

BEN

I can't sin until I'm twelve.

GUSSIE

Who told you that lie?

BEN

Sister Sue Willie Hollis when she came through here with her tent revival.

GUSSIE

Shoot! I went me to one of them tent churches once. The preacher was a big foreign man who couldn't even speak the good Lord's English. Up there trying to convert me who had read the book from Genesis to Revelations. I asked him if there was a heaven before there was an earth. He said "yes." I asked him who was up there. He said,

"The Lord and the angels." And that's as much about it as that rascal knew.

BEN

Wasn't that enough?

GUSSIE

Maybe for somebody like you, but for a preacher—and somebody like me who knows my Bible well—Did you know that the devil was an angel before the earth was built?

BEN

He was?

GUSSIE

Well, he was. Up there in that beautiful heavenly garden carrying on like a sinner on Saturday night. Just as two-faced as he could be. Doing all his little sinning behind the Lord's back and thought the Lord didn't know about it. But the Lord knows everything, boy, and He sat a trap for him.

BEN

What was the devil doing?

GUSSIE

Up there chasing after them girl angels and playing cards. The good Lord kicked his behind right out of there. And do you know, the Lord was busy making Adam and here come the devil sailing down to earth. He landed on a rock and broke his arm to pieces—blood just spewed. And before the Lord could get Adam sewed up, seven drops of the devil's blood got inside him. And right today all you men got the devil in you. You're nothing but animals—old dogs!

BEN

You seemed to be right pleased with old Matthew Morris.

GUSSIE

Reverend Morris is a fine, upright, God-fearing man.

BEN

He's an undertaker, and anybody who embalms the dead has no business preaching.

GUSSIE

Somebody's got to do it. You'd just as soon let the dead rot away with no respect, huh?

BEN

No, I'd cremate 'em.

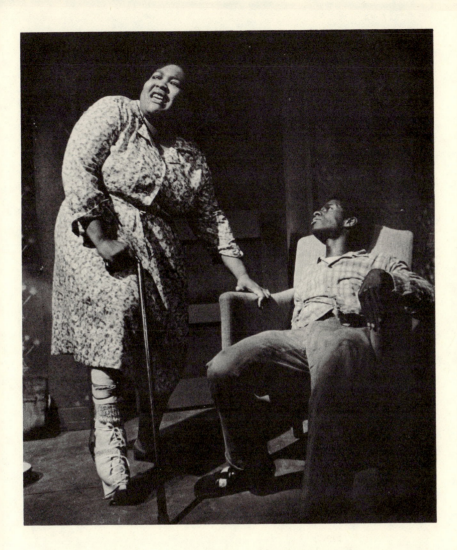

Ben and Gussie talking

GUSSIE

Who put that sinful idea into you, that traveling preacher-woman?

BEN

I read it in geography. In India they always cremate their dead. It's more sanitary.

GUSSIE

I'm glad I ain't no Indian then. The Bible says: "Ashes to ash. Dust to dust."

BEN

When I die, I'll turn to rust. Take my body and let it burn, and put my ashes in a golden urn.

GUSSIE

The only thing you and your daddy's got in common is a name. If you were my child—

BEN

I know you want to beat me.

GUSSIE

Beat some sense in your mannish head.

BEN

I make all A's! I even made A's from Mr. Tolbert when he was teaching here—and he was a graduate of Harvard University!

GUSSIE

Just who is this old Mr. Tolbert you and Ida Ray keep mentioning?

BEN

He was the smartest man you'd ever want to meet.

GUSSIE

Then what was he doing down here?

BEN

Teaching. Mama said that he was a crusader. He came all the way from Providence, Rhode Island, to teach for a year right here in Earth, Texas, and he lived with us while he was here. You've never seen such activity in this old house. We used to sit around listening to him talk for hours. He'd tell us all sorts of things we'd never heard of before. And he'd let us read his books. He told Mama that I was exceptional—and he got me to start my library. He still sends me books for it.

GUSSIE

What kind of old books?

BEN

You've seen 'em. I have classical books—*A Tale of Two Cities, The Adventures of Tom Sawyer.* I even have me a Negro library—books by such famous authors as Richard Wright, Langston Hughes, and James Baldwin—

GUSSIE

I ain't never heard of none of 'em.

BEN

'Cause you've never read a book!

GUSSIE

The Bible is a book!

BEN

Anybody can thumb through the Bible.

GUSSIE

All that junk you're reading sure ain't gonna get you to the promised land. Oh, I looked at one of them old books you got in yonder—wasn't nothing in it but a lot of old words. Why don't you get you some books with some pretty pictures in 'em?

BEN

I've got one in there you might like—it's called *Baby Pony.*

GUSSIE

Well . . . all this reading and schooling ain't everything. It's religion and mother wit that got me this far in life. You're gonna be a sorry man when you grow up. If you listen to me, boy, I can fix up your future.

BEN

I don't want to be no preacher!

GUSSIE

Because your mama didn't make you go to Sunday school. You've got to have ambition, boy. What're you gonna be when you come of age?

BEN

I'm gonna be—like Mr. Tolbert—a grown man of *dignity!*

GUSSIE

If you ain't a mess! Letting that old uppity schoolteacher and Cora and Ida fill your head full of junk like that. You'd better be something that's gonna put some money in your pockets. Now you sit down here and let me tell you the miracle in my life. I've had the sign of God come to me.

BEN

When?

GUSSIE

A long time ago. Listen. This is something that's meant for only my close kin.

BEN

What?

GUSSIE

You see this leg? It's the miracle. I know folks wonder why I painted it white—they got all sorts of reasons.

BEN

You just want to attract attention.

GUSSIE

Old Ida Ray told you that but it's only partially true. Sure, I want to attract attention—you know why?

BEN

No.

GUSSIE

So that I can spread His word. If I can save me a soul a year—just a single soul—that means an extra year for me up there in His land.

BEN

You're supposed to live in heaven eternally.

GUSSIE

Stop being smart and listen to me. Sit still. (*She extends her leg toward him.*) Go on take a good look at it. I've seen you sneaking glimpses when my back's turned.

BEN

I don't want to look at that old thing!

GUSSIE

Be quiet and let me go on. And you concentrate on what I'm saying. This story can lead you to glory. What does this leg look like to you?

BEN

A big fat pencil that's been whittled down to nothing and chewed on.

GUSSIE

Sticks and stones may break my bones, baby, but words is for the birds. Shoot. I used to be like you—a real big sin-

ner. Lived in sin for almost forty years. Used to sell boot-
leg whiskey. And drink. I could tear up a quart of liquor!
Trying to keep up with that rotten grandpa of yours.
Sometimes I'd get drunk and be out for days. One day I
woke up with a hangover this big. Your uncle Leroy was
just a baby then. He was laying over in a corner half dead.
While I was passed out rats had nibbled on him and
roaches and ants had almost covered his body. It was an
awful thing to see and it was a warning from the Lord. I
had to slow down. I had to break away from your granddaddy's sinful ways and give my attention to my boys. I
got myself together and nursed Leroy back to health and I
lived in me a church from then on.

BEN

How did you lose your leg?

GUSSIE

It was a stone that broke the bone—a cornerstone, but let
me finish what I had to say first. I got me a new set of
righteous friends and I was happy. I tried for years to save
your grandfather, but the devil had his hands around that
man's heart and he wouldn't turn him loose. I was the one
who was responsible for our church being built in Forney.
A stone church with a slate roof that couldn't burn. A bolt
of lightning struck that foreign preacher's tent in the midst
of one of his sermons. It caught fire and burned down
umpteen people. That's why we wanted us a brick church.
I helped lay the bricks myself. When it was completed—all
except the cornerstone, we held a picnic. Barbeque, pies,
big freezers of ice cream. Oh, it was an occasion. At exactly five o'clock that old foreign preacher drove his mule
and wagon into the churchyard. He was a broken, sinful
man if I had ever seen one. He testified and told us that
he had been a hypocrite; that he had asked the Lord's
forgiveness and that he wanted to join up with us. And he
had brung us a marble cornerstone—all engraved. There
was praying and rejoicing that day. I stood atop that
wagon leading the songs. Old Sister Crawford got happy
and let out a merciful yell—WOOOOOOOOWWW, JE-
SUS!—right into that mule's ear. He bucked and the next
thing I knew I was laying on the ground, and that marble
stone was resting across this leg. It took eight strong men
to move it. And while all this was happening your grand-

daddy was out drunk and fornicating with the floozies. Lord, I was a bloody mess. Bones crushed to pieces like toothpicks—you could just pluck 'em out by the hands full.

BEN

I'll bet it hurt.

GUSSIE

I didn't feel a thing, child. Not even when they cut my leg off. I was suffering for my Jesus and I didn't feel a thing. The church give me this leg—pure grade D Georgia pine.

BEN

Why did you paint it?

GUSSIE

Because I had been washed with the blood of the lamb. I was reborn! Bathed in sweet salvation—saved! And I'm happy to say that I'm more active now than ever. That's my miracle.

BEN

It is something.

GUSSIE

Be my friend, boy, and get on the good side of life.

BEN

I am.

GUSSIE

Well, I guess it's not so much what a person does, it's what goes on in his mind. I've seen you thinking, child. Where's old Ida Ray?

BEN

She's getting dressed.

GUSSIE

Probably in there taking a nap with her lazy self. Boy, how come you won't open your eyes to the things around you?

BEN

My eyes are always opened.

GUSSIE

Yeah, you see everything and you don't see nothing. Don't you know old Ida Ray don't like you?

BEN

She likes me a lot better than you do!

GUSSIE

You're a burden to her, boy. A young gal like that wants

to be out sporting and you're in her way. Ah, don't play like you don't know what I'm talking about. I watched you last night—don't nothing slip by me. You asked her if she wanted you to meet her after church and she said no —and you sat up in there watching for her to come home and she wasn't alone either, was she?

BEN

I don't know what you're talking about.

GUSSIE

Don't lie to me. You know that man brung her home last night. I seen 'em too. Giggling and acting right giddy. Who does she think she is anyway—trying to spark! But let me tell you, son, who ever that dog was with her has got her going, and she's gonna marry him and kick your behind right out in the cold. You'll find out who your friend is then.

BEN

I . . . I . . . I don't know what you're talking about!

GUSSIE

Um-huh.

BEN

How bad did those rats bite Uncle Leroy?

GUSSIE

Bad enough, but, oh, I fixed 'em. I got me some New Fidelity Rat and Roach Paste. You put it on bread like a sandwich. It looks right moldy and it smokes when you first spread it. They used to think I was giving them a real treat. I'd cover the top of it with a little jelly or a little bitty piece of cheese. They'd bite into it and it would tear their insides out just like that. They'd roll over then and there—eyes bulging out and all fours sticking up.

BEN

That's how Bo looked when he died. You think that New Fidelity Paste could kill something as big as a dog?

GUSSIE

It could kill you if I gave you enough.

BEN

Oh.

IDA RAY

(*Entering. She moves to porch. She is dressed for work.*)
Gonna be another scorcher today.

GUSSIE

Be it the will of the good Lord.

IDA

Miss Gussie, you know I've been thinking, and it would be sort of nice if you—

GUSSIE

What?

IDA

Cora and Marvin used to often talk about what a fine housekeeper and cook you are.

GUSSIE

I'm proud to say I've never had no complaints.

IDA

Wouldn't it be nice, Ben, if Miss Gussie would treat us to one of her meals?

BEN

I don't know . . .

IDA

Your daddy used to marvel over her lemon pies.

BEN

He did talk about 'em.

GUSSIE

Well, once you've tasted the nectar off the vine, plain old water don't mean much. But I can't do much in a kitchen in all this heat, Ida.

IDA

Once I get busy doing something I like I forget about the heat completely. And there's always a nice breeze blowing through.

GUSSIE

I ain't never felt it, child.

IDA

Miss Gussie, you'd sure be doing me a favor if you'd fix Ben Marvin a hot lunch. He seldom eats when I'm not here. You know how children are.

GUSSIE

I taught my boys how to cook for themselves before they were seven years old. It's a shame Cora let this child grow up ignorant, but these modern wives—

BEN

I'm not ignorant!

IDA

Ben! (*She gives him a hard look.*) There's a lot to be done around here. I've made out a little list.

GUSSIE

What's this first one? I ain't got my glasses on.

BEN

(*Reading*) Mop kitchen, wash dishes, clean . . .

IDA

I've cleaned up my room already and your bed's made.

GUSSIE

(*Studies list for a moment.*) When you get to be my age you just have to sit and rest and thank the Lord you're alive and breathing. Can't take on the burdens of the young like you used to could.

IDA

I haven't been feeling too well, lately, and—I'm so tired when I get home. These are just simple things.

GUSSIE

It ain't that I don't want to be helpful, Ida, but this leg of mine bothers me something awful at times.

IDA

Ben Marvin, you do the heavy things, hear?

GUSSIE

There ain't nothing on this list that this boy can't do his-self, Ida. Young'ns have to be taught to work if they're to amount to anything. Lord, I'm tired and daybreak's coming up. Boy, bring me my hat.

IDA

Miss Gussie, where're you off to this early?

GUSSIE

Down the road for a spell. Guess I'll have a little coffee with Sister Sedrick—although the Lord knows she fills a sorry cup.

IDA

That poor soul has seven children and lots of housework to do, and Mr. Myron's job has played out.

GUSSIE

I told 'em to put things in the hands of the Lord. Bring me my tambourine and drum, boy, I think I'll get me a little session going while I'm down there. (*Ben exits for things.*)

IDA

Miss Gussie, I think you ought to stay home this morning and keep an eye on Ben Marvin. Like you said, you don't know what devilment a child his age might get into.

GUSSIE

Don't worry about this boy, child. He ain't gonna do a thing but collect wood and stack it behind the barn. Got enough back there already to last three winters.

IDA

If you're so tired, you ought to stay here and rest. You have no business roaming up and down this road. (*Ben enters with hat, tambourine, and drum.*)

GUSSIE

I ain't got much longer for this old world, child. I want to see me the sights and talk with the folks before I pass on.

IDA

There's nothing to see around here that you haven't already seen, and the folks are tired of you.

GUSSIE

What did you say?

IDA

Folks are beginning to find you a nuisance.

GUSSIE

(*Hurt*) They like me a heap better than they do you because I'm friendly and helpful—and a Christian.

BEN

You're eating all of Miss Sedrick's food.

GUSSIE

That's a lie! She's never sat a decent plate before me.

IDA

All the same, you stay here and take care of this house, you hear me?

GUSSIE

I ain't no maid.

IDA

Miss Gussie . . .

GUSSIE

Ida, child, you're yelling at me like I'm deaf.

IDA

I don't mean to yell, but—

GUSSIE

(*To Ben*) Give me my hat son, you're squeezing the flowers.

IDA

Miss Gussie, I didn't mean to hurt your feelings, it's just that—

GUSSIE

I know you're trying to make me do your work, but like I told you I ain't nobody's maid, child. I came way out here to take care of old Cora, and you didn't give me a cent.

IDA

Now you listen here, Miss Gussie, I feed you and put a roof over your head. You didn't bring a cent with you when you came—the ticket that brought you here was bought with money out of my pocket. And as far as your taking care of Cora is concerned, I wrote and told you how things were—I asked you if you wanted to come and you said yes—nobody forced you. Now you're just being lazy and stubborn, that's all. I've gone out of my way to treat you nice, and you know you're not any kin to me at all.

GUSSIE

I'm gonna take me a little stroll and see how come the folks around here don't like me.

IDA

Miss Gussie, I told you to stay home!

GUSSIE

I'm a grown woman, child, I don't have to mind you. (*She starts toward the road.*) See yawl this evening, the good Lord willing. I just got to get away from this house of sin where I can't serve my Jesus when I get up in the morning. (*She exits singing.*)

IDA

(*Calls after her.*) If you're so miserable here go on back to Forney—I'll gladly buy you a ticket anytime you're ready. (*To Ben*) That old critter is more than a notion.

BEN

Yeah. She killed a hundred rats with New Fidelity Rat and Roach Paste, and she told me how she lost her leg.

IDA

I'm not interested. Come on in and help me with the dishes. (*They exit into the kitchen.*)

BEN

You believe she poisoned Granddaddy?

IDA

I wouldn't put it past her.

BEN

Me neither. (*There is silence as they begin working, Ida washing the dishes and Ben drying them and putting them in the cupboard. On his way back to the sink he spies the calendar.*) The calendar says frost today!

IDA

You believe it in this heat?

BEN

Just the same I'm taking my rocker back.

IDA

I don't mind. She's taken it from me anyway.

BEN

I'm gonna tell her—this is my chair during winter and nobody else sits in it but me. Boy, I hope it freezes and I can light my fire.

IDA

You're a strange one, Ben Marvin. I have yet to see a young boy like you who just loves sitting before that old fireplace in an old rocking chair night after night after night.

BEN

That's where I make my plans (*Ida clutches back of chair, cringes for a moment.*) What's the matter, Ida Ray?

IDA

Oh. Oh . . . God . . . Another one of those pains.

BEN

You'd better go see Dr. Green.

IDA

(*Trying to be cheerful*) It's hot in this kitchen. This dress is sticking to me like another layer of skin. Why in the world don't you ever sweat in all this heat?

BEN

I donno.

> (*Ida gets the broom and begins sweeping. She hums an old blues song. Ben joins in, then to amuse her, improvises a few dance steps. He takes her into his arms and dances her about the room, then sits*

her in a chair and begins his floor show. He begins to sing.)

BEN

Oh,
She had a wooden leg!
All stiff at the knee
Just like a wooden peg
It was just a limb off the old pine tree
Pure Georgia pine
A good grade D!

(*During the song Miss Gussie enters and stands in the doorway. Ida sees her, but Ben does not. When he does spy the old woman, he begins to giggle uncontrollably. Ida is amused, but conceals it. The old woman is upright and shocked.*)

IDA

Ben Marvin! Where did you learn that song? You ought to be ashamed of yourself, boy. (*He giggles.*) Apologize to Miss Gussie. You hear me?

GUSSIE

Aint' no need to put yourself out.

IDA

Ben Marvin, are you going to apologize?

GUSSIE

You're just as much to blame as he is.

IDA

Miss Gussie, I'm terribly sorry.

GUSSIE

Huh!

IDA

I thought you were walking—

GUSSIE

I had to come back for my pocketbook—and a good thing too. I can see how I'm sassed and made fun of when my back's turned.

BEN

Snooping!

IDA

Boy, I'm gonna take off this shoe! Miss Gussie, he didn't mean any harm. It's just an old song he heard on the radio.

GUSSIE

I know you don't like me, Ida Ray.

IDA

Say what?

GUSSIE

You needn't try to lie. I seen the gleam of hate in your eyes the very day I come here. But let me tell you this, child. My son worked like a slave to pay for this house and died before he could enjoy it good. But he had foresight, child. He knew you and old Cora wasn't no good, so he sent me the deed to this place before he died. This is my property you living in—*and* soon as my pension check gets here I'm gonna see me a lawyer.

BEN

This is not your house either!

IDA

I worked just as hard as Marvin did to pay for this house and so did Cora. And when we bought it they gave me a third interest in it. I have the deed, honey. You may have one of those photostats that Marvin had made, but this is my house—my property and Ben's. I don't know what you're talking about.

GUSSIE

I'm gonna take it up with a lawyer.

IDA

You do what you want to do, it's not gonna worry me a bit.

GUSSIE

All of my family has had long life spans—all of us. Wasn't no cause for my boy to die suddenly like that at his age—except he had a helping hand from somebody.

IDA

Marvin died of natural causes—it's down in black and white on the death certificate!

GUSSIE

I seen that old thing, but a death certificate ain't a fart. Your old sister stole my boy. Brought him out here and ruined him.

IDA

Miss Gussie, I was taught not to argue with a fool. You

know as well as I do that no woman can steal a grown man. Cora and Marvin loved each other, they got married and left Forney to get away from you. And believe me honey, I can see why.

GUSSIE

He wouldn't have left if she hadn't poisoned his mind against me—Marvin loved his mama.

IDA

I never would have known it from what he said about you.

GUSSIE

I just want you to know that I know things. I never aimed to be no burden to nobody. Me and the good Lord walks hand in hand.

BEN

You don't do nothing!

IDA

Ben Marvin, be quiet, and Miss Gussie, don't you say another word.

GUSSIE

This is a free country, child, and I got a right to say my piece. I told Marvin old Cora wasn't no good, but men are weak to sinner women. I was training that boy to be a preacher, and Cora come along and took him. He was gonna be a rich preacher and send Melvin and Leroy off to school, and all of 'em together was gonna build me a brick house. Then old Cora took him and brought him out here and ruined all our lives. Leroy's in the pen and Melvin's dead because of your sister.

IDA

You pack your things and hit that road before I get back, you hear me? Be gone!

GUSSIE

It don't matter to me. They kicked Jesus out of the temple. But I can turn the other cheek, child.

IDA

You turn it in the direction of Forney and make it!

GUSSIE

Ahhhhhhhhhh! (*Takes butcher knife and slams it into the table. The others stand in fear and silence. Gussie composes herself.*) I'm gonna cook you up the last supper, child. Fix you up a treat you'll never forget. (*Exiting outside*) I'm gonna run into town and get me a few things.

BEN

You forgot your suitcase!

GUSSIE

I'll be back.

BEN

Is she really leaving, Ida Ray?

IDA

Um-huh. And you forget about what was said, you hear me?

BEN

(*Nods*) Where'll she go?

IDA

I don't know and care less.

BEN

Didn't I hear you and Mama say something about her not being able to go back to Forney?

IDA

Haven't I told you about eavesdropping?

BEN

I couldn't help it if you talked loud.

IDA

I hear that she was in some sort of trouble concerning the folks she worked for.

BEN

What kind of trouble?

IDA

I don't know, so don't ask me.

BEN

Where'll she go then? She don't have any kin.

IDA

There're homes that'll take the old in.

BEN

Does she know about them?

IDA

That old woman is as strong and healthy as I am. She's shrewd enough not to starve. She's got sense and she can make it. She made it all these years without me. How come you're so concerned all of a sudden? I thought that you were eager for her to leave.

Ida Ray comforting Ben

BEN

I am, but she is right pitiful sometimes like you said—with that leg and all—and she's trying to be nice to you before she leaves.

IDA

She's not staying, Ben Marvin, and that's for sure. I've stood all that I can stand. If I let her stay it'll be the same thing over and over again. (*Picks up the old woman's plate.*) She didn't eat a thing. And look at this toast.

BEN

(*Examining it*) I'll bet that's New Fidelity Rat Paste!!

IDA

Wipe the table off.

BEN

(*Doing as commanded*) Ida Ray?

IDA

Huh?

BEN

Do you love me?

IDA

What a question to ask at this hour in the morning.

BEN

I just want to know.

IDA

Boy, you know I love you. Whatever prompted such a question?

BEN

Well . . . I . . .

IDA

I know that old woman has tried and tried to turn you against me, but you're too intelligent to be taken in by somebody like that. Cora taught you to be independent— to think for yourself and to stand on your own two feet. To be proud.

BEN

It's not her or anything that she said.

IDA

(*Embraces him.*) I know. You miss your mama, don't you. (*Ben nods.*) I do too sugar, but we've got to keep our chins up—that's what she'd want us to do. This old house gets terribly lonely sometimes, but I never let it get me down because I've got you—and you've got me. Look, if you get lonely today, why don't you go down and play with Joe Sedrick or the little Simpson boy?

BEN

No. I'm gonna collect my wood. And I don't get lonesome —not often. Mama wouldn't want me to.

IDA

That's a good boy. And you have nothing to worry about, do you?

BEN

Yes, I do too! You think things'll be different when she leaves? I mean like they were before—with just me and you and—

IDA

Of course they will, sugar.

BEN

I don't think so.

IDA

Why not?

BEN

I saw you coming home from church last night—and I know why you didn't want me to meet you now.

IDA

Oh, that's it. Ben you can't go on holding a grudge against somebody like that. Reverend Morris admits now that he was wrong. He's very fond of you.

BEN

Do you plan to marry him?

IDA

(*Stunned by the boy's bluntness*) Well . . . er . . . we have talked about it.

BEN

If you do you're crazy! He's ignorant and crazy and ugly too!

IDA

Ben Marvin!

BEN

It's true. He's got a great big belly and rotten teeth and he thinks he's cute! Daddy never liked him and I don't either. And if you marry him I'm leaving!

IDA

Ben Marvin, you're old enough to understand things, sugar. Reverend Morris is a respected man in this community. He was your mother's pastor—your father's pastor. Both he and I are lonely and we have a lot in common.

BEN

What?

IDA

We enjoy each other's company for one thing.

BEN

Don't you enjoy my company?

IDA

Of course I do. Ben Marvin, you're being selfish and unreasonable. Cora would be surprised at you. She didn't raise you this way. You know that you can't have me to yourself always—just like I won't have you. One day you'll leave here sugar and it'll hurt me to my heart, but I know you're going to leave. And once you get out of this dull place you're never coming back. Reverend Morris and I have talked about you a lot. He honestly likes and respects you. Together we can send you off to college if you continue to do as well in school as you've been doing.

BEN

I don't want that old man to give me nothing!

IDA

I've got to be off to work. (*Starts to door.*) Ben, don't let this bother you. You're too sensitive sometimes. We've only talked about it . . . nothing more. Now you be a good boy, hear? (*She exits outside.*) Help the old woman pack if she wants you to.

BEN

Ida, do you really want to get married?

IDA

All women dream of marrying and having a home and a family of her own, sugar.

BEN

Why didn't you marry Mr. Tolbert when he was here? You liked him, didn't you?

IDA

Of course I liked him.

BEN

Then why didn't you marry him?

IDA

Well . . . Mr. Tolbert had a girl friend up East, son.

BEN

Would you have married him if he had asked you?

IDA

Well . . . I . . . Ben, boy, he didn't ask me, and you stop questioning me this way! I'll be late for work. (*She starts off.*)

BEN

(*Moves onto the porch.*) I wasn't playing, Ida Ray. If you marry that man I'm leaving!! (*He dashes from the porch and exits out of sight before Ida can answer. She stands for a moment, then shakes her head from side to side.*)

IDA

Ben! Ben Marvin! . . . Lord . . . today . . . (*She turns and heads down the road slowly.*)

(*The lights dim.*)
Curtain

SCENE 2 *Noon. Ben enters the yard with an armful of wood. He carries it into the living room and places it beside the fireplace. The fireplace has been stuffed with papers and pieces of wood and is ready to be lit. The rocker has been moved from the back porch and placed before the fireplace. The boy hums excitedly as he works. He rushes from the house, stands atop the porch and gazes momentarily into the sky. The day has changed. The sky is a much paler blue now, and during this scene changes to a cold, windy white. Miss Gussie enters into the yard. Ben tries to hide under the steps, but it is too late; the old woman has seen him.*

GUSSIE

Boy!

BEN

Huh?

GUSSIE

You say "ma'am" to me.

BEN

I was brought up to say "yes" and "no."

GUSSIE

Respect thy elders, devil! Repent: for the kingdom of heaven is at hand.

BEN

I don't care! Where've you been anyway?

GUSSIE

To get me some paint.

BEN

You could have painted a barn as long as you've been gone.

GUSSIE

I made a few visits.

BEN

I hope you didn't go by Miss Sedrick's. I'm tired of Joe telling me to keep you home.

GUSSIE

I did go by there and Miss Sedrick said that she was more than glad to see me. I told her all about how I'm treated here.

BEN

We treat you fine!

GUSSIE

Stop yelling at me.

BEN

You had no business talking about us like that.

GUSSIE

Hush your mouth and come into this kitchen and let me fix you a bite to eat.

BEN

I don't want any of your food.

GUSSIE

You're a living beanpole. Ida Ray is starving you to death and you're too dumb to realize it.

BEN

What time are you going back to Forney?

GUSSIE

When I get good and ready. Child, you should be ashamed of yourself talking to me this way. I came way out here to nurse your sick mama and to see you, and you treat me this-a-way. But remember: That except your righteousness shall exceed the righteousness of the scribes and Pharisees, ye shall in no case enter into the kingdom

of heaven. Where's my rocker? I've got to sit down and
rest these weary bones.

BEN

There's a chair.

GUSSIE

I want *my* rocker!

BEN

That's Ida Ray's rocker during the summer and mine during the winter.

GUSSIE

Oh, you're a hard one all right. The devil has firm grips on
you.

BEN

He ain't got nothing!

GUSSIE

You'd better take heed to the old and the experienced before it's too late. I've lived through it all. I don't have
much longer to be here, so treat me nice, boy, or be
barred eternally from heaven.

BEN

Huh!

GUSSIE

I'm gonna have a personal talk with the Lord the minute I
pass through those gates—about you. Now get me that
rocker.

BEN

Shoot! (*Marches angrily into the house and fetches
rocker.*)

GUSSIE

And you stop that cussin'.

BEN

(*Mumbling*) Can't do nothing!

GUSSIE

I believe it's cooling off a bit. The sky is almost as white
as my leg. I'm gonna start supper directly, then we're
gonna clean up this house spotless. (*Ben enters with
chair.*) Where's that list of things Ida left here for us to do?

BEN

I don't know.

GUSSIE

Look at you. Sticking that lip out at your poor old dying
grandmother. Ain't there no love in your heart for me?

BEN

You don't love me!

GUSSIE

Child, no matter how bad you are, no matter how your mama and Ida turned you against me, I love you. You're all I got left in this world now.

BEN

You got Uncle Leroy.

GUSSIE

No, child. He's in the pen for life. I won't see him no more till he reaches the promised land. I'm alone child and lonely. My only comfort has been the Lord. (*Sings: "Abide with Me." Extends hand to boy.*) Sit here in my lap and let me rock you like I used to rock your daddy when he was a little boy. (*The boy sits.*) I never have held you in my arms, have I? You're right heavy, but I don't mind. I love my boys—all of 'em—including you.

BEN

You really love me?

GUSSIE

Just like I love the Lord. Here I brought you some candy back from town.

BEN

It's melted.

GUSSIE

Put it in the icebox.

BEN

I will.

GUSSIE

Well, ain't you gonna thank me?

BEN

Thanks . . . Grandmama.

GUSSIE

I declare, that's the first time you've ever called me that, Mr. Benjamin Marvin.

BEN

That's the first time you've ever called me Benjamin. (*He notices the sack that she has brought with her from town.*) What else did you buy?

GUSSIE

A tube of roach paste. I thought I seen a roach in my room this morning.

BEN

We don't have roaches.

GUSSIE

All the same it's best to be prepared.

BEN

That's a mighty big tube.

GUSSIE

On sale. I got me a can of paint too. My leg needs a new coat.

BEN

It looks okay to me.

GUSSIE

I like to look my best when I travel.

BEN

What time do you plan to leave?

GUSSIE

Er . . . as soon as my check gets in.

BEN

You've been waiting on that check a long time.

GUSSIE

Sometimes the mail is slow, but it should be here any minute now.

BEN

My money got here a month after mama died.

GUSSIE

Your insurance money? (*He nods.*) Five hundred dollars —what're you gonna do with all that money?

BEN

I'm gonna use it to go to college.

GUSSIE

You should give a tenth of that to the Lord.

BEN

I'm keeping every penny of that money in the bank.

GUSSIE

Whatever you give to the Lord you always get back two-fold.

BEN

I'm satisfied with my 3 percent interest.

GUSSIE

I saw Reverend Morris this morning. He asked about you.

BEN

Don't mention him around me.

GUSSIE

We had a long talk. He told me how you carried on at your daddy's wake before all those people. The dead's not to be feared, son.

BEN

And not to be touched either. Every time I think about it I get a real funny feeling.

GUSSIE

You didn't act that way when Cora died.

BEN

I know, but I was just seven when Daddy died.

GUSSIE

Reverend Morris was trying to do the right thing.

BEN

I don't want to talk about it.

GUSSIE

Children are supposed to touch their kinfolks when they die. You touch them a last farewell and you'll never be scaired of the dead for the rest of your life.

BEN

That's what you think.

GUSSIE

I've washed and dressed many a dead person. I'm glad Reverend Morris made you touch your daddy—he was doing the right thing. They tell me it made you some sick.

BEN

I was in bed all summer and part of the fall.

GUSSIE

And after that you never sweated, huh? Not even on the hottest days?

BEN

I haven't sweated since I could remember.

GUSSIE

Folks around here think it's sort of mysterious . . . that plus the fact that you act right grown-up sometimes for a boy your age. This could be a miracle, you know. A sign from the Lord asking you to serve Him. Boy, if you were a preacher I'd dress you in a white satin robe and take you from town to town to spread the Holy Ghost.

BEN

Thought you didn't like those moving churches.

GUSSIE

I don't. You'd preach in brick churches that were established—not in some old tent that would burn. God willing, we could make us pots of money. I could teach you how to preach. I'm a deaconess.

BEN

I've been to church in my day. I reckon I know how to preach if I wanted to.

GUSSIE

Have you ever preached, boy?

BEN

We used to play church sometimes.

GUSSIE

Preachers get rich—wouldn't you like to be rich?

BEN

Yeah.

GUSSIE

With money you can do anything—buy fine property, big cars, clothes. You could travel the world over and still have plenty of money in your pocket. What would you do with all that money, boy?

BEN

I'd give it to Ida.

GUSSIE

Of course you would. You're fond of your old grandmother—you're just too stubborn to admit it. All of my children were fond of me. Every one of my sons promised to buy me a house. They would have done it too if things hadn't gone wrong.

BEN

Didn't Grandpa buy you one?

GUSSIE

Shoot! That old rascal was full of promises and liquor.

BEN

Then why did you marry him?

GUSSIE

I was young and easy to impress. Lord, that man was a diamond in the rough, a dap-daddy—big and good-looking and flashy. I listened to him and let him twist my very stockings. After we married I found out that all of his old talk wasn't nothing but air! Son, I see something good in

you and I'm aiming to bring it out. How would you like to
go back home with me?

BEN

I don't know.

GUSSIE

Think of all the sinning souls we could save together—and
all the money we'd make.

BEN

If you can get so rich preaching, why don't you preach?

GUSSIE

You ever hear of a woman prophet?

BEN

Sister Sue Willie Hollis.

GUSSIE

Shoot! I'm talking about in the Bible. Women can be dea-
conesses and ushers and sing in the choir, but the word is
to be delivered by a man. Come on and go with me.

BEN

Ida Ray wouldn't let me go.

GUSSIE

I'm more kin to you than that gal is—I'm your grandmama,
she's just your auntie. Anyway, she don't have to know. I
checked on the buses when I was in town. We can get one
out of here before she wakes up.

BEN

I can't run off!

GUSSIE

Why not? You'd be with me—working for the Lord.

BEN

Sister Sue Willie told me you had to be called to preach.

GUSSIE

What does she know about it?

BEN

She knows a lot more than you do.

GUSSIE

Who's supposed to call you?

BEN

The Lord.

GUSSIE

He's given you the sign and you and that woman are too
dumb to see it.

BEN

What sign?

GUSSIE

You're not sweating! That's the will of the Lord, boy.

BEN

Shoot!

GUSSIE

Your trouble is you don't believe.

BEN

How do you know?

GUSSIE

You don't go to church.

BEN

And I'm not going as long as old Matthew Morris is preaching, but that don't mean I don't believe. My mama used to go to church—she taught me the Bible, and I go to Sister Sue Willie's church every time she comes to town. Ida goes to church.

GUSSIE

You can see what kind of Christian woman old Ida is by the way she treats me. Putting me out in the world when folk're already starting to bed down for the winter.

BEN

You brought it on yourself. If you had acted decent it never would have happened.

GUSSIE

That gal never liked me because I stand for right. And if Cora was such a good Christian, how come she stole my boy?

BEN

She didn't steal Daddy! Anyway—you're trying to steal me.

GUSSIE

I don't steal, child! I'd be crazy to steal anything as honery as you. Now run in there and get my tambourine and bring that drum. Let's have us a little holy session before I start fixing supper.

BEN

Don't you ever get tired of going into those trances?

GUSSIE

I don't ever tire of doing for my Jesus. Now hurry while

the sun's still behind the clouds. (*She begins to limber up a bit, singing a religious song—slowly and quietly.*) You beat the drum for me. I want a rhythm like this. Start it slow at first, then you get faster and faster. (*She starts the song and beats the tambourine. Ben beats the drum.*) Sing with me, child. Listen to the music and sing and you'll feel the spirit creeping up through your toes and your hair'll stand on end. Praise the Lord! Hallelujah! Sing, child! Feel the glory that a true Christian is feeling. (*She begins to shake herself until she is removed from reality. The song gets louder and faster as does the old woman's dance. She collapses into the rocker, her eyes bulging. She gasps for breath. Ben moves quickly to her not knowing what to do. She goes into trance.*)

BEN

Grandma? Grandma?

GUSSIE

Can't breathe . . . (*Ben rushes into the house and gets a glass of water. He gives it to her. Slowly she comes around.*)

BEN

Grandmama, you all right? (*She nods.*) How do you feel?

GUSSIE

I feel fine now—like I was reborn almost. What was that you give me to drink.

BEN

Huh?

GUSSIE

Whatever it was it really brought me back to life quick. Serving the Lord can sometimes wear a poor soul out, but you sure fixed me up quick. I feel like a new woman. Amen! (*She looks at the boy.*) Say Amen with me.

BEN

Amen.

GUSSIE

God bless you.

BEN

How do you feel when you get that way?

GUSSIE

What way?

BEN

In one of those trances?

GUSSIE

Child, it's like the thrill of love. Once you've experienced it you have to go back for more and more.

BEN

Can anybody feel it?

GUSSIE

No, child, it's reserved for those of us that's loved by Jesus.

BEN

Jesus loves everybody.

GUSSIE

Shoot! That's what you think. He don't love old Ida Ray anymore than I do.

BEN

You believe what you want to believe.

GUSSIE

I believe what I know.

BEN

I believe what I read.

GUSSIE

There's only one book worth reading and that's the book of facts—the Holy Bible. All this junk you read ain't worth a fart.

BEN

Ida don't allow me to use that word.

GUSSIE

Well, ain't she cute.

BEN

You're supposed to be a real Christian lady and you honest-to-goodness don't like Ida Ray, do you?

GUSSIE

I am a real honest-to-goodness Christian lady and I don't like her—never have and never will—and that's the God's truth.

BEN

The Bible says "love thy enemies."

GUSSIE

Don't I know it? Didn't I say I was gonna fix her up a treat? Why, child, I'm gonna fix her up a meal that's gonna lay her right out on this floor.

BEN

Huh?

GUSSIE

Light the stove for me so I can get started.

BEN

Ida Ray might not be hungry when she gets in.

GUSSIE

That gal's always hungry.

BEN

She's going to church tonight so she might eat at the Lappas'.

GUSSIE

You light me that stove, boy, and let me get in here and work for the Lord. (*They enter the kitchen. Ben starts the fire and the old woman busies herself with the cooking.*) Give me that bowl. Now go on outside and play. I don't want nobody in my kitchen but me.

BEN

Can't I help?

GUSSIE

No. I won't have you stealing my recipes. Now get on out of here.

BEN

What are you cooking?

GUSSIE

Oh, I think I'll do a little stew.

BEN

I can peel the potatoes!

GUSSIE

Scat!

(*Ben exits slowly into the front yard. He is disturbed over Gussie's sudden desire to be helpful. He is about to sneak to the kitchen window when there is a hiss from behind the bush in the front yard. Ben stops short. Miss Sue Willie Hollis sticks her head out. She is in her early thirties—plump, youthful, and naive in matters other than religious. She is dressed in a silk print dress, a conservative hat and shoes. She wears little or no makeup. Her pulpit manner is obvious. Sister Sue Willie has never known a man intimately, and she longs to. Because of her occupation she feels that this is im-*

possible. Her one desire now is to wait until Ben is old enough to seduce her or be seduced by her.)

SISTER SUE

SSsssssssssssssssstttttttttttt! Little Daddy!

BEN

Sister Sue Willie! What are you doing here?

SISTER SUE

Passing through on my way to Muleshoe. I just had to see you, honey. Myyyyyyy, you've grown in these past few months. Your chest has filled out and you're getting muscles.

BEN

Yes'um, but I can't talk long now.

SISTER SUE

Ida ain't around, is she?

BEN

She's at work, but my grandmother's home.

SISTER SUE

Then it's safe for me to come out, huh? (*She enters into the yard.*) Lord, I've been perched behind that bush for hours waiting to see you. Boy, you're getting finer every day. Open your mouth and let me see your teeth. (*She examines his teeth.*) Perfect! I just adore men with perfect teeth. Turn around and let me look you over good. Goodness gracious, if you ain't something! Firming up and maturing every minute. The little girls around here ain't been putting their hands on you, have they? (*He shakes his head no.*) That's good. You know there're still Delilahs in this world, baby, and they will clip your hair just as sure as I'm standing here. But you save yourself for your Sister Sue Hollis, hear?

BEN

Yes'um. Sister Sue Willie, you know that I enjoy talking to you but right now I've got to—

SISTER SUE

Ah Little Daddy, you're not trying to get away from Sister Sue are you? I ran all the way here from town just to gaze upon you—and behold! You're a light in the darkness. Seek, baby, and ye shall find! Knock and the door shall be opened unto thee. Ask and it shall be given. Ask, Little

Daddy, just ask. Wooooooooooooo! Blessed are the pure—
hallelujah! Let me just touch you, baby. Don't you feel
nothing?

BEN

I donno.

SISTER SUE

I'll tell you what I feel. Little drops of water trinkling
down my spine and hot wind blowing in my ears.
Ooooooowwwwwww, what a feeling. Hallelujah! Move in
closer to me, sugar, and give your Sister Sue a big hug.

(*Ben is embraced by the woman. She refuses to let
him go. He tries to push away.*)

BEN

It's hot out here.

SISTER SUE

Oh, honey, don't I know it! Let me sit. I'm weak in the
knees. How old are you now?

BEN

Going on twelve.

SISTER SUE

(*Counting on her fingers*) Thirteen, fourteen, fifteen,
sixteen. Four more years and you'll be a plum-ripe and
ready for plucking. (*She looks at him longingly for a
moment, then catches herself.*) Lord, this is a shame.

BEN

What?

SISTER SUE

You're too young to understand right now, but like I've
told you—the Lord pointed you out to me and one day
you've got to help me do His work.

BEN

All of yawl want to make me a preacher!

SISTER SUE

What yawl? Don't tell me somebody else is trying to get
into my playground?

BEN

Huh?

SISTER SUE

Who else is been after you?

BEN

You and my grandmother.

SISTER SUE

O! Well, Little Daddy, it's destined to be. I don't know what you've got, but whatever it is I spotted it a long time ago—and it sure has affected me. You're going to be a beautiful man—and you must work with me—and the Lord, too, of course—when the time comes.

BEN

How'll I know when the time comes?

SISTER SUE

You'll know it all right. You'll have pains, baby. You'll feel like your insides are just busting out of your skin. You just look at yourself in the mirror and one day you'll say, "I'm a man!" That'll be the time, and I want you to come running.

BEN

Suppose He called me now.

SISTER SUE

Then I wouldn't hesitate to take you along with me. I could put you in training for the great day. You could drive for me and take up collection. Lord, I'd give you anything you wanted. That's the will of the Lord, baby. Ask and ye shall be given all. Little Daddy, you reckon you ready to go right now?

BEN

I donno. I'm sorta worried.

SISTER SUE

About what, sugar? You'd be safe with me.

BEN

I know, but it's about Ida . . .

SISTER SUE

She hasn't been treating you mean since your mama died, has she?

BEN

No, but she and my grandmother don't get along and . . . I'm scared that my grandmama's gonna try to kill her.

SISTER SUE

Oh, Little Daddy, you're just letting your mind play tricks on you. Your folks never did like me none too well, but that don't mean they're the kind who'd kill up each other. Folks don't kill up each other on this side of the state, no how.

BEN

There's a first time for everything.

SISTER SUE

(*Looks at him longingly again.*) Yeah, that very first time. OWwwwwwwww, Little Daddy, just talk to me.

BEN

Look here. (*He removes the tube of roach paste from his pocket.*) This is poison. My grandmother just bought a great big tube of it and she's in there cooking supper for Ida.

SISTER SUE

Baby, don't trouble your mind with nothing trivial like this.

BEN

Suppose Ida eats that stuff!

SISTER SUE

Lord, you're really worried aren't you? (*Touches his face with her hands.*) I know what it is to worry too, sugar— especially when you've got nobody to go to. Isn't it awful that life is such a lonely thing? And it's most lonely when you don't have a friend. I'm loved by people all over this state and I don't have a single friend to talk to. Child . . . if you lived with me . . . you'd talk to me sometimes and be my friend, wouldn't you? (*Ben nods.*) Oh, God bless you. God bless you! Now, let me see that tube. (*Reads*) Here it is. Give whoever takes this stuff by mistake a quart of soda water.

BEN

What kind of soda water?

SISTER SUE

Bicarbonate of soda water. You got any bicarbonate?

BEN

Um-huh. Will it work?

SISTER SUE

Sure it will. It says so here in black and white. Read it for yourself. But you have nothing to worry about.

BEN

I really do appreciate this, hear. I feel a lot more relieved now. Ida Ray can be stubborn sometimes, you know.

SISTER SUE

Oh, before I forget, I brought you something.

BEN

What is it?

SISTER SUE

Two religious miracles—the ninth and tenth wonders of the Christian world. (*She removes a package from the bush and unwraps two pictures.*)

BEN

What are they?

SISTER SUE

This is the smiling face of Jesus that glows in the dark, no less.

BEN

What?

SISTER SUE

Hang it in your room, and at night when it gets dark Jesus' face'll just bust out smiling at you.

BEN

What's this one?

SISTER SUE

It's the face of Jesus and Mary at the same time.

BEN

Huh?

SISTER SUE

Walk over there. Now who do you see?

BEN

Jesus.

SISTER SUE

Now walk to the other side. What do you see?

BEN

Lord, if that picture hasn't changed to the Virgin Mary my name's not Ben Marvin McDaniels! Where did you get these ninth and tenth wonders of the world, Sister Sue Willie?

SISTER SUE

Don't tell a soul, Little Daddy, but the Lord touched me one morning and I painted 'em with blood and flames.

BEN

This is something!

SISTER SUE

And they're yours, Little Daddy. Gifts from the Almighty. Take 'em now and every time you look at them, think about me. Oh, Little Daddy, think about me, hear? In every conceivable way I want you to think about me. Look at me good now. (*She turns around slowly before him.*) And remember that I'm all yours—and you've got to be all mine. Yield not to temptation! You understand what I'm talking about? Of course you don't, but you will one day, and that's when I want you to hit that highway and hightail it in my direction. I travels east and west—west and east. Just ask for me by name and we're bound to meet up. And then, oooooooowwwwwwweeeeeee, Little Daddy! Hug me again and let me get away from here before I lose complete control of myself. (*Miss Gussie enters into the front room, glances out of the door and sees Ben and Sister Sue embracing.*) Kiss your sweet Sister Sue, Little Daddy, right here on her lips like the men kiss the girls in the picture show.

BEN

(*Embarrassed*) Naw . . .

SISTER SUE

Oh, come on, Little Daddy. Just try it and see. (*He kisses her quickly.*) Whew! Wasn't that the joy of salvation! Praise the Lord! Sweet Jesus!

GUSSIE

Ben Marvin, you bring yourself into this house! Disgracing our good family name in public! And you, hussy, get away from here!

SISTER SUE

(*Exiting*) Bye, baby, and remember: I travels east and west—west and east.

BEN

Bye, Sister Sue Willie! Thanks for these wonders!

GUSSIE

I'll wonder your backside! Fornicating with a grown woman in the broad daylight! I thought that you were a child of God—you're just like your granddaddy! Nothing but the devil's boy. Pick up that tambourine and sing praises to the Lord and ask Him to forgive your behind.

BEN

Well . . . I . . .

GUSSIE

Shut up and sing! (*She picks up the drum and starts beating it.*) Sing, you rascal! (*Ben starts singing.*) Louder! Sing until sweet redemption fills your sinning soul. Louder! Sing it louder! Get in step! Sing it! Praise the Lord and sing! (*Ben sings, starts shaking, goes into trance and falls to floor. When Gussie realizes he is in a trance, she is frightened. She reaches over and lifts his wrist up, lets it go and his hand flops to floor.*) Boy! Boy! (*She crosses over for pitcher of water and returns. Throws water in his face. Ben awakens.*) Praise the Lord! (*She helps him up.*) Now. Let's sit down and rest a spell. You feeling all right? I just witnessed a miracle, child. You went under, you know that? (*Ben nods yes.*) You remember anything? (*He nods yes again.*) You were under all right. A child of God and you don't know it! He that receiveth a prophet in the name of a prophet shall receive a prophet's reward; and he that receiveth a righteous man in the name of a righteous man shall receive a righteous man's reward! You the prophet and me the righteous.

BEN

I told you I was a Christian.

GUSSIE

I seen it with my own eyes . . . just then.

BEN

Everything was blurred and hazy.

GUSSIE

The Lord has you in His grips!

BEN

I'm scaired.

GUSSIE

No need to be. You're saved, child. Redeemed.

BEN

I never felt like that before in my whole life . . .

GUSSIE

The prophet Benjamin!

BEN

Am I really a prophet?

GUSSIE

Just as sure as there're stars in the sky. Slew the wicked— spare them no mercy. Stand and battle the devil face to face.

BEN

How is a prophet supposed to feel?

GUSSIE

Full of love for the Lord and full of hate for the Lord's enemies.

BEN

I feel the same as I did before—a little dizzy and winded,
but . . .

GUSSIE

Inspiration is the Lord. It comes and goes in spurts. Live
right and always be prepared for the moment when the
good Lord decides to touch you again. He'll fix it up so
that you can work miracles—heal the sick; make the blind
see.

BEN

David was a boy prophet. He killed Goliath.

GUSSIE

Done it in the name of the Lord. And you have to be like
David and slew the Lord's enemies.

BEN

How'll I know who they are?

GUSSIE

You'll just know—the Lord'll tell you.

BEN

The only one I can think of right now is old Matthew
Morris.

GUSSIE

Ah, boy!

BEN

He was the one who brought Ida Ray home last night.

GUSSIE

Did the Lord tell you that?

BEN

He didn't have to tell me. I saw it with my own eyes.

GUSSIE

Them hypocrites! No wonder she wants to get rid of me.
So that she and that rascal can move into my son's house.
I recognized greed in that man's eyes the first time I saw
him. Grinning and pretending. And just as sure as Ida Ray
gets rid of me she's gonna git rid of you and take your little money.

BEN

I don't believe she'd do that.

GUSSIE

You don't know what a woman'll do once a man like that
gets ahold of her. Now, boy, you've really got to go with
me. If you don't the Lord'll put His wrath on you—strike
you down—turn you into a pillow of salt like He did Lot's

wife. We've got to hightail it out of here at daybreak—and don't you look back at the fire!

BEN

What fire?

GUSSIE

One thing you've got to promise me though. You've got to swear on the Bible that you'll build me a house—a brick one with a slate roof that won't catch fire. We can use that money you got in the bank for the down payment.

BEN

Mama told me not to swear—and I'm not spending my money.

GUSSIE

I'm your mama now.

BEN

You can't just come here and take me like I'm yours. I don't even know you that good.

GUSSIE

I'm your kin, ain't I?

BEN

I've got kin I've never seen before that live in the city, that don't mean that I want to go off and live with them.

GUSSIE

You're getting mean again, boy. Provoking me like your grandaddy used to do. Ummmmmmmmmm! Don't this supper smell good I'm cooking? I used to be a cook during my day, you know. I used to wouldn't eat me nothing but fillet mignons, lobster imperial, and breast of capon Eugene.

BEN

Then why are you cooking stew now?

GUSSIE

Rich folks eat stew, child.

BEN

You cooked for rich folks?

GUSSIE

Up until the time they died a little while back. Couldn't stand 'em and they knew it.

BEN

Why didn't they fire you?

GUSSIE

I don't be fired by nobody! I quits. Anyway, I was the best cook in the county. All that money and they just barely paid me enough to make ends meet. I slaved, boy, for thirty years for them damned Merryweathers—raised them young 'uns, washed dirty drawers, cleaned toilets, and cooked! And what they paid me wasn't worth a fart.

BEN

You could have quit.

GUSSIE

Jobs ain't easy to come by—not at my age. But I made up for what they didn't pay me in other ways. I'd always get the biggest and best steak, and I was wasteful on purpose. They used to give parties all the time—drinking until they passed out. You wouldn't suspect small-town folks to carry on like that, but they did. I took my Bible to work one day and I told old lady Merryweather, "Miss Merryweather," I said, "Put that drink down. The time is at hand. Prepare to meet your God!"

BEN

What did she say?

GUSSIE

Told me to go to hell! Shoot! It didn't faze me a bit because I took it to the Lord. The Lord come to me one day while I was stewing and said, "Fix 'em."

BEN

What did you do?

GUSSIE

I ain't saying nothing, but they stuffed themselves on my stew, then got all stewed up on liquor and went to sleep with one of them gas heaters just ablazing. Somehow that hose come aloose and they all died—seven old Merryweathers. And do you know them rascals didn't leave me a cent!

BEN

I'm glad we don't burn gas.

GUSSIE

Anything that burns is dangerous.

BEN

Is that why you can't go back to Forney?

GUSSIE

Who told you that? I can go anywhere I please. I walks with the Lord, child, He's my shepherd.

BEN

How did my granddaddy die?

GUSSIE

Ask the Lord—you're his prophet.

BEN

The next time I go off into a trance, I am. He may tell me something you don't want to hear.

GUSSIE

That'll be the day.

BEN

Did granddaddy like your stew?

GUSSIE

Loved it. Ate a big pot of it the day he died. It's getting right cold. I'm glad you brought that wood in here.

BEN

I'm gonna light the fireplace if there's frost.

GUSSIE

I'll have to fix up a big fire in here in the morning for Ida. Now, let's start cleaning this house. Get the broom. Hurry now, because I want you to paint my leg for me later on.

BEN

If I leave here what's gonna happen to Ida?

GUSSIE

The good Lord already has His eyes hooked on her.

BEN

Suppose the Lord tells me to stay here?

GUSSIE

He's not gonna tell you nothing like that.

BEN

How do you know?

GUSSIE

Because I'm representing the Lord as far as you're concerned.

BEN

I'm the prophet, you're not!

GUSSIE

But I've worked for the Lord longer than you have, Mr. Smarty!

BEN

That don't mean a thing. The Lord gave me something that would turn you for a flip.

GUSSIE
He ain't give you nothing.

BEN
That's what you think. I've got something that you've never seen before.

GUSSIE
What is it?

BEN
I have the magic pictures of Jesus.

GUSSIE
What in the world are you talking about, boy?

BEN
You look at it one way and it's the face of Jesus. You look at it another way and it's Jesus' mother.

GUSSIE
I don't believe it.

BEN
I'll show it to you—but you have to be careful.

GUSSIE
Shoot.

BEN
I can say a magic word to that picture and you'll see some miracles happen.

GUSSIE
I've seen one today and that was enough for me. It was a blessing to see the Lord touch you like that.

BEN
You stay in here while I get it. I'll get it. I don't want you finding my hiding place.

GUSSIE
I ain't gonna tell nobody.

BEN
You just stay in here. (*He exits for the picture.*)

GUSSIE
Magic pictures and words—child foolishness!

BEN
(*Entering*) Stand right there. What do you see?

GUSSIE
Oh, it ain't nobody but Jesus.

BEN
(*He crosses to the other side of the room.*) Who do you see?

GUSSIE

(*Stunned*) If it ain't Mary holding a great big heart in her hands! Boy, where did you get that picture?

BEN

I painted it with blood and flames.

GUSSIE

Child, hush your mouth!

BEN

If I'm lying may I roast in hell.

GUSSIE

Let me sit and get a little air. This is really been a day, I tell you. You must have been in contact with the Lord longer than I thought.

BEN

Sister Sue Willie says I've always been in contact with Him.

GUSSIE

Let me see if I can test you. Close your eyes. Go on, close 'em. Now think on something religious—this leg of mine.

BEN

What do you want me to think?

GUSSIE

Anything holy.

BEN

I can recite some scriptures.

GUSSIE

Can you do that?

BEN

The mouth of strange women is a deep pit; he that is abhorred of the Lord shall fall therein.

GUSSIE

Child . . .

BEN

Beware of false prophets, which come to you in sheep's clothing, but inwardly they are ravening wolves.

GUSSIE

The Son of man shall send forth his angels, and they shall gather out of his kingdom all things that offend, and them which do iniquity; and shall cast them into a furnace of fire: there shall be wailing and gnashing of teeth.

BEN

Mene mene tekel upharsin.

GUSSIE
What's that, child?

BEN
It's in the Bible. It was written on the wall. "He has counted, counted, weighed, and they assess."

GUSSIE
Praise the Lord, child.

BEN
AH BAH KEE BAH AH BAH SHUMBA! BAH KEE BAH AH BAH SHUMBA AH!

GUSSIE
The unknown tongue! Child, where did you learn to speak the tongue like that?

BEN
It came to me when I touched my daddy's face.

GUSSIE
I'm feeling right dizzy. (*She closes her eyes.*) My head is just spinning around.

BEN
Let me get something for you. (*He rushes into the kitchen. Fills a glass of water and pours in some baking powder. It foams. He returns.*)

GUSSIE
Hurry!

BEN
Drink it quick before it loses its power.

GUSSIE
What is it?

BEN
Drink it!

GUSSIE
(*Downs the drink.*) Good Lord, boy, what was that?

BEN
Ambrosia.

GUSSIE
Am who?

BEN
Don't you feel better?

GUSSIE
(*Thinks for a moment.*) Lord, if I don't today. Boy, what was that you give me?

BEN

I told you—ambrosia.

GUSSIE

Where'd you get it?

BEN

I just held my hand up and it was there. You had blacked out—

GUSSIE

I don't remember nothing like that happening to me.

BEN

'Cause you had blacked out—for twenty minutes. I had a time trying to get you back to life.

GUSSIE

Child, you trying to frighten me?

BEN

No. You had really gone under.

GUSSIE

And you took care of me and brought me back? (*He nods.*) See. You love your grandma Gussie—and you're a prophet. Now can I count on you to go with me?

BEN

I can't leave Ida Ray.

GUSSIE

You'll leave her one day just like all my boys left me. Some gal'll get you. Think about all that money we could make. Can't you just see us living in a brick house—eating . . . beef à la Stroganoff—crab Rangoon. This is your one big opportunity.

BEN

I can go with Sister Sue Willie if I want to.

GUSSIE

That floozie? Over my dead body.

BEN

Well . . . let me think about it.

GUSSIE

That's right . . . go on think . . .

BEN

But I'm not promising you . . .

GUSSIE

While you're thinking, open this paint and start on my leg. I got a brush and some turpentine in that bag. I want two good coats on it. (*Ben puts a piece of paper beneath her leg, opens the paint, and begins painting.*) Boy, somebody in my family has got to satisfy me before I pass on. Looks like the Lord sent me to you.

BEN

What else do you want me to do?

GUSSIE

Well, I tell you. Life is just one nightmare after another—and it won't end until the Lord takes you away. Did you know that your rotten granddaddy gave me what the French folks got?

BEN

What's that?

GUSSIE

I can't tell you exactly—but it's a disease—and I can tell you what it done to me. My last baby was born a monster!

BEN

Uncle Leroy?

GUSSIE

No, I had another boy after him. His head was as big as a pumpkin and he had eyes no bigger than blackeye peas. His lips wasn't formed and you could see inside his mouth all the time. And his little hands were like claws. Your grandaddy had give me what the French folks got—and that baby had it too. I asked the doctor if that baby would live. He said he thought so but that he'd be dependent all his life—a halfwit. I asked the Lord if my baby would live and He was much kinder. That baby died and me and the Lord vowed vengeance on your granddaddy—black vengeance with no mercy!

BEN

I see why you didn't like him.

GUSSIE

Do you know that I taught your daddy the Bible and that he saved fifteen people when he was eight years old? If he had listened to me he'd be alive today and pastoring a big church in some city right now. No, he had to run off with your mama and die. My boys disappointed me, and they're either in the pen or scattered about in graveyards. Ain't it funny. Almost everybody I used to know is dead.

BEN

It may be funny to you, but it ain't so funny to me. Didn't Grandpa leave you nothing when he died?

GUSSIE

Shoot! Left me a hard way to go. You go on to work on that leg.

BEN

I'm working. (*There is silence for a moment.*) Why're you staring into space like that?

GUSSIE

Just thinking, child.

BEN

About what?

GUSSIE

My soul ain't at ease. The Lord ain't so pleased with me as I pretend He is. You can help, I do believe.

BEN

I'll do whatever I can.

GUSSIE

You can do a lot 'cause you're a prophet who's made the contact.

BEN

I'm sort of cold all of a sudden.

GUSSIE

The breath of the Lord's on you. Take my hand, child. Now say a prayer for me and save this poor old soul before it's too late.

BEN

Too late for what?

GUSSIE

I need redeeming bad. I'M REPENTING, MY JESUS!

BEN

Too late for what?

GUSSIE

I'm on probation with the Lord, child. I sinned for forty years, and I have to live the life of the righteous for forty years before my soul can come to rest. I have eight more years to go—until today when the good Lord showed Hisself in you. You can free my soul. Wash my sin away and I can live the rest of my life as I see fit. Pray for me.

BEN

If I pray for you will you promise to leave me alone and go away from here without bothering me and Ida Ray?

GUSSIE

If it be the will of the Lord. Quick, boy! Pray!

BEN

(*Speaking as he has heard ministers speak.*) It's the will of the Lord. He just told me. (*He prays.*) Dear Jesus, please have mercy on this poor old sinner woman who has roamed this earth from before dawn to sunset.

GUSSIE

Please, Jesus . . .

BEN

Whose husband left her with nothin', and whose sons didn't buy her a house of her own to sleep in. Take her in your arms like the lamb and—

GUSSIE

FREE MY SOUL!

BEN

Free her soul so that she can be on her way in life's journey. Hear me, Jesus, I ask you. Amen.

GUSSIE

(*She sits for a moment. Ben touches her face with his hands.*) Hallelujah! ! ! Praise His Sweet Name! You done it, child! (*Rises, raises her hands to glory.*) You put new breath back into this old body! Now run in there and get me a cigarette from under the mattress. It's good to be alive! Oh, sweet Jesus. This child prayed and the life come back—and my soul has been cleansed like the lamb and I'm free once more! While I sat here an angel of the Lord come to me and said, "That child'll be preaching in temples before the week's out. Soon as you finish my leg, pack your things.

BEN

I'M NOT LEAVING HERE!

GUSSIE

It's the will of the Lord, and you're going too! Nothing'll stop it. Get me my cigarettes, boy. We'll be lighting out of here before daybreak. And don't you tell old Ida Ray either.

BEN

You promised me!

GUSSIE

A promise ain't worth a fart. Bring my cigarettes now. (*Ben, in anger and fear, stamps into the house.*) I'm your rock and your foundation. (*She begins breaking dishes, knocks over chairs during remainder of speech, leaving the kitchen in shambles.*) Smart Miss Ida Ray! I don't need this old shack of yourn. The good Lord's done sent me the light and I'm gonna get me a real pretty new house to own before I die—even if it's just for one day! Brother Ben! Bring the Bible and let's prepare ourself for glory, boy!

(*The lights dim as Ben enters into the living room tremendously disturbed.*)

Blackout

SCENE 3 *Night. The evening is dark and cold. The sound of the wind is heard throughout this scene whistling in the distance. At the conclusion of the scene the wind is violent and haunting. Once again the rocking chair is placed before the fireplace. Ben Marvin stands for a moment before the fireplace staring at the clock. There is frost. At a certain hour the boy will light his fire. Ida Ray enters the yard, pauses for a moment. It is obvious that she is sick. She composes herself and moves to the back porch. She has just returned from work and is exceedingly tired and cold. She carries a small package with her. When she reaches the porch she is stunned momentarily by the spilled and tracked paint.*

IDA

Ben Marvin! Ben Marvin!

BEN

Here I am, Ida. (*Rushes to porch.*)

IDA

What in the world's been going on here? Look at this porch—paint everywhere.

BEN

I painted her leg—

IDA

(*Enters kitchen.*) Look at this floor! Miss Gussie! Miss Gussie!

BEN

She's packing.

IDA

I don't care what she's doing! Miss Gussie, you come here to me this minute!

BEN

She's leaving, Ida Ray.

GUSSIE

(*Entering from her room, singing*)
Amazing grace
How sweet the sound . . .

IDA

Look at my house!

GUSSIE

That saved a wretch like me . . .

BEN

I told her she was tracking it up!

GUSSIE

I once was lost
But now I'm found . . .

IDA

A grown woman ought to know better.

GUSSIE

Was blind, but now I see . . .

(*To Ida*) Say what you want to say, but the Holy Ghost come to me and I've found peace.

Through many dangers . . .

IDA

I don't care what you've found. That paint's still dripping all over the place. You get out in the backyard this minute and sit until it dries!

GUSSIE

It's cold out there, girl.

IDA

I don't care!

GUSSIE

I ain't gonna let myself freeze to death when I'm in my own son's house.

IDA

(*Pulls up a chair.*) Put a piece of newspaper under her,

Ben Marvin. And don't you move—you hear me? (*The old woman sits and starts singing again.*) You get some turpentine and clean up this paint, boy.

BEN

I will.

IDA

(*Moving into the living room*) You didn't even close the windows.

BEN

I'm gonna light my fire and sit. I've got everything ready.

IDA

You don't need a fire as hot as it is in here.

BEN

She's been . . . cooking. That old kitchen stove is still red-hot—that's why the windows are opened.

IDA

Miss Gussie, I've got a headache and I wish you wouldn't sing so loud.

GUSSIE

Just trying to talk to my Jesus.

BEN

She told me that I was a prophet.

IDA

Uh!

BEN

I went into a trance and the day turned gray and cold!

IDA

You weren't in a trance—and you certainly had nothing to do with the day turning cold. I told you to leave that old woman alone. She's a religious fanatic.

BEN

What's that?

IDA

A person who gets carried away with religion to the point where it makes them crazy.

BEN

She went under and I brought her back to life!

IDA

Boy, I'm tired and I've got no time to listen to your foolishness.

BEN

But I did! Ask her.

IDA

Folks don't die and come back to life.

BEN

Jesus did.

IDA

You think she's Jesus?

BEN

No, but . . . well . . . she didn't die exactly, she just went under and I . . . (*Ida gives him a hard stare.*) What have you got in that bag?

IDA

A bottle of brandy. Miss Lappas asked me to pick it up for her party tomorrow evening.

BEN

Did Miss Lappas fire you?

IDA

What?

BEN

Didn't you register?

IDA

Finally. I went down during my lunch hour. The office was closed. I guess they saw me coming. I would have gone back to work, but I was sick and I just couldn't walk another step. I sat on the porch to rest. The Sheriff came up and asked me to move and I refused. I told him I paid taxes and I was gonna sit there just like those old white men sat there. He must have seen in my eyes that I meant it because he left me alone. Soon they opened the office back up and I voted. Half the town was milling around in the street.

BEN

Weren't you afraid?

IDA

I've been afraid all my life . . . but I just didn't care any-more.

BEN

Does Miss Lappas know?

IDA

I told her . . . and I told her I'd quit if she wanted me to.

BEN

What did she say?

IDA

That she was having this party tomorrow and she needed my help. We would talk about it some other time.

BEN

Oh. I'm real proud of you, Ida, and I'm sorry I carried on so this morning.

IDA

It's all right, baby, and here . . . Mr. Tolbert sent this package.

BEN

New books! (*Opens package.*) I wonder what he sent me this time? It's three, Ida! *The Rise and Fall of the Roman Empire!*

IDA

That's nice.

BEN

You still don't feel too well, do you?

IDA

No, I don't, sugar. I hardly got anything done today. Miss Lappas was rather peeved. If I don't feel any better tomorrow I think I'll pay Dr. Green a visit.

BEN

She's leaving in the morning as soon as her pension check comes in. That should make you feel better.

IDA

She doesn't get a pension.

BEN

She must get money from somewhere. She's always buying cigarettes and stuff in town.

IDA

I haven't said anything about it, but she's been going in my purse from time to time.

BEN

Stealing?

IDA

Well, she hasn't taken much.

BEN

She won't steal anymore.

IDA

You can't teach old dogs new tricks, Ben Marvin.

BEN

I redeemed her!

IDA

What makes you think you could redeem somebody?

BEN

Sister Sue Willie said . . .

IDA

I don't care what lie that woman told you. She's the biggest hypocrite in the state. I'm surprised you let her take you in like this.

GUSSIE

I'm tired of sitting in here in this chair all by myself.

IDA

Don't you move until every inch of that leg dries!

GUSSIE

Go on, treat me this-a-way, Ida Ray, after I spent the day cooking you up this big pot of stew. I've got the table set and everything, and you ain't said a word.

BEN

She bought a lot of New Fidelity Rat Paste today!

IDA

With my money, no doubt. (*Enters kitchen.*) Well, it does smell good and I'm starving.

GUSSIE

Come to the feast, child.

BEN

Didn't you say you ate at Miss Lappas'?

IDA

No, I didn't say that. I couldn't keep a thing down all day. (*Gussie chuckles to herself.*)

BEN

You're gonna be late for church! Why don't you eat when you get back?

IDA

Because I'm hungry now.

GUSSIE

Stew is my speciality. Have a heaping bowlful, child.

BEN

I can fix you a quick sandwich, Ida Ray!

IDA

Ben Marvin, what's wrong with you? Get me a plate and behave.

BEN

That old stew is probably cold!

GUSSIE

My food ain't cold either. Just help yourself to it, Ida. Eat all you want.

BEN

(*To Ida, who is getting a helping of the stew.*) Ida Ray, you'd better not eat that stuff!

IDA

Boy!

GUSSIE

That's good food, child—sticks to the bones. Why don't you eat you a plateful?

IDA

It smells good, Miss Gussie.

GUSSIE

It is, child.

BEN

Ida, she plans to . . . (*He rushes to her and knocks the plate from her hands.*)

IDA

Ben Marvin, look what you've done, boy!

BEN

I've been trying to tell you . . .

IDA

Tell me what?

(*Gussie has taken the pot from the stove and is sampling the stew herself. Ben has not noticed this.*)

BEN

She put poison in that stuff . . . I know she did. She plans to kill you!!

GUSSIE

Child . . .

IDA

Your mind just runs wild sometimes . . .

BEN

But she does, Ida.

GUSSIE

There's plenty more, Ida, child. Sure is delicious.

IDA

I don't know what gets into you.

BEN

She had that big tube of roach paste when she was in here cooking and I can't find it nowhere. I looked all over for it . . .

IDA

You apologize to Miss Gussie and start getting that paint up before it dries.

BEN

I'm sorry.

GUSSIE

You ought to be. I've got feeling, you know, and sometimes you can be a mean mistreater.

BEN

I said that I'm sorry and I hope you're not mad at me.

GUSSIE

No, child. (*Ida sits at table and begins eating.*)

BEN

I hope you don't hold no grudges.

GUSSIE

We're still friends, I guess. (*She winks at him.*)

BEN

(*Stares at her for a moment.*) Can I stay all night with Joe Sedrick?

IDA

Miss Sedrick has trouble enough without you.

BEN

Just this once, Ida, please.

IDA

No! And I mean it—so don't ask me anymore.
(*The boy stands lost and dejected for a moment, he
turns away helplessly, moves into the living room,
and begins work on the floor.*)

GUSSIE

How does it taste, child?

IDA

You put a little too much salt on it, but otherwise . . .

GUSSIE

Well seasoned. All of my food is well seasoned.

IDA

I bought your bus ticket today. The bus leaves for Forney at eleven thirty. I'll have to work, but I'll take your bag down and check it when I leave in the morning. Ben can walk you to the station.

GUSSIE

Child, I don't want to go back to Forney. Ain't you satisfied with my cooking, Ida?

IDA

You cook very well, but I've thought it through carefully and I've made up my mind. I think it'll be best for all of us if you leave.

GUSSIE

But child, I can't go back to Forney!

IDA

What kind of trouble were you in back there?

GUSSIE

I wasn't in no trouble.

IDA

Then what's to keep you from going home?

GUSSIE

Well . . . memories, child. Ain't nothing there for me but unpleasant memories.

IDA

We all have to learn to live with the past, Miss Gussie. This house holds some unpleasant memories for me, but I've learned to live with them.

GUSSIE

You'd put an old woman out in the cold?

IDA

Don't try to play on my sympathies—you're not helpless. You told Ben that you get a pension.

GUSSIE

They stopped sending it.

IDA

Why?

GUSSIE

I didn't tell nobody where I was coming to when I left.

IDA

They know you're not dead. You've been here for a little over three months—I think they'll keep your checks at the post office for you that long. You should have a good bit of change waiting for you when you get home.

GUSSIE

I sort of like the peace and quiet around here. Folks're all right nice and kindly . . .

IDA

Miss Gussie, I've made up my mind now.

GUSSIE

Well, child, if that's what you've done, I don't reckon I can change it none. Every tree that bringeth not forth good fruit is hewn down, and cast into the fire! (*She stares at Ida for a moment.*) Wherefore by their fruits ye shall know them.

IDA

(*Restlessly*) I . . . I'd better get ready for church.

GUSSIE

Sit a spell longer, child. I have a few words I want to pass on to you.

IDA

I don't have too much time.

GUSSIE

It'll take only a second. You look right pale anyway.

IDA

Well . . .

GUSSIE

The good book says: In what place 'soever ye enter into an house, there abide till ye depart from that place. And whosoever shall not receive you, nor hear you, when ye depart thence, shake off the dust under your feet for a testimony against them . . .

IDA

I've read the Bible.

GUSSIE

I'm gonna tell you how come I can't go back to Forney.

IDA

You don't have to if you don't want to. It's really none of my business.

GUSSIE

The family that I worked for died—asphyxiated—all seven of 'em. A good clean death that seemed almost natural, but the book says that sin's to be swept away by fire. The Lord told me that just as sure as I'm sitting here, but I didn't listen. And do you know what happened? That oldest Merryweather boy—old Roger, who's a Major in the army come home to the funeral and ordered an autopsy. Know what they found? It wasn't only gas that killed 'em, they had been poisoned with arsenic!

IDA

Why are you telling me this?

GUSSIE

I just think you should know, child, Miss Merryweather just loved flowers and she always used sprays and powders and things on 'em. She told me what arsenic was.

IDA

Did you put it in their food?

GUSSIE

They hushed up the investigation—thought old lady Merryweather done it! Old Roger wasn't satisfied and wasn't gonna let it rest—that's how come I came out here when you wrote to me.

IDA

I thought you came because you wanted to be helpful.

GUSSIE

Shoot!

IDA

Why did you kill all those people?

GUSSIE

Because they fired me! After thirty years of slaving for practically nothing, they fired me. Said I was too old to do the work. Kicked me out into the world without a penny. I was left to die. I pleaded with old Lady Merryweather. She cussed me and tole me to get! The old man didn't say a word—nor did any of their grown children. Fired with nothing to do but die.

IDA

That was no reason.

GUSSIE

An eye for an eye, child!

IDA

Cora was improving when you came here.

GUSSIE

She acted right spry sometimes, didn't she?

IDA

Then she suddenly took a turn for the worse.

GUSSIE

The good Lord didn't like her.

IDA

You mean you didn't like her. Miss Gussie, I'm not saying anything, but I'm going to the Sheriff and ask them to perform an autopsy on Cora . . .

GUSSIE

Child, you're old enough to know that the law don't care nothing about you and me in little towns like this. We can do anything and they'll close their eyes to it—so long as it don't involve them. And I ain't dumb by no means—I used to listen to "I Love a Mystery" and "Inner Sanctum"—and I read the Bible. Who'd suspect an old soul like me having enough sense to use something like arsenic. They'd be apt to think I would use something as silly as that old roach paste that Ben's so scaired of.

IDA

The law here is just, and you're gonna get your due reward. I'm gonna tell them everything. Ben Marvin! Ben Marvin!

BEN

Yeah!

IDA

Run and ask Mrs. Simpson to come over here right this minute.

GUSSIE

Now, Ida.

BEN

Okay. (*He exits.*)

GUSSIE

Ben Marvin, you come back here, boy!

IDA

He's gone already.

GUSSIE

Well . . . it don't matter anymore to me. Why're you holding your stomach like that Ida?

IDA

You know I've been having these spells off and on lately.

GUSSIE

I know it very well, child. (*Laughs to herself.*) I wish you could just see yourself now, child. The sweat that's on your face and that faraway look you got in your eye. Ain't you dizzy and sleepy yet?

IDA

(*Ida is stunned.*) You didn't! (*Gussie laughs softly and hysterically and holds up a little bag of arsenic.*) But you ate some of that stuff too—(*The old woman nods and removes a little bag of powder from her pocket. Ida tries to rise but is too weak.*) Oh, Miss Gussie, how could you?

GUSSIE

That's right, child. Go get in the bed. Make it look natural.

IDA

Ben! Ben Marvin!

GUSSIE

Hush you! He can't hear you anyhow. Yawl think I'm so dumb, but don't underestimate Miss Gussie Black. You've just took the final dose. And there ain't nothing nobody can do for you.

IDA

Ummm . . .

GUSSIE

PREPARE TO MEET YOUR MAKER! Repent, child! The time is at hand. I've been putting little pinches of my arsenic in your food for several weeks now.

IDA

Oh . . . OH, GOD! Ohhh, God. What about Ben? Ohhhh . . .

GUSSIE

It'll be over before you know it. Come on in here to bed. (*She struggles with Ida to get her to the bedroom.*)

IDA

Let . . . me go! Ben. What about him? Did you . . .?

GUSSIE

No, child, He's my kin. My blood kin and he's a prophet. Can't keep your eyes open can you? The pain ain't so bad now though, is it? Come on in here to bed, child. And you pray and ask to be forgiven. And remember: Don't monkey with me. I'll put the hurt on you real bad—won't I, Jesus? We've got us another sinner ready for the hell pot. Child, you're as heavy as a hip-pi-mo-pottimus! (*She exits with Ida into Ida's bedroom. She returns with Ida's pocketbook*) Seventeen dollars! Well, I got this ticket and Ben's got his money. (*She tosses purse back into the the room.*) And I plan to destroy the evidence, child! I'm gonna set this place to blazing when I leave here in the morning. Me and brother Ben's going to the city and start us the Gussie Black and Grandson Tabernacle. Praise the Lord!

BEN

(*Enters running.*) Miss Simpson's gone to church, Ida!

GUSSIE

Ah, that gal left here in a huff.

BEN

Did she say for me to meet her? (*The old woman nods.*) Look at you dripping paint, and I've already cleaned up in here—get on back into that kitchen! I mean now!

GUSSIE

(*Moving into the kitchen, humming*) What's in this bag Ida brought here?

BEN

She brought some brandy home.

GUSSIE

Didn't I tell you she wasn't no good?

BEN

It's for Miss Lappas' party tomorrow!

GUSSIE

Well, tomorrow this time me and you'll be spreading the word and climbing to the promised land.

BEN

I've thought about it and I don't want to go.

GUSSIE

Boy, you turning your back on the Lord?

BEN

No, but . . .

GUSSIE

Fill me a cup of water.

BEN

You'd better sit down—Ida was mad.

GUSSIE

Oh, I done appeased her. Ain't you hungry? You haven't eaten a thing today.

BEN

I don't want to die!

GUSSIE

You ought to be ashamed of yourself . . .

BEN

Let me see you eat some more of that stew . . .

GUSSIE

You saw me eating some a minute ago, didn't you?

BEN
You might have been faking.
GUSSIE
Shoot, boy!
BEN
And you sit down—your leg's still dripping paint.
GUSSIE
(*Sitting*) I told you not to put all that thinner in it.
BEN
You ought to have bought some quick-drying!
GUSSIE
Shoot! Bring me my rocker in here.
BEN
I was good enough to let you use it today, but if you think you're getting it tonight, you got another think coming.
GUSSIE
Any old chair ought to suit a young boy like you.
BEN
Well, it don't.
GUSSIE
You've gotten right sinful since Ida Ray's been here.
BEN
Pay it no mind.
GUSSIE
What did she say to you?
BEN
Nothing.
GUSSIE
Once I get you out from under her influence . . .
BEN
I'm not going with you!
GUSSIE
You're going even if I have to put you to sleep and carry you to that bus.
BEN
Shoot! You're too old to pick up a toothpick.
GUSSIE
When they cut off my leg all my strength rose up to my shoulders and arms. Feel this muscle.
BEN
I'm busy. Besides, you can't go anywhere—you don't have

any money.

GUSSIE

Where there's a will there's a way, boy.

BEN

I don't plan to take up with no thief.

GUSSIE

That's why I've got to get you away from old Ida Ray— round here stealing whiskey . . .

BEN

Ida Ray don't steal.

GUSSIE

Not anymore, she don't. I'm all you've got. What would you have if Ida and that Matthew Morris run off together.

BEN

They're not gonna run off!

GUSSIE

Supposin' they did.

BEN

Then . . . I'd have my books!

GUSSIE

You think more of them old books than you do me?

BEN

Yes! . . . sometimes.

GUSSIE

See there. You're not so hard as you try to be. Books! Shoot!

BEN

I'll be glad when you get on that bus. Now I'm just gonna do my work and pay you no mind—so don't talk to me.

(*He begins on the kitchen floor.*)

GUSSIE

(*After a moment*) You look like your grandpapa squatting down like that.

BEN

Did you try to make him a preacher?

GUSSIE

Thought you didn't want to talk to me?

BEN

I don't! I just wanted to know if you tried to make Grandpa a preacher.

GUSSIE

That devil?

BEN

I wouldn't marry nobody I didn't love.

GUSSIE

He promised to buy me things, child. A home, pretty clothes, hard liquor.

BEN

Did you ever drink any more after you got converted?

GUSSIE

I told you I was on probation with the Lord—how could I drink anything? You know, now that I've been reborn I can let my hair down and backtrack a bit. Let me see that bottle, boy.

BEN

It's not ours.

GUSSIE

Don't I know it? (*She gets up and gets the bag of liquor.*)

BEN

You'd better stay in that chair!

GUSSIE

Apricot brandy! Ain't it golden-looking? Been close to forty years since I had me anything stronger than beer— excusing eggnog at Christmastime.

BEN

It's a sin to drink!

GUSSIE

Read your Bible—they're drinking all the way through it. Anyway, when you get to be my age a little spirits is good for the heart. Ask any doctor.

BEN

Don't you open that! It's Miss Lappas'!

GUSSIE

I'm just gonna take a swallow—she won't know the difference.

BEN

Ida will and she's gonna light into you.

GUSSIE

Stop talking so loud! (*She grins, smells the contents of the bottle.*) Umm, smells like the good old days when your grandpapa was twisting my young mind. (*She drinks.*) Tasty, just like I remember, too.

BEN

You give me that bottle.

GUSSIE
Clean up that floor, boy, and leave me be!

BEN
I'm gonna tell Ida Ray!

GUSSIE
Shoot! (*Takes another drink.*) Umm-uh! It's a thrill to feel this pleasant burn trickle down.

BEN
You like that old stuff?

GUSSIE
Don't I? This'll put the fire back in the furnace, boy.

BEN
You keep on drinking it and you're gonna be drunk.

GUSSIE
I ain't been drunk since I could remember.

BEN
If you pass out I'm gonna let the rats and roaches eat you.

GUSSIE
Do and your days'll be numbered.

BEN
I'm gonna tell everybody around here that you drink whiskey!

GUSSIE
You do that and I'll tell 'em about you!

BEN
What?

GUSSIE
How you and that old woman preacher was out in the front yard doing something bad!

BEN
Ooooooowwwwwwwwwww!

GUSSIE
I seen you! All that hugging and kissing and you putting the joy of salvation in her soul!

BEN
You ought to be ashamed of yourself!

GUSSIE
Shoot, I ain't 'shamed of nothing. I used to be 'shamed because I had this wooden leg. Little old children like you used to laugh and make fun of me—called me Miss Peg Leg—"Peggy" for short. But I learned to turn the other cheek and let the Lord take care of 'em.

BEN

It's almost time for me to light my fire.

GUSSIE

Don't need to light no fire! I'm sweating already—just burning up.

BEN

(He exits into the front room, stands silently for a moment staring at the clock before the fireplace. The clock strikes. Excitedly he lights the fire and slowly, almost mysteriously, he sits in the rocker. He begins rocking slowly, beaming with joy to himself. There is silence for a moment. Ben in his chair reading his new books, the old woman in her chair with her bottle. Gussie is restless. She gets up and moves to the living-room door. She relaxes, stretches, takes a long drink from the bottle, moves to the table, and puts the bottle down. She hobbles into the front room.)

You'd better keep still in there.

GUSSIE

I ain't in there, I'm in here. And I ain't keeping still—this ain't no jail and you ain't my keeper.

BEN

(Half rising) You get back in that kitchen and sit down!

GUSSIE

Oh, leave me alone, boy! I'm grown. You don't be telling me what to do. What're you doing in here anyway?

BEN

I'm sitting—minding my own business and trying to read.

GUSSIE

Read about what?

BEN

None of your business! Now go on back in there and sit down and leave me alone!

GUSSIE

I ain't going nowhere!

BEN

You're dripping paint!

GUSSIE

Hush up and let your poor old grandma sit and get warm before this fire.

BEN

The kitchen's warm.

GUSSIE

I want to sit here. It's too warm in there.

BEN

I've told you that this is my chair, and I'm not letting you have it. It's the first frost, and this chair belongs to me—I don't even let Ida Ray sit in it, and I'm sure not going to let you have it. Now get out of here and leave me alone.

GUSSIE

Why is this old chair so special?

BEN

My daddy gave me this chair. He said every man ought to have a rocker of his own to sit before the fire and think in.

GUSSIE

You ain't no man yet.

BEN

Well, I'm gonna sit here anyway and think and make my plans.

GUSSIE

Think and plan about what?

BEN

None of your business.

GUSSIE

"Have nourished children and they rebel, but goodness and mercy shall follow me." You know it grieved the Lord that he had made man.

BEN

Will you get out of here—you old—religious fanatic!

GUSSIE

Where did you learn that big word?

BEN

Prophets know a lot of things.

GUSSIE

What does it mean?

BEN

Somebody who's crazy in the head.

GUSSIE

I may not have too much education, but I've got some real good sense.

BEN
You take it in the kitchen, then.

GUSSIE
What do you think about?

BEN
(*Disgusted*) Grandmama!

GUSSIE
Don't start that yelling now—the old have to be comforted.

BEN
If I tell you will you leave me alone? (*She nods.*) I think about different things. I sit here and close my eyes and I can see things in the past and the present and sometimes in the future.

GUSSIE
What do you see in the past, huh?

BEN
You're supposed to leave me alone.

GUSSIE
I'm going to if you'll just answer that.

BEN
Lately everytime I close my eyes I see you.

GUSSIE
What am I doing?

BEN
Meddling in somebody else's business.

GUSSIE
You don't see nothing!

BEN
(*Looks at her sharply, then closes his eyes.*) I see you right now. And I see three little boys and an old drunk man.

GUSSIE
Go on.

BEN
One of those boys looks like my daddy.

GUSSIE
I don't care about them. What am I doing?

BEN
There's my daddy's face—just like it was when he died.

GUSSIE
I'm interested in me.

BEN

Now you've come back again. You're spreading that old roach paste.

GUSSIE

How can you see all that?

BEN

I'm a prophet, remember? You're spreading a mighty lot of it. It must be enough to kill a grown man.

GUSSIE

Child . . .

BEN

I can't make out what it is you're putting it on.

GUSSIE

Is it a baked potato?

BEN

Yeah, I do believe it is.

GUSSIE

Lord . . . (*She is dazed momentarily. Ben stares at her.*) Them wood rats liked baked potatoes. I used to chunk it under the house to 'em. Boy, get up out of that chair and let me sit down! I'm tired. (*She forces him up and sits.*) And you stop all this here thinking about the past—ain't nothing but the devil in you.

BEN

That's my chair and I want it!

GUSSIE

A lot of things I wanted in life I couldn't get. What did you put all of that wood in this fire for, I'm burning up.

BEN

BECAUSE I WANTED TO!

GUSSIE

I told you I needed some wood for in the morning. (*She takes a piece of newspaper and puts it beneath her leg.*) The least you could do is help a poor old cripple woman make herself comfortable.

BEN

I saw something else when I was sitting there.

GUSSIE

I ain't interested in your mess, boy.

BEN

I saw Grandpapa!

GUSSIE

You hush up now. I don't want to hear any more.

BEN

I just thought I'd tell you.

GUSSIE

Well . . . don't.

BEN

He was sitting at a table eating dinner . . . chewing and sweating, sweating and chewing, and breathing hard . . .

GUSSIE

Yeah, he was having a feast on that stew, wasn't he? (*She catches herself.*)

BEN

Then I saw him stretched out dead!

GUSSIE

You hush up talking about the dead, boy. Ain't you got no respect?

BEN

YOU KILLED HIM WITH ROACH—

GUSSIE

DAMN IT, BOY, SHUT UP! (*Ben is frightened now.*) I ain't silly enough to put roach paste in somebody's stew. Have you ever smelled that stuff? Now stop all this talk about the dead and go in there and get me that bottle. I mean now! (*Ben goes into the kitchen and gets the bottle and gives it to her.*)

BEN

You've drank almost half of it!

GUSSIE

(*Takes a long drink.*) Now go in there and bring me my purse.

BEN

Where is it?

GUSSIE

Under my mattress. (*Ben exits into her room. The old woman gets up, throws Ben's books in the fire, takes another drink, spies the turpentine and tosses it about the kitchen. She is about to spread it about the living room when Ben returns.*)

BEN

What're you doing putting all that stuff down in here for?

GUSSIE

You half cleaned—look at those spots.

BEN

You just wait until Ida Ray gets home!

GUSSIE

(*Yawns, takes another drink, and sits in the rocker again.*)
Give me my purse. (*She removes a cigarette and lights
it.*)

BEN

What did you do with my books?

GUSSIE

I ain't seen 'em.

BEN

What did you do with my books? Where did you hide
them?

GUSSIE

Boy!

BEN

You tell me where my books are!

GUSSIE

I burnt 'em up!

BEN

You what?

GUSSIE

I chunked 'em in the fire, set 'em on fire. You're a prophet,
boy, and filth ain't for you! You got to lean on me.

BEN

You burned my new books?

GUSSIE

Didn't I! And I'd do it again.

BEN

I really do believe you killed Grandpa . . .

GUSSIE

Leave me be, child . . .

BEN

I'm going into a trance and ask him! (*He gets the tambourine and begins to sing and dance, imitating the old
woman this time.*)

GUSSIE

Cut out all that racket! (*The boy ignores her. He stops
short at the peak of his song, his eyes wide open.*)

BEN

Granddaddy? Is that you? (*The old woman perks up a bit. She looks at the boy. She is not sure whether he is really under or not. She rises and waves her hand before his face. He does not respond. This convinces her that he is under.*) She . . . She . . . did?

GUSSIE

That bastard got just what he deserved—didn't he, Jesus! Sure I fixed him a meal he never forgot. That lazy bastard—giving me that disease, stealing my little money to buy liquor, courting floozies. I had me four hundred dollars saved up once, and he stole it and run off and spent it all up on some strumpet and come back home to me. That money was for the down payment on a house! Yeah, I got rid of him all right. It was right funny too. He died buck naked on all fours—must have thought that young gal give him a heart attack. I cried at his funeral though—you should have seen them tears I shed—just like I shed for your mama and just like I'm gonna shed for old Ida Ray . . .

(*Ben stares at her stunned. She drowsily returns the stare.*)

. . . if I lives to see her die.

BEN

Did you do something to my mama?

GUSSIE

I don't feel like talking no more.

BEN

Did you kill my mama?

GUSSIE

Jesus talks to me. I'm put here to free the world of sin . . . just like you. If you can't talk to 'em and bring 'em to God —then you have to do the next best thing. Remove their butts from here and let 'em burn in the eternal fire! The Lord talks to me, don't You? You tell me what to do and I do it!

BEN

DID YOU KILL MY MAMA?

GUSSIE

Lord, tell this boy I'm a Christian lady. Anybody can pass on anytime—that ain't no big thing. Shoot! (*She sits.*) This is my house now if I want to stay here—and like it says in the good song, "I shall not be moved! Just like a tree planted by the river—I shall not be moved." I'm gonna be right here and you're gonna be here with me cause you're my blood kin. I'm all you've got now and you're all I got. Look in Ida's room and bring me her fan—I'm sweating. (*Ben backs away from her slowly toward the room. The old woman realizes now what she has done, but it is too late. She rushes awkwardly over to stop the boy.*) Wait! That's all right, I don't need it . . . (*But he has opened the door. She holds him and he pushes her away.*)

BEN

Thought you said Ida Ray had gone to church!

GUSSIE

Is that gal still in there? She said she was gonna take a nap . . .

BEN

Ida Ray!

GUSSIE

Leave her alone! Let her rest—she's tired.

BEN

Ida Ray wouldn't miss church for nothing—no matter how tired she is. Ida Ray! (*He breaks away and rushes into the room.*) Ida Ray!

GUSSIE

Come out of there, boy . . . dammit! (*She wanders slowly back to the chair and sits for a moment, then takes a long drink.*)

BEN

IDA RAY! (*There is a loud scream from within the room. Gussie sits worried and confused and pathetic. Ben bursts from the room, his face covered with tears. He stands for a moment wide-eyed and staring with deep hate at the old women. She cannot look him in the eye.*)

GUSSIE

(*Pathetically*) Stop that crying, boy! I can't stand it. (*Ben screams again like a madman and lunges forward. He grabs the old woman about the neck and begins to choke her. She struggles desperately; manages to push him away with her wooden leg.*) Touch me again and die . . . you little bastard! (*She is breathing slowly and deeply.*) Touch me . . . and die! (*They stare at each other.*) I'm all you got now. We got to work together . . . (*She cannot reach the boy. Unconsciously she lifts the bottle and drinks again. Her eyelids are heavy. Ben watches as she slowly falls asleep.*) The will of . . . the Lord . . . must have its . . . way . . . fan me . . . boy . . . I'm all you got. . . .

BEN

You may think you're all I've got, but I've got news for you. I've got *me*, old woman—and I've got my freedom! And like Mr. Tolbert used to say to me—"You've got to have determination" . . . now I've got it. It's you who don't have nothing—you don't have a . . . *fart!* (*The old woman snores loudly, ignoring the boy completely.*) That spark is burning on that newspaper . . . (*The old woman is asleep now, her head back and her mouth opened.*) That heat is making the paint pucker. You listening to me? That paper will be on fire beneath your leg. I'm not gonna tell you anymore . . . I've got to go to Muleshoe tonight . . . Sister Sue Willie's gonna be there waiting on me. Old woman, your leg might burn with all that thinner on it. (*He puts on his coat and buttons it. He starts for the door, picks up the turpentine can and tosses it into the center of the room near the old woman.*) You hear me? (*She does not answer. He turns, his head high, and rushes from the house. He stops in the yard and thinks for a moment.*) Shoot! And I'm not gonna look back at the flames!

    (*He rushes off down the road as the lights begin to dim. The fireplace area glows brighter and brighter.*)

The curtain falls

CONTRIBUTIONS IN AFRO-AMERICAN AND AFRICAN STUDIES